THE CANADIAN CONSTITUTION
AND
THE COURTS

THE CANADIAN CONSTITUTION
AND
THE COURTS

THE FUNCTION AND SCOPE
OF JUDICIAL REVIEW

THIRD EDITION

The Honourable Barry L. Strayer
B.A., LL.B. (Sask.), B.C.L. (Oxon.), S.J.D. (Harvard)
Judge, Federal Court of Canada—Trial Division

Butterworths
Toronto and Vancouver

The Canadian Constitution and the Courts

© 1988 Butterworths, A division of Reed Inc.

Printed and bound in Canada

The Butterworth Group of Companies

Canada:
Butterworths, Toronto and Vancouver
United Kingdom:
Butterworth & Co. (Publishers) Ltd., London and Edinburgh
Australia:
Butterworths Pty Ltd., Sydney, Melbourne, Brisbane, Adelaide and Perth
New Zealand:
Butterworths (New Zealand) Ltd., Wellington and Auckland
Singapore:
Butterworth & Co. (Asia) Pte. Ltd., Singapore
South Africa:
Butterworth Publishers (SA) (Pty) Ltd., Durban and Pretoria
United States:
Butterworth Legal Publishers, Boston, Seattle, Austin and St. Paul
D & S Publishers, Clearwater

Canadian Cataloguing in Publication Data

Strayer, Barry L. (Barry Lee), 1932–
  The Canadian constitution and the courts

3rd ed.
Includes bibliographical references and index.
ISBN 0–409–80631–5

1. Judicial review—Canada.   2. Canada—
Constitutional law.   I. Title.

KE4248.S77 1988   347.71′012   C87–095089–4   KF4483.J8S85 1988

Sponsoring Editor: Paul Truster
Executive Editor (P. & A.): Lebby Hines
Managing Editor: Linda Kee
Supervisory Editor: Marie Graham
Freelance Projects Coordinator/Cover Design: Catherine Haskell
Editor: June Masuda
Production: Jill Thomson

Preface

This edition reflects, I believe, the dramatic changes which have occurred in constitutional judicial review during the four years since the last edition was published. These changes include a major increase in the number of cases involving constitutional issues, the dominance of Charter questions in constitutional litigation, and the greatly heightened profile of the Supreme Court of Canada as innovating leader in the interpretation of the new constitutional provisions. Correspondingly, the reader will find in this book a new emphasis on the Charter and on the jurisprudence of the Supreme Court of Canada. At the same time, I have sought to maintain a continuity between the judicial review of the past and that of the present, and to accord appropriate space to developments in the judicial review process as it relates to distribution of power issues.

Readers will note, and some may lament, that there is still no extended development in the book of a particular theory of judicial review upon which any given decision is tested. There is, particularly in Chapters 2 and 10, a serious consideration of the legitimacy of judicial review, and the preservation of that legitimacy. But I have not embraced either of the extremes popular to current judicial review theory, those of "interpretivism" and of "non-interpretivism". As with most dichotomous analyses, neither option is fully satisfying, howsoever useful they may be in contrasting the implications and results of either approach if carried to its logical conclusion. "Interpretivism", sometimes denigrated as "historicism", involves essentially a reliance by courts on the text of the constitution as the main source of guidance in applying constitutional requirements to the matter in hand. "Non-interpretivism" involves minimal concern with the text, but rather judicial resort to philosophy, morals, general (usually intuitively-determined) principles of constitutionalism, "integrity", etc.

I believe it will emerge from a reading of this book that I favour a resort to "interpretivism" as the most important starting place. I argue for this particularly in relation to the Charter because it is of very recent adoption: its words and concepts are contemporary, not (as with the U.S. Bill of Rights) the language of centuries past. Further, I indicate a preference for what might elsewhere be dismissed as "historicism": that is, a resort to the *travaux préparatoires* leading to the *Constitution Act, 1982* which may elucidate the political will upon which its legitimacy (and the legitimacy of judicial review under the Charter) ultimately rests. I further suggest that a resort to those sources will put the Charter in its proper context—that of an instrument designed not only to protect individual rights but also to preserve as much as possible the pre-existing norm of parliamentary sovereignty. That history shaped the Charter just as much as the perceived iniquities of rule by a strong British executive and Parliament shaped the Constitution of the United States and its first 10 amendments. Such history cannot be irrelevant to an interpretation of the words of constitutional instruments. This is not to say that the text or its history will resolve all questions. There is clearly a role for "non-interpretivism", and a resort to constitutional policy (as conceived by the courts), but only where the primary sources have not provided adequate guidance. This is an approach most suitable to the present, in these years closely following the adoption of the Charter. It will not necessarily represent the right set of priorities for judicial review three or four decades from now.

The law is described essentially as it stood on May 1, 1987, with a few exceptions involving important recent jurisprudence and rule changes in the Supreme Court of Canada. I have only briefly noted the constitutional changes which may flow from the agreement of the First Ministers of June 3, 1987, as these have not yet been formally adopted.

I wish to acknowledge gratefully the research grant provided by the Social Sciences and Humanities Research Council which enabled me to undertake this task. I especially thank my Research Assistant, Ruth Grealis, and my secretary, Francine Roy, for their thorough and tireless work in connection with this revision. I am grateful to former Dean H.A. Hubbard and Madeleine Dupont of the Common Law Faculty, University of Ottawa, who assisted with the administration of my research funds. I valued greatly the research facilities and assistance provided by the Human Rights Research and Education Centre, University of Ottawa, and particularly the help of its Librarian, Iva Caccia. I also appreciate the patience and assistance of my wife Eleanor during the year involved in the completion of this work.

The net royalties from this edition will go to the College of Law, University of Saskatchewan, for the provision of a prize in constitutional law.

B.L. Strayer
Ottawa
August 1987

Contents

Table of Cases

Chapter 1

Nature and History of Judicial Review

A. NATURE OF JUDICIAL REVIEW

The constitution is a set of rules governing in certain ways the conduct of Governments. Like most sets of rules, it is generally observed voluntarily by those whose actions it governs. But there are times when it is not observed, even though the non-observance may be unintended or even unperceived. Very frequently the breach is not perceived because the constitution is general in its terms and its application to specific and novel situations is far from clear.

Where governmental action does not conform to the constitution, there is no assurance that conformity will be enforced. Parties affected may not notice the violation or they may acquiesce in it. There are no "constitutional police" to ferret out constitutionally invalid behaviour and see that it is punished. Certainly the courts have no power to initiate a review of governmental action to enforce the constitution.

The courts nevertheless play a major role in ensuring that governmental action generally corresponds to constitutional requirements and limitations. There is commonly someone, an individual, a corporation, or frequently another level of government, who has an interest in stopping invalid action. Where ordinary protests do not avail, such interested party may be able to raise before a court the issue of constitutional validity and thus achieve judicial review of the governmental behaviour in question. The court will then determine whether it is or is not in conformity with the constitution.

Throughout most of our history such judicial review in Canada has mainly been concerned with the validity of federal or provincial legislation. While that will remain an important form of judicial review, the portions of the constitution adopted in 1982,[1] in particular the *Canadian Charter of Rights and Freedoms*, impose new norms on the conduct of the executive branch of government, conduct which may not have any basis in legislation. Thus judicial review for the enforcement of the constitution now frequently involves an examination of executive, instead of legislative, action.

---

[1] *Constitution Act, 1982*, enacted by *Canada Act*, 1982, c. 11, Schedule B (U.K.).

It should be noted at the outset of a work such as this that judicial review is not and cannot be the only device for applying constitutional norms. Every element of government, whether executive, legislative, or judicial, shares the responsibility of ensuring that such norms are observed. It is not possible to leave all of this responsibility to the courts as they would be unable to cope with the sheer volume and the quasi-political burden this would impose. Nor would it be healthy for the body politic of a parliamentary democracy such as ours, where we expect elected representatives to be the principal decision-makers.

While it is apparent, therefore, that judicial review is not an exclusive, nor invariably effective, means of ensuring that the constitution is observed, it is of pervasive importance to the maintenance of constitutional government. Apart from offering a final resolution for many specific disputes, constitutional decisions of the courts have profoundly influenced the common understanding of governments as to their respective powers and responsibilities. As the Canadian constitution until recently has nowhere mentioned judicial review, it is legitimate to inquire as to the source of this fundamental mechanism of our governmental system.

B. JUDICIAL REVIEW AND THE COMMON LAW

The concept of judicial review of legislation in Canada is not an inheritance from the common law. We have come to accept it as a fundamental, authorized by that unwritten law which is the source of so much of the judicial power. But it must be acknowledged that English common law as received by Canada had rejected the claim of some judges to the right to review acts of Parliament for validity. The practice which came to be so widely accepted within the Imperial system with respect to colonial legislation was an outgrowth of that particular system, implicit in the royal instructions, charters, or Imperial statutes creating the colonial Legislatures.

It is true that English courts had more than once asserted a power to pass judgment on the validity of parliamentary legislation. The most outstanding example of this was found in Lord Coke's pronouncement in *Dr. Bonham's Case*:[2] "And it appears in our books, that in many cases, the common law will controul Acts of Parliament, and sometimes adjudge them to be utterly void: for when an Act of Parliament is against common right and reason, or repugnant, or impossible to be performed, the common law will controul it, and adjudge such Act to be void". This appeal to a fundamental law was obviously expedient for one apprehensive of the power struggle between Parliament and the Crown which was developing in the early seventeenth century. While some other English

---

[2](1610), 8 Co. Rep. 114a at 118a, 77 E.R. 646 at 652 (K.B.).

judges accepted and applied Coke's *dictum*, and the principle received some support from contemporary digests and treatises, its star was in the descent by the start of the eighteenth century and had fallen into oblivion by the middle of the nineteenth.[3] In the end, the supremacy of Parliament was accepted in England in preference to the supremacy of the courts. At the end of the last century Maitland[4] was able to dismiss in a few words the concept of judicial review: "Just now and then in the last of the Middle Ages and thence onwards into the eighteenth century, we hear the judges claiming some vague right of disregarding statutes which are directly at variance with the common law, or the law of God, or the royal prerogative. Had much come of this claim, our constitution must have taken a very different shape from that which we see at the present day. Little came of it . . . [T]he theory is but a speculative dogma".

It is not surprising, however, that the concept of a higher law (imposed by the judges) controlling Parliament commended itself to the North American colonies which subsequently formed the United States of America. The views of Coke and his seventeenth-century supporters were well known in the colonies settled in that period.[5] In the following century these colonies developed a strong antipathy to Parliament and to the principles of parliamentary supremacy. This antipathy, combined with the philosophy of natural rights popularized in revolutionary America, gave fertile ground for the seeds sown by Coke. Some courts in the 13 colonies were able to pass judgment on colonial legislation, invoking a higher principle such as "natural law" or the "common law".[6] This set the stage for judicial review based on the limitations of written constitutions, a development which culminated in the celebrated *Marbury v. Madison*.[7]

In the colonies which were later to become part of the Dominion of Canada, there is little evidence that Coke's *dictum* ever had any serious influence. Many factors contributed to this situation. For example, settlement in the English-speaking areas was insignificant until the eighteenth century, well after the English civil wars of the preceding century had established the supremacy of Parliament to the general satisfaction of the populace. During and after the American Revolution loyal supporters of the Crown in the northern colonies, many of them fugitives from that upheaval, were also inclined to reject the natural rights theories which had contributed to the open breach between England and their neighbours.

Among the French settlers there was even more antipathy toward

---

[3]Plucknett, "Bonham's Case and Judicial Review" (1926), 40 *Harv. L. Rev.* 30, *passim*.
[4]2 Maitland, *Collected Papers* (1911), 481.
[5]Plucknett, *supra*, note 3, at pp. 61–62; McGovney, "The British Origin of Judicial Review of Legislation" (1944), 93 *U. Pa. L. Rev.* 1 at 7–8.
[6]Plucknett, *supra*, note 3, at pp. 61–68.
[7]1 Cranch 137, 5 U.S. 87 (1803).

the republicanism and what they regarded as the excesses of democracy to the south. The Imperial Parliament was not to them the inevitable oppressor; the *Quebec Act, 1774*,[8] which to the 13 colonies was one of the "Intolerable Acts", was to them a guarantee of their law and religion.

Apart from these factors, when the Dominion of Canada finally emerged as an entity in 1867 positivism was in the ascendancy in England. The whole letter and spirit of the *British North America Act 1867*[9] bears witness to this fact. The Act is as prosaic as any municipal charter. Absent are the ringing declarations of the United States Constitution and its amendments, declarations of eternal principles such as "justice", "liberty", "freedom", or "due process". The Act assumes the collective supremacy of the legislative branch: Parliament and the provincial Legislatures are given powers which, according to the Privy Council, "cover the whole area of self-government within the whole area of Canada".[10] While this oversimplifies the situation, there are only a few sections of the original Act which prevent legislative action at both the federal and provincial levels. These include the guarantees with respect to the use of English and French (s. 133), denominational schools (s. 93), an annual session of Parliament (s. 20), and duty-free movements of goods among provinces (s. 121). It is arguable that there are some other guarantees expressed or implied in the Act.[11] But these guarantees are limited and in the main inherently related to the federal and bicultural nature of the Canadian state. They do not reflect any general belief in 1867 that the people of Canada required protection against omnipotent Legislatures.

As a result, constitutional judicial review in Canada until recently was concerned almost exclusively with the division of powers between the provinces and the federal authorities. The courts refused to concern themselves with the wisdom or fairness of legislation,[12] or even the possibility of abuse of a legislative power,[13] so long as the impugned legislation was not being used as a means of invading a forbidden area under the guise of exercising a power given to the enacting Legislature.[14] That

---

[8] 14 Geo. III, c. 83 (U.K.).

[9] 1867, 30 & 31 Vict., c. 3 (U.K.) (*now Constitution Act, 1867*).

[10] *A.G. Ont. v. A.G. Can.*, [1912] A.C. 571 at 581, 3 D.L.R. 509 (P.C.).

[11] See *e.g.* Laskin, "An Inquiry into the Diefenbaker Bill of Rights" (1959), 37 *Can. Bar Rev.* 77 at 99–100.

[12] See *e.g. A.G. Ont. v. A.G. Can., supra*, note 10 at p. 583; *Royal Bank of Canada v. The King*, [1913] A.C. 283 at 296, [1911–13] All E.R. Rep. 846, 3 W.W.R. 994, 9 D.L.R. 337 (P.C.); *Co-operative Committee on Japanese Canadians v. A.G. Can.*, [1947] A.C. 87 at 102, [1947] 1 D.L.R. 577 (P.C.); *Amax Potash Ltd. v. Sask.*, [1977] 2 S.C.R. 576 at 590, [1976] 6 W.W.R. 61, 71 D.L.R. (3d) 1 at 10, 11 N.R. 222.

[13] *Bank of Toronto v. Lambe* (1887), 12 App. Cas. 575 at 587 (P.C.); *A.G. Can. v. A.G. Ont.*, [1898] A.C. 700 at 712–13 (P.C.).

[14] See *e.g. A.G. Ont. v. Reciprocal Insurers*, [1924] A.C. 328, [1924] 2 W.W.R. 397,

is, provided that the federal authorities did not infringe on provincial powers, nor the provinces on the federal power, the courts would not interfere.

It was only with the adoption of the *Constitution Act, 1982*[15] that Canadian courts faced the prospect of enforcing wide-ranging qualitative limitations on all legislative and administrative powers. The *Constitution Act, 1982*, apart from effecting the "patriation" of the Canadian constitution by providing for an amending formula and terminating the remaining formal amending authority of Westminster, also made some substantive additions to the constitution including the *Canadian Charter of Rights and Freedoms*. This Charter binds both levels of government and imposes limitations on them by guaranteeing certain fundamental and democratic rights, as well as rights of free movement, legal rights, egalitarian rights and linguistic rights. Thus it obliges the courts to apply the same limitations to both Parliament and the Legislatures as to the manner in which they exercise legislative power that is otherwise within their respective jurisdictions. Also, by their nature some of the guaranteed rights impose restrictions on how administrative authority is exercised, and here again the courts have new and different supervisory powers unconnected to the traditional surveillance of the distribution of legislative powers.

In its origins, however, judicial review in Canada was a product of the Imperial system, based on a jurisdiction implicit in the Imperial statutes which distributed legislative power with respect to Canadian affairs. It was not based on a specific mandate nor on a jurisdiction inherent in Anglo-Canadian courts by virtue of the common law. Its primary focus was the protection of federalism, not of individual rights.

C. PRE-CONFEDERATION PRACTICE

1. The Imperial System and Judicial Review

Throughout the Empire, colonial Legislatures were Legislatures of limited power. Apart from their territorial limitations (they could not pass extra-territorial legislation), they were enjoined from enacting laws conflicting with those of the mother land. The extent of this latter restriction was for many years in doubt. As early as 1696 an Imperial statute entitled

---

[1924] 1 D.L.R. 789, 41 C.C.C. 336 (P.C.); *A.G. Alta. v. A.G. Can.*, [1939] A.C. 117, [1938] 3 W.W.R. 337, [1938] 4 D.L.R. 433 (P.C.); *Can. Fed. of Agriculture v. A.G. Que.*, [1951] A.C. 179, [1950] 4 D.L.R. 689.

[15]*Supra*, note 1.

An act for preventing frauds, and regulating abuses in the plantation trade[16] had provided:

> IX. And it is further enacted and declared by the authority aforesaid, That all laws, by-laws, usages or customs, at this time, or which hereafter shall be in practice, or endeavoured or pretended to be in force or practice, in any of the said plantations, which are in any wise repugnant to the before mentioned laws, or any of them, so far as they do relate to the said plantations, or any of them, or which are any ways repugnant to this present act, *or to any other law hereafter to be made in this kingdom, so far as such law shall relate to and mention the said plantations*, are illegal, null and void, to all intents and purposes whatsoever.

This statute clearly indicates that a colonial law would not be void unless it conflicted with an English statute either existing or future (''law hereafter to be *made* in this kingdom''), which specifically applied to the colony or colonies.

The colonial charters, granted in the exercise of the royal prerogative and usually in the form of instructions to the governor with respect to the establishment of a colonial legislative body, were not always as specific. While they generally restricted the legislative power, the extent of the limitation was not clear. Typical of such instructions were those issued to Governor Edward Cornwallis by letters patent in 1749 with respect to establishment of the first representative assembly in the colonies now forming part of Canada. The commission provided that the Governor, with the advice and consent of this assembly, ''shall have full power and authority to make, constitute and ordain Laws, Statutes and Ordinances for the Publick peace, welfare and good government of our said province . . . which said Laws, Statutes and Ordinances are not to be repugnant but as near as may be agreeable to the Laws and Statutes of this our Kingdom of Great Britain''.[17]

The commission to Governor Murray of Quebec in 1763 authorizing an assembly (which was never elected or summoned) had an identical wording[18] and the pre-Confederation prerogative constitutions of other colonies now part of Canada had similar or identical provisions.[19]

What did this clause mean? To what ''Laws and Statutes of this our Kingdom of Great Britain'' did it refer? Did it include all the law, including the common law, and all the statutes including those which did not specifically apply to the colonies? It is clear that some colonial courts

---

[16]1696, 7 & 8 Will. III, c. 22, s. 9 (Imp.), (emphasis added).

[17]Akins, *Selections from the Public Documents of the Province of Nova Scotia* (1869), 497 at 500.

[18]Shortt and Doughty, *Documents Relating to the Constitutional History of Canada, 1759–1791* (1918), 173 at 175.

[19]See Read, ''The Early Provincial Constitutions'' (1948), 26 *Can. Bar Rev.* 621, *passim*.

took a narrow view of this royal injunction. In testing the validity of colonial statutes they took into account only those Imperial statutes clearly extending to the colony.[20] In other parts of the Empire this restriction on the legislative power was given a much wider meaning.[21] Largely as a result of the enthusiasm of Mr. Justice Boothby in South Australia for striking down colonial laws on the basis of repugnancy,[22] the rule was clarified and narrowed by the *Colonial Laws Validity Act, 1865*.[23] This Act provided that colonial laws would be void only for repugnancy to "any Act of Parliament extending to the colony to which such law may relate, or . . . to any order or regulation made under authority of such Act of Parliament, or having in the colony the force or effect of such Act". In the meantime, the united province of Canada had already achieved this position by Imperial statute.[24]

This background is important now only to the extent that it helped to set the stage for judicial review throughout the Empire. The *Colonial Laws Validity Act, 1865*, continued until 1982[25] with respect to one set of Imperial statutes extending to Canada, that is, the B.N.A. Acts. While the *Statute of Westminster, 1931*, released both Parliament and the provincial Legislatures from the general prohibition of the *Colonial Laws Validity Act* against passing laws repugnant to Imperial statutes, the B.N.A. Acts were kept under the protection of the 1865 Act.[26] When a Canadian court struck down a statute for constitutional invalidity, it was inarticulately applying the *Colonial Laws Validity Act*, holding void the Canadian statute for repugnancy to the provisions of the B.N.A. Act distributing power between Parliament and Legislatures.[27] It may be noted in passing

---

[20]See *Uniacke v. Dickson* (1848), 2 N.S.R. 287 (Ch.).

[21]See *e.g. Winthrop v. Lechmere* (1727), 3 *Acts of the Privy Council (Colonial Series)* (1910), at 139–50.

[22]For the consequences to Mr. Justice Boothby of his actions, see Todd, *Parliamentary Government in the British Colonies*, 2nd ed. (1894), at 846–54; Keith, *Responsible Government in the Dominions* (1912), vol. 1 at 402ff.

[23]28 & 29 Vict., c. 63, s. 2 (U.K.). See also s. 3.

[24]*Union Act*, 1840, 3 & 4 Vict., c. 35, s. 3 (U.K.).

[25]By virtue of item 17 of the schedule to the *Constitution Act, 1982, supra*, note 1, s. 7(1) of the *Statute of Westminster*, 1931, 22 Geo. V, c. 4 (U.K.), which had continued the applicability of the *Colonial Laws Validity Act* to preserve the supremacy of the B.N.A. Acts over federal or provincial laws, was repealed with respect to Canada. It was replaced in effect by s. 52 of the *Constitution Act, 1982*, which makes the "Constitution of Canada" the "supreme law of Canada". The "Constitution of Canada" is defined in that section so as to include, *inter alia*, what were the B.N.A. Acts. These developments are discussed more fully *infra*, pp. 31–33.

[26]*Statute of Westminster*, 1931, 22 & 23 Geo. V, c. 4, s. 7 (U.K.); the B.N.A. Acts, 1867–1930 were all so protected therein.

[27]In earlier times the courts sometimes expressly applied the *Colonial Laws Validity Act, 1865*. See *e.g. R. v. Chandler; Re Hazleton* (1869), 12 N.B.R. 556 (C.A.).

that neither the *Colonial Laws Validity Act* nor the B.N.A. Acts specifically empowered the courts to exercise this power. The judiciary simply continued a practice which was implicitly permitted by earlier charters and statutes of the Imperial system.

In the northern colonies which now form part of Canada, there had been courts in operation from the early days of British rule. The first such court was established in 1721 at Annapolis Royal, by order in council of Governor Phillips, which court was to have the same powers and procedures as did the General Court in Virginia.[28] Less than two months after the fall of Quebec Governor Murray established a court, and there has been an unbroken succession of judicial institutions in Canada since that time.[29]

There is, however, no clear evidence that prior to Confederation any of these courts actually struck down a colonial statute for invalidity. They apparently were prepared to hold invalid other exercises of legislative power where such power had been delegated to the executive branch. The Supreme Court of Prince Edward Island[30] in 1856 held invalid an order of the lieutenant governor in council on the grounds that it was not authorized by the statute under which it was passed. A Lower Canadian court held void letters patent of the local governor which purported to give precedence to a judge newly appointed to its bench. The decision was reversed by the Privy Council,[31] but on substantive grounds not connected with the right of review of the colonial court. Also, in New Brunswick the Supreme Court, while rejecting the argument that it could hold a colonial statute invalid simply because it interfered with property rights, clearly recognized in *obiter* that it could hold invalid a statute which was repugnant to Imperial law extending to the colony.[32]

These reported decisions all indicate an awareness in the courts of the northern colonies that they could supervise the exercise of limited powers granted under charters or statutes. Whether the courts in what is now Canada ever invalidated *ultra vires* legislation is not clear, but it may be assumed fairly confidently that at the time of Confederation they would have been prepared to do so in a proper case. If the legislative instrument of a colonial lieutenant governor in council could be set aside for want of authority, the same could be done to a colonial statute which exceeded the legislative powers conferred on the colonial assembly.

The practice in other parts of the Empire would have reassured British North American courts in this regard. There is evidence that in the eight-

---

[28] 3 *Nova Scotia Archives*, at 28–29, quoted in Chisholm, "An Approaching Bicentenary" (1918), 38 *Can. L.T.* 727 at 728.
[29] Riddell, "The First British Courts in Canada" (1924), 33 *Yale L.J.* 571.
[30] *Bourke v. Murphy* (1856), 1 P.E.I. L.R. 126 (S.C.).
[31] *Re Bedard* (1849), 7 Moo. P.C. 23, 13 E.R. 788, 1 Can. Rep. 328 (P.C.).
[32] *R. v. Kerr* (1838), Ber. 367, 2 N.B.R. 553 (S.C.).

eenth century the courts in the colonies to the south had reviewed the validity of colonial statutes[33] and had even attempted to review orders of the Privy Council.[34] The Judicial Committee of the Privy Council itself had implicitly approved the practice of judicial review in colonial courts. In the case of *Cameron v. Kyte*[35] in 1835 the Judicial Committee upheld a decision of the Supreme Court of Civil Justice of the West Indian colony of Bernice, in which that court had treated a regulation passed by the governor as being of no effect. The regulation was a legislative instrument purporting to reduce the commission payable to the vendue master, a public official who conducted all public auctions. The local court had given judgment for the vendue master for the full amount of his commission, thus refusing to apply the governor's regulation. With respect to this decision the Privy Council judgment stated: "But if the Governor be an officer, merely with a *limited authority* from the Crown, his assumption of an act of sovereign power, out of the limits of the authority so given to him, would be purely void, and the Courts of the colony over which he presided could not give it any legal effect".[36] This points up the essential element of judicial review in the Empire: a "limited authority", the purported exercise of which could always be examined for validity by the courts.

English courts did not hesitate to test the validity of colonial legislative instruments, even those issued by the Imperial authorities. In the well-known case of *Campbell v. Hall*[37] Lord Mansfield held invalid letters patent issued in London fixing a duty of four and one-half per cent on all sugar exported from Grenada. Here again limited authority was being exercised: the royal prerogative with respect to the colony was subject to restrictions imposed by Parliament and to restrictions resulting from previous prerogative acts done with respect to the colony. The latter type of restriction was decisive here, because previous letters patent in April 1764 had authorized the summoning of a legislative assembly (which was in fact summoned in 1765). The letters patent with respect to the export duty were issued in July 1764. In an action brought in England against Hall, the collector of the export duty, for a return of sums paid pursuant to the latter letters patent, Lord Mansfield held them to be invalid because the King had precluded himself from further legislative action with respect to the colony once he authorized the summoning of a local Legislature.

Legislative or quasi-legislative action of colonial assemblies also

---

[33]McGovney, "The British Origin of Judicial Review of Legislation" (1944), 93 *U. Pa. L. Rev.* 1, *passim.*

[34]Davis, "The Case of Frost v. Leighton" (1896–7), 2 *Am. Hist. Rev.* 229; Smith, *Appeals to the Privy Council from the American Plantations* (1965), at 328–33.

[35](1835), 3 Knapp's P.C. 332, 12 E.R. 678.

[36]3 Knapp's P.C. at 334, 12 E.R. at 683 (emphasis added).

[37](1774), 1 Cowp. 204, 98 E.R. 1045 (K.B.).

came before domestic English courts. In *Watson's Case*[38] an application was made in the English King's Bench for *habeas corpus* on behalf of Watson who was being detained at Liverpool awaiting transportation to Van Diemen's Land. Conditionally pardoned for offences against the state in Upper Canada, he had been ordered transported and was in transit when this application was made. The validity of Upper Canadian legislation authorizing this procedure was challenged, and the King's Bench, after thorough consideration, upheld it as being authorized by the *Constitutional Act, 1791*.[39]

This practice in other colonial courts and in the domestic English courts must have been known to the pre-Confederation courts in British North America, and they must have accepted it as a proper exercise of judicial power. More important even than these precedents, however, would be the practice of the Privy Council as the supreme appellate tribunal of the Empire. The history and functions of that body deserve special examination.

2. The Privy Council and Judicial Review

The king as the fountain-head of justice is an ancient concept in English law.[40] With the creation of the ordinary courts for handling domestic judicial business, the judicial power of the king's prerogative courts became more and more reduced. The Star Chamber continued to exercise powers with respect to domestic matters until its activities were finally stopped by Act of Parliament in 1640.[41] This statute not only abolished the Star Chamber and similar tribunals, but also forbade the King and his Privy Council from exercising judicial power in matters which the ordinary courts of law were already empowered to hear.

This prohibition did not apparently extend to matters arising within the King's domains beyond England: such matters were not necessarily within the jurisdiction of English courts.[42] It was not surprising then that questions arising within the colonies might be considered to fall within that residual royal prerogative of justice. As early as the fifteenth century, appeals to the Privy Council from the Channel Islands had been regulated, and in an order of 1674 the trade and plantations committee of the Council

---

[38](1839), 9 Ad. & El. 731, 112 E.R. 1389 (K.B.).

[39]31 Geo. III, c. 31 (U.K.).

[40]See *e.g.* Bracton, *Treatise on the Laws and Customs of England*, Twiss ed. (1878–83), fol. 107.

[41]*Habeas Corpus Act*, 1640, 16 Car. I, c. 10 (Imp.).

[42]See Smith, *supra*, note 34, at pp. 3–5.

was assigned the duty of dealing with such matters.[43] In the eighteenth century further orders in council provided generally for appeals from the colonies.[44] It was said in *obiter* by Lord Macclesfield in a 1724 Chancery case[45] that English domestic courts could not deal with appeals from colonial courts, that such appeals must go to the King in council.

The modern era of the Privy Council's judicial work began in 1833 when the Judicial Committee was first created by statute.[46] Until this time the composition of the committee which heard appeals was often unsatisfactory, with many lay members. The 1833 Act created the "Judicial Committee of the Privy Council" to be composed of the president of the Privy Council, the Lord Chancellor, the Lord Chief Justice, and various judges. The Act gave the committee jurisdiction over Admiralty appeals from the colonies, and conferred on it power to hear all appeals which the King or the King in council had previously been authorized to hear. A further statute of 1844[47] extended the committee's jurisdiction by authorizing appeals from the lower colonial courts, even with respect to those jurisdictions where local law only permitted appeals to the Judicial Committee from the final court of appeal in the colony. The basic jurisdiction of the committee did not change significantly thereafter until after the *Statute of Westminster, 1931*,[48] though a number of statutes altered its composition by making eligible for membership various other English and colonial judges.[49]

After the middle of the seventeenth century the colonial charters generally specified a right of appeal from colonial courts to the Privy Council.[50] There was usually a limitation to the effect that decisions of the local courts would be final unless there was more than a specified minimum amount involved. Where so authorized by its charter the local Legislature could further limit, abolish, or extend the appeal as of right.[51] The 1844 Act which extended the jurisdiction of the Judicial Committee apparently empowered the Queen in council to circumvent local limita-

---

[43]*Supra*, at p. 70.

[44]Finlason, *The History, Constitution and Character of the Judicial Committee of the Privy Council* (1878), at 37–39; Pierson, *Canada and the Privy Council* (1960), at 6–7.

[45]*Fryer v. Bernard* (1724), 2 P. Wms. 261 at 262, 24 E.R. 722 at 723 (Ch.).

[46]*Judicial Committee Act*, 1833, 3 & 4 Wm. IV, c. 41 (U.K.).

[47]The *Judicial Committee Act*, 1844, 7 & 8 Vict., c. 69, s. 1 (U.K.).

[48]1931, 22 Geo. V, c. 4 (U.K.).

[49]See *e.g. Judicial Committee Act*, 1881, 44 & 45 Vict., c. 3 (U.K.); *Judicial Committee Amendment Act*, 1895, 58 & 59 Vict., c. 44 (U.K.); *Appellate Jurisdiction Act*, 1908, 8 Edw. VII (U.K.), c. 51; *Appellate Jurisdiction Act*, 1913, 3 & 4 Geo. V, c. 21 (U.K.).

[50]See Read, "The Early Provincial Constitutions" (1948), 26 *Can. Bar Rev.* 621.

[51]*Cuvillier v. Aylwin* (1832), 2 Knapp's P.C. 72, 12 E.R. 406; *disapproved* in *Cushing v. Dupuy* (1880), 5 App. Cas. 409 at 417, 42 L.T. 445 (P.C.).

tions on appeals as of right from the lower courts.[52] While colonial law might restrict or abolish appeals as of right from the highest court in the colony, there remained the power of the Judicial Committee to grant special leave to appeal from any colonial court. This was a continuation of the old prerogative power of the Crown as the fountain-head of justice. The challenge to this power by the Parliament of Canada, and the failure of that challenge, will be discussed later.

Within this framework of appellate jurisdiction, the Privy Council was able and willing to review the validity of colonial legislation from time to time. There is evidence of this power being used at least four times with respect to legislation in the American colonies prior to 1776 and the Revolution,[53] the first instance being the case of *Winthrop v. Lechmere*[54] in 1726. After the American Revolution the Privy Council apparently did not have the occasion to use the power for some time.

We have already seen that in 1835 in the case of *Cameron v. Kyte*[55] the Judicial Committee affirmed the judgment of the Supreme Court of Civil Justice of Bernice, striking down the order of the governor which had reduced the vendue master's commission. In *Kielley v. Carson*,[56] in 1842, the committee heard an appeal from the Supreme Court of Judicature of Newfoundland which turned on the validity of a resolution of the Legislature of that colony. The plaintiff had, pursuant to the resolution, been imprisoned for contempt of the Legislature with respect to certain remarks he had made outside that assembly. He sued the speaker and others for assault, battery, and false imprisonment, contending that the Legislature had no power to commit for contempt. The local court had dismissed the action, but the Judicial Committee allowed the appeal. It found that the Legislature had no authority to punish for contempt not committed in the face of the Legislature. Such action was outside the grant of powers in the commission which, in 1832, had conferred on the inhabitants the right to have a legislative assembly. It was said that such a power could not be implied in the mere authority to have an assembly.

In *Re Cape Breton*[57] the Judicial Committee was asked to consider the validity of royal instructions issued in London in 1820 to the governor of Nova Scotia. The commission indicated that Cape Breton Island was to be annexed to Nova Scotia. A petition was presented to the Queen opposing this action, it being contended *inter alia* that the prerogative

---

[52]*Judicial Committee Act, 1844*, 7 & 8 Vict., c. 69, s. 1 (U.K.).

[53]McGovney, "The British Origin of Judicial Review of Legislation" (1944), 93 *U. Pa. L. Rev.* 1 at 13–34.

[54](1727), 3 *Acts of the Privy Council (Colonial Series)* 1910, at 139–50.

[55]*Supra*, note 35 and accompanying text.

[56](1842), 4 Moo. P.C.C. 63, 13 E.R. 225.

[57](1846), 5 Moo. P.C.C. 259, 13 E.R. 489.

power to annex Cape Breton to another colony had been irrevocably divested by the Crown when it had granted letters patent in 1784 authorizing a separate government and assembly for the island. The Queen's advisors referred the petition to the Judicial Committee for a determination of the legal, as opposed to the policy, questions[58] and that body rejected the petition. The decision was in the form of a report simply expressing the opinion that the inhabitants of the island were not entitled as of right to a constitution of their own.

There is nothing to indicate that the Judicial Committee or its predecessor, the Committee on Trade and Plantations, ever suffered from any doubts about the propriety of reviewing the exercise of subordinate legislative authority with respect to the colonies. Its practice would undoubtedly have been well known throughout the Empire, providing strong precedents for the exercise of a similar power by colonial courts.

It could be argued, of course, that the Privy Council in reviewing colonial legislation was performing a political function. The royal power of disallowance of colonial legislation was well recognized. Since 1631, when the laws of the newly constituted royal province of Virginia were first sent to England for royal assent, the Crown had played a vital political role in the colonial legislative process.[59] In the royal province of Massachusetts, for example, in the period 1691–1775 some 59 statutes were disallowed.[60] Of these, some 13 were disallowed because they were "repugnant to the Laws of England" or otherwise exceeded the powers granted under the colonial charter.[61] At first blush it might seem difficult to distinguish this procedure, where the King's advisors would recommend disallowance of a colonial Act for excess of jurisdiction, from that procedure by which his Privy Council would advise that a colonial law was invalid because of a similar excess. Could it be argued that the committee was really performing a political function in reviewing colonial legislation, a function to which colonial courts themselves could not aspire? It has been pointed out that in the modern constitution the Privy Council would be subject to the control of Parliament,[62] and therefore it could be considered purely a political body. It has also been noted that

---

[58]By the *Judicial Committee Act*, 1833, 3 & 4 Will. IV, c. 41, s. 4 (U.K.), the sovereign was given power to refer to the Judicial Committee "any such other matters whatsoever as His Majesty shall think fit".

[59]Dorland, *The Royal Disallowance in Massachusetts*, Bulletin No. 22, Departments of History and Political and Economic Science, Queen's University, Kingston (1917), at 1–5.

[60]*Ibid.*, at p. 5.

[61]*Ibid.*, at pp. 6, 23.

[62]Haines, "Judicial Review of Legislation in Canada" (1915), 28 *Harv. L. Rev.* 565 at 587–88.

in one aspect of its work the Judicial Committee acted more like a political than a judicial agency: it did not publish dissenting opinions but instead revealed only one conclusion, advice for the sovereign unqualified by the dissents of those members of the committee who had been overruled by the majority.[63] One would expect the members of a purely judicial tribunal to be free to express the views to which they are led by their reason and conscience, not forced to conceal their honestly held opinions for the sake of unanimity.

In spite of the foregoing it must surely be conceded that, in review of legislation on appeal from the colonies, the committee was exercising a judicial function. Firstly, the power of disallowance and the power of judicial review are distinguishable. The effect of disallowance is to nullify the statute as of the date it is disallowed. A judicial determination of invalidity means that it was void *ab initio*. Disallowance was used for a variety of reasons unassociated with validity.[64] As we have seen, the Judicial Committee or its forerunner dealt with the validity of royal instruments other than those to which the power of disallowance would apply. Secondly, the Committee on Trade and Plantations or the Judicial Committee did in substance act in a judicial manner in dealing with appeals. As early as the *Winthrop* case in 1727 lawyers were engaged in presenting argument and the proceedings were apparently conducted like those in court. Thirdly, when the new committee was established by statute in 1833, it was composed predominantly of judicial, not political officers. The adjective ''Judicial'' used in the title clearly indicates the intention of Parliament. After 1833 the changes made in its composition were directed to strengthening the committee's judicial character.

We can thus see that, as Confederation approached, the judges and lawyers in the colonies of British North America must have been familiar to some degree with the British doctrine of judicial review of colonial legislation. Courts in other colonies had exercised this function, some British North American courts had at least exercised an analogous function, and the English courts had not hesitated to deal with colonial legislative validity where it was relevant to their proceedings. The Judicial Committee, as the supreme judicial body of the colonial system, had provided ample precedents for judicial review. Its practice would have led the colonial courts to consider the question of validity where necessary, in anticipation of that issue being dealt with in London on appeal.

The constitutional law of the Empire in 1867 thus embraced the principle that where legislative powers were granted subject to limitations the courts would enforce those limitations. The B.N.A. Act was drafted and enacted in this context.

---

[63]Finlason, *The History, Constitution and Character of the Judicial Committee of the Privy Council* (1878), at iii–xi.

[64]Dorland, *supra*, note 59 at p. 6.

D. CONFEDERATION AND AFTER

1. Expectations at Confederation

It is surprising that the question of judicial review and the position of the courts in relation to the new Parliament and Legislatures of Canada was not given more express consideration at the time of Confederation. The records of the Quebec Conference of 1864 do not suggest that this matter was discussed directly, though there was some interest in the possible creation of a general court of appeal. In the Confederation Debates in the Parliament of the Province of Canada in 1865 little mention is made of it and the comments which do appear are not very helpful.

Sir John A. Macdonald, Attorney General West, minimized the problem, through either shrewdness or naïveté. In the Confederation Debates he explained the virtues of the proposed constitution as outlined in the Quebec Resolutions of the previous year:

> We have given the General Legislature all the great subjects of legislation. We have conferred on them, not only specifically and in detail, all the powers which are incident to sovereignty, but we have expressly declared that all subjects of general interest not distinctly and exclusively conferred upon the local governments and local legislatures, shall be conferred upon the General Government and Legislature. We have thus avoided that great source of weakness which has been the cause of the disruption of the United States. *We have avoided all conflict of jurisdiction and authority.* . . .[65]

> . . . .

> Besides all the powers that are specifically given in the 37th and last item of this portion of the Constitution, confers [*sic*] on the General Legislature the general mass of sovereign legislation, the power to legislate on "all matters of a general character, not specifically and exclusively reserved for the local governments and legislatures." This is precisely the provision which is wanting in the Constitution of the United States. It is here that we find the weakness of the American system — the point where the American Constitution breaks down.[66]

> There are numerous subjects which belong, of right, both to the Local and the General Parliaments. In all these cases it is provided, in order to prevent a conflict of authority, that where there is concurrent jurisdiction in the General and Local Parliaments, the same rule should apply as now applies in cases where there is concurrent jurisdiction in the Imperial and

---

[65] *Parliamentary Debates on the Subject of Confederation*, 8th Parl., 3rd sess. at 33 (1865) (emphasis added).

[66] *Ibid.*, at p. 41. The "37th item" referred to is head 37 of s. 29 of the Quebec Resolutions of 1864. Section 29 was the original draft of what is now s. 91 of the *Constitution Act, 1867*, dealing with federal powers.

in the Provincial Parliaments, and that when the legislation of the one is adverse to or contradictory to the legislation of the other, in all such cases the action of the General Parliament must overrule, ex necessitate, the action of the Local Legislature.[67]

Though Macdonald did not deal directly with the question of judicial review, these excerpts suggest he did not consider that any serious "conflict of jurisdiction or authority" would arise. If both Parliament and Legislature had authority, the Act of Parliament would prevail. Perhaps one may assume that he expected the courts to determine who did have legislative authority in such cases. One might suspect, however, that Sir John may have foreseen a role for the Canadian Parliament similar to that of the Imperial Parliament. That is, the Canadian Parliament would be a sovereign body subject to no external restraints, whose legislation would not be subject to review by the courts. The Quebec Resolutions and, later, the B.N.A. Act[68] did put the federal cabinet in the position that the Imperial cabinet had formerly occupied with respect to the power of disallowance of provincial legislation. If the federal executive clearly was to assume certain powers of the Imperial executive, it would not be difficult to conclude that the federal Parliament was to be put in the same position as the Imperial Parliament. Its legislation would be supreme over legislation of the inferior provincial assemblies, subject only to the exercise in London of the power of disallowance retained there with respect to federal enactments.

There is other evidence that immediately after confederation Macdonald assumed that the proper and perhaps the only control on invalid provincial legislation would be the power of disallowance resting with the governor general. He explained to the provinces the use of the power on this basis in 1868, and he privately expressed fears that federal cabinets full of " 'states rights' advocates" might in the future refuse to exercise the power.[69] If it were assumed that the protection against invalid provincial legislation was the governor general's power of disallowance it should further have been assumed that the protection against invalid federal legislation was the Queen's power of disallowance. In such a system, the courts would have no important role.

---

[67]*Ibid.*, at p. 42. Macdonald is here summarizing the effect of s. 45 of the Quebec Resolutions. There is no counterpart of this section in the present *Constitution Act*, although the courts have reached essentially the same result by the "paramountcy" rule.

[68]1867, 30 & 31 Vict., c. 3, ss. 55–57, 90 (U.K.), based on ss. 50 and 51 of the Quebec Resolutions.

[69]Farr, *The Colonial Office and Canada, 1867–1887* (1955), at 110. He later appears to have thought that judicial review should apply to provincial laws: see Russell, "The Political Role of the Supreme Court of Canada in its First Century" (1975), 53 *Can. Bar Rev.* 576 at 577.

The information concerning Macdonald's views on the subject of judicial review is inconclusive. He may have assumed that the courts would exercise this power. His apparent familiarity with the constitution of the United States should have suggested this to him. Or he may have assumed that other arrangements — a general supremacy of the federal Parliament and the powers of disallowance — would serve the same purpose in the new Dominion.

Other members speaking in the Confederation Debates reveal the confusion prevailing on this subject. The following exchange occurred between A. A. Dorion (Hochelaga), an opponent of Confederation, and the Hon. George E. Cartier (Montreal East), Attorney General East:

> HON. MR. DORION: . . . In case of difference between the Federal Power and the local governments, what authority will intervene for its settlement?
> HON. ATTY. GEN. CARTIER: It will be the Imperial Government.
> HON. MR. DORION: In effect there will be no other authority than that of the Imperial Government, and we know too well the value assigned to the complaints of Lower Canadians by the Imperial Government.
> HON. ATTY. GEN. CARTIER: The delegates understood the matter better than that. Neither the Imperial Government nor the General Government will interfere, but the courts of justice will decide all questions in relation to which there may be differences between the two powers.
> A VOICE: The Commissioners' courts (Hear, Hear).
> HON. MR. DORION: Undoubtedly, One magistrate will decide that a law passed by the Federal Legislature is not law, whilst another will decide that it is law, and thus the differences instead of being between the legislatures will be between the several courts of justice.
> HON. ATTY. GEN. CARTIER: Should the General Legislature pass a law beyond the limits of its functions, it will be null and void *pleno jure*.
> HON. MR. DORION: Yes, I understand that, and it is doubtless to decide questions of this kind that it is proposed to establish Federal courts.
> HON. ATTY. GEN. CARTIER: No, No! They will be established only to apply and adjudicate upon the Federal laws.
> HON. MR. DORION: . . . If the differences between the Federal and the Local Parliaments are not to be submitted to the decision of a Supreme Federal Court, I do not see who can possibly decide them (Hear, Hear).[70]

Mr. Dorion proceeded to state his fears that a federal court of appeal would have at best only one Lower Canadian ("who may be selected out of the English population") and that Lower Canadian interests would inevitably suffer before such a court.

Cartier's remarks as quoted are remarkably unedifying. He first casually explains that the Imperial Government will decide disputes over jurisdiction. When this proves objectionable to his compatriot, he suggests

---

[70]*Supra*, note 65 at p. 690.

that the courts will decide "differences". He then is forced to say that it will not be the federal courts, the creatures of Parliament, which will decide.

One might have expected the two principal law officers of the government, Attorneys-General Macdonald and Cartier, to have been more precise and lucid on this not insignificant subject. At least it may be said that Cartier was consistent in his ambiguity.[71] It may be concluded, perhaps, that the Government was trying to avoid stirring up the issue on which Dorion touched. If there was to be judicial review, which courts should exercise it? Would it be a Canadian court, appointed by the federal Government and composed predominantly of English-speaking Protestant Canadians? To avoid this issue, the problem was glossed over. The jurisdiction of the Privy Council was in no way affected, and the proposed constitution did not in fact create a "General Court of Appeal". As enacted, it only empowered the federal Parliament to create such a court if it saw fit.[72]

If the members of the Government found it necessary to skirt the issue, it was still possible for a backbencher to express what must have been obvious to many. Joseph Cauchon (Montmorency) subsequently commented on the remarks of A. A. Dorion, some of which were quoted above. Cauchon noted the practice in the United States. "If any conflict arises between the Federal Legislature and that of the states, it is decided by the judicial tribunals . . . Why then should the case be otherwise so far as we are concerned?"[73]

The discussion of the B.N.A. Act in committee in the House of Commons at Westminster indicates an awareness of the problem, but two possible cures for invalid legislation were again suggested. In answer to the question of how conflicts of jurisdiction would be settled, Mr. C. B. Adderly, parliamentary under-secretary of the Colonial Office, said "he did not think that any serious conflict of the kind anticipated by the honourable member could take place so long as a supreme power was vested in the Governor General to veto Acts". Another member complained that there was no Supreme Court, such as existed in the United States, to decide as to the validity of federal laws. The former colonial secretary, Edward Cardwell, in reply to this criticism said:

> [he] was afraid that the defect pointed out by the honourable and learned Member was not one which, in the present state of feeling in the North American Provinces, it was possible to remedy. As matters now stood if

---

[71]See his answer to a question asked by Joseph Cauchon (Montmorency) concerning the jurisdiction of the proposed Supreme Court, *supra*, at p. 576.

[72]B.N.A. Act, s. 101, based on s. 31 of the Quebec Resolutions.

[73]*Supra*, note 65, at p. 698.

the Legislature of Canada acted *ultra vires*, the question would first be raised in the Colonial Law Courts; and would ultimately be settled by the Privy Council at home. No doubt it was a defect, but this point had undergone consideration by the delegates, who thought it would be better to leave things in this state.[74]

Here again we see both disallowance and judicial review suggested as devices for curing excesses of legislative authority. Again we hear the overtone of the internal struggle between the two major linguistic groups in Canada, making impolitic any further clarification of the situation.

2. Post-Confederation Practice of the Courts

Whatever the views of statesmen, whatever the political difficulties inherent in judicial review, the Canadian courts after Confederation showed themselves ready to pass judgment on the validity of legislation. In 1869 the Supreme Court of New Brunswick in *R. v. Chandler; Re Hazleton*[75] held invalid a statute of that province on the grounds that it related to bankruptcy, a federal matter. The court distinguished its decision 30 years earlier in *R. v. Kerr*[76] wherein the court had refused to hold an Act of the local Legislature invalid on the ground that it was unjust or interfered with private property. In the *Chandler* case it was pointed out that, whatever the merits of *Kerr*, there had been a substantial change brought about by the enactment of the B.N.A. Act. In the case of *L'Union St-Jacques de Montreal v. Bélisle*[77] the Quebec Circuit Court in 1870 held invalid a provincial statute on the grounds that it related to the federal matter of insolvency. This decision was upheld two years later by the Quebec Court of Queen's Bench.[78] Also in 1872, the Quebec Court of Queen's Bench held invalid a provincial statute establishing the Court of the Fire Commissioners, and the appeal from this decision apparently gave the Judicial Committee its first opportunity to construe the B.N.A. Act.[79] In 1871 in Ontario the Court of Chancery had to consider the validity of a private Act of the provincial Legislature which in effect altered the disposition made by the will of a deceased. The court upheld

---

[74]185 *H.C. Debates*, 3rd ser., at 1319–20 (1867). Perhaps the Colonial Office officials did not share Cardwell's belief that the lack of a supreme court was a "defect". Sir Frederic Rogers, Permanent Under-Secretary, in 1869 could see nothing "inadequate or unsatisfactory" in questions of validity of laws being decided by local courts subject to an appeal to the Judicial Committee. See Farr, *supra*, note 69 at pp. 111–12.

[75](1869), 12 N.B.R. 556 (C.A.).

[76](1838), Ber. 367, 2 N.B.R. 553 (S.C.).

[77](1870), 15 L.C. Jur. 212 (Que. Circ. Ct.).

[78](1872), 20 L.C. Jur. 29 (Que. Q.B.), revd L.R. 6 P.C. 31.

[79]*R. v. Coote* (1873), L.R. 4 P.C. 599, 9 Moo. P.C.C. N.S. 463, 17 E.R. 587.

the statute, and the Court of Appeal affirmed this decision after further examination of the validity of the law.[80] The Nova Scotia Supreme Court took up constitutional review in *Keefe v. McLennan*[81] in 1876. The court upheld a local statute establishing a system of issuing licenses for retail liquor outlets. It rejected the argument that this related to "trade and commerce", a federal matter.

The newly created Supreme Court of Canada officially acquired its judicial functions on January 11, 1876.[82] The first reported decision in which it considered the constitutional validity of any statute was *Severn v. The Queen*[83] in 1878. The court, without showing any hesitation concerning its right to do so, reviewed the validity of an Ontario statute and reversed a decision of the Court of Queen's Bench for that province which had held the statute to be valid. The Supreme Court took the view that the Ontario license on brewers was invalid as a restraint on "trade and commerce". A year later the court had occasion to review the validity of a federal statute, the *Dominion Controverted Elections Act, 1874*, in the case of *Valin v. Langlois*.[84] It was argued there that Parliament could not validly impose a duty on provincial courts to try controverted federal election cases. The Supreme Court upheld the Act. Chief Justice Ritchie took this opportunity to state his views on the role of the court in the federal structure. Referring to the question before them, he said:

This, if not the most important, is one of the most important questions that can come before this court, inasmuch as it involves, in an eminent degree, the respective legislative rights and powers of the Dominion Parliament and the Local Legislatures, and its logical conclusion and effect must extend far beyond the question now at issue. In view of the great diversity of judicial opinion that has characterized the decisions of the provincial tribunals in some provinces, and the judges in all, while it would seem to justify the wisdom of the Dominion Parliament, in providing for the establishment of a Court of Appeal such as this, where such diversity shall be considered and an authoritative declaration of the law be enunciated, so it enhances the responsibility of those called on in the midst of such conflict of opinion to declare authoritatively the principles by which both federal and local legislation are governed.[85]

And so the Canadian courts were launched on a course from which they have never swerved. The ease with which they could take up judicial

---

[80]*Re Goodhue; Torey v. Goodhue* (1872), 19 Gr. 366 (Ont. C.A.).
[81](1876), 11 N.S.R. (R. & C.) 5, 2 Cart. 400 (S.C.).
[82]See *Taylor v. The Queen* (1876), 1 S.C.R. 65.
[83](1878), 2 S.C.R. 70.
[84](1879), 3 S.C.R. 1, affd 5 App. Cas. 115 (P.C.).
[85]*Ibid.*, at pp. 9–10 S.C.R.

review of legislation after Confederation must have been the result of the situation existing prior to 1867. There was a continuity of judicial practice because the Imperial structure had not changed basically. Colonial laws (the Dominion of Canada was really only a colony) still were subject to overriding Imperial laws. The *Colonial Laws Validity Act, 1865*, could be relied on by a court in order to strike down a provincial or federal statute, just as the courts before 1865 could strike down any colonial statute for being "repugnant to the laws of England". Colonial Legislatures, whether Dominion or provincial, were limited Legislatures, and the courts could enforce the limitations.

The expectation of some that problems of invalidity would be dealt with through the power of disallowance was never realized. In the first place, the power of disallowance did not inherently exclude other forms of review of legislation. While the exercise, or threatened exercise, of the power did prevent considerable invalid legislation taking effect, the use of the power for this purpose was gradually discontinued. By agreement, London's power of disallowance over federal legislation had been eliminated by 1930.[86] By 1935, the federal Government had asserted that its power of disallowance over provincial legislation ought not to be used solely on the grounds of legislative invalidity. It was conceded that the courts were the proper agencies to determine whether a statute was *ultra vires* of a provincial Legislature.[87]

It is fortunate that disallowance did not become the principal means for enforcing the B.N.A. Act's restrictions on legislative power. Disallowance had to be exercised on the advice of political officers of a senior government. Many issues quite irrelevant to constitutionality could bear on the decision about its use. Disallowance could be exercised only within one year after enactment in the case of provincial legislation and two years in the case of federal legislation.[88] Constitutional problems not apparent at first might subsequently arise after the limitation period had expired. Regulations made pursuant to a statute and going beyond the constitutional authority of the government passing them could not be nullified because disallowance only extended to statutes. Also, if disallowance were relied on solely, rights could be affected by an invalid statute which would be effective upon enactment and continue to operate until disallowed. In a system which embraces judicial review, the citizen

---

[86]*Report of the Conference on the Operation of Dominion Legislation and Merchant Shipping, 1929* (1929), at 20.

[87]See La Forest, *Disallowance and Reservation of Provincial Legislation* (1955), at 76–77. While invalid provincial legislation has been occasionally disallowed since, the federal Government has claimed some other ground in addition to invalidity: *ibid.*, at 77–82, 99–101.

[88]B.N.A. Act, 1867, 30 & 31 Vict., c. 3, ss. 56, 90 (U.K.).

is enabled to treat an invalid statute as void *ab initio* and to assert this position in court if the need arises.

3. The Present Framework of Judicial Review

(a) Evolution of the Supreme Court

The most significant development in the judicial structure since 1867 has been the rise of the Supreme Court of Canada and the fall of the Judicial Committee of the Privy Council as the final court of constitutional adjudication. The B.N.A. Act did not establish the Supreme Court. Section 101 merely provided that

> 101. The Parliament of Canada, may, notwithstanding anything in this Act, from Time to Time, provide for the Constitution, Maintenance, and Organization of a General Court of Appeal for Canada, and for the Establishment of any additional Courts for the better Administration of the Laws of Canada.

There were probably sound political reasons for not expressly creating this court at the time of Confederation. Macdonald but touched on the problem when he remarked during the Confederation Debates that "There are many arguments for and against the establishment of such a court".[89] In fact, the Supreme Court issue was bound up with the sensitive subject of judicial review. The problems involved and the attitude of French-speaking Canada to a new Canadian tribunal have been adverted to previously.[90] French Canadians feared that a final Court of Appeal for the whole of the Dominion would be composed predominantly of English-speaking protestant common lawyers who would neither understand the civil law nor be impartial where language or religious issues were involved. Henri A. Taschereau (Beauce), speaking in the Confederation Debates, asserted that his compatriots would "assuredly be less satisfied with the decisions of a Federal Court of Appeal than with those of Her Majesty's Privy Council".[91] Cartier, in response to a question concerning the possible Court of Appeal, reassured the House in these words: "but I do hold, and the spirit of the conference at Quebec indicated, that the appeal to the judicial committee of Her Majesty's Privy Council must always exist, even if the Court in question is established".[92] On this basis the Lower Canadians permitted s. 101 of the B.N.A. Act to become law.

So delicate was the situation that no serious attempt was made for

---

[89]*Supra*, note 65 at p. 41.
[90]See notes 70 to 73, *supra*, and accompanying text.
[91]*Supra*, note 65 at p. 897.
[92]*Supra*, at p. 576.

several years to establish a final Court of Appeal for the new Dominion. Appeals continued to go directly from the provincial courts to the Judicial Committee. In 1875, during the Mackenzie government, legislation was enacted establishing the Supreme Court and the Exchequer Court.[93] Generally speaking, the court was given jurisdiction to hear appeals from the final judgments of the court of final resort in each of the provinces.[94] Provisions of this Act with respect to appeals to the Privy Council will be considered later.

As we have seen, there were two types of appeal to the Judicial Committee, those as of right and those with leave. The *Judicial Committee Act, 1833*[95] simply provided that the committee should hear appeals "which, either by virtue of this Act, or of any Law, Statute, or Custom, may be brought before His Majesty or His Majesty in Council". As the Act did not, except with respect to certain specialized matters, create any new right of appeal, it seemed to leave it to the particular law relating to the colonies and the law with respect to the royal prerogative of justice to fix the scope of appeals. The *Judicial Committee Act, 1844*[96] went further in specifically authorizing Her Majesty "to provide for the Admission of any Appeal or Appeals to Her Majesty in Council from any Judgments, Sentences, Decrees, or Orders of any Court of Justice within any British Colony or Possession abroad". Although the main purpose of this statute seems to have been to overcome colonial restrictions which prevented appeals from courts other than final appellate courts, it was broad enough to authorize an order in council permitting any appeal in any case from any colonial court. In this way the royal prerogative of justice was formalized by statute.

From the foregoing it may be seen that the appeal as of right was fixed by colonial law, the appeal by leave of the Judicial Committee being provided for by Imperial statute. The appeal as of right was usually defined monetarily, the decision of the local court being "final" except where the amount involved was, for example, over £300. In the earlier colonial period the right of appeal was set out in the charter or the commission to the governor,[97] and the colonies were not permitted to alter it.[98] The

---

[93]*Supreme and Exchequer Courts Act*, S.C. 1875, c. 11. For a discussion of earlier bills on this subject see Snell and Vaughan, *The Supreme Court of Canada: History of the Institution* (Toronto: University of Toronto Press, 1985), at pp. 5–10.

[94]*Ibid.*, s. 17.

[95]3 & 4 Wm. IV, c. 41, s. 3 (U.K.).

[96]7 & 8 Vict., c. 69, s. 1 (U.K.).

[97]See *e.g.* Read, "The Early Provincial Constitutions" (1948), 26 *Can. Bar Rev.* 620 *passim*. Shortt and Doughty, *Documents Relating to the Constitutional History of Canada, 1759–1791* (1918), at 676–83.

[98]The Legislature of the Massachusetts Bay Colony in 1691 attempted to impose a limitation on appeals to the Privy Council. The statute was disallowed by London because it was said the Legislature had no authority to alter the right of appeal. Dorland, *The*

Constitutional Act, 1791[99] creating Upper Canada and Lower Canada authorized the Legislatures of those colonies to legislate with respect to appeals from colonial courts. Both colonies were quick to exercise the power, restricting appeals to matters involving more than £500.[100] It was apparently thought at one time that the colonial Legislatures had been empowered by the 1791 Act to restrict the appeal with leave, the so-called prerogative appeal, as well as the appeal as of right.[101] Later Privy Council decisions made it clear, however, that whether or not this power had been conferred, a colonial Legislature would have to legislate specifically in this regard to restrict the prerogative appeal.[102] This finding was simply an application of the general rule that the court will not imply that a Crown prerogative has been taken away by statute. Prior to Confederation there is no indication that any of the British North American colonies did succeed in limiting the "prerogative" appeal with leave.

The B.N.A. Act did not deal with Privy Council appeals expressly, but it may implicitly have granted some legislative power on the subject. The provinces were given jurisdiction over

> 92(14) The Administration of Justice in the Province, including the Constitution, Maintenance, and Organization of Provincial Courts, both of Civil and of Criminal Jurisdiction, and including Procedure in Civil Matters in those Courts.

As we have seen, Parliament was empowered by s. 101 to legislate with respect to a "General Court of Appeal for Canada". It was unclear whether the power to create local courts involved some power to regulate appeals from their judgments subject, at least, to Imperial statutes or

---

Royal Disallowance in Massachusetts, Bulletin No. 22, Departments of History and Political and Economic Science, Queen's University, Kingston (1917), at 24.

[99] 31 Geo. III, c. 31, s. 34 (U.K.). Some doubt has been expressed that this section really authorized colonial limitations on the appeal as of right: see Duff C.J. in *Reference Re Supreme Court Act Amendment Act*, [1940] S.C.R. 49 at 65, [1940] 1 D.L.R. 289 (*sub nom. Reference Re Privy Council Appeals*), affd. (*sub nom. A.G. Ont. v. A.G. Can.*) [1947] A.C. 127, [1947] 1 All E.R. 137, [1947] 1 W.W.R. 305, [1947] 1 D.L.R. 801 (P.C.), at p. 145 *per* Jowitt L.C. But the terms of the section seem reasonably clear and the Privy Council has assumed the validity of limitations enacted under it: see *Re Marois* (1862), 15 Moo. P.C.C. 189, 15 E.R. 465; *Nadan v. The King*, [1926] A.C. 482 at 493, 134 L.T. 706.

[100] *An Act for the Division of the Province of Lower Canada, for the amending of the Judicature thereof, and for the repealing certain Laws therein mentioned, 1794*, 34 Geo. III, c. 6, s. 30 (L.C.); *An Act to establish a Superior Court of Civil and Criminal Jurisdiction and to regulate the Court of Appeal*, 34 Geo. III, c. 2, s. 36 (1794) (U.C.).

[101] *Cuvillier v. Aylwin* (1832), 2 Knapp's P.C. 72, 12 E.R. 406.

[102] *Re Marois, supra*, note 99; *Cushing v. Dupuy* (1880), 5 App. Cas. 409, 42 L.T. 445 (P.C.).

orders in council. Ontario and Quebec, as successors to Upper and Lower Canada, continued to legislate in relation to appeals as of right from provincial courts to the Privy Council.[103] Imperial orders in council were passed under the *Judicial Committee Act, 1844* with respect to the other provinces, regulating appeals as of right where the provinces themselves had not done so.[104] Appeals from the provincial courts by leave of the Judicial Committee were not affected. All in all, the system of appeals from provincial courts as of right or by leave gave rise to few controversies.

It was otherwise with respect to the Supreme Court of Canada. The very creation of the court was jeopardized by a controversy over the appealability of its decisions. The Act establishing the Supreme Court did not purport to interfere with appeals from provincial courts to the Judicial Committee. But with respect to appeals from the new federal tribunal, s. 47 provided that "[t]he judgement of the Supreme Court shall in all cases be final and conclusive . . . Saving any right which Her Majesty may be graciously pleased to exercise by virtue of Her Royal Prerogative".[105] The Imperial authorities threatened disallowance of the whole Act on the ground that it purported to bar appeals from the Supreme Court to the Privy Council. It was only after the Canadian Government conceded that the Act did not extend to appeals by leave, the "prerogative" appeals, that London agreed to allow the Act to take effect.[106] The net result was that there were no appeals as of right from the Supreme

---

[103] After Confederation Ontario and Quebec would have to justify their legislation under s. 92(14), "The Administration of Justice in the Province . . ." In *Reference Re Supreme Court Act Amendment Act, supra,* note 99, three of the judges (Duff C.J., at p. 57 S.C.R. Rinfret J., at 72, and Judson J., at 128) held that s. 92(14) did not authorize provincial limitations on appeals from provincial courts to the Privy Council. On appeal to the Privy Council in this case, *supra,* note 99, at 152 A.C., Lord Jowitt L.C. expressed doubts as to the provincial power but declined to decide the question. It is submitted that, on principle, the provinces did have the power to regulate appeals from provincial courts subject to both overriding federal legislation under s. 101 and, until the *Statute of Westminster,* 1931, 22 Geo. V, c. 4 (U.K.), overriding Imperial laws. The provincial aspect of this subject is in relation to "Administration of Justice in the Province, including the Constitution, Maintenance and Organization of Provincial Courts . . . " It does not cease to be "in the Province" merely because the appeals may be heard elsewhere. See, *infra,* note 113.

[104] The statutes and orders in council are reproduced in Cameron, *The Canadian Constitution* (1915), at 30, 32, 145–165.

[105] *Supreme and Exchequer Courts Act,* S.C. 1875, c. 11, s. 47.

[106] A detailed account of the struggle may be found in Farr, *The Colonial Office and Canada,* 1867–1887 (1955), c. 5. See also Underhill, "Edward Blake, the Supreme Court Act, and the Appeal to the Privy Council, 1875–6" (1938), 19 *Can. Hist. Rev.* 245, and "Edward Blake's Interview with Lord Cairns on the Supreme Court Act, July 5, 1876", 19 *Can. Hist. Rev.* 292; MacKinnon, "The Establishment of the Supreme Court of Canada" (1946), 27 *Can. Hist. Rev.* 258.

Court of Canada to the Judicial Committee, but appeals by leave were permitted. The committee was circumspect in granting leave to appeal from the Supreme Court. Summing up the committee's policy in 1926, Viscount Haldane said:

> In Canada there are a number of cases in which leave to appeal is granted because Canada is not a unitary state, and because it is the desire of Canada itself that the Sovereign should retain the power of exercising his prerogative; but that does not apply to internal disputes not concerned with constitutional questions, but relating to matters of fact. There the rule against giving leave to appeal from the Supreme Court of Canada is strictly observed where no great constitutional question, or question of law, emerges.[107]

Despite Haldane's complacent assumption concerning the "desire of Canada itself", the Parliament of that country, during the 75 years after the creation of the Supreme Court, passed a number of measures with the purpose of making its judgments final. In 1887 a statute was enacted purporting to abolish all appeals in criminal matters from any court in Canada to any tribunal in the United Kingdom.[108] Sir John Thompson, Minister of Justice, in introducing the measure indicated that he thought the bill only expressed what was already understood to be the law. It is difficult to take this suggestion seriously, but the Act appears to have passed without significant opposition.[109] This provision was carried forward as s. 1025 of the *Criminal Code*[110] in the statutes of 1906, and was not effectively challenged until the decision in *Nadan v. The King*[111] in 1926. The Judicial Committee, though it refused leave to appeal in that case, held that s. 1025 was invalid and that there still existed a prerogative appeal in criminal cases. It was held that the *Criminal Code*

---

[107]*Hull v. M'Kenna*, [1926] I.R. 402 at 405.

[108]*An Act to amend the law respecting Procedure in Criminal Cases*, S.C. 1887, c. 50, am. 1888, c. 43.

[109][1887] 2 *Can. H.C. Debates*, at 644–46. It is probable that this bill was introduced as a result of the appeal taken in the case of *Riel v. The Queen* (1885), 10 App. Cas. 675. Riel, the leader of the Northwest Rebellion, had been convicted of treason and his conviction was upheld by the Queen's Bench of Manitoba on appeal from the territorial court in Regina. His application for leave to appeal to the Judicial Committee was refused. This may be the "recent case" to which Sir John Thompson referred, in which Crown counsel were instructed to argue against the right of appeal but in which the appeal was dismissed on other grounds. See *Can. H.C. Debates, supra*, at 644. There was some impatience felt over delays in administration of criminal justice because of such appeals being taken.

[110]R.S.C. 1906, c. 146.

[111][1926] A.C. 482, 134 L.T. 706 (P.C.).

provision was repugnant to Imperial statutes, namely, the *Judicial Committee Acts* of 1833 and 1844 which had authorized the Crown to permit appeals in any cases from any colonial courts. By virtue of the *Colonial Laws Validity Act, 1865*,[112] this repugnancy made the Canadian statute void. In addition, it was held to be void on the rather questionable ground that it would have extra-territorial effect.[113]

The final chapter in the abolition of Privy Council appeals began with the passing of the *Statute of Westminster, 1931*.[114] This Act, as we have seen, permitted Canadian Legislatures to legislate in a manner inconsistent with existing Imperial statutes. By s. 3, Parliament was also empowered to legislate extra-territorially. Taking its cue, Parliament in 1933 added a section to the *Criminal Code* similar to the old s. 1025.[115] This time, the provision cutting off appeals in all criminal cases from all courts was upheld,[116] the Judicial Committee relying on the changes effected by the *Statute of Westminster, 1931*. After the Second World War, and after a further decision of the Judicial Committee[117] which established that Parliament had the right to terminate all appeals both civil and criminal, the last step was taken. In 1949 the *Supreme Court Act* was amended to prohibit appeals from any judgment of any court in Canada to the Judicial Committee. The *Judicial Committee Acts* of 1833 and 1844 were repealed by the Canadian Parliament insofar as they applied to Canada.[118] This bond of Empire was cut in response to a growing nationalism in Canada, but not without considerable controversy.[119]

As a result, the Supreme Court of Canada was made what its name implied: a final court for Canadians. Henceforth, the constitution would be authoritatively interpreted on Canadian soil by those familiar with the context in which it was to operate. But would the abolition of appeals

---

[112]28 & 29 Vict., c. 63, s. 2 (U.K.). See note 23, *supra*, and accompanying text.

[113]The conclusion that this was an extra-territorial measure because the Judicial Committee sat in London seems specious. Had it not been for the Imperial connection with its doctrine of paramountcy of certain Imperial laws, no one would ever have suggested that the regulation of appeals and the creation of a court of final resort was not a purely local matter. The Privy Council later recognized this in *British Coal Corporation v. The King*, [1935] A.C. 500 at 521, [1935] All E.R. Rep. 139. The operative obstacle to termination of appeals before the *Statute of Westminster* was surely the problem of repugnance to the *Judicial Committee Acts*.

[114]22 Geo. V, c. 4, (U.K.): See note 26, *supra*, and accompanying text.

[115]*An Act to amend the Criminal Code*, S.C. 1933, c. 53, s. 17.

[116]*British Coal Corporation v. The King, supra*, note 113.

[117]*A.G. Ont. v. A.G. Can.*, [1947] A.C. 127, [1947] 1 All E.R. 137, [1947] 1 W.W.R. 305, [1947] 1 D.L.R. 801 (P.C.).

[118]*An Act to amend the Supreme Court Act*, S.C. 1949 (2nd Sess.), c. 37, s. 3.

[119]See Pierson, *Canada and the Privy Council* (1960), at 69–94; Snell and Vaughan, *supra*, note 93, at pp. 186–89.

bring real independence to the Supreme Court? Would the court be free to take bold initiatives in developing the law, or would it be bound as before by its own past decisions and those of the Imperial tribunal?

Prior to the abolition of appeals to the Privy Council, it appeared that the Supreme Court was bound by its own previous decisions, and by decisions of the Privy Council in appeals from Canada.[120] With its new status as a final appellate court, the Supreme Court was at liberty to reassess its attitude to *stare decisis*. Torn between models such as the House of Lords with its then rigid adherence to precedent, and the United States Supreme Court with its candid revisionism, it might at least have been expected to abandon *stare decisis* in constitutional matters.[121] The formal rigidity of a federal constitution requires some flexibility of interpretation. This is in contrast to other areas of law where the courts can be extricated from bad precedents by statutory change. Secondly, the constitution is not otherwise readily susceptible to modification in the light of changing social and economic conditions. Judicial review provides a means of constitutional development if the courts will seize the opportunity. The Privy Council never fully perceived this role of judicial review in a state with a written constitution. One of the expectations of those who advocated finality for Supreme Court decisions was that the Canadian tribunal would be more capable of, and disposed to perform, such a role.

Although it took some years after abolition of Privy Council appeals to do so, and only after the House of Lords had announced its intention to override its own decisions where appropriate,[122] the Supreme Court signalled in 1967[123] its willingness to reverse itself in a proper case. It has since proceeded to do so[124] and even overruled a constitutional decision of the Privy Council.[125]

---

[120]For a discussion on the authorities see Joanes, "Stare Decisis in the Supreme Court of Canada" (1958), 36 *Can. Bar Rev.* 175.

[121]See *ibid.*, at 193–200; Laskin, "The Supreme Court of Canada: A Final Court of and for Canadians" (1951), 29 *Can. Bar Rev.* 1038, at 1073.

[122]See Note, [1966] 3 All E.R. 77, (*sub nom.* Practice Statement (Judicial Precedent)) [1966] 1 W.L.R. 1234 (H.L.).

[123]*Binus v. The Queen* [1967] S.C.R. 594, [1968] 1 C.C.C. 227, 2 C.R.N.S. 118.

[124]*E.g.* in *R. v. Paquette*, [1977] 2 S.C.R. 189, 70 D.L.R. (3d) 129, 11 N.R. 451, 30 C.C.C. (2d) 417, 39 C.R.N.S. 257; *McNamara Const. (Western) Ltd. v. The Queen*, [1977] 2 S.C.R. 654, 75 D.L.R. (3d) 273, 13 N.R. 181 (*sub nom. Canada v. McNamara Const. (Western) Ltd.; Canada v. J. Stevenson & Assoc.*); *Vetrovec v. The Queen* [1982] 1 S.C.R. 811 at 830; *Semble, MacDonald v. City of Montreal*, [1986] 1 S.C.R. 460 at 512; and see Curtis, "Stare Decisis at Common Law in Canada" (1978), 12 *U.B.C.L. Rev.* 1.

[125]*Reference re Agricultural Products Marketing Act*, [1978] 2 S.C.R. 1198, 84 D.L.R. (3d) 257, 19 N.R. 361, overruling *Lower Mainland Dairy Products Sales Adjustment*

The court's position on *stare decisis* is important but will not be determinative of its success over time as a source of dynamism in the development of the constitution. That success, while affected by the court's attitude to precedent, will ultimately be judged on its ability to develop or distinguish past decisions to allow the constitution to operate in a changing world in broad conformity to the principles on which it was established.

This ascendancy of the Supreme Court as a final appellate body has left in its wake some continuing controversy as to its legitimacy in matters of judicial review under the constitution. This controversy has centred on the status of the court as a body created by Parliament, whose members are appointed and paid by federal authorities with a tenure dependent on federal laws. Its jurisdiction is seemingly also dependent on the laws of Parliament. Yet it is expected to be the guardian of the constitution and adjudicate fairly between the two levels of Government. This criticism has some validity as a matter of logic, particularly as it relates to the establishment and jurisdiction of the court which, in a federal system, should be guaranteed by the constitution. It is not convincing when critics suggest that because the members of the court are federally-appointed there must as a result be some institutional bias in favour of the federal authority. Serious examinations of the court's jurisprudence reveal no such bias.[126] Curiously, the same argument is not made against the federal appointment of judges of provincial superior, district, and county courts even though these courts must also sometimes decide constitutional issues.

Because of these concerns, mainly voiced by some provincial spokesmen, as to the legitimacy of the court, federal-provincial discussions on "putting the Supreme Court in the constitution" have proceeded intermittently since 1968. There has been a general assumption that the existence of the court should be protected by the constitution from the unilateral power of abolition theoretically available to the Parliament of Canada. It has also been generally accepted that some other provisions concerning the court should be entrenched, but there is continuing debate over what these should be. Elements under discussion have been the method of appointment of judges (with an emphasis on some provincial involvement in the process), the number and geographical distribution of judges, security of tenure, jurisdiction of the court, and the handling of appeals in Quebec civil law matters. The main purpose to be achieved

---

Committee v. Crystal Dairy, Ltd., [1933] A.C. 168, [1932] 3 W.W.R. 639, [1933] 1 D.L.R. 82 (P.C.).

[126]Hogg, "Is the Supreme Court of Canada Biased in Constitutional Cases?" (1979), 57 *Can. Bar Rev.* 721; L'Ecuyer, *La Cour suprême du Canada et le partage des compétences 1949–1978* (Gouvernement du Québec, Ministère des Affaires intergouvernementales, 1978). See also c. 10, *infra*.

is to make the court in form as well as fact a national institution independent of either level of Government and thus to strengthen its acceptability as the final adjudicator in constitutional matters.

At one point, at the Constitutional Conference of federal and provincial first ministers at Victoria in June 1971, there was agreement on the text of a Canadian Constitutional Charter which contained such provisions concerning the Supreme Court. This charter was ultimately not proceeded with to adoption. These proposals were further analyzed during the 1970's by various bodies. They were advanced with some elaboration by the federal Government in its Constitutional Amendment Bill[127] (Bill C-60) of 1978 which led to further inconclusive federal-provincial discussions in 1978–80.[128] Federal-provincial discussions then broke off and were not resumed until November 1981 at which time the contents of the *Constitution Act, 1982*[129] were agreed to by the governments of Canada and of all provinces except Quebec. It is this agreement embodied in the *Constitution Act, 1982*, which does contain some limited constitutional provisions concerning the Supreme Court.

The references to the Supreme Court in the 1982 Act are not the product of the federal-provincial discussions between 1968 and 1980, but instead were drafted by the eight provinces which had during 1980–81 opposed unilateral action by the Parliament of Canada to patriate the constitution. Those eight provinces[130] had agreed in April 1981 to an amending formula on the basis of which they would be prepared to see the constitution "patriated" (that is, the formal amending power transferred to Canada from Westminster). As part of the final settlement this formula was accepted by the federal Government and the two other provinces which had been supporting it. The formula as incorporated into the *Constitution Act* makes two references to the Supreme Court. Section 41 requires that any "amendment to the Constitution of Canada in relation to . . . *(d)* the composition of the Supreme Court of Canada" must have the consent of both Houses of Parliament and of the legislative assemblies of all provinces. Section 42 requires that an "amendment to the Consti-

---

[127]Bill C-60, 30th Parliament, 3rd Sess., 1978. This bill was not proceeded with after consideration by a joint committee of the Senate and House of Commons.

[128]The Victoria Charter and various subsequent constitutional proposals on the Supreme Court are set out in *Proposals on the Constitution 1971–78* (Canadian Intergovernmental Conference Secretariat, Ottawa, 1978) at pp. 291–311. Many of these are discussed in Jones, "A Constitutionally Guaranteed Role for the Courts" (1979), 57 *Can. Bar Rev.* 669; Lederman, "Current Proposals for Reform of the Supreme Court of Canada" (1979), 57 *Can. Bar Rev.* 687; Décary, "La Cour suprême et la dualité canadienne" (1979), 57 *Can. Bar Rev.* 702; and Beckton and MacKay, *The Courts and the Charter*, (Toronto: University of Toronto Press, 1985), at pp. 97–106.

[129]*Constitution Act, 1982* enacted by *Canada Act*, 1982, c. 11, Sch. B. (U.K.).

[130]All but Ontario and New Brunswick.

tution of Canada in relation to . . . *(d)* subject to paragraph 41*(d)*, the Supreme Court of Canada'' shall have the consent of both Houses of Parliament and of the legislative assemblies of at least two-thirds of the provinces that have at least 50% of the population of all provinces.

The application of these new provisions has been debated as to how they limit, if at all, the previously unqualified power of Parliament under s. 101 of the Constitution Act, 1867 to ''provide for the Constitution, Maintenance, and Organization of a General Court of Appeal for Canada'' and thus to enact or amend the *Supreme Court Act*.[131] Sections 41 and 42 require certain provincial consents for amendments to the ''Constitution of Canada'' in relation to the Supreme Court, but what existing provisions concerning the Supreme Court are part of the ''Constitution of Canada''? There is no exhaustive definition of the term ''Constitution of Canada''. Subsection 52(2) and the schedule of the *Constitution Act, 1982* provide a list of statutes which the constitution ''includes''. While the list does not purport to be exhaustive, the *Supreme Court Act* is not listed and it is unlikely that it can be considered part of the Constitution of Canada. If it is not, seemingly the only existing provision of the Constitution of Canada protected by ss. 41 and 42 would be s. 101 of the *Constitution Act, 1867*, quoted in part above, since that Act is listed as being part of the constitution. Sections 41 and 42 would presumably then govern further amendments to s. 101 and any new additions to the constitution that would govern matters referred to in those sections. Ordinary amendments to the *Supreme Court Act* would not, however, be affected. This would appear to be the preferable interpretation because otherwise para. 42(1)*(d)* would mean that no amendment of any sort, even a matter dealing, for example, with officers of the court or its procedures, could be made to the *Supreme Court Act* without the consent of seven provinces.[132]

Such additions to the constitution concerning the Supreme Court may well be made in the near future. On June 3, 1987, the first ministers agreed to seek legislative aproval of a number of amendments, including provisions that would constitutionally preserve the Supreme Court, fix its size, guarantee three judges from Quebec, and require that judges be

---

[131]R.S.C. 1970, c. S-19.

[132]Hogg, *Constitutional Law of Canada*, 2nd ed. (Toronto: Carswell, 1985), at 62–65 adopts this interpretation. But see Cheffins, ''The Constitution Act, 1982 and the Amending Formula: Political and Legal Implications'' (1982), 4 *Supreme Court L.R.* 43, where it is suggested that the whole of the *Supreme Court Act* is now entrenched as part of the Constitution; and Lederman, ''Constitutional Procedure and the Reform of the Supreme Court of Canada'' (1985), 26 *Cah. de D*. 195 at 195–99, where it is suggested that a number of ''essential'' sections of the Supreme Court have been constitutionally entrenched by these provisions.

federally appointed from among persons nominated by provincial governments. Apart from addressing many of the concerns noted above as to the appearance of independence of the court, these amendments would, if adopted by the necessary legislative resolutions, be substantive constitutional provisions to which the protection of the amending formula could attach. That formula will, if the agreement is implemented, be altered to require unanimous consent of the provinces for any constitutional amendment in relation to the Supreme Court.

(b) Supremacy of the Constitution Confirmed

Finally, what was once a by-product of the Imperial system has finally become an explicit principle of the Canadian constitution. The *Constitution Act, 1982*, s. 52(1) provides that

> 52(1) The constitution of Canada is the supreme law of Canada, and any law that is inconsistent with the provisions of the Constitution is, to the extent of the inconsistency, of no force or effect.

At the same time the Act repeals[133] s. 7(1) of the *Statute of Westminster* which had preserved the application of the *Colonial Laws Validity Act* so as to underpin the paramountcy over Canadian laws of one Imperial statute, the B.N.A. Act.[134] Now we need look no farther than s. 52 of the *Constitution Act, 1982* for the principle of supremacy of the constitution, for a partial definition of the constitution covering the core statutes, and for the intended consequence of supremacy: that is, the invalidity of inconsistent laws. While the section does not specifically provide for judicial review to determine if there is inconsistency, its adoption after 115 years of such judicial review under the constitution implies that the courts are to continue to exercise such a role.

Some decisions since the coming into force of the *Constitution Act, 1982*, have referred specifically to s. 52 as adopting the principle of supremacy of the constitution.[135] The Supreme Court of Canada, however, has confirmed that s. 52 simply continues the same "invalidity doctrine" as was contained in s. 2 of the *Colonial Laws Validity Act*, meaning that

---

[133]Schedule, item 17.

[134]*Supra*, notes 25, 26 and accompanying text.

[135]See, *e.g.*, *R. v. Currie* (1983), 33 C.R. (3d) 227 at 233 (N.S.C.A.); leave to appeal to S.C.C., judgment reserved Jan. 25, 1984; *Reynolds v. A.G.B.C.*, [1984] 5 W.W.R. 270 at 274 (B.C.C.A.); leave to appeal to S.C.C. granted Oct. 22, 1984; *Re Martin; Children's Aid Society of Winnipeg v. Martin et al.* (1983), 25 Man. R. (2d) 143 at 149 (C.A.).

any court can treat as invalid any law inconsistent with the constitution.[136]

(c) Judicial Review Extended

Section 52 of the *Constitution Act, 1982* addresses the situation of laws inconsistent with the constitution and assumes judicial review to be a means to determine whether there is such inconsistency. Section 24, a part of the *Canadian Charter of Rights and Freedoms* contained within the *Constitution Act*, goes further. It provides:

> 24(1) Anyone whose rights or freedoms, as guaranteed by this Charter, have been infringed or denied may apply to a court of competent jurisdiction to obtain such remedy as the court considers appropriate and just in the circumstances.
>
> (2) Where, in proceedings under subsection (1), a court concludes that evidence was obtained in a manner that infringed or denied any rights or freedoms guaranteed by this Charter, the evidence shall be excluded if it is established that, having regard to all the circumstances, the admission of it in the proceedings would bring the administration of justice into disrepute.

It will be noted that this enforcement section applies only to the Charter. It specifically assures a role for the courts and seemingly contemplates a wide range of judicial remedies based on findings that rights or freedoms have been infringed, not just (as in s. 52) a finding of invalidity because laws relied on by a party are inconsistent with the constitution. In many cases the result would be the same, of course, because usually a Government official or agency, when accused of violating the constitution, can point to a law which purports to authorize the activity in question. It is then the validity of the law which is put in dispute. But the Charter guarantees many individual rights which are susceptible to an administrative intrusion or denial that may have no basis in law: for example, the denial of counsel at a police station, or arbitrary searches on a street corner. It was one of the anomalies of the *Canadian Bill of Rights*,[137] a federal statutory statement of rights that was supposed to prevail over other inconsistent federal laws, that such purely administrative denials

---

[136]See *R. v. Big M Drug Mart Ltd.*, [1985] 1 S.C.R. 295 at 312–13, 315–16; *Reference re Language Rights in Manitoba*, [1985] 1 S.C.R. 721 at 745–46; *Operation Dismantle Inc. et al. v. The Queen et al.*, [1985] 1 S.C.R. 441 at 482–83, 18 D.L.R. (4th) 481 at 511–12. The Court has also observed that the adoption of the Charter by "the elected representatives of the people of Canada . . . entrusted the courts" with the responsibility of judicial review in relation to it: *Reference re Section 94(2) of the Motor Vehicle Act, R.S.B.C. 1979, c. 288,* [1985] 2 S.C.R. 486 at 497.

[137]R.S.C. 1970, Appendix III.

of rights declared by the bill to exist were seemingly without remedy.[138] That difficulty has been avoided for the Charter.

It is not yet entirely clear what the total effect of s. 24 will be. It probably creates no new remedies as such, but it does provide a new criterion — *i.e.*, violation of the constitution — for the granting of remedies already within the jurisdiction of the court in question.[139]

---

[138]See, *e.g.*, Tarnopolsky, "A New Bill of Rights in the Light of the Interpretation of the Present One by the Supreme Court of Canada" *1978 Lectures L.S.U.C.* 161 at 172–77.

[139]See generally *Mills v. R.*, [1986] 1 S.C.R. 863 and, *infra*, at pp. 46, 47, 70–72, 299–310.

Chapter 2

Judicial Review and Parliamentary Democracy

We have seen that judicial review has become an established feature of constitutional government in Canada. Yet there are some who have argued, and with more intensity in the face of the extension of judicial review through the entrenchment of rights and freedoms, that judicial review is basically inconsistent with the parliamentary democracy which is central to our constitution.[1] It is said that one fundamental principle of our constitution is that Legislatures are supreme and the courts must apply their enactments without "second-guessing" the legislative branch; another is that the voice of the majority, as represented by elected Legislatures, must prevail over that of non-elected judges if democracy is to prevail. The principle of parliamentary supremacy is justified on legal and historic grounds, and the principle of majority rule is presented as both a consequence of, and moral justification for, parliamentary supremacy. (Few would argue that parliamentary supremacy in its origins had much to do with majoritarian democracy as we know it today.)

An attempt will be made here to see how judicial review does relate to these two principles and what conditions or limits on its exercise are implied by the Canadian constitutional system.

A. PARLIAMENTARY SUPREMACY: COURTS VERSUS LEGISLATURES

1. In the United Kingdom

The claims of parliamentary supremacy in Canada have strong legal and historical roots in the United Kingdom. The preamble of the *British North America Act, 1867*,[2] states the intention to create a union "with a

---

[1] See, *e.g.* Schmeiser, "The Case against Entrenchment of a Canadian Bill of Rights" (1973), 1 *Dalhousie L.J.* 15. During the more than decade of debate leading up to the adoption of the *Canadian Charter of Rights and Freedoms* several provincial Governments opposed it because of the inconsistency they perceived between entrenchment of rights and parliamentary democracy.

[2] 1867, 30 & 31 Vict., c. 3 (U.K.) (now *Constitution Act, 1867*).

Constitution similar in Principle to that of the United Kingdom''. In the constitution of the United Kingdom, Parliament has been supreme in law since it became supreme in fact in the seventeenth century.[3] It declared its supremacy as early as 1642, and the *Bill of Rights, 1688*, was certainly predicated on that supremacy when it stated that ''the freedome of speech and debates or proceedings in Parlyament ought not to be impeached or questioned in any court or place out of Parlyament.''[4] Here Parliament firmly limited the jurisdiction of the courts in one important aspect.

In Dicey's[5] classical formulation of the supremacy of Parliament, the jurisdiction of the courts was always subject to limitation by Parliament and certainly did not include the power to determine the validity of legislation. ''English judges do not claim or exercise any power to repeal a Statute, whilst Acts of Parliament may override and constantly do override the law of the judges. Judicial legislation is, in short, subordinate legislation, carried on with the assent and subject to the supervision of Parliament.'' According to Dicey, one of the ''traits of Parliamentary sovereignty as it exists in England'' was ''the non-existence of any judicial or other authority having the right to nullify an Act of Parliament, or to treat it as void or unconstitutional.''[6]

Parliament had unlimited power, save that it had no power to limit itself. Therefore there was no role for courts in applying limitations on Parliament by way of judicial review, even self-denying limitations which Parliament might have purported to impose. A more modern statement of the proposition is to the effect that the ''rule of recognition'', by which courts decide what is law, is logically independent of that law, and therefore the rule that courts obey statutes cannot be dependent on or altered by statute. That rule or *grundnorm* has its source elsewhere in history and politics, not in statutory law.[7] Based on such reasoning a House of Lords committee has concluded, for example, that it would be impossible to entrench a Bill of Rights in United Kingdom law in a way which would ensure that later laws inconsistent with it would be held invalid by the courts. In their view, even a ''manner and form'' require-

---

[3]See McIlwain, *The High Court of Parliament and its Supremacy* (1910), at 336–46, 389–90; Winterton, ''Parliamentary Supremacy and the Judiciary'' (1981), 97 *L.Q. Rev.* 265 at 273.

[4]1 Wm. III & Mary, 2nd sess. c. 2, (Imp.), preamble, The Subject's Rights, No. 9.

[5]Dicey, *Introduction to the Study of the Law of the Constitution*, 10th ed. (London: Macmillan, 1959), pp. 60–61.

[6]*Ibid.*, at p. 91. See also *British Railways Bd. v. Pickin*, [1974] A.C. 765 at 789 (H.L.); *Manuel et al. v. A.G.*, [1982] 3 All E.R. 822 at 827–28 (C.A.).

[7]See, *e.g.* H. W. R. Wade, *Constitutional Fundamentals* (London: Stevens, 1980), at pp. 26–27.

ment within the Bill to the effect that future laws which are to override it successfully, would have to do so expressly, would not be effective.[8]

Yet there are those in the United Kingdom who think that the conventional view of parliamentary supremacy goes too far. First it is thought that there are some external limits placed on the power of Parliament by the Treaty of Union with Scotland of 1706. That treaty may have created a "fundamental law" which could prevent Parliament from enacting certain types of legislation.[9] But even the Scottish Court of Session was unwilling to assert in 1953 that it had jurisdiction to determine whether official action conflicted with this "fundamental law". At issue in the case of *MacCormick v. Lord Advocate*[10] was the right of Her Majesty to use the numeral II in her title of "Queen Elizabeth II". The petitioners sought to interdict the publication pursuant to Act of Parliament of a proclamation entitling the sovereign in this fashion. It was alleged, *inter alia*, that the use of the numeral II would be a violation of the Treaty of Union. The Lord President (Lords Carmont and Russell concurring) expressed the view that neither a Scottish nor an English court could entertain proceedings to determine whether there had been a breach of the fundamental law. To the question whether such an issue "is determinable as a justiciable issue in the Courts of either Scotland or England, in the same fashion as an issue of constitutional *vires* would be cognisable by the Supreme Courts of the United States, or of South Africa or Australia"[11] a negative answer was given.

Others contend that even if Parliament may not limit its substantive powers, it may impose certain procedural limitations on itself through "manner and form" requirements which the courts could be obliged to enforce.[12] For example, Parliament could provide that a Bill of Rights should override all subsequent legislation unless in that subsequent legislation Parliament has stated an intention to the contrary. Another method might be to require a special parliamentary majority, for example, two-thirds, to amend a Bill of Rights. Or Parliament could delegate a portion of its authority to another body, either internal to it (for instance, one

---

[8]Report of the Select Committee on a Bill of Rights (House of Lords, 1978), paras. 13–17.

[9]See *e.g.,* Mitchell, "Sovereignty of Parliament: Yet Again" (1963), 79 *L.Q. Rev.* 196, at 202–06; MacCormick, "Does the United Kingdom have a Constitution? Reflections on MacCormick v. Lord Advocate" (1978), 29 *No. 1 L.Q.* 1. But see Gough, *Fundamental Law in English Constitutional History* (1955), at 179–80.

[10][1953] Sess. Cas. 396, [1953] S.L.T. 255.

[11]*Ibid.*, at pp. 412–13 Sess. Cas.

[12]See, *e.g.* Winterton, "The British Grundnorm: Parliamentary Supremacy Re-examined" (1976), 92 *L.Q. Rev.* 591, and other writers referred to therein.

House plus the Crown, as it did in the *Parliament Acts* of 1911 and 1949[13]) or external (as in the case of the regulation-making bodies of the European Communities). It is argued that Parliament, if it prescribes its own procedures or delegates its own authority, must thereafter observe these arrangements until it takes a formal decision to change them.

Much of the modern debate in the United Kingdom has centred on its entry into the European Communities. When the United Kingdom entered, it enacted the *European Communities Act, 1972*[14] which provides that its obligations under the various communities treaties shall be part of the law of the United Kingdom and thus be given legal effect notwithstanding other laws. The issue remains as to whether a future Act of Parliament clearly in conflict with an existing regulation of a community would be enforced by British courts. Is s. 2 of the *European Communities Act, 1972* an effective "manner and form" requirement to the effect that in order to alter regulations of the Community it is necessary to resort to the community body to which the United Kingdom Parliament has delegated law-making powers over such matters? Some argue that it is and that entrenchment and judicial review have already been achieved in this fashion even within the general framework of parliamentary supremacy.[15]

The courts have given effect to community law in the face of domestic law which at first blush appeared to be divergent from the former, but usually on the basis of construing the domestic law so as to render it consistent with community law. It appears likely that if Parliament enacted new legislation clearly intended to override community law British courts would apply the new domestic law on the basis of traditional concepts of parliamentary sovereignty.[16]

2. In Canada

As noted above, Canada must in some way have inherited the concept of parliamentary supremacy since the preamble to the B.N.A. Act says

---

[13]1911, 1 & 2 Geo. V, c. 13 (U.K.) and 1949, 12, 13 & 14 Geo. VI, c. 103 (U.K.).

[14]1972, c. 68 (U.K.).

[15]See, *e.g.* Winterton, *supra*, note 12; Lester, "Fundamental Rights in the United Kingdom: the Law and the British Constitution" (1976), 125 *U. Pa. L. Rev.* 337.

[16]See, *e.g.*, Macarthys Ltd. v. Smith, [1979] 3 All E.R. 325 (C.A.); *Garden Cottage Foods Ltd. v. Milk Marketing Bd.*, [1983] 2 All E.R. 770 (H.L.); Furmston et al. (eds.), *The Effect on English Domestic Law of Membership of the European Communities and of Ratification of the European Convention on Human Rights* (Boston: Klüwer, 1983), at pp. 32–68, 387–428; Drzemczewski, *European Human Rights Convention in Domestic Law: A Comparative Study* (Oxford: Clarendon Press, 1983), at pp. 177–87; 51 *Halsbury's Laws of England*, 4th ed. (1986), at pp. 387–89, 396–98.

we are to have a "constitution similar in principle to that of the United Kingdom". Yet judicial review of legislative action has thrived in Canada while in the United Kingdom its legitimacy is still very questionable.

What then are the arguments in support of judicial review in Canada and how does our situation differ from that of the British? In the former colonial system, it seems to have been assumed that Her Majesty's colonial courts had a duty to enforce the restrictions imposed by Imperial statute. The Imperial law officers in 1861 stated the proposition in this manner.

> The powers of the Colonial Legislature being conferred by Act of the Imperial Parliament, and limited by the same enactment, and so, valid or invalid, as they keep within or transgress the prescribed limits, the Supreme Court of South Australia is, in our opinion, bound (and certainly at liberty) to satisfy itself of the legal validity of any Act of the Colonial Legislature, the provisions of which it is called upon to administer.[17]

A similar view was propounded in *obiter* by Lord Selborne in an 1878 Privy Council decision.

> The Indian Legislature has powers expressly limited by the Act of the Imperial Parliament which created it, and it can, of course, do nothing beyond the limits which circumscribe these powers. . . . The established Courts of Justice, when a question arises whether the prescribed limits have been exceeded, must of necessity determine that question; and the only way in which they can properly do so, is by looking to the terms of the instrument by which, affirmatively, the legislative powers were created, and by which, negatively, they are restricted.[18]

This statement was approved by the Supreme Court of Canada in the following year.[19]

This view of the power of colonial courts in relation to colonial legislation needed to be reconciled with the theories of parliamentary sovereignty previously mentioned. Dicey, the great expounder of parliamentary sovereignty, argued that in a federal state the various Legislatures

---

[17]Quoted in Keith, *Responsible Government in the Dominions* (1912), Vol. 1, at 405. See also Todd, *Parliamentary Government in the British Colonies*, 2nd ed. (1894), at 301–02.

[18]*R. v. Burah* (1878), 3 App. Cas. 889 at 904–905 (P.C.). Approved in *James v. Commonwealth of Australia*, [1936] A.C. 578 at 613, [1936] 2 All E.R. 1449 (P.C.). See also *Harris v. Minister of Interior*, [1952] 2 S. Af. 428, [1952] 1 T.L.R. 1245 (*sub nom. Harris v. Dönges*) (C.A.); *Minister of Interior v. Harris*, [1952] 4 S. Af. 769 at 779 (C.A.).

[19]*Valin v. Langlois* (1880), 3 S.C.R. 1 at 17–18.

were essentially the same as joint stock companies, limited in their power by the Charter which created them. Speaking of the situation in the United States and Canada he said "Congress and the London, Chatham, and Dover Railway are in truth each of them nothing more than subordinate law making bodies. Their power differs not in degree, but in kind, from the authority of the sovereign Parliament of the United Kingdom".[20] From this it followed, according to Dicey, that just as a court could quash a company by-law if *ultra vires*, so it could set aside an invalid statute in a federal state. Dicey was not alone in comparing Legislatures of limited powers to corporations. Baron Parke, in *Kielley v. Carson*[21] in 1842, had stated that it was no more possible to imply a power of the Newfoundland Legislature to commit for a contempt perpetrated outside the Legislature than it would be to imply a power in a company to commit for contempt.[22] Lord Watson, in the famous Local Prohibition case (*A.G. Ont. v. A.G. Can.*)[23] in 1896, held, *inter alia*, that the power of the Parliament of Canada to "regulate" trade did not include the power to prohibit trade. In coming to this conclusion he relied solely on the authority of *City of Toronto v. Virgo*,[24] a Privy Council decision of the previous year, which dealt with the powers of a municipal corporation to pass by-laws pursuant to its statutory authority to regulate a trade. Lord Watson imposed the same restrictive interpretation on the legislative power of the Parliament of Canada as had been imposed on the by-law making power of the City of Toronto. Over a generation later Street, in his authoritative work *The Doctrine of Ultra Vires*, similarly compared such Legislatures to corporations and concluded that "whenever powers have been exceeded, it is the business of the Courts to restrict them."[25]

Essential to this analogy with ordinary corporate action is the assumption that the courts must necessarily recognize and enforce any limitations on the exercise of legislative power. Another way of expressing this is to say that the courts must apply not only part of the law, but the whole of the law germane to any case coming before them. If there are relevant constitutional limitations, these are part of the law which must be taken into account. Dicey, drawing on American practice and experience, said that "the American judge must in giving judgment obey the terms of the constitution, just as his English brother must in giving judgment obey every Act of Parliament bearing on the case."[26] He then

---

[20] Dicey, "Federal Government" (1885), 1 *L.Q. Rev.* 80 at 85. See also Dicey, *supra*, note 5, at pp. 150–51.

[21] (1842), 4 Moo. P.C.C. 63, 13 E.R. 225.

[22] *Ibid.*, at p. 89 Moo. P.C.C., p. 235 E.R.

[23] [1896] A.C. 348 at 363, 74 L.T. 533 (P.C.).

[24] [1896] A.C. 88 (P.C.).

[25] Street, *The Doctrine of Ultra Vires* (1930), at 416–17.

[26] Dicey, *supra*, note 5, at 159.

proceeded to generalize from the situation in the United States and to conclude that this is a feature essential to all federal states. At least one Canadian judge expressly followed American decisions in coming to a similar conclusion. Chief Justice Meredith of the Quebec Superior Court in *Langlois v. Valin*[27] in 1879, was faced with an argument that the courts must give effect to any statute coming before them if its unconstitutionality was not pleaded. After referring with approval to Chief Justice Marshall's judgment in *Marbury v. Madison*,[28] he dismissed this argument in the following terms: "To me it seems plain that a statute, emanating from a legislature not having power to pass it, is not law; and that it is as much the duty of a judge to disregard the provisions of such a statute, as it is his duty to obey the law of the land."[29]

While one may accept the conclusion that, unlike the United Kingdom, constitutional limitations exist in Canada on legislative and governmental authority which the courts should enforce, one might question some of these rationales and in particular the implications which could otherwise flow from them. The Governments created by the B.N.A. Act were something more than municipal corporations or joint stock companies. This was made clear by the Privy Council with respect to provincial Legislatures (and at least as much can be said for the Parliament of Canada) in *Hodge v. The Queen* in 1883. It was argued in that case that a provincial Legislature had no power to delegate the law-making authority to a municipal agency. The maxim *delegatus non potest delegare* was relied on. In refuting this, Sir Barnes Peacock, in his judgment, said of the provincial Legislatures that:[30]

> They are in no sense delegates of or acting under any mandate from the Imperial Parliament. When the British North America Act enacted that there should be a legislature for Ontario, and that its legislative assembly should have exclusive authority to make laws for the Province and for provincial purposes in relation to the matters enumerated in sect. 92, it conferred powers not in any sense to be exercised by delegation from or as agents of the Imperial Parliament, but authority as plenary and as ample within the limits prescribed by sect. 92 as the Imperial Parliament in the plenitude of its power possessed and could bestow.

From this it may be seen that the Canadian Legislatures were given a genuinely sovereign legislative character, and that certain restrictive rules suitable for the interpretation of municipal or corporate by-laws were not readily applicable.

---

[27](1879), 5 Que. L.R. 1, *affd* 3 S.C.R. 1, affd 5 App. Cas. 115 (P.C.).

[28]1 Cranch 137, 5 U.S. 87 (1803).

[29]*Supra*, note 27 at p. 17 Que. L.R.

[30](1883), 9 App. Cas. 117 at 132, 50 L.T. 301 (P.C.). See also *Liquidators of Maritime Bank v. Receiver General of New Brunswick*, [1892] A.C. 437 at 441–43 (P.C.).

Instead of simply adopting the corporate analogy it is perhaps better to return to the nature of parliamentary supremacy in the United Kingdom and see how it relates to that in Canada. It is generally accepted that the rule that the laws of the United Kingdom Parliament are supreme and must be followed by the courts is not itself a legal rule but a fundamental political and historic fact, the *grundnorm* of the British constitution.[31] Perhaps surprisingly, the *grundnorm* (the basic rule accepted as a political fact from which flows the legitimacy of our laws) of the Canadian constitution is *also* that the laws of the *United Kingdom* Parliament are supreme. This was more apparent between the time of the *Quebec Act, 1774*[32] and confederation. No doubts were expressed in 1867 as to whether Westminster could enact binding law for Canada, and her fiat had political legitimacy at that time as well as legal legitimacy. Not long after confederation it became apparent that *political* legitimacy for law-making for Canada attached to Canadian political authorities and that Westminster would generally not legislate for Canada except at Canadian request. Progressively such legislation came to be confined to amendments to the B.N.A. Acts, and only those made at the request of the Parliament of Canada.[33] It was also accepted that legislation for Canada on any other subject would only be adopted at Canada's request and this convention was made law by the *Statute of Westminster, 1931*,[34] s. 4. That statute expressly did not apply to amendments to the B.N.A. Acts but it continued to be accepted that such amendments would not be made without the request of the Parliament of Canada. Again in 1931 there was no serious question in Canada as to the legal necessity or legitimacy of United Kingdom legislation in this area (that is, the amendment of the B.N.A. Acts) that had never been assigned to the authority of Canadian Legislatures. As the Supreme Court of Canada said in 1981, "the one constant since the enactment of the *British North America Act* in 1867 has been the legal authority of the United Kingdom Parliament to amend it."[35]

This situation continued unchanged until 1982 when, by the *Canada Act 1982*,[36] the United Kingdom Parliament expressly renounced its authority to legislate for Canada in any way by providing in s. 2 that:

---

[31]See, *e.g.* Wade, *supra*, note 7, at p. 26.

[32]1774, 14 Geo. III, c. 38 (U.K.).

[33]See, *e.g.* Government of Canada, *The Amendment of the Constitution of Canada* (1965) at 10–16; Government of Canada, *The Role of the United Kingdom in the Amendment of The Canadian Constitution* (1981) at 5–9; Rand, "Some Aspects of Canadian Constitutionalism" (1960), 38 *Can. Bar Rev.* 135 at 145.

[34]1931, 22 Geo. V, c. 4 (U.K.).

[35]*Re Resolution to Amend the Constitution*, [1981] 1 S.C.R. 753 at 807, 125 D.L.R. (3d) 1 at 47, 39 N.R. 1, 34 Nfld. & P.E.I.R. 1, 95 A.P.R. 1, 11 Man. R. (2d) 1, [1981] 6 W.W.R. 1 (*sub nom. A.G. Man. v. A.G. Can.*), 1 C.R.R. 59.

[36]1982, c. 11 (U.K.).

No Act of the Parliament of the United Kingdom passed after the Constitution Act, 1982 comes into force shall extend to Canada as part of its law.

At the same time s. 1 enacted the *Constitution Act, 1982* which provides for a Canadian procedure for constitutional amendment and also provides that "the Constitution of Canada is the supreme law of Canada".

While some may still delight in logical fancies that by the nature of parliamentary supremacy what Westminster has done it can equally undo and thus some day "expatriate" the Canadian constitution, even Dicey conceded that Parliament could abandon or transfer its sovereignty.[37] Moreover the unlikelihood of a British Parliament gratuitously asserting control over the Canadian constitution once again is only exceeded by that of such actions being recognized either by the people, the Governments, or the courts of Canada.[38]

In short, we have had a modification in our *grundnorm*. We still recognize that the constitutional laws as enacted by Westminster for Canada, including the *Canada Act 1982* and its schedule, the *Constitution Act, 1982*, are the supreme law of Canada, but we now also recognize that in the future the supreme law-making authority (that is, the authority to amend the constitution, to make the law by which laws are made and governed) will belong to those Canadian legislative bodies prescribed in the new constitutional amending formula.

Given this *grundnorm*, that the constitutional laws prescribed for us in the past by Westminster or adopted in Canada in the future by a procedure prescribed by Westminster are the supreme laws, it readily follows that the courts should decide cases in accordance with those laws. The courts need not regard Canadian legislative bodies as "sovereign" in exactly the same sense that Westminster is sovereign because that is not the *grundnorm* of our constitution. Yet that does not mean that they should be regarded as corporations or municipalities. For the most part, they have been made in the image of Westminster. They have the dignities and implied powers of a sovereign Parliament.

Thus while Parliament and Legislatures have legislative authority limited now by both the distribution of powers and the Charter guarantees of individual rights and freedoms, within the areas of authority left to each they enjoy parliamentary supremacy. This means that, like Westminster, they make laws which, if otherwise valid, the courts must respect. It also means that they cannot bind their successors. This has caused particular conceptual difficulties in the interpretation of the statutory *Canadian Bill of Rights*[39] of 1960 which provided that federal laws,

---

[37]Dicey, *supra*, note 5 at pp. 68–69.
[38]For a discussion of these issues see Strayer, "The Patriation and Legitimacy of the Canadian Constitution" (Cronkite Lectures, 1982).
[39]S.C. 1960, c. 44 (now R.S.C. 1970, App. III).

past or future, should be "construed and applied" so as not to abridge certain rights unless the federal law in question specifically provides that it is to apply notwithstanding the *Canadian Bill of Rights*. The courts have been reluctant to give the Bill full effect, and one of the difficulties seemingly has been that of reconciling such a directive to the courts with parliamentary sovereignty.[40] The better view would seem to be that the concepts of judicial review and parliamentary sovereignty can be reconciled on the basis that although Parliament is sovereign in the areas assigned to it, it can limit itself by a "manner and form" requirement. That is, until such time as it may repeal the *Canadian Bill of Rights* it can only legislate effectively in contravention of the Bill if it does so in express language.[41]

Parliament and the Legislatures also have important legislative powers, including the powers of creation and regulation of the courts themselves, which can affect the availability and means of judicial review.

Section 92 of the B.N.A. Act provides in part as follows:

> 92. In each Province the Legislature may exclusively make Laws in relation to Matters coming within the Classes of Subjects next hereinafter enumerated . . .

> 14. The Administration of Justice in the Province, including the Constitution, Maintenance, and Organization of Provincial Courts, both of Civil and of Criminal Jurisdiction, and including Procedure in Civil Matters in those Courts.

Section 101 provides that

> 101. The Parliament of Canada may, notwithstanding anything in this Act, from Time to Time provide for the Constitution, Maintenance, and Organization of a General Court of Appeal for Canada, and for the Establishment of any additional Courts for the better Administration of the Laws of Canada.

These sections seemingly put the very existence of the courts, and their jurisdiction, at the mercy of the legislative branch of both levels of Government. Parliament and the provincial Legislatures are surely distinguishable in this manner from business or municipal corporations.

---

[40]See, *e.g. A.G. Can. v. Lavell; Isaac v. Bedard,* [1974] S.C.R. 1349 at 1361, 38 D.L.R. (3d) 481 at 491–92.

[41]See, *e.g.* Tarnopolsky, *The Canadian Bill of Rights,* 2nd ed. (Toronto: McClelland & Stewart, 1975), at 143; Hogg, *Constitutional Law of Canada,* 2nd ed. (Toronto: Carswell, 1985), at 643–45; and see note 12, *supra,* and accompanying text for the comparable debate in the U.K.

These latter bodies have no power to regulate the courts which might be called on to review their by-laws. But subject to other conditions, to be discussed later, it would seem that Parliament and the Legislatures might limit judicial review of their own legislation.

As previously noted, Dicey and others have supported their case for the inherent right of judicial review in Canada by reference to principles and practices of judicial review in the United States. The analogy is far from perfect. The constitution of the United States specifically guarantees the existence of, and confers certain jurisdiction on, the federal judiciary. Article III states:

> Section 1. The judicial Power of the United States shall be vested in one Supreme Court, and in such inferior Courts as the Congress may from time to time ordain and establish . . .
> Section 2. The judicial powers shall extend to all Cases, in Law and Equity, arising under this Constitution . . .

Thus the creation of the Supreme Court was in effect required by the constitution, and wherever federal courts were created they were to exercise the "judicial power" which would extend to all cases "arising under this Constitution". In the seminal case of *Marbury v. Madison* Chief Justice Marshall, while stressing the logical necessity of courts enforcing constitutional limitations wherever a written constitution may be found, also relied on these specific provisions of the American constitution.[42]

> The judicial power of the United States is extended to all cases arising under the constitution. Could it be the intention of those who gave this power, to say, that in using it, the constitution should not be looked into? That a case arising under the constitution should be decided, without examining the instrument under which it arises? This is too extravagant to be maintained. In some cases, then, the constitution must be looked into by the judges. And if they can open it at all what part of it are they forbidden to read or to obey?

Similarly, Article VI imposes like obligations on the state judiciary where it provides that:

> this Constitution . . . shall be the supreme Law of the Land; and the Judges in every State shall be bound thereby, any Thing in the Constitution or Laws of any State to the Contrary notwithstanding.

Here again, the state judges are bound to apply constitutional limitations and no Legislature can interfere with their power to do so.

---

[42]1 Cranch 137 at 178–79, 5 U.S. 87 at 112 (1803).

These specific guarantees of judicial review are reinforced by the concept of separation of powers which pervades American constitutional law at both the federal and the state level. By this concept, the judicial branch is considered to be co-ordinate with the legislative and executive branches of Government. The courts are not superior to the other branches but on occasion they must, in a case properly before them, refuse to give effect to actions of the other branches of Government when these conflict with the constitution. This is a function which cannot be denied the courts by the Legislature or executive. It is true that Congress can limit the jurisdiction of the Supreme Court and of the lower federal courts in various ways as to the kind of cases they hear. Article III, s. 2, only specifies a certain limited original jurisdiction for the Supreme Court, and otherwise allows Congress to create exceptions to the Court's general appellate jurisdiction conferred by the constitution. It is also left to Congress to confer such subject-matter jurisdiction as it chooses on other Federal courts but the above-quoted provisions ensure that once created they can exercise the function of judicial review for the enforcement of the constitution. Moreover, it is doubtful how far Congress can go in its control over subject-matter jurisdiction so as to impede judicial review.[43] This situation is in contrast to that under the constitution of the United Kingdom where Parliament is considered to be supreme, where the executive holds office only so long as it has the confidence of the House of Commons, and where the courts have only such jurisdiction and functions as Parliament confers on or leaves to them.

While the Canadian constitution resembles that of the United States in its federalism and its entrenchment of rights and freedoms, it has not expressly guaranteed judicial review to the same extent. Not until the *Constitution Act, 1982* have we moved in this direction, and the consequences of that step are not yet certain.

First, the *Canadian Charter of Rights and Freedoms* provides:

> 24(1) Anyone whose rights or freedoms, as guaranteed by this Charter, have been infringed or denied may apply to a court of competent jurisdiction to obtain such remedy as the court considers appropriate and just in the circumstances.
>
> (2) Where, in proceedings under subsection (1), a court concludes that evidence was obtained in a manner that infringed or denied any rights or freedoms guaranteed by this Charter, the evidence shall be excluded if it is established that, having regard to all the circumstances, the admission of it in the proceedings would bring the administration of justice into disrepute.

---

[43]See, *e.g.* Tribe, *Constitutional Choices* (Cambridge, Mass.: Harvard University Press, 1985), c. 5.

The question arises as to whether s-s. (1) guarantees every court the subject-matter jurisdiction and function to review legislative or administrative action alleged to contravene the Charter, or whether it only enables a court otherwise authorized to hear such a case to grant whichever of its normal remedies it thinks appropriate. The latter interpretation seems to be generally accepted.[44] Also this section applies only to the enforcement of the Charter and not to the rest of the constitution.

As discussed in Chapter 1,[45] there are also some references to the Supreme Court in the new constitutional amendment formula. They require the consent of the Senate, House of Commons, and some or all provincial legislative assemblies for amendments "to the Constitution of Canada" in relation to the Supreme Court. This may have restricted in some way the otherwise unlimited power of Parliament to legislate for the Supreme Court under s. 101 of the B.N.A. Act as quoted above. But since these provisions only apply to amendments to the constitution and since the *Supreme Court Act* is apparently not part of the constitution, it is hard to see what direct effect they may have until such time as the Supreme Court is put into the constitution. Then presumably provincial consent will be required and once the constitution is so amended those provisions respecting the court will be changeable only with the appropriate provincial consent as required by ss. 41 and 42 of the *Constitution Act, 1982* or their successors.

Another, but older, textual basis has been suggested by some for a guarantee of the judicial power not unlike that referred to in Article III of the United States constitution. In *Ottawa Valley Power Co. v. Hydro-Electric Power Commn.*[46] the Ontario Court of Appeal was considering the validity of a statutory provision which prohibited any action being taken against the defendant commission with respect to certain contracts. The contracts in question had been declared invalid by the provincial Legislature. It was held that this declaration was *ultra vires* as involving civil rights outside the province. In addition, Fisher J.A. stated in *obiter* that the effect of the prohibition against these contractual actions, involving, as they might, certain constitutional issues was

> to take away from the Supreme Court one at least of the essential characteristics of a Superior Court. The British North America Act does not, it is true, guarantee the continued existence of the Superior Court in each of the Provinces. But it is quite clear that both secs. 96 and 127 [*sic*] are founded upon an unwritten guarantee of the continuance of the Superior

---

44 See, *infra* at pp. 70–72.

45 *Supra*, at pp. 31, 32.

46 [1937] O.R. 265, [1936] 4 D.L.R. 594 (C.A.), revg [1937] O.R. at 266, [1936] 3 D.L.R. 468 (H.C.).

Courts in the Provinces. To alter the essential character of the Supreme
Court as a Superior Court in any vital particular, is contrary to the spirit
of The British North America Act, and tantamount to an unauthorized
repeal of that Statute in that respect.[47]

Professor Lederman took up this argument and elaborated it. He asserted
that ss. 96 to 101 of the B.N.A. Act disclosed an intention to reproduce
provincial and federal superior courts "in the image of the English central
royal courts".[48] From this assumption he proceeded to the conclusion
that, just as the central royal courts had the jurisdiction to supervise the
exercise of powers by other public officers and agencies, so it must be
presumed that Canadian superior courts were guaranteed a similar jurisdiction including the supervision of the various Legislatures.[49]

This analysis is open to question. It ignores the basic fact that the
jurisdiction of the "central royal courts" was subject to limitation by
Parliament. Parliament could and still can prevent judicial review of the
actions of public officers or agencies.[50] Moreover, the "central royal
courts" never had the power to review Acts of Parliament for validity,
in spite of the pretensions of Coke and others.[51]

The Supreme Court of Canada has, however, adopted a view similar
to that of Professor Lederman in ascribing to s. 96 a special role in the
protection of judicial review on constitutional grounds. It has held that
provincial superior courts are "the basic constitutional concepts [*sic*] of
judicature of this country" whose judicial power in constitutional matters
is "fundamental to a federal system as described in the *Constitution
Act*".[52] It has thus held that provincial superior courts cannot be denied
the power to determine the jurisdiction of Parliament,[53] or of federal[54] or
provincial[55] administrative tribunals.

---

[47]*Supra*, at p. 333 O.R. See also *Independent Order of Foresters v. Lethbridge Northern
Irrigation District*, [1938] 2 W.W.R. 194 at 221, [1938] 3 D.L.R. 89 at 102–03 (Alta.
C.A.), affg [1937] 3 W.W.R. 424, [1937] 4 D.L.R. 398 (Alta. S.C.).

[48]Lederman, "The Independence of the Judiciary" (1956), 34 *Can. Bar Rev.* 769 (Part
I), 1139 (Part II), at 1160, 1175; "The Supreme Court of Canada and the Canadian
Judicial System", (1975) Transactions of the Royal Society of Canada, 4th Series, Vol.
XIII, 209 at 222–24.

[49]"The Independence of the Judiciary", *supra*, at 1174–75, 1176–77.

[50]See *e.g. Smith v. East Elloe R.D.C.*, [1956] A.C. 736, [1956] 1 All E.R. 855 (H.L.);
R. v. Secretary of State for the Environment; Ex p. Ostler, [1977] Q.B. 122, [1976] 3
All E.R. 90 (C.A.); Garner, "The Exclusion of Judicial Review" (1981), 125 *Sol. J.*
192.

[51]See *Dr. Bonham's Case* (1610), 8 Co. Rep. 114a at 118a, 77 E.R. 646 at 652 (K.B.).
See also, *supra*, at pp. 2, 3.

[52]*A.G. Can. v. Law Society of B.C.*, [1982] 2 S.C.R. 307 at 328.

[53]*Ibid.*

[54]*Canada Labour Relations Board et al. v. Paul L'Anglais Inc. et al.*, [1983] 1 S.C.R.
147.

[55]*Crevier v. A.G. Que.*, [1981] 2 S.C.R. 220, 127 D.L.R. (3d) 1, 38 N.R. 541. See
infra, at pp. 86–97.

One problem with this approach is that, if the true textual guarantee of constitutional judicial review is found in the constitutional provisions concerning provincial superior courts, then by implication there are no similar guarantees of constitutional powers for courts dependent for their existence on s. 101 of the *Constitution Act, 1867* (including both the Federal Court and the Supreme Court of Canada). This can give rise to anomalies.[56] It may be more helpful to start with the principle stated in s. 52 of the *Constitution Act, 1982* that the Constitution is

> . . . the supreme law of Canada, and any law that is inconsistent with the provisions of the Constitution is, to the extent of the inconsistency, of no force or effect.

This is a direction to every court, which must guide it in dealing with every case properly brought before it in accordance with the legislation (federal or provincial) which defines its jurisdiction. Such legislation should only be ignored to the extent that it will prevent the principle of s. 52 being vindicated in *any* suitable forum.

Although the textual basis in the constitution for judicial review may be debatable, the general implications in its favour are compelling. Notwithstanding the intent of the constitution to create legislative bodies with a form of parliamentary sovereignty similar to that of the United Kingdom, they were at the same time to be Legislatures in a federal system with a distribution of legislative powers. While in the abstract it may be argued that judicial review is not inevitable in a federal system as some survive without it,[57] given the Imperial system at the time of Confederation and the prior history of judicial review it was surely implicit that the limitations on legislative power would, where necessary, be enforced by the courts.[58] So parliamentary sovereignty in Canada was always qualified to that extent. The recent entrenchment of rights in the Charter has only extended the scope of that qualification: it has not introduced a new concept.

---

[56]See, *e.g. Brink's Canada Ltd. v. Canada Labour Relations Board et al.*, [1985] 1 F.C. 898 (T.D.).

[57]See, *e.g.* Wheare, *Federal Government*, 4th ed. (1963), at 17, and 64–65; Roussy, *Le contrôle judiciaire de la constitutionnalité des lois fédérales aux Etats-Unis et en Suisse* (1969), at 126–56.

[58]For a similar rationale in Australia see *Baxter v. Comm'rs of Taxation (N.S.W.)* (1907), 4 C.L.R. 1087; Lane, *The Australian Federal System*, 2nd ed. (1979), at 1143–44. Sawer, *Australian Federalism in the Courts* (1967), at 76 *ff.* And see Lyon, "The Central Fallacy of Canadian Constitutional Law" (1976), 22 *McGill L.J.* 40.

Charter has only extended the scope of that qualification: it has not introduced a new concept.

That the Supreme Court remains firmly committed to its role in judicial review was clearly reiterated in the case of *Amax Potash Ltd. v. Govt. of Sask.* where the court said[59]

> The Courts will not question the wisdom of enactments which, by the terms of the Canadian Constitution are within the competence of the Legislatures, but it is the high duty of this Court to insure that the legislatures do not transgress the limits of their constitutional mandate and engage in the illegal exercise of power.

It is submitted, however, that like parliamentary sovereignty, the right of judicial review is not in all respects absolute, and that there are occasionally conflicting principles which may support some limitation on the jurisdiction of the courts to test constitutional validity. Apart from s. 24 of the Charter, the constitution in no place specifically provides for judicial review nor does it otherwise specifically guarantee the jurisdiction of the courts in this regard. There is an implication in favour of judicial review, but that implication can be taken no farther than the protection of the constitution may demand, and it is subject to other limitations both expressed and implied in the constitution. For example, express limitations arise out of the grants of power to Parliament and the Legislatures in ss. 101 and 92(14) of the B.N.A. Act respectively, to regulate the "Constitution, Maintenance, and Organization" of the courts. Implied limitations may be found in the fact that the B.N.A. Act created quasi-sovereign legislative bodies, and executives which were to exercise the Crown prerogatives.[60] Limitations are also suggested by the fact that our constitution does not dictate a separation of powers among co-equal branches of Government. It is therefore even more appropriate in our system that courts defer at times to the judgment of legislative bodies which in many respects remain supreme.

We must as a result avoid easy generalizations and ascertain to what extent the constitution requires and protects judicial review. In order to do this it is necessary to examine various legislative and non-legislative attempts to limit judicial review, and the judicial reaction to these attempts. This will be undertaken in Chapters 3 and 4.

---

[59][1977] 2 S.C.R. 576 at 590, [1976] 6 W.W.R. 61, 71 D.L.R. (3d) 1 at 10, 11 N.R. 222. See also *Reference re Language Rights in Manitoba*, [1985] 1 S.C.R. 721 at 745–46; *Reference re Section 94(2) of the Motor Vehicle Act, R.S.B.C. 1979, c. 288*, [1985] 2 S.C.R. 486 at 496–97.

[60]See cases cited, *supra*, note 30.

B. DEMOCRACY: COURTS VERSUS PEOPLE

1. The Anti-Majoritarian Issue

As part of the concern over the seeming inconsistency between judicial review and parliamentary democracy, it is also argued by its critics that judicial review runs counter to majoritarian principles. That is, it is argued that in a democratic society governmental decisions should be made by, or directly on behalf of, current majorities, and certainly not by someone independent of the majority will such as a judge with long tenure. Because Legislatures are directly elected and are thus thought to be, if not the perfect, at least the best available, agents of the public will, this provides a democratic justification for the constitutional supremacy of these bodies over non-elected agencies such as courts. Parliamentary supremacy is not an end in itself but the means for implementing the will of the people.

Much has been written in the last twenty-five years in Canada and the United States on the general relationship between judicial review and majoritarian democracy. Serious doubts have been raised and examined as to the legitimacy of judicial review. In the United States much of the debate has been inspired by the post-Second World War judicial activism and revisionism of the Supreme Court, particularly the "Warren Court".[61] In Canada much, though not all, of the debate has focused on the desirability and consequences of entrenching certain rights and freedoms in the constitution.[62] Some of it has also been associated with the movement for reform, and entrenchment in the constitution, of the Supreme Court.

---

[61]See, *e.g.* Bickel, *The Least Dangerous Branch* (1962); Cox, *The Role of the Supreme Court in American Government* (1976); Dworkin, *Taking Rights Seriously* (1977); Horowitz, *The Courts and Social Policy* (1977); Choper, *Judicial Review and the National Political Process* (1980); Ely, *Democracy and Distrust* (1980); Cappelletti, "The 'Mighty Problem' of Judicial Review and the Contribution of Comparative Analysis" (1980), 53 *So. Cal. L. Rev.* 409; Perry, *The Constitution, the Courts and Human Rights: an Inquiry into the Legitimacy of Constitutional Policymaking by the Judiciary* (New Haven: Yale University Press, 1982); Agresto, *The Supreme Court and Constitutional Democracy* (New York: Cornell University Press, 1984); Tribe, *Constitutional Choices* (Cambridge, Mass.: Harvard University Press, 1985); Dworkin, *Law's Empire* (1986), at pp. 355–99. For a view of many of these issues from a Canadian perspective see Gold, "The Rhetoric of Constitutional Argumentation" (1985), 35 *U. of T. L.J.* 154.

[62]See, *e.g.* Russell, "A Democratic Approach to Civil Liberties" (1969), 19 *U. Tor. L.J.* 109; Schmeiser, "The Case Against Entrenchment of a Canadian Bill of Rights" (1973), 1 *Dalhousie L.J.* 15; Smiley, "Courts, Legislatures, and the Protection of Human Rights", in Friedland (ed.) *Courts and Trials: a Multidisciplinary Approach* (1975), at 89; Weiler, "Of Judges and Rights, or Should Canada have a Constitutional Bill of

The major conceptual criticism of judicial review is, then, that it inevitably involves policy decisions which are much more than mere textual exegesis or logical deduction from established legal principles. These decisions require value judgments typical of the legislative process. Yet most judges are appointed to their office with security of tenure effectively for the remainder of their career. If they ever were representative of their society (and, it is said, by definition they are not because they are of necessity drawn from an elite minority) they cease to be so after years of splendid isolation from the experience of the common man.

The "policy" nature of the judicial role is found to some extent in the protection of federalism. Realist critics argue, and with justification, that the interpretation of constitutional heads of power in a changing world, and the characterization of challenged laws, is only in part an exercise in logic and is to a large extent one of value judgment. There are some who would seemingly prefer to limit even this aspect of judicial review.[63] But apparently most of the critics of judicial review would accept its legitimacy in the maintenance of federalism because it is seen as at best a necessary evil associated with a generally desirable federal system of Government.

Most of the concern about judicial policy-making is focused on judicial protection of individual or collective rights. This is because bills of rights use general terms such as "equal protection", "due process", "freedom of speech", "the right to a speedy . . . trial", and "cruel and unusual punishment". These terms lack further definition in the constitution because it would be impossible to foresee all of the situations in the indefinite future to which they might be applied and it would be unwise to restrict their use by too much precision. As a result, the courts have to attribute some meaning to these very general words in the particular situation which happens to come before them. In the United States where the *Bill of Rights* expresses many of the guaranteed rights and freedoms in fairly absolute terms, the courts have had to find some rationale for balancing such interests against the interests of others which may seem equally valid. They have done so without any specific constitutional mandate. In the process the U.S. Supreme Court has seemingly reversed itself or distinguished its own previous decisions with sufficient frequency to add credibility to the view that it is engaged in a continuing

---

Rights" (1980) *Dalhousie Rev.* 205; Schmeiser, "The Entrenchment of a Bill of Rights" (1981) 19 *Alta. L. Rev.* 375 and various sources referred to therein. Weiler, *In the Last Resort* (Toronto: Carswell, 1974), especially chs. 6 and 7, deals with many of these issues in the context of an analysis of the Supreme Court of Canada. See also Gold, *supra*, note 61.

[63]See, *e.g.* Weiler, *supra*, at ch. 6, *passim*; Schmeiser, 1973 article, *supra*; Choper, *supra*, note 61, c. 4.

policy-making process. For the critics of judicial review in Canada this has provided demonstrable evidence that entrenchment of rights and freedoms in the constitution can only lead to similar law-making by appointed judges instead of, and often in conflict with, elected Legislatures. Not only will such judicial review bring unwanted additions to existing laws, it will also strike down popular measures for the general welfare because of some judicially-imagined conflict with constitutionally enshrined rights and freedoms of some individual or minority.

There is some force to the argument that judicial review might sometimes produce results which would not at that moment be supported by a majority of the population if they were consulted. But to oppose judicial review and the entrenchment of the constitutional norms on which it is based for that reason is to assume that in a democracy all important decisions and all binding rules must reflect the majority view at all times. The slightest experience with our political system tells us this is not so. In the first place, there are anti-majoritarian features in the parliamentary system itself. The electoral system with its rule that the candidate with a plurality may win, combined with a multi-party system, means that Parliaments and Legislatures are commonly elected by a minority of the population. The Senate, appointed for a term to age 75 by the Government of the day, is surely not a majoritarian institution even though it enjoys equal legal power with the House of Commons. Even assuming that a legislative majority is truly elected by a majority of electors, that selection is but a "snapshot" of public opinion which may be quite different six months or a year later. Yet majority Governments are assured up to five years in office if they wish it. It is obvious that Governments often do necessary but unpopular things in the early years of their mandate, when voter retribution is not imminent, that they would not dare to do in an election year. It is doubtful that certain measures, if the public were consulted specifically about them, would ever have majority support: measures such as tax increases or the abolition of capital punishment.

A few critics specifically recognize that federalism itself is an anti-majoritarian institution because it, and the judicial review that sanctions it, can frustrate at times the will of the majority clearly expressed in *ultra vires* legislation. But many of the apostles of provincial rights have insisted that in matters of constitutional amendment national majorities cannot prevail over provincial Governments or Legislatures. And many of those who have attacked the entrenchment of rights and freedoms because of its anti-majoritarian tendencies have been less than enthusiastic about the use, for constitutional amendment purposes, of the referendum, which surely is the most direct form of majoritarian democracy.

It is instead more realistic to view a democratic system of Government as one in which the majority generally acquiesces in a hierarchy of norms varying in importance and intended duration. The Canadian experience with the B.N.A. Act is a prime example of such a norm. It would be impossible to demonstrate that a majority of Canadians, even in 1867, expressly voted for it. Certainly those in contemporary Canada have never been given the opportunity to do so. Yet the efficacy of the B.N.A. Act must rest on a general public acceptance of the principles of government and federalism which it embodies. It is surely not based on a "command" of the British Parliament that any Canadian would find compelling. Whenever the courts hold invalid statutes duly enacted by elected Legislatures they are, in effect, enforcing these ongoing norms of the B.N.A. Act against passing electoral majorities. Yet this is accepted because Canadians have tacitly approved of the principle, intended to be of long duration, of a federal system where powers are reasonably divided between the federal and provincial authorities. This principle, they agree, is to transcend short-term legislative action which might endanger it.

It is then not a foreign concept to introduce another lasting principle, that of the protection of certain rights and freedoms against legislative or administrative action which might in the short term serve what the public in a more reflective moment would concede to be goals of lesser importance. While one may quarrel with any given hierarchy of norms, the idea of having a hierarchy is not antithetical to democracy.

It may equally be argued that judicial review has long been acquiesced in by the public and is thus not inimical to democracy. Admittedly the system of selection and tenure of judges is not designed to make them responsive to changing political trends. But while the judges need not follow changeable currents of public opinion from day to day they are expected to enforce the durable principles found in statutory and common law and, above all, the most durable principles found in the constitution. Until the public will is translated into statutory or constitutional amendment the courts must follow the last formal expression of will as found in the existing instruments. As the Supreme Court of Canada pointed out recently in *Reference re Section 94(2) of the Motor Vehicle Act, R.S.B.C. 1979, c. 288*[64]

> It ought not to be forgotten that the historic decision to entrench the *Charter* in our Constitution was taken not by the courts but by the elected representatives of the people of Canada. It was those representatives who extended the scope of constitutional adjudication and entrusted the courts with this new and onerous responsibility. Adjudication under the *Charter* must be approached free of any lingering doubts as to its legitimacy.

Thus judicial review, instead of being antithetical to democracy, is supportive of it. In theory at least it is not a matter of judges imposing

---

[64]*Supra*, note 59, at 497.

their will in conflict with the popular will; it is a matter of judges forcibly reminding the public and its elected representatives that some immediately attractive goal is in conflict with more pervasive and durable norms previously accepted by this society. More importantly, perhaps, the courts support both the general public and its elected representatives when they review the activities of officials and agencies to ensure that they conform with the constitutional rules that both public and legislatures want observed.[65] And they can also help the people police the Legislatures and officialdom in enforcing the provisions of the constitution that provide for the proper functioning and representativeness of the electoral system.[66] In the United States this has been demonstrated most markedly with the apportionment cases which have enforced "equal protection of the laws" by requiring state Legislatures to create electoral districts of approximately equal populations.

It is of course true that judges do and must indulge in value judgments in applying general constitutional norms to current, specific, problems. But it is inevitable that constitutions be general in terms if they are not to be unduly restrictive of change.

As the Supreme Court of Canada has recently reconfirmed, a constitutional provision such as s. 8 of the Charter must be interpreted from a "broad perspective" with a "purposive analysis".[67] Caution is, of course, also important in constitutional adjudication because it cannot be readily corrected as can, for example, the unsatisfactory interpretation of a statute.

The danger of legislative power being "transferred to the judiciary" has been much exaggerated. Even in its most activist form, judicial review is interstitial, sporadic, and fortuitous. The judges can only "legislate" in those matters which happen to be brought before them. These are specific cases, not categories of social or economic problems, and the courts' decisions immediately apply only to the actual parties before them. Moreover, unlike legislation, judicial decisions before being finalized are normally subject to repeated reconsideration and refinement through the system of appeals.

The judges then perform a role which is generally accepted, as is the constitution itself, by a democratic society which has delegated to them certain functions of constitutional interpretation and interpolation. It is unrealistic to say that these functions do not involve some value

---

[65]A recent study shows that in the first few years of the Charter some 66% of the cases have involved challenges to administrative action, not legislation: Morton & Withey, "Charting the Charter, 1982–85: A Statistical Analysis", 1987 Canadian Human Rights Yearbook (forthcoming).

[66]See Ely, *supra,* note 61 expecially c.4.

[67]*Hunter et al. v. Southam Inc.*, [1984] 2 S.C.R. 145 at 155–56.

judgments. These value judgments are tolerated provided they do not depart too abruptly from general principles in which that society appears to have acquiesced. They are also much more likely to be tolerated if they display as much consistency as possible, and if the courts clearly appear to be indulging in them reluctantly and for a lack of another means for problems to be resolved.

Courts must recognize that this role is complementary to those of the executive and the legislature; that each has responsibilities in the observance and functioning of the constitution.[68] It is recognition of these constraints which will maintain the legitimacy of judicial policy-making. This is equally true of judicial review performed by the Supreme Court of Canada, even though changes in its constitutional status, method of selection, etc. would reinforce its position as the ultimate tribunal in a federal system.[69]

Before leaving the subject of majoritarian democracy it should also be noted, although the issue is beyond the scope of this book, that true democracy arguably does not yield every decision to majorities and that the most democratic society is that in which the maximum scope for decision-making (that is, freedom) has been left to the individual.[70] If this is so, constitutional guarantees of individual rights and liberties which Governments cannot infringe and courts can protect, are most supportive of democracy even if not of majoritarian democracy.

2. The Functional Issue

A variation of the concern for democratic government is that, even if judicial review to protect rights and freedoms does not offend unduly against an otherwise dominant majoritarianism it is not the best, or perhaps even a very good or wise, method of protecting those rights and freedoms.[71] This argument takes various forms.

It is said that judges are not by training or experience best suited for making political judgments. Nor do their courts offer a proper forum for doing so. Unlike Legislatures, courts are not in a given case open to representations from members of the public or any group not connected

---

[68]See Lederman, ''The Power of the Judges and the New Canadian Charter of Rights and Freedoms'' (1982), *Charter Edition U.B.C. L. Rev.* 1; Agresto, *supra*, note 61, at pp. 77–95.

[69]*Supra*, at pp. 29–32.

[70]See, *e.g.* West and Winer, ''The Search for a Constitution'' (1980), 6 *Can. Public Policy* 1.

[71]See, *e.g.* Horowitz, *supra*, note 61; Russell, Smiley, Weiler (1980 article), *supra*, note 62.

with the case who may wish to advocate certain solutions to the problem under consideration. Courts do not have available to them an unlimited range of expertise on social and economic problems as Legislatures theoretically do. Courts see only an extreme form of a problem, the one that litigants think is the "hard case" that will attract judicial sympathy, whereas Legislatures can take a balanced view of a total range of similar or related problems. Judicial processes are slow and costly and inaccessible to the average citizen whereas legislative and administrative agencies are not. So, it is said, even if a given democracy is committed to the protection of certain individual rights and freedoms, judicial review is not the best means of achieving that objective.

This reasoning may provide an argument against total reliance on judicial review but it surely does not demonstrate that the courts should not be resorted to at all. It seems to be predicated on the assumption that if judicial review cannot provide the ideal solution to every problem, it has no utility. But again it must be remembered that judicial review is a last resort, normally invoked when all other solutions have seemed impossible. It is a particular safeguard for unpopular minorities who may not find the political system to be responsive to their needs.

It is also arguable that, with ever more congested timetables of Legislatures, the courts are better positioned to give effect to constitutionally-recognized rights than are legislators. One can compare, for example, the rather limited output of Legislatures since 1982 in amendments to bring federal and provincial laws into line with the Charter, with the plethora of judicial decisions during the same period which have given the Charter practical effect in so many areas.

Sometimes the functional criticism is put in slightly different terms: that too much is expected of entrenchment of rights and judicial review, with the result that governments and Legislatures do not do their best to respect rights, or they do not put in place other mechanisms which might be more effective. On the first point it remains to be seen whether the entrenchment in Canada of a Charter of Rights will create an indifference in Governments and Legislatures to "good" government and a focus solely on "legal" government. But there is no logical reason why entrenchment should preclude the continuing development of other protections for rights. Perhaps the rhetoric of the supporters of entrenchment has sometimes suggested that entrenchment is the complete solution. During the 15 years of active debate in Canada before the entrenchment of the Charter, however, remarkable progress was in fact made in the development of other protections for human rights. More human rights laws and commissions were adopted so as to cover all jurisdictions, and ombudsmen were established at the provincial level. In 1976 Canada acceded to the International Covenant on Civil and Political Rights and its Protocol by which individuals were enabled for the first time to take complaints of rights violations by Canada (*i.e.* by federal or provincial Governments) directly to the United Nations. The public attention given to the possible constitutional entrenchment of rights did not hamper these developments.

3. The Anti-Federalism Issue

It is also argued that this entrenchment in the national constitution of a Charter of Rights and Freedoms equally binding on federal and provincial authorities, to be interpreted ultimately by one Supreme Court, will impose uniform standards on all Governments and thus stifle the diversity which is the great advantage of federalism.[72] Whether one finds this a persuasive argument against entrenchment and judicial review will depend on his views of federalism, the relative value of rights and local particularism, and the state of our national consensus.

It is true that entrenchment of rights and their interpretation will tend to make more uniform the treatment of rights and freedoms in Canada, leaving less scope for originality in their abridgement by provinces. Although the Charter is not likely to upset the pursuit of major provincial policies crucial to the maintenance of federalism, it is an important new instrument of national integration[73] and undoubtedly this has been an important factor in both the support and the opposition which it has generated. Assuming that all who pay at least lip service to federalism would accept that integration and national uniformity is justified with respect to those matters upon which Canadians in all regions are generally agreed, the real issue here is: do we have a national consensus on the priority of these rights and freedoms over every day governmental decisions? The Parliament of Canada, the Government of Canada, and the Governments of the nine provinces which agreed to entrenchment of the Charter appear to have come to the conclusion that there was such a consensus.

C. THE CHARTER AND PARLIAMENTARY DEMOCRACY

1. Section 1

As we have seen, many conceptual and practical concerns have shaped the debate over entrenchment and judicial review. While some

---

[72]See, *e.g.* Russell, and Schmeiser (1973 article), *supra*, note 62.
[73]See Russell, ''The Political Purposes of the Canadian Charter of Rights and Freedoms'' (1983), 61 *Can. Bar Rev.* 30 at 40–43.

of this debate has brought into question judicial review in the protection of federalism (that is, the maintenance of the distribution of powers), most of the emphasis has been on the constitutional entrenchment of rights and freedoms and the judicial review which flows from that. Concerns have been expressed about the inconsistency of such a development with parliamentary supremacy and majoritarian democracy. This debate profoundly affected the nature of the *Canadian Charter of Rights and Freedoms* as ultimately adopted in the *Constitution Act, 1982*.

In an effort to reassure those who attached more importance to legislative supremacy, the version of s. 1 of the Charter first presented to Parliament provided as follows.[74]

1. The *Canadian Charter of Rights and Freedoms* guarantees the rights and freedoms set out in it subject only to such reasonable limits as are generally accepted in a free and democratic society with a parliamentary system of government.

This wording was strongly criticized by some groups appearing before the Joint Parliamentary Committee on the Constitution, on the grounds that it placed little if any restraint on legislative bodies. Instead of imposing some kind of objective test, it only required that limits be "generally accepted". The reference to a "parliamentary system of government", while intended to be reassuring to the advocates of legislative supremacy, was seen by human rights advocates as a complete acceptance of the status quo: that anything a parliamentary body might enact would by definition be "accepted" in a free and democratic society.

As a result s. 1 was extensively modified so that as adopted it reads:

1. The *Canadian Charter of Rights and Freedoms* guarantees the rights and freedoms set out in it subject only to such reasonable limits prescribed by law as can be demonstrably justified in a free and democratic society.

One can see in the resulting text an effort to reconcile entrenchment of individual rights with parliamentary democracy. The section clearly recognizes that guaranteed rights and freedoms are not absolute but must yield to certain limitations. (This is in contrast to the U.S. *Bill of Rights* which generally proclaims rights in absolute terms so that the courts have had to debate the possibilities of limitation.) Since those limits must be "prescribed by law" to be effective, this leaves Legislatures with the

---

[74]Proposed resolution on the Constitution, tabled House of Commons, Oct. 6, 1980, Hansard Debates, 1st session, 32nd Parliament, vol. III at 2307 to 3518 and Tabled at 3274.

right to restrict them. Thus legislative power is preserved, but only as long as the limitations imposed can be shown to be "justified in a free and democratic society". So we have elements of both parliamentary supremacy and majoritarian democracy ultimately protected by this section from the effects of entrenchment. What is fundamentally changed is that now there is a presumption in favour of these rights and freedoms which will necessarily prevail if Legislatures do not give specific attention to their limitation, and may prevail even in the face of legislation if Governments cannot demonstrate its justification before a court.

Some leading judicial decisions to date have indicated that s. 1 is to be applied strictly, and that the section has qualified legislative supremacy in a major way. It has been held that a direct denial or negation of a right otherwise guaranteed by the Charter is not a mere "limit" such as is permitted by s. 1. Direct denial of rights otherwise guaranteed must be effected under s. 33 if at all.[75] The "limit", if framed as such, must of course be within the jurisdiction of the body prescribing it[76] and it must, to be a "prescribed" limit, provide some form of criteria to guide those applying restrictions on individual rights otherwise guaranteed by the Charter rather than leaving such restrictions wholly to the discretion of administrators.[77] Once it is clear that a guaranteed right or freedom is restricted by a law or official act, then the onus shifts to the party relying on s. 1 to justify such restriction: that is, the normal presumption of validity of statutes has no place here. This onus can, apparently, be met by argument or evidence or both, depending on the circumstances, although evidence will generally be necessary. The evidentiary onus is proof on the balance of probabilities.[78]

In determining what is reasonable and justified in a free and democratic society, the courts obviously do have to make subjective judgments about the wisdom of legislation. The Supreme Court of Canada has prescribed certain criteria to apply in this process. In the *Oakes* case it held that both the ends and the means of the prescribed limitations must be tested. As to the ends or objective, this must be sufficiently important — related to societal concerns both pressing and substantial — to warrant restriction of individual rights and freedoms. As for the means employed,

---

[75]*A.G. Qué. v. Que. Assn. of Protestant School Boards et al.*, [1984] 2 S.C.R. 66 at 84, 86; *R. v. Big M Drug Mart Ltd.*, [1985] 1 S.C.R. 295 at 353.

[76]*Big M* case, *ibid.*

[77]*Re Ont. Film and Video Appreciation Soc. and Ont. Board of Censors* (1984), 5 D.L.R. (4th) 766 (Ont. C.A.); leave to appeal to S.C.C. granted April 4, 1984, but appeal discontinued Dec. 17, 1985; *Luscher v. Deputy Minister, Revenue Canada, Customs and Excise*, [1985] 1 F.C. 85 (C.A.); *R. v. Therens*, [1985] 1 S.C.R. 613 at 621.

[78]*R. v. Oakes*, [1986] 1 S.C.R. 103 at 137–38. See also *Law Soc. of Upper Canada v. Skapinker*, [1984] 1 S.C.R. 357 at 383–84.

they must be proportional to the ends: fair, not arbitrary; rationally connected to the objective; impairing rights no more than necessary; and generally proportional in their severity of effect to the importance of the objectives being served.[79]

Thus it may be seen that while the saving clause in s. 1 which commences "subject only to . . ." was originally intended to preserve a large measure of parliamentary supremacy, as revised and as interpreted it attenuates that supremacy in a very fundamental way. It involves the courts, in a proper case where the issue is necessarily before them, in the assessment and supervision of legislative policy. It must be remembered, however, that s. 1 does not give the courts a general licence to seek and destroy bad legislation. Section 1 is not a constitutional imperative that all legislation must be in accordance with the requirements (as judicially defined) of a "free and democratic society". The criteria set out in s. 1 relate only to "limits" placed on those specific rights and freedoms guaranteed in the Charter; and it is only when those limits are relied on in court as a defence to an allegation of constitutional invalidity that a judge is properly charged with the responsibility of applying tests such as "reasonable", "justified", and "free and democratic society".

2. Section 33

This section provides:

33(1) Parliament or the legislature of a province may expressly declare in an Act of Parliament or of the legislature, as the case may be, that the Act or a provision thereof shall operate notwithstanding a provision included in section 2 or sections 7 to 15 of this Charter.

(2) An Act or a provision of an Act in respect of which a declaration made under this section is in effect shall have such operation as it would have but for the provision of this Charter referred to in the declaration.

(3) A declaration made under subsection (1) shall cease to have effect five years after it comes into force or on such earlier date as may be specified in the declaration.

(4) Parliament or a legislature of a province may re-enact a declaration made under subsection (1).

(5) Subsection (3) applies in respect of a re-enactment made under subsection (4).

This is the most striking effort in the Charter to preserve the concept of parliamentary democracy while protecting individual rights and freedoms as effectively as possible. In theory and in law legislative bodies remain

---

[79]*Oakes* case, *ibid.* at pp. 138–40.

supreme with respect to the subjects covered by this section. Yet as a practical matter it is relatively difficult for Legislatures to abridge these guaranteed rights and freedoms. Inertia is of no avail. Legislators have to make a specific decision to abridge rights and overtly act on it or the Charter guarantees in s. 2 or ss. 7 to 15 operate. Any declaration is effective for no more than five years, at the termination of which time they either have to take further action to renew it or it will lapse, leaving the guarantees supreme.

Section 33 was adopted as one of the final conditions for obtaining the agreement of those provincial governments previously opposed to entrenchment of a Charter. Those governments advocating entrenchment understood the wording of s. 33, as finally settled, to establish strict conditions for the use of this legislative power to override guaranteed rights and freedoms. In particular it was generally understood by them that a declaration made under s. 33 would have to specify both the Charter right to be abridged and the legislative provisions intended to operate in spite of that right. But whether this is the proper interpretation of the actual words employed in s. 33 is a question that has been squarely raised before the courts. Notwithstanding the assumptions of many governments agreeing to s. 33 that it could and would be used only sparingly, the National Assembly of Quebec (the only province whose government had not agreed to the constitutional amendments incorporated in the *Constitution Act, 1982*) adopted, soon after the coming into force of the Charter, *An Act respecting the Constitution Act, 1982.*[80] This statute purported to make all past statutes of Quebec override all of the rights in ss. 2, and 7 to 15 of the Charter; that is, all the rights which s. 33 permits to be overridden. There was no effort made to specify which rights were being overridden by which statutes. Similarly, thereafter until about the end of 1985 the National Assembly of Quebec continued to enact a similar declaration in each new statute declaring that such law should operate notwithstanding the provisions of ss. 2, and 7 to 15 of the Charter. In the meantime the 1982 general overriding statute was attacked in the Quebec courts. Though upheld in the Superior Court,[81] the Act was held invalid by the Quebec Court of Appeal on the grounds that it did not specify adequately the particular rights being abridged by a particular statute.[82] The court held this to be a requirement for two reasons. First, because of the wording of s. 33(1), which refers to an ''Act or a provision thereof'' of the overriding legislation, but only to a ''provision included'' in a section of the Charter when speaking of the provision that must be

---

[80]S.Q. 1982, c. 21.

[81]*Alliance des Professeurs de Montréal et al. v. A.G. of Qué. et al.* (1983), 5 D.L.R. (4th) 157.

[82](1985), 21 D.L.R. (4th) 354; leave to appeal to S.C.C. granted Sept. 30, 1985.

declared to be intentionally abridged by the Legislature, the court held that it does not suffice to refer to simply a series of Charter sections. Second, because this power to override is seen as extraordinary and exceptional, the court said it must be strictly applied so as to require the proposers of legislation to "link" the abridged right with the abridging legislation in order to permit informed debate by legislators and the public. Before the Supreme Court decided an appeal in this case, the declaration in *An Act respecting the Constitution Act, 1982* was allowed to lapse at the end of the five year period allowed in s. 33 of the Charter, without being renewed. Declarations in legislation adopted between 1982 and 1985 will, in form at least, continue until their five years expire, subject to whatever final judicial determination is made as to their validity.

Apart from the use made by the Quebec National Assembly as described above, s. 33 has been used on one other occasion. It was invoked by the Legislature of Saskatchewan in 1986 in a statute dealing with a specific labour dispute and in relation to a specific right to be abridged, namely freedom of association, referred to in one of the provisions in s. 2 of the Charter.[83] This was done after a court decision[84] had held that similar legislation was invalid as an abridgement of this particular freedom.

Whatever the merits of the particular use of s. 33 in the Quebec and Saskatchewan examples, it is probable that those governments agreeing to the inclusion of this override clause in the Charter anticipated that it would be used in the kind of sequence of events that occurred in Saskatchewan. That is, where a law had been struck down by the courts as in conflict with the Charter, and where the Legislature nevertheless remained convinced that such a law was of sufficient importance, it could expressly take the political responsibility for overriding, with legislation, specific rights which would normally be protected by the Charter. In this way there would be a reinforcement of the powers of both courts and Legislatures. Courts could be more astute to strike down laws in conflict with the Charter, knowing that Legislatures could still prevail by the use of s. 33 if the public need for such legislation should be deemed to be sufficiently great as to justify the overriding of these private rights or freedoms. And the Legislature could then face this issue squarely and adopt the necessary declaration under s. 33 if it consciously concluded that such a measure was sufficiently important and politically justifiable.

Section 33 allows a legislative override of "fundamental" freedoms (speech, belief, press, assembly, association, etc.), legal rights, and equality rights. It does not permit such override with respect to "democratic"

---

[83]S.S. 1984–85–86, c. 111, s. 9.
[84]*Re Retail, Wholesale & Dept. Store Union Locs. 544 et al. v. Govt. of Sask.* (1985), 19 D.L.R. (4th) 609 (Sask. C.A.), revd [1987] 3 W.W.R. 673 (S.C.C.).

rights (the right to vote, to candidacy, the requirement of regular legislative sessions and elections), nor to mobility rights or linguistic rights. This means, *inter alia*, that the democratic rights in ss. 3 to 5 which protect the integrity of the electoral and parliamentary systems are not subject to legislative supremacy. This again furthers the reconciliation between entrenchment and parliamentary democracy because judicial review in relation to these sections could only reinforce the democratic process (although to be consistent the fundamental freedoms in s. 2 should also have been left outside the ambit of the legislative override).

3. Some Problem Areas

Although ss. 1 and 33 have modified the judicial role by imposing qualifications or exceptions to judicial review, the Charter as a whole has confronted the courts with a vast range of new decisional responsibility. The scope of this responsibility has been only partly perceived so far. One can readily get a sense of it simply from looking at the contents of almost any law report published since the coming into force of the Charter, and there see the number of cases in which the Charter has been a factor.

The majority of these cases have invoked legal rights of a procedural nature, as found in ss. 7 to 11 of the Charter. They have evoked concepts of fairness which are familiar to courts and which have counterparts in common or statutory law. As a result, they have not obliged the courts to make difficult choices of a substantive nature which would tend to bring into question the legitimacy of the judicial role.

While the analysis of Charter decisions as a whole is not within the nature or purpose of this book, it may be useful to look briefly at a few Charter provisions which appear to have more potential for creating role-problems for the courts.

Section 7 asserts the right not to be deprived of "life, liberty and security of the person" "except in accordance with the principles of fundamental justice". It is apparent from the legislative history that, rightly or wrongly, this wording was chosen to avoid the broader concept of substantive, as opposed to procedural, rights, attributed to the phrase "due process of law" as found in similar provisions of the Fifth and Fourteenth Amendments to the U.S. Constitution.[85]

In the majority of cases thus far where s. 7 has been applied, it has

---

[85]See *e.g. Proceedings of the Special Joint Committee on the Constitution*, January 27, 1981, at 46: 32–4. For earlier proposals using this same language, see Gibson, *The Law of the Charter: General Principles* (Toronto: Carswell, 1986), at pp. 32, 36. See also Romanow, Whyte, Leeson, *Canada . . . Notwithstanding: The Making of the Constitution 1976-82* (Toronto: Carswell/Methuen, 1984), at pp. 245–46.

been invoked as a procedural guarantee, and the courts have been able to rely on familiar concepts of procedural fairness in giving it content. The Supreme Court of Canada has, however, in *Reference re Section 94(2) of the Motor Vehicle Act, R.S.B.C. 1979, c. 288*[86] rejected the procedural-substantive dichotomy as a basis for constraining judicial review of the policy of legislation. While eschewing the role of adjudicating wisdom or policy of laws, the court held invalid a provincial law which imposed imprisonment with respect to an offence for which there was no requirement of *mens rea*. While not characterizing this as a procedural question, the court found it to offend the "principles of fundamental justice" protected by s. 7. The principles of fundamental justice were not defined, but described as[87]

> found in the basic tenets of our legal system. They do not lie in the realm of general public policy but in the inherent domain of the judiciary as guardian of the justice system.

This it was said

> provides meaningful content for the s. 7 guarantee all the while avoiding adjudication of policy matters.

While legislators might previously have thought that whether a particular offence deserves imprisonment is a matter of policy, this is apparently not the case for the purposes of judicial review under s. 7 of the Charter. But at the very least it can be said that the identification of the "basic tenets of our legal system", for the purposes of establishing the "principles of fundamental justice", is going to require the courts to make many choices, articulate those choices, and apply them in novel ways. This will at the very least create the impression of judicial activism.

Again, s. 15 will oblige the courts to make a number of difficult choices among possible interpretations, choices which may have greatly varying impacts. This section provides that every individual is "equal before and under the law" and has the right to "equal protection and equal benefit of the law without discrimination" and in particular without discrimination based on certain grounds specified therein. The courts have already had to face problems such as: what is "equality" (*i.e.*, do certain differences among certain individuals necessitate unequal treatment)?[88]

---

[86]*Supra*, note 59. See also *R. v. Morgentaler et al.* (1985), 22 D.L.R. (4th) 641 at 668–74 (Ont. C.A.); S.C.C. judgment on appeal reserved Oct. 10, 1986.

[87]*Supra*, note 59, at p. 503.

[88]See, *e.g. Re Blainey and Ont. Hockey Assn. et al.* (1986), 54 O.R. (2d) 513 (C.A.), leave to appeal to S.C.C. refused 58 O.R. (2d) 274n; *R. v. Swain* (1986), 53 O.R. (2d) 609 (C.A.); *Re Shewchuk and Ricard et al.*, [1986] 4 W.W.R. 289 (B.C.C.A.).

Or, what is "discrimination"?[89] Or, does it matter whether the discrimination complained of is on one of the grounds specified in s. 15?[90] Judicial innovation in the application of this section will be as difficult as it is inevitable, because it touches on profound social issues as to what distinctions are permissible or desirable in the state's relations with its citizens.

Another area with considerable scope for judicial creativity, in theory at least, is that of minority language educational rights in s. 23. Under s-s. 23(2), the specified rights to minority official language education in any province applies wherever the number of entitled children "is sufficient to warrant the provision to them out of public funds" of such instruction.

Cases decided under s. 23 have illustrated the difficulties which the courts will face if they have to decide whether in a given situation the numbers of entitled children warrant the provision of instruction. So far, the tendency has been to insist that in the first instance these decisions should be left to the Legislature, with the courts being only a last resort if the Legislature does not make proper provision in this respect.[91]

All these Charter sections — and there are several others as well — oblige the courts to make choices of an unfamiliar kind. These are choices which may be seen as traditionally more legislative than judicial in nature. The adoption of the Charter was the expression of a consensus for the judicialization of certain public policy issues. The challenge for the courts is to ascertain the extent of that consensus; to so interpret the Charter as to make it a mandate for the protection of values truly intended to be embodied in the constitution and for no more; but to recognize that with the passage of time the proper application of those fundamental values will have to evolve along with Canadian society.

D. CONCLUSION

It is possible, then, to reconcile judicial review, for the protection of federalism or for the protection of rights and freedoms, with a system of parliamentary democracy. The "supremacy" of our legislative bodies has never been quite the same as that of Westminster, because they have always worked within certain external limitations. Yet within these lim-

---

[89] *Smith, Kline & French Laboratories Ltd. et al. v. A.G. Can.*, [1986] 1 F.C. 274 (T.D.), affd 34 D.L.R. (4th) 586 (C.A.), leave to appeal to S.C.C. refused April 9, 1987; *Andrews v. Law Soc. of B.C. et al.*, [1986] 4 W.W.R. 242, leave to appeal to S.C.C. granted Nov. 27, 1986.

[90] *Ibid.*

[91] *Reference re Education Act of Ont. and Minority Language Education Rights* (1984), 10 D.L.R. (4th) 491 at 521–22 (Ont. C.A.); *Mahe et al. v. The Queen in right of Alta.* (1985), 22 D.L.R. (4th) 24 at 43 (Alta. Q.B.).

itations they are supreme and this creates a potential for legislation affecting judicial review that may distinguish our system from one with a constitutional separation of powers. Judicial review can also be reconciled with democracy if democracy is seen to be based on the acceptance by a society of its system of government combined with the lawful and peaceful means to change it should it become unacceptable. The delegation of certain authority, even law-making authority, to judges through judicial review is part of that consensus in Canada, but it is one which cannot be taken for granted and its legitimacy must be nurtured and protected by Governments and the courts themselves.

While the *Canadian Charter of Rights and Freedoms* has been designed to avoid many of the potential conflicts between courts and Legislatures or between courts and people, it brings with it many possibilities for judicial innovation. These pose new opportunities, new problems, and new dangers, for judicial review.

Chapter 3

Legislative Controls on the Power of Review

It has been shown in the preceding chapter that there are competing principles involved wherever Canadian legislative bodies seek to limit the power of judicial review. On the one hand, there is clearly power in Parliament and the Legislatures to govern the constitution and jurisdiction of the courts, to deny rights to citizens, or to impose restrictions on access to the courts. On the other hand, the reliance on judicial review for protection of the constitution implies that these legislative powers cannot be exercised in such a way as to facilitate its violation.

In other words, legislative bodies may not in the guise of legislating with respect to matters otherwise within their jurisdiction, in essence legislate so as to exceed their jurisdiction and prevent the courts from reviewing their actions. This is only a particular application of the general rule against colourability: legislation which on its face appears valid may be found invalid if its essential object and effect is to deal with some matter beyond the jurisdiction of the enacting Legislature.[1]

This chapter will deal in detail with the principal types of controls on judicial review imposed by legislative bodies. With respect to each it will be necessary to examine how far the legislative body may go in imposing limitations before it runs afoul of some constitutional imperative.

A. STATUTORY ASSIGNMENT OF JURISDICTION

It was noted in Chapter 2 that Parliament by s. 101 of the *Constitution Act, 1867*, and provincial Legislatures by head 92(14) thereof, have the legislative power to establish certain courts and to provide for their "Constitution, Maintenance, and Organization". This has always been recognized to include the power to define their jurisdiction, subject to particular constitutional constraints and the normal distribution of powers. Some

---

[1]See *e.g. Madden v. Nelson & Fort Sheppard Ry.*, [1889] A.C. 626, 81 L.T. 276 (P.C.); *A.G. Ont. v. Reciprocal Insurers*, [1924] A.C. 328, 130 L.T. 738, [1924] 2 W.W.R. 397, [1924] 1 D.L.R. 789, 41 C.C.C. 336 (P.C.); *Can. Fed. of Agriculture v. A.G. Que.*, [1951] A.C. 179, 66 T.L.R. 774, [1950] 4 D.L.R. 689 (P.C.); Finkelstein (ed.), *Laskin's Canadian Constitutional Law*, 5th ed. (Toronto: Carswell 1986), at pp. 309–11; Hogg, *Constitutional Law of Canada*, 2nd ed., (Toronto: Carswell, 1985), at 322.

of the constitutional restraints on Legislatures imposing such jurisdictional limitations will be examined later in this chapter.

Generally speaking, no court has an exclusive jurisdiction over constitutional matters nor is any court precluded from dealing with constitutional issues. Every court is obliged, by s. 52 of the *Constitution Act, 1982*, to apply the constitution as "the law of Canada" should this become relevant in any case over which the court has jurisdiction[2] by virtue of statutory authority granted to it with respect to the (non-constitutional) subject-matter of, the parties to, and the remedies sought in, the dispute.

The impact of statutory grants or limits on a court's jurisdiction in relation to constitutional litigation has been brought into question by s. 24 of the Charter. This section provides:

> 24.(1) Anyone whose rights or freedoms, as guaranteed by this Charter, have been infringed or denied may apply to a court of competent jurisdiction to obtain such remedy as the court considers appropriate and just in the circumstances.
>
> (2) Where, in proceedings under subsection (1), a court concludes that evidence was obtained in a manner that infringed or denied any rights or freedoms guaranteed by this Charter, the evidence shall be excluded if it is established that, having regard to all the circumstances, the admission of it in the proceedings would bring the administration of justice into disrepute.

For present purposes, the words "court of competent jurisdiction" in s-s. (1) pose the relevant questions. Do they implicitly empower any court to give a constitutional remedy? Is any court "of competent jurisdiction" for this purpose? Or can any court give any remedy for an infringement of the constitution even if such remedy would not normally be within its remedial powers?

These questions have been answered to a large extent in the jurisprudence to date. Three judges of the Supreme Court of Canada as early as the *Singh* case of 1985 observed that this phrase in s-s. 24(1) "premises the existence of jurisdiction from a source external to the Charter itself".[3] Those judges who applied the Charter to a decision of the Immigration Appeal Board limited the scope of their review to that permitted to the Federal Court of Appeal by s. 28 of the *Federal Court Act*,[4] the court from which the appeal was brought to the Supreme Court. Charter criteria were therefore not applied to associated administrative decisions which could not be the subject of judicial review by the Federal Court of Appeal.

The more recent decision of the Supreme Court in *Mills v. The*

---

[2] *R. v. Big M Drug Mart Ltd.*, [1985] 1 S.C.R. 295 at 315–16.
[3] *Singh et al. v. Min. of Employment and Immigration*, [1985] 1 S.C.R. 177 at 222.
[4] R.S.C. 1970 (2nd Supp.), c. 10.

Queen[5] appears to have adopted the standard test for "competent juris-diction". To be of competent jurisdiction, a court must by its constitutive laws (normally statutes) have jurisdiction as to the person impleaded before it, the subject-matter of the cause, and the remedy being sought. This threefold test, applied earlier by the Ontario Court of Appeal in respect of s-s. 24(1),[6] was quoted[7] with approval by McIntyre J. in a judgment concurred in by a majority of the panel which heard the *Mills* case. With respect, this appears to be most in accord with the wording of s-s. 24(1), using as it does the standard phrase "court of competent jurisdiction". If the Charter had intended to confer general jurisdiction on all courts to adjudicate any Charter matter it would surely have been worded otherwise.

Given the wording of s-s. 24(1) there might have been more of a dispute as to whether "competent jurisdiction" really required that the court be otherwise authorized to give the precise remedy being sought in a Charter case. After all, the subsection says that in a competent court anyone may "obtain such remedy as the court considers appropriate". Arguably, a "court of competent jurisdiction" might be defined in terms of the parties and subject-matter, with a court competent in respect of these two factors being empowered by s-s. 24(1) to grant *any* remedy.[8] Such an approach would, however, be potentially disruptive of the normal division of functions in the judicial system and is not lightly to be pre-sumed. In the *Mills* case itself this interpretation appears to have been rejected implicitly by the Supreme Court of Canada when it held that a magistrate presiding over a preliminary inquiry could not grant a stay of proceedings, as a remedy for violation of the Charter right under s. 11(b) to be tried within a reasonable time. The only remedies available to such a magistrate are a committal to stand trial or a discharge, based on the existence or non-existence of a *prima facie* case. Further, it was said that exclusion of evidence, as contemplated in s-s. 24(2), is also a remedy which must be granted in accordance with s-s. 24(1), that is by a court of competent jurisdiction. Any evidence to be excluded on Charter grounds must therefore be excluded by the trial judge,[9] and this will normally occur at the trial itself.[10]

---

[5][1986] 1 S.C.R. 863. Folld in *Carter v. The Queen*, [1986] 1 S.C.R. 981. See also *U.S.A. v. Allard*, May 14, 1987 (S.C.C.).

[6]*R. v. Morgentaler et al.* (1984), 41 C.R. (3d) 262 at 271 (Ont. C.A.).

[7]*Mills* case, *supra*, note 5, at p. 960.

[8]This possibility is suggested, *e.g.* in Gibson, *The Law of the Charter: General Principles* (Toronto: Carswell, 1986), at pp. 283–84; Hogg, *Constitutional Law of Canada*, 2nd ed. (Toronto: Carswell, 1985), at p. 696.

[9]*Mills* case, *supra*, note 5, at 954–55.

[10]See, *e.g. Re Blackwoods Beverages Ltd. et al. and The Queen et al.* (1984), 16 C.C.C. (3d) 363 (Man. C.A.).

The result is that normally it will be the legislative definition of a court's jurisdiction — in terms of parties, subject-matter, and remedy — that will determine if it is a "court of competent jurisdiction" for the purposes of granting a remedy under s. 24.

One problem area, however, which remains unclear is as to the extent that Parliament can, through the exercise of its power under s. 101 of the *Constitution Act, 1867*, deny jurisdiction to provincial superior courts in Charter matters. It will be recalled that s. 101 provides that Parliament may

> . . . notwithstanding anything in this Act . . . provide for . . . the Establishment of any additional Courts for the better Administration of the Laws of Canada.

The pervasive effect of the opening words of s. 101, "notwithstanding anything in this Act", were confirmed by the Supreme Court of Canada and the Judicial Committee of the Privy Council in respect of Parliament's power to make the Supreme Court the obligatory and final court of appeal from provincial superior courts.[11] Nevertheless the provisions of s. 18 of the *Federal Court Act*,[12] enacted by Parliament under s. 101, were held not to be effective to confer exclusive jurisdiction on the Federal Court in respect of determining the validity of federal laws. It was so held by the Supreme Court on the basis that Parliament could not by this means deprive the superior courts of the provinces of the power to declare a federal law invalid, "a judicial power fundamental to a federal system".[13] It remains to be seen whether the same rule will be applied to s. 24 Charter cases. While, if any court is called upon to enforce or apply a law it may surely take into account the validity or invalidity of that law, whether measured against the distribution of legislative powers or the Charter, it is not as obvious that every provincial superior court needs to have inherent jurisdiction to grant declarations of conflict between federal laws and the Charter. The rationale quoted above for the conclusion that provincial superior courts must have the power to declare a conflict with the constitutional distribution of powers was that this is "essential to a federal system". Charter guarantees are not essential to a federal system. If Parliament purports to abridge Charter rights, this raises a serious issue between the citizen and federal authorities, but it does not threaten the

---

[11]*Reference re Supreme Court Act Amendment Act*, [1940] S.C.R. 49 at 63–64, affd [1947] A.C. 127 at 152 (*sub nom. A.G. Ont. v. A.G. Can. and A.G. Que.*).

[12]*Supra*, note 4.

[13]*A.G. Can. et al. v. Law Soc. of B.C. et al. and A.G. Ont. et al.; Jabour v. Law Soc. of B.C. et al. and A.G. Can. et al.*, [1982] 2 S.C.R. 307 at 328.

federal system. Given the decision in *Mills*, it may be p⌐
that a Charter issue involving federal laws need not be co.
every court at every stage, so long as it is litigable in som⌐
provided by the statutes assigning jurisdiction over the relev⌐
(*i.e.*, the federal government), the relevant subject-matter, and ⌐ relevant remedy.[14]

B. PROCEDURAL REQUIREMENTS

The most common procedural prerequisite to judicial review is the
service of notice on the appropriate attorney general advising him of an
impending attack on the validity of a particular piece of legislation.

The importance of government participation in constitutional litigation became apparent almost as soon as judicial review began in the
Anglo-American legal world. In 1727 in *Winthrop v. Lechmere*,[15] the
first recorded appeal from the American colonies involving validity of a
colonial statute, the Privy Council held a Connecticut intestacy law to
be invalid. The soundness of this decision was seriously questioned as it
held, in effect, that a colonial Legislature had no power to alter in the
colony the rule of primogeniture which applied, under English law, in
England. *Winthrop v. Lechmere* was a purely private piece of litigation,
but the effects of it in Connecticut were far-reaching. When 20 years
later the validity of a similar law was about to be considered by the Privy
Council in the case of *Clark v. Tousey*,[16] the Connecticut Legislature
voted to lend Tousey £500 to assist him in employing good counsel to
present the case for the statute. An opposite result from that in *Winthrop
v. Lechmere* was obtained and the statute was upheld.[17]

In Canada, *Russell v. The Queen*[18] is a leading example of an early
decision which upheld Dominion legislation without participation of any
provincial attorney general in the proceedings. The appellant had been
convicted at Fredericton, New Brunswick, under the *Canada Temperance
Act, 1878*. He sought *certiorari* to quash the conviction, contending that
the Act was *ultra vires* of Parliament on the grounds that it was legislation

---

[14]Cases consistent with this approach include *Jackson v. Min. of Finance, Dept. of Nat.
Revenue for Taxation* (1982), 4 C.R.R. 271 (Sask. Q.B.); *Pêcheries M.P.Q. Ltée et
al. v. Haché et al.* (1986), 25 D.L.R. (4th) 66 (N.B.Q.B.); and *Re Gandam and Min.
of Employment and Immigration* (1982), 140 D.L.R. (3d) 363 (Sask. Q.B.).

[15](1727), 3 *Acts of the Privy Council (Colonial Series)* 1910, at 139–50.

[16]See McGovney, "The British Origin of Judicial Review of Legislation" (1944–45), 93
U. Pa. L. Rev. 1.

[17]*Supra*, note 16.

[18](1882), 7 App. Cas. 829, 46 L.T. 889 (P.C.).

in relation to property and civil rights in the province, matters of a local or private nature, or licensing (all of these matters being within provincial jurisdiction under s. 92 of the *British North America Act*). The Privy Council upheld the validity of the *Canada Temperance Act*, and the decision was subsequently[19] understood to mean that this law was within the federal power to legislate for the "peace, order, and good government of Canada" as provided by the opening words of s. 91. This was one of the most important and controversial decisions ever rendered in the interpretation of the B.N.A. Act, and it was rendered in a proceeding between a private prosecutor and an accused person. Neither the Attorney General of Canada nor the Attorney General of any province was represented. There was some subsequent feeling that the decision might have been otherwise had one or more of the provinces been heard,[20] though in fairness it must be noted that the counsel leading the unsuccessful attack on the federal legislation was no less a personage than J. P. Benjamin, Q.C., former Attorney General of the Confederate States.

It is probably no coincidence that machinery was introduced in Canada soon thereafter to ensure that the appropriate attorneys general would be notified of, and permitted to appear in, constitutional litigation. Legislation to this end was passed in Quebec in 1882,[21] Ontario in 1883,[22] and subsequently in all other provinces except, apparently, Prince Edward Island.

The tendency, in those provinces with such legislation, has been to broaden the coverage of notice requirements. This has been particularly noticeable since the adoption of the *Canadian Charter of Rights and Freedoms*.

One of the most comprehensive of the modern notice requirements is s. 8 of the *Constitutional Questions Act* of Saskatchewan as amended in 1984.[23]

> **8**(1) In this section:
> (a) 'law' includes an Act of the Parliament of Canada or of the

---

[19]In the local prohibition case of *A.G. Ont. v. A.G. Can.*, [1896] A.C. 348 at 362, 74 L.T. 533 (P.C.).

[20]This seems to be the implication of Lord Watson's comments in *A.G. Ont. v. A.G. Can.*, *supra*, note 19 at p. 362 A.C. See also *Re Board of Commerce* (1920), 60 S.C.R. 456 at 507–508, [1920] 3 W.W.R. 658, 54 D.L.R. 354 at 391, opinion divided, no judgment rendered; [1922] 1 A.C. 191, [1922] 1 W.W.R. 20, 60 D.L.R. 513 (P.C.). *Re Natural Products Marketing Act*, [1936] S.C.R. 398 at 420, [1936] 3 D.L.R. 622 at 638–39, 66 C.C.C. 180, affd [1937] A.C. 377 (*sub nom. A.G. B.C. v. A.G. Can.*), [1937] 1 W.W.R. 328, [1937] 1 D.L.R. 691, 67 C.C.C. 337.

[21]*An Act to Facilitate the intervention of the Crown in Civil Cases in which the Constitutionality of a Federal or Provincial Act is in Question*, S.Q. 1882, c. 4, s. 1.

[22]*An Act for the Better Administration of Justice in this Province*, S.O. 1883, c. 6, s. 6.

[23]R.S.S. 1978, c. C-29 as amended by S.S. 1983–84, c. 31, s. 2.

Legislature and includes a proclamation, regulation or Order in Council made pursuant to any such Act;

(b) 'regulation' means a regulation as defined in *The Regulations Act*;

(c) 'remedy' means a remedy provided pursuant to section 24 of the *Canadian Charter of Rights and Freedoms* but does not include a remedy of exclusion of evidence or a remedy consequential on exclusion of evidence.

(2) When, in a court of Saskatchewan:

(a) the constitutional validity or constitutional applicability of any law is brought into question; or

(b) an application is made to obtain a remedy;

the court shall not adjudge the law to be invalid or inapplicable nor shall it grant the remedy until after notice is served on the Attorney General of Canada and on the Attorney General for Saskatchewan in accordance with this section.

(3) When, in a court of Saskatchewan, the validity or applicability of a proclamation, regulation or Order in Council made or purportedly made in the execution of a power given by an Act of the Legislature is brought into question on grounds other than those mentioned in subsection (2), the court shall not adjudge the proclamation, regulation or Order in Council to be invalid until after notice is served on the Attorney General for Saskatchewan in accordance with this section.

(4) Subject to subsection (5), a notice mentioned in subsection (2) or (3) is required to be served at least 14 days before the day of argument.

(5) The court may, on an *ex parte* application made for the purpose, order an abridgement of the time for service of a notice mentioned in subsection (2) or (3).

(6) A notice mentioned in subsection (2) or (3) is required:

(a) to be headed in the action, cause, matter or proceeding in which the question arises or application is made;

(b) to state:

(i) the law or provision thereof in question; or

(ii) the right or freedom alleged to be infringed or denied;

(c) to state the day and place for the argument of the question; and

(d) to give the particulars that are necessary to show the point to be argued.

(7) The Attorney General for Saskatchewan is entitled as of right to appear and be heard either in person or through counsel in any action, cause, matter or proceeding to which subsection (2) or (3) applies.

(8) The Attorney General of Canada is entitled as of right to appear and be heard either in person or through counsel in any action, cause, matter or proceeding to which subsection (2) applies.

(9) Where the Attorney General of Canada or the Attorney General for Saskatchewan appears in an action, cause, matter or proceeding to which subsection (2) or (3) applies, he is a party for the purposes of appeal from an adjudication therein respecting the validity or applicability of a law or respecting entitlement to a remedy.

There are several aspects to be noted here. First, the notice requirement

applies with respect to challenges to both federal and provincial legislation. Such a challenge may be to its validity or its application. The
reference to "application" has been added since the advent of the Charter
and presumably was thought to be necessary to cover situations where a
court is to be asked to "read down" a statute so as to avoid conflict with
a right or freedom guaranteed by the Charter. It also now covers cases
where a remedy is being sought (*i.e.*, to vindicate a guaranteed right or
freedom) pursuant to s. 24 of the Charter. Further it appears to require
notice on both the Attorney General of Canada and the Attorney General
of Saskatchewan, regardless of whose law is in issue. As before, it applies
to proceedings of any kind (*i.e.*, under either federal or provincial law)
in any court of Saskatchewan, and it purports to prohibit any adjudication
of invalidity or inapplicability of a law unless the required notice has
been given. The section also calls for notice to be given to the provincial
Attorney General where delegated legislation made pursuant to provincial
law is attacked on non-constitutional grounds.

Similar legislation has been adopted in British Columbia,[24] Nova
Scotia,[25] and Manitoba,[26] although the Nova Scotia provision does not
require notice to the Attorney General of Canada. Ontario has broadened
its previous notice requirement so as to make it apply where there is an
issue of "constitutional applicability", as well as of validity, of a federal
or provincial law or regulation. Notice to both the federal and provincial
attorneys general is required.[27] Alberta's law has not been changed since
the Charter, but is similar in effect to Ontario's except that it does not
cover questions of "applicability of laws".[28] New Brunswick's statute
appears to be similar in coverage to that of Ontario but it does not prohibit
adjudication of invalidity where no notice has been given.[29] Newfoundland's law addresses questions of "validity" only and prohibits adjudication where notice has not been given.[30]

In Quebec art. 95 of the *Code of Civil Procedure* as recently amended[31]
continues to apply to attacks on federal or provincial legislation. It now
applies both to questions of validity and of applicability, and specific
reference is made to attacks based on the *Canadian Charter of Rights
and Freedoms*. Notice is also required in non-constitutional challenges

---

[24] S.B.C. 1982, c. 5, amending *Constitutional Question Act*, R.S.B.C. 1979, c. 63, s. 8.
[25] S.N.S. 1985, c. 15, s. 1, amending *Constitutional Questions Act*, R.S.N.S. 1967, c. 51.
[26] *The Constitutional Questions Act*, C.C.S.M., c. C180, s. 7.
[27] *Courts of Justice Act, 1984*, S.O. 1984, c. 11, s. 122.
[28] *Judicature Act*, R.S.A. 1980, c. J-1, s. 25, am. 1981, c. 51, s. 2.
[29] *Judicature Act*, R.S.N.B. 1973, c. J-2, s. 22, am. 1980, c. 28, s. 5; 1982, c. 3, s. 39(1);
  1983, c. 43, s. 6.
[30] *The Judicature Act, 1986*, S.N. 1986, c. 42, s. 57.
[31] R.S.Q. 1977, c. C-25, am. 1985, c. 29, s. 6.

based on the provincial *Charter of Human Rights and Freedoms*. Unlike its predecessor, the new art. 95 now prohibits an adjudication of such issues if no notice has been given. This article only requires that notice be given to the provincial Attorney General in any of these cases.

While there is no comparable federal statute, the rules of the Supreme Court of Canada have, since 1905, provided for notice to the Attorney General where the validity of a statute is challenged. Formerly the rules required such notice only to the Attorney General of Canada where a federal statute was involved, and only to that Attorney General and the Attorney General of the particular province where a provincial statute was questioned.[32] The rule is now somewhat broader:[33]

> 32.(1) When a party to an appeal
> (*a*) intends to raise a question as to the constitutional validity or the constitutional applicability of a statute of the Parliament of Canada or of a legislature of a province or of Regulations made thereunder, or
> (*b*) intends to urge the inoperability of a statute of the Parliament of Canada or of a legislature of a province or of regulations made thereunder,
> such party shall, upon notice to the other parties, apply to the Chief Justice or a Judge for the purpose of stating the question, within thirty days from the granting of leave to appeal or within thirty days from the filing of the notice of appeal in an appeal with leave of the court of final resort in a province, the Federal Court of Appeal, or in an appeal as of right.
>
> (2) The parties to a reference under section 55 of the Act shall follow the procedure set out in subsection (1).
>
> (3) The time referred to in subsection (1) may be extended by the Court or a Judge.
>
> (4) Upon a motion, the Chief Justice or a Judge shall state the question or question and direct service of the question or questions upon the Attorney General of Canada and the attorneys general of all the provinces within the time fixed by the Chief Justice or Judge together with notice that any of them who intends to intervene, whether or not the attorney general wishes to be heard, shall, within a time fixed in the notice that is not less than four weeks after the date of the notice, file a notice of intervention in Form C.
>
> (5) Any order made by the Chief Justice or a Judge pursuant to this Rule shall be prepared for the signature of the Registrar by the party making the motion and all such orders shall be included in and form part of the case on appeal.
>
> (6) A constitutional question or questions to be raised pursuant to this Rule shall be included in Part I of the factum.

---

[32]*Supreme Court Rules*, 1945, Rules 18 and 19 as originally promulgated.
[33]*Supreme Court Rules*, SOR/83–74, am. SOR/84–821; SOR 87–292.

(7) Any attorney general, after leave to intervene has been granted under Rule 18 shall follow the procedure set out in subsection (1) to state a constitutional question or questions except the question shall be stated within 15 days after leave to intervene has been granted.

(8) Where an attorney general is an intervener in the Courts below, he may upon notice to the other parties or interveners, apply to the Chief Justice or a Judge for the purpose of stating the question or questions within 30 days from the granting of leave to appeal or within 30 days from the filing of the notice of appeal,

(*a*) in an appeal with leave of the court of final resort in a province or of the Federal Court of Appeal; or

(*b*) in an appeal as of right.

This rule does not purport to deny the court jurisdiction on the constitutional issues where no application is made first to have the points in question stated, or where notice of them is not subsequently served on attorneys general. It appears, however, that the court will not attempt to deal with the constitutional issues if such a process has not been followed. In *Northern Telecom Ltd. v. Communications Workers of Canada* an order of the Canada Labour Relations Board certifying the union was under attack. This order was challenged in the courts on the question of the jurisdiction of the board and it became apparent that this essentially involved a constitutional issue as to whether the employer was a federal work or undertaking. On appeal from the Federal Court of Appeal, which had dismissed the application to set aside the order, the Supreme Court held that there was not the necessary evidence to enable it to determine this issue, which had not been addressed either before the board or the Federal Court of Appeal. Moreover, no application had been made under Rule 17, the predecessor to Rule 32. Dickson J., delivering judgment for the court, stated:[34]

> I am inclined toward the view that, in the absence of the vital constitutional facts, this Court would be ill-advised to essay to resolve the constitutional issue which lurks in the question upon which leave to appeal has been granted. One must keep in mind that it is not merely the private interests of the two parties before the Court that are involved in a constitutional case. By definition, the interests of two levels of government are also engaged. In this case, the appellant did not apply to the Court, pursuant to Rule 17 of the *Supreme Court Rules*, for the purpose of having a constitutional question stated. If the appellant had intended to raise the question as to the constitutional applicability of the *Canada Labour Code*, then the obligation was upon the appellant to assure that the constitutional issue was properly raised. As no constitutional question was stated nor notice served upon the respective Attorneys General, the Court lacks the

---

[34][1980] 1 S.C.R. 115 at 139–40, 98 D.L.R. (3d) 1 at 19, 28 N.R. 107.

traditional procedural safeguards that would normally attend such a case and the benefit of interventions by the governments concerned.

As a result, the court declined to deal with the constitutional issue and dismissed the appeal on the basis that the appellant company had not shown reversible error on the part of the board.

While it appears that the lack of an application and notice under Rule 17 was not the exclusive reason for the refusal of the Supreme Court to deal with the constitutional issue, it was probably a weighty factor. Moreover, the rationale for the Rule 17 (now Rule 32) process is articulated: that constitutional issues transcend the interests of the immediate private parties before the court and it is important that the public interest be protected by the clear definition of the issues the court is going to address and by the opportunity for governments to express their views thereon.

The Rules of the Federal Court of Appeal do not appear to be as demanding in this respect. Rule 1101[35] simply provides that where "any constitutional question or any question of general importance" is raised before the court then a party *may* serve notice on any interested Attorney General, the court itself *may* bring the matter to the attention of any interested Attorney General, and in such case, or apparently independent of such notice, any Attorney General *may* apply for leave to intervene and participate in the hearing. These are all enabling provisions, but seemingly not conditions precedent to the consideration of a constitutional issue.

Statutory requirements of notice as a precondition for judicial review were strictly applied in several cases prior to the Charter, and courts refused to consider or decide the question of constitutionality where notice had not been given.[36] The decision in *Mohr v. North American Life Assur.* is particularly significant, because the proceedings therein arose under a federal statute and the impugned legislation was an amendment to that statute. The Saskatchewan Court of Appeal concluded, however, that because no notice had been served on the Attorney General as required by provincial law "this Court is therefore precluded from holding that the amendment is invalid under the provisions of this [*Constitutional Questions*] Act". In other words, provincial law prevented a superior court, in a proceeding under a federal statute, from examining that federal statute for constitutional validity.

---

[35]*Federal Court Rules*, C.R.C. 1978, c. 663.
[36]*E.g. McLeod v. Security Trust Co.*, [1940] 1 W.W.R. 423, [1940] 2 D.L.R. 697 (Alta. S.C.); *Mohr v. North American Life Assur. Co.*, [1941] 1 W.W.R. 15, [1941] 1 D.L.R. 427 (Sask. C.A.); *Pelletier v. Imperial Oil Ltd.*, [1941] 2 W.W.R. 75 (Sask. Dist. Ct.), affd [1941] 3 W.W.R. 739, [1941] 4 D.L.R. 732 (Sask. C.A.).

Since the advent of the Charter there has been a renewed debate as to the applicability of such notice requirements in relation to Charter issues. As already noted, special provision has been made by legislation in British Columbia, Saskatchewan, Manitoba, Nova Scotia and Quebec to ensure that notice is required in Charter cases, both with respect to claims that a law is invalid for conflict with the Charter, and to claims that a law should not be applied (*i.e.*, that it should be "read down") so as to avoid conflict with the Charter. The British Columbia, Saskatchewan, Manitoba, and Nova Scotia requirements also apply where any Charter remedy is sought under s-s. 24(1) but make a specific exception with respect to objections raised to the admission of evidence pursuant to s-s. 24(2) of the Charter on the grounds that it was obtained in violation of Charter guarantees. In the latter kind of case no notice is required. The Quebec provision is silent on the matter of notice where a remedy other than a finding of the invalidity or inapplicability of a law is sought. Presumably where these express provisions in provincial statutes concerning notice for Charter issues apply, they will preclude adjudication of such issues where no notice is given.

It remains to consider whether, in the provinces where there has been no amendment to notice provisions, they should apply to Charter cases. While it has been held in some cases that notice is not required in respect of Charter issues[37] this does not seem justifiable in principle. The Charter is as much a part of the constitution as is the distribution of powers and its imperatives are equally important. The same reasons, the same interests, which have justified notice requirements for distribution of powers questions apply equally to Charter issues. It is important that the Attorney General's position be put to the court for its assistance and for the protection of the public interest in support of the legislation or of its application. These considerations apply whether the contention is that the legislation is invalid, or that it cannot validly apply, because of conflict with the Charter. This in fact is the position adopted by the Alberta Court of Appeal in two cases, *Re Broddy et al. and Director of Vital Statistics*[38] and *R. v. Stanger et al.*[39] Even though the Alberta statute only refers to proceedings involving "constitutional validity" the Court held that notice must be given as a precondition of a determination that a statute must be read down or held invalid because of the Charter. An Ontario Divisional

---

[37]See, *e.g. R. v. Leggo* (1982), 69 C.C.C. (2d) 443 (Alta. Prov. Ct.); *R. v. Oakes* (1982), 38 O.R. (2d) 598 (Prov. Ct.), affd on other grounds 145 D.L.R. (3d) 123 (Ont. C.A.), affd [1986] 1 S.C.R. 103. See also *Gandam v. Min. of Employment and Immigration* (1982), 140 D.L.R. (3d) 363 (Sask. Q.B.), holding that inconsistency with the Charter is not a matter of constitutional invalidity.

[38](1982), 142 D.L.R. (3d) 151.

[39][1983] 5 W.W.R. 331.

Court has taken the same position with respect to a Charter challenge to validity of sections of an Ontario statute. It refused to consider such a contention because of want of notice.[40] It will be recalled that the Ontario statute requires notice only in cases involving "constitutional validity or constitutional applicability" without specific reference to the Charter.[41]

In provinces such as Alberta and Ontario where there is no notice requirement with respect to Charter remedies other than findings of invalidity or inapplicability of laws, there may remain questions as to whether notice will be required. It must be kept in mind that by s. 32 of the Charter it applies to "the Parliament and government of Canada" and to "the legislature and government of each province". It therefore guarantees its rights and freedoms against both legislative and administrative action which might abridge them. As a result, there are many Charter-based complaints which do not bring into question the validity or applicability of legislation. To these the notice requirements would seem to have no application except in those provinces (British Columbia, Saskatchewan, Manitoba, Nova Scotia) where they have been expressly extended to cover all Charter-based remedies other than the exclusion of evidence.

The relevant legislation in Alberta apparently does not make the Attorney General who appears in response to the notice a party to the action in which the constitutional issue is raised. Nor does Rule 32 of the *Rules of the Supreme Court of Canada* do this; it merely permits the Attorney General to apply to intervene. It has been held that in this type of procedure notice does not make the Attorney General or the Crown a party to the action,[42] and the court is not thereby entitled to award any substantive relief against the Crown which it could not otherwise have granted in the absence of notice and appearance.[43] Thus such immunity from suit as the Crown may have enjoyed as part of the Crown prerogative was not destroyed by a statutory provision for notice and appearance. Also, when the Attorney General appears in this way as intervener or even as a party to argue the constitutional question alone, it is not customary to award costs against him. The New Brunswick statute specifically authorizes the appropriate Attorney General to "intervene as a party",[44] but it also prohibits the awarding of costs for or against the

---

[40]*Re Butler and Bd. of Governors of York University et al.* (1983), 3 D.L.R. (4th) 763.

[41]See also Cavarzan, *Note* (1984), 62 *Can. Bar Rev.* 75.

[42]*Florence Mining Co. Ltd. v. Cobalt Lake Mining Co. Ltd.* (1909), 18 O.L.R. 275, at 284 (C.A.), affd on other grounds 43 O.L.R. 474 (P.C.). *Beauharnois Light, Heat & Power v. Hydro-Electric Power Comn.*, [1937] O.R. 796, [1937] 3 D.L.R. 458 at 463 (C.A.).

[43]*Florence Mining* case, *supra*.

[44]*Judicature Act*, R.S.N.B. 1973, c. J-2, s. 22, as amended.

Crown and allows the Crown to limit its participation to the constitutional question alone. The Ontario statute,[45] as revised in 1984, provides that where the Attorney General (federal or provincial) makes submissions in such proceedings, he or she

> shall be deemed to be a party to the proceedings for the purpose of any appeal in respect of the constitutional question.

The British Columbia, Saskatchewan, Newfoundland and Manitoba statutes as recently amended are now similar to Ontario's. The effect of these provisions is not entirely clear, but it would appear that the Attorney General would be a party for a very limited purpose only. He would be entitled as a party to initiate an appeal whereas as a mere intervener he could not.[46] No remedy could be given against the Crown which would not otherwise be available apart from this section, however. Although such provisions say nothing about costs, one would assume that the courts would refrain from awarding costs for or against the Attorney General in such proceedings in accordance with the general practice prior to the amendment of these sections.

The former Quebec provision, art. 114 of the *Code of Civil Procedure* which was replaced in 1965, did not expressly make the Attorney General a party but the effect seemed to be the same as that of the present Ontario, British Columbia, Saskatchewan, Newfoundland and Manitoba statutes. Article 114 provided that, where the Attorney General intervened, "the judgment of the Court must mention such intervention and such conclusions on which it renders judgment *as if the Attorney General were a party to the suit*."[47] It was held in *A.G. Que. v. Bérubé*[48] that an Attorney General who intervened pursuant to this article was in a position analogous to an ordinary party and could maintain the proceedings by himself even if the original parties of like interest withdrew. The Supreme Court of Canada in fact held that such an intervention by an Attorney General in Quebec created a *lis* between himself and the party attacking the legislation. In *Switzman v. Elbling*[49] the provincial Attorney General intervened pursuant to art. 114 because the validity of the so-called "Padlock Act"[50] was in question. The plaintiff landlord had commenced action against the defendant tenant to have his lease set aside and to claim

---

[45]*Courts of Justice Act, 1984*, S.O. 1984, c. 11, s. 122(5).
[46]*A.G. Alta. v. Kazakewich*, [1937] S.C.R. 427, [1937] 3 D.L.R. 574.
[47]Emphasis added.
[48][1945] Que. K.B. 77, [1945] 4 D.L.R. at 306, affd without reference to the point [1945] S.C.R. 600 (*sub nom. A.G. Que. v. A.G. Can.*), [1945] 4 D.L.R. 305, 84 C.C.C. 369.
[49][1957] S.C.R. 285, 7 D.L.R. (2d) 337, 117 C.C.C. 129.
[50]*An Act to Protect the Province against Communistic Propaganda*, R.S.Q. 1941, c. 52.

damages, on the grounds that the leased premises had been used for purposes prohibited by the statute. The defendant as part of his defence challenged the validity of the Act and served notice on the Attorney General. The plaintiff succeeded in the trial and appellate courts in Quebec. When the defendant appellant reached the Supreme Court of Canada with his appeal it was argued that there was no *lis inter partes* before the court because the term of the original lease had, in the meantime, expired. It was said that the appellant therefore had no interest to assert before the Supreme Court. The plaintiff-respondent in fact took no part in the appeal. Chief Justice Kerwin disposed of this objection by holding that the intervention of the Attorney General of Quebec raised an issue between him and the appellant as to the constitutionality of the statute. This issue was enough to permit the court to hear the appeal.[51]

The present *Code of Civil Procedure* appears to achieve the same result by simpler means. Article 492 provides that

> The attorney-general may, *ex officio*, appeal from a final judgment rendered in an action raising a ground of public order, as if he were a party to the action.

It apparently does not matter whether the Attorney General has received notice or has intervened below, so far as his right of appeal is concerned.

From the foregoing it may be seen that constitutional adjudication by provincial courts has been restricted to some extent by provincial legislation. To the extent that the Supreme Court rules accomplish the same purpose, that is, facilitating government participation in constitutional litigation, they are self-imposed by the court and do not raise an absolute bar to adjudication. But in the face of assertions of the inherent right of judicial review in a federal state, how can one justify the provincial statutes which prevent provincial courts from considering constitutional validity where notice to the Attorney General is not given?

The constitutional basis for provincial notice requirements must be found in s. 92(14) of the *Constitution Act, 1867* giving the provinces jurisdiction, it will be recalled, over

> The Administration of Justice in the Province, including the Constitution, Maintenance, and Organization of Provincial Courts, both of Civil and of Criminal Jurisdiction, and including Procedure in Civil Matters in those Courts.

If one looks at the notice requirement as a limitation on the jurisdiction of the courts, this probably can be justified as a matter of "Constitution"

---

[51]*Supra*, note 49 at 286–87 S.C.R.

or "Organization". If one looks upon it as a procedural matter only (and perhaps this is all it is) it could be justified, in civil actions, as "Procedure in Civil Matters".

These justifications are more readily acceptable where the proceeding before the provincial court is itself one over which the province has jurisdiction. This would include most civil actions (being matters of "Property and Civil Rights in the Province") or prosecutions for violations of provincial statutes ("The Imposition of Punishment . . . for enforcing any Law of the Province" under s. 92(15)). Doubts might be raised, however, about the validity of the provincial notice requirement where the provincial court is involved in a proceeding essentially within federal jurisdiction. Parliament can confer jurisdiction on provincial courts with respect to matters within federal legislative competence,[52] and can also regulate procedure in relation to these matters. In such proceedings can the provincial Legislature still limit the jurisdiction of its courts through notice requirements?

The better view would appear to be that such notice requirements essentially involve the practice and procedure of the court and therefore fall within provincial power. They do not become, for example, criminal law or procedure just because they apply to the raising of a constitutional point in a case under the *Criminal Code*. This was the view taken by the Alberta Court of Appeal in *R. v. Stanger et al.*[53] where it held that in such a case where no notice had been given, the court would not refuse to hear the issue but would decline to deal with it in the absence of notice. This was seen as a procedural, not a substantive, matter "as no one is precluded from ultimately securing relief under the Charter". This is true, of course, only if the party wishing to raise the constitutional issue is prepared to give the notice and the court is prepared, if necessary, to allow an adjournment to make it possible for adequate notice to be given.

The rules of court of the Supreme Court of Canada and the Federal Court are delegated legislation presumably justifiable under Parliament's jurisdiction in s. 101 of the B.N.A. Act to "provide for the Constitution, Maintenance, and Organization of a General Court of Appeal for Canada, and for the Establishment of any additional Courts for the better Administration of the Laws of Canada." This jurisdiction over the Supreme Court as a "General Court of Appeal" appears to be plenary, even where the court is dealing with appeals in matters of provincial law,[54] and thus even if Rule 32 goes to jurisdiction it would be valid. In the Federal

---

[52]*Valin v. Langlois* (1879), 5 App. Cas. 115 (P.C.); *Re Vancini* (1904), 34 S.C.R. 621, 8 C.C.C. 228.

[53]*Supra*, note 39, at pp. 358–59. See also Cavarzan, *supra*, note 41.

[54]*A.G. Ont. v. A.G. Can.*, [1947] A.C. 127, [1947] 1 All E.R. 137, [1947] 1 W.W.R. 305, [1947] 1 D.L.R. 801 (P.C.).

Court, Rule 1101 seems to be purely procedural, but in any event the matters dealt with by that court are necessarily confined to laws enacted or adopted by Parliament.[55]

A question remains whether these requirements of notice to the Attorney General can be reconciled with general principles of judicial review. When strictly applied, notice requirements can inhibit or even preclude an adjudication by a court on the constitutional validity of a statute involved in proceedings before it. If one takes an absolute approach to judicial review, and argues that the courts must always be entitled to review because they are "superior courts" or because they must apply the "whole law", or because they are operating in a federal system, such limitations on adjudication should be held invalid. It is submitted, however, that such an approach is unjustified. These procedural limitations are a legitimate exercise of the grant of power to the provinces to create and regulate the jurisdiction of their courts. This is the power which justifies the provincial requirements of notice to the Attorney General as a condition precedent to constitutional adjudication. Similarly, Parliament in the exercise of its jurisdiction over federal courts and the criminal law, and incidentally to the regulation of other federal matters, could introduce similar restrictions in any proceedings in federal courts or brought under federal law.

It might be thought that Laskin J., writing for the majority of the Supreme Court in *Thorson v. A.G. Can.*,[56] had foreclosed that argument when he said

Any attempt by Parliament or a Legislature to fix conditions precedent, as by way of requiring consent of some public officer or authority, to the determination of an issue of constitutionality of legislation cannot foreclose the Courts merely because the conditions remain unsatisfied. . . .

However, notice requirements are not colourable devices essentially directed to the prevention of judicial review. The practical effect of these requirements must surely be to facilitate rather than to hamper the functioning of a federal system. They do not operate as an absolute bar to adjudication, but merely create conditions precedent with which it is not difficult to comply. They ensure that the appropriate Governments have an opportunity to be represented so that the constitutional issues may be thoroughly canvassed by those having a continuing concern and interest with respect to the validity of legislation. The desirability of notice to

---

[55]See *e.g. McNamara Const. (Western) Ltd. v. The Queen*, [1977] 2 S.C.R. 654, 75 D.L.R. (3d) 273, 13 N.R. 181 (*sub nom. Canada v. McNamara Const. (Western) Ltd.; Canada v. J. Stevenson & Assoc.*).

[56][1975] 1 S.C.R. 138 at 151, 43 D.L.R. (3d) 1 at 11, 1 N.R. 225.

the Attorney General has been judicially recognized even where not strictly required by statute.[57] The notice procedure has advantages over a system where constitutional decisions with far-reaching consequences may be made in litigation between private parties,[58] sometimes in shareholders' or other similar actions where the conflict between the parties is more apparent than real.[59] Although the notice requirements may on occasion limit the exercise of judicial review, through their imposition the fundamental objective of making the courts effective agents in the application of the constitution can be achieved. Therefore it may be reasonable to interpret Laskin J.'s comment in the *Thorson* case as being limited to the kind of situation to which he refers, where the condition may be impossible for the litigant to meet and may have no relationship to ensuring effective judicial review.

C. "PRIVATIVE CLAUSES" EXCLUDING JUDICIAL REVIEW

Another type of statutory limitation on judicial review has appeared in legislation establishing various administrative tribunals or agencies. It is not uncommon for these statutes to contain a "privative clause" which purports to limit or prohibit review by the courts of administrative decisions. The significance and effect of these clauses in administrative law have been extensively discussed by others,[60] and need not be explained further at this point. But their special implications for judicial review of legislation should be noted.

A typical privative clause may provide that:

---

[57]*Charter Airways Ltd. v. A.G. Can.* (1955), 17 W.W.R. 129, 1 D.L.R. (2d) 110, 73 C.R.T.C. 330 (Alta. C.A.); *R. v. Dickson and Corman* (1982), 145 D.L.R. (3d) 164 at 176 (Ont. G.S.P.).

[58]See Dickson J.'s comments in *Northern Telecom Ltd. v. Communications Workers of Canada*, [1980] 1 S.C.R. 115, 98 D.L.R. (3d) 1, 28 N.R. 107, at note 34 and accompanying text.

[59]See *e.g.* Grant, "Judicial Review in Canada: Procedural Aspects" (1964), 42 *Can. Bar Rev.* 195 at 214–21. And see *Union Colliery Co. of B.C., Ltd. v. Bryden,* [1899] A.C. 580 at 584, 81 L.T. 277 (P.C.).

[60]*E.g., de Smith's Judicial Review of Administrative Action*, 4th ed., Evans, ed. (London: Stevens, 1980), c. 7; Pépin et Ouellette, *Principes de contentieux administratif* (2nd ed., 1982, Les Editions Yvon Blais, inc.) at 439–47; Mullan, *Administrative Law*, 2nd ed. (1979), at 3–87; Kavanagh, *A Guide to Judicial Review*, 2nd ed. (Toronto: Carswell, 1984), c. 7; Lyon, "Comment" (1980), 58 *Can. Bar Rev.* 646; Carter, "The Privative Clause in Canadian Administrative Law, 1944–1985: A Doctrinal Examination" (1986), 64 *Can. Bar Rev.* 241.

No decision, order, direction, declaration or ruling of the Board shall be questioned or reviewed in any court, and no order shall be made, or process entered, or proceedings taken in any court, whether by way of injunction, declaratory judgment, certiorari, mandamus, prohibition, quo warranto or otherwise, to question, review, prohibit or restrain the Board or any of its proceedings.[61]

The section quoted prohibits the use of a declaratory action, *certiorari* or any other remedy to bring the correctness of a board decision into question before a court. What then if the decision of the board involved a determination as to the constitutional scope of the board's jurisdiction? If a provincial labour relations board held, for example, that its statute authorized it to regulate employees of interprovincial bus companies, could this decision be protected from judicial review so that the validity of the statute, as applied to these proceedings, could not be challenged?

The reluctance of the courts to give effect to federal or provincial privative clauses is well known.[62] The courts have in general held that privative clauses are no bar to judicial review where the board has exceeded, or refused properly to exercise, its jurisdiction. The rationale of this principle has often been unclear, with at least two possibilities being suggested at various times.

Some judges appear to take the view that the right of judicial review of administrative action is to be presumed unless the Legislature has clearly excluded it.[63] The difficulty with this approach is that the Legislature has usually expressed itself quite emphatically in favour of excluding judicial review but the courts have nevertheless persisted in exercising jurisdiction. If the review of decisions in such circumstances were really dependent on the presumption in favour of this judicial power or the presumption in favour of the right of access of the citizen to the courts, then the courts should decline to act in the face of a clear privative clause.

The proper and traditional application of these presumptions may be seen in *Smith v. East Elloe R.D.C.*[64] where the House of Lords, in 1956, gave effect to a privative clause which said that "a compulsory purchase order . . . shall not . . . be questioned in any legal proceedings whatsoever". It was argued that this clause could not be deemed to apply where an order was made in bad faith. But the House of Lords found

---

[61]*Labour Relations Act*, R.S.O. 1980, c. 228, s. 108.

[62]See materials cited, *supra*, note 60. And see, *e.g. Metropolitan Life Ins. Co. v. I.U.O.E., Local 796*, [1970] S.C.R. 425, 11 D.L.R. (3d) 336.

[63]*E.g. Toronto Newspaper Guild v. Globe Printing Co.*, [1953] 2 S.C.R. 18 at 38, [1953] 3 D.L.R. 561 at 581, 106 C.C.C. 225; apparently approved in *Metropolitan Life, supra*, note 62 at p. 436 S.C.R.

[64][1956] A.C. 736, [1956] 1 All E.R. 855 (H.L.).

nothing ambiguous about the privative clause and observed that "plain words must be given their plain meaning".[65] Thus judicial review was effectively excluded.

The effectiveness of privative clauses in England has since been statutorily diminished,[66] and further attenuated judicially,[67] but has not been eliminated.[68] It is submitted that the *East Elloe* case represents the correct use of the relevant canons of statutory interpretation. The presumption in favour of judicial review can be applied only in the absence of clear words to the contrary. Upon re-examination of the privative clause earlier quoted[69] one is struck by the seemingly plain meaning of phrases such as "no decision . . . shall be questioned . . . in any court, and no order shall be made . . . by way of injunction, declaratory judgment, certiorari, mandamus, prohibition, quo warranto or otherwise". Yet the courts have managed to find such words inapplicable where defects of jurisdiction are alleged against an administrative tribunal.[70] This judicial avoidance of express legislative directions could not, at least in its origins, be defended on the basis of any canon of statutory interpretation although it may perhaps now be argued that long legislative acquiescence in such judicial review implies an intent that it should occur.[71] The Supreme Court has recently confirmed, however, that clearly-expressed privative clauses can preclude judicial review based on non-jurisdictional grounds,[72] or transfer from provincial superior courts to the Federal Court judicial review other than that involving the distribution of powers.[73]

This leads to the other rationale for ignoring privative clauses: that there is some constitutional guarantee of judicial review which overrides the attempts of the Legislatures to make final the decisions of tribunals. This is a very different basis for judicial review: that the courts need not confine themselves to seeking the intention of the Legislature but may override the wishes of the Legislature and review administrative acts by virtue of a constitutional grant of power for that purpose. The scope of such a constitutional guarantee has evolved slowly and uncertainly.

---

[65]*Ibid.*, at p. 751 A.C.

[66]*Tribunals and Inquiries Act*, 1958, 6 & 7 Eliz. II, c. 66, s. 11(1) (U.K.).

[67]See, *e.g.* *Anisminic v. Foreign Compensation Comn.*, [1969] 2 A.C. 147, [1969] 1 All E.R. 208 (H.L.).

[68]See, *e.g.* Garner, "The Exclusion of Judicial Review" (1981), 125 *Sol. J.* 192; Evans, *supra*, note 60.

[69]*Supra* note 61 and accompanying text.

[70]*Supra*, note 60.

[71]See Mullan, "The Jurisdictional Fact Doctrine in the Supreme Court of Canada: A Mitigating Plea" (1972), 10 *Osgoode Hall L.J.* 440.

[72]*Crevier v. A.G. Que.*, [1981] 2 S.C.R. 220, 127 D.L.R. (3d) 1, 38 N.R. 541.

[73]*Canada Labour Relations Board et al. v. Paul L'Anglais Inc. et al.*, [1983] 1 S.C.R. 147 at 154.

Over the years the courts have made vague references to a constitutional guarantee of judicial review of administrative tribunals in questions of jurisdiction of those tribunals, or in some cases have reached decisions that could only be explained on the basis that such a guarantee exists.[74]

Professor Lederman has long contended that there is a constitutional guarantee of judicial review in spite of privative clauses. In his view[75] both federal and provincial superior courts have a constitutionally protected jurisdiction similar to that of the "English central royal courts" which enjoyed the power of supervision over public officials by means of the prerogative writs. According to him, when the B.N.A. Act referred to "superior courts" it implicitly guaranteed to such courts the jurisdiction of the English superior courts. This guaranteed power of review extends at least to questions of fairness of procedure and the jurisdiction of the tribunal. As mentioned in chapter 2, this theory was at least open to question on the grounds that, in the context of the B.N.A. Act, Parliament and the Legislatures were empowered to legislate with respect to the "Constitution, Maintenance, and Organization" of the superior courts. This legislative power could well include the right to limit the jurisdiction of the courts in the same way that the United Kingdom Parliament may on occasion exclude the jurisdiction of the English courts in certain matters.[76]

The concept of a constitutionally guaranteed right of review has been tested more fully in the provincial field where it has been partly rejected and partly accepted. The Supreme Court has upheld and applied provincial privative clauses excluding judicial review of inferior tribunals on questions of law[77] or of alleged denial of natural justice.[78] Recently, however, in the *Crevier* case, it has for the first time clearly and firmly held that a province may not validly confer on an inferior tribunal the final authority, free from review by a superior court, of determining what matters are or are not within its jurisdiction. This decision was based on the implicit limitations of s. 96 of the *Constitution Act, 1867,* which prevent

---

[74]*E.g. Toronto Newspaper Guild v. Globe Printing Co.,* [1953] 2 S.C.R. 18 at 28, [1953] 3 D.L.R. 561, 106 C.C.C. 225. *Town of Dauphin v. Director of Public Welfare* (1956), 64 Man. R. 142, 19 W.W.R. 97, 5 D.L.R. (2d) 275, 117 C.C.C. 45, 24 C.R. 238.

[75]Lederman, "The Independence of the Judiciary" (1956), 34 *Can. Bar Rev.* 769 (Part I), 1139 (Part II), at 1160, 1175; "The Supreme Court of Canada and the Canadian Judicial System" (1975) *Transactions of the Royal Society of Canada,* Fourth Series, Vol. XIII, 209 at 222–24. For similar views see Lyon, "Comment" (1971), 49 *Can. Bar Rev.* 365.

[76]See *e.g. Smith v. East Elloe R.D.C., supra,* note 64.

[77]*Farrell v. Workmen's Compensation Bd.,* [1962] S.C.R. 48, 37 W.W.R. 39, 31 D.L.R. (2d) 177: approved in *Crevier* case, *supra,* note 72 at pp. 234–35 S.C.R.

[78]*Executors of Woodward Estate v. Minister of Finance,* [1973] S.C.R. 120, 27 D.L.R. (3d) 608.

a province from creating and appointing a tribunal which has the characteristics of a superior court (such appointments being within the authority conferred on the Governor General by s. 96). There has, of course, been a long and difficult succession of cases on what characteristics make a provincial tribunal into a "superior court" within the meaning of s. 96.[79] More recent decisions have emphasized a functional approach, looking at the nature of the tribunal's powers in context and avoiding striking down tribunals simply because of partial or superficial similarities to judicial powers.[80] The Supreme Court in *Crevier v. A.G. Que.* has finally dropped the language of statutory interpretation and said that to give a tribunal exclusive authority to determine its own jurisdiction is to attempt unconstitutionally to make it a superior court. Laskin C.J., on behalf of the court, observed that

> . . . I can think of nothing that is more the hallmark of a superior court than the vesting of power in a provincial statutory tribunal to determine the limits of its jurisdiction without appeal or other review.[81]

While this case did not involve any constitutional issue of jurisdiction, but only a question of whether the decision of the tribunal was within the scope of the regulations under which it operated, the court said that such issues of jurisdiction "are not far removed from issues of constitutionality".[82] Elsewhere, it referred to "the well-accepted limitation on the power of provincial statutory tribunals to make unreviewable determinations of constitutionality".[83] It did not specify the source of this "well-accepted limitation" but clearly the *Crevier* decision, in confirming a constitutional barrier against tribunals making final determinations of

---

[79]See *e.g. Reference re Adoption Act*, [1938] S.C.R. 398, [1938] 3 D.L.R. 497, 71 C.C.C. 110; *Labour Relations Bd. for Sask. v. John East Iron Works*, [1949] A.C. 134, [1948] 2 W.W.R. 1055, [1948] 4 D.L.R. 673; *Dupont v. Inglis*, [1958] S.C.R. 535, 14 D.L.R. (2d) 417; *A.G. Ont. v. Victoria Medical Building Ltd.*, [1960] S.C.R. 32, 21 D.L.R. (2d) 97; *Brooks v. Pavlick*, [1964] S.C.R. 108, 42 D.L.R. (2d) 572; *Tomko v. Labour Relations Bd.*, [1977] 1 S.C.R. 112, 14 N.S.R. (2d) 191, 69 D.L.R. (3d) 250, 7 N.R. 317, 10 N.R. 35, 76 C.L.L.C. 14, 005; *A.G. Que. v. Farrah*, [1978] 2 S.C.R. 638, 86 D.L.R. (3d) 161, 21 N.R. 595; Pépin, "The Problem of Section 96 of the Constitution Act, 1867" in Beckton and MacKay (eds.), *The Courts and the Charter* (1985), at 223.

[80]See *e.g. Tomko* case, *supra; Reference re Residential Tenancies Act*, [1981] 1 S.C.R. 714 at 729–736, 123 D.L.R. (3d) 554 at 567–73, 37 N.R. 158; *Massey-Ferguson Industries Ltd. v. Gov't of Sask.*, [1981] 2 S.C.R. 413 at 429; *A.G. Qué. v. Udeco Inc. et al; Laliberté, Lanctôt, Morin & Associés v. Udeco Inc. et al.*, [1984] 2 S.C.R. 502.

[81]*Supra*, note 72 at pp. 13–14 D.L.R., p. 558 N.R.

[82]*Supra*, note 72 at p. 14 D.L.R., p. 559 N.R.

[83]*Supra*, at p. 13 D.L.R., p. 558 N.R.

the scope of their statutory jurisdiction was, *a fortiori*, establishing a similar barrier against such final determinations of constitutional jurisdiction.

Some other questions remain for further clarification. First, what other issues will be embraced within the concept of "jurisdiction" in the future? Courts in the past have shown great originality in being able to identify almost any alleged defect in a tribunal's decision as going to jurisdiction. While the Supreme Court specifically distinguishes "errors of law" from issues of jurisdiction and confirms that privative clauses may "effectively oust judicial review on questions of law and, indeed on other issues not touching jurisdiction", it also recognizes that "there may be differences of opinion as to what are questions of jurisdiction".[84] This is, surely, a remarkable understatement.[85]

Secondly, what are the implications of the *Crevier* decision for federal tribunals? While Professor Lederman would, apparently, contend that there is equally a core of superior court jurisdiction to review federal tribunals,[86] this does not necessarily follow from *Crevier* which by its terms only holds that a province may not appoint a tribunal that exercises superior court functions such as final determination of its own jurisdiction. Privative clauses preventing judicial review of federal tribunals or agencies by provincial superior courts have been elsewhere upheld. It has been held that Parliament can provide for a special appeal tribunal with an ultimate appeal from it on points of law to the Supreme Court and exclude recourse to provincial courts.[87] Or, judicial review of the decision of a federal agency can be made the exclusive jurisdiction of the Federal Court, as it has been by s. 18 of the *Federal Court Act*,[88] although this may not prevent a provincial court from determining in other proceedings if the decision was within the constitutional authority of the federal government.[89] These cases did not of course address the question of whether Parliament could abolish judicial review of its agencies altogether, since there had simply been a federal judicial review process substituted for that of the provincial superior courts which at one time exercised such authority.

The combined effect of two 1983 decisions of the Supreme Court

---

[84]*Supra.*
[85]See Macdonald, "Comment" (1983), 17 *U.B.C. L. Rev.* 111 at 138–39.
[86]*Supra*, note 75.
[87]*Pringle v. Fraser*, [1972] S.C.R. 821, 26 D.L.R. (3d) 28.
[88]S.C. 1970–71–72, c. 1; *Commonwealth of Puerto Rico v. Hernandez*, [1975] 1 S.C.R. 228, 41 D.L.R. (3d) 549.
[89]*Per* Beetz J. in *A.G. Can. v. Canard*, [1976] 1 S.C.R. 170 at 216, [1975] 3 W.W.R. 1, 52 D.L.R. (3d) 548 at 583, 4 N.R. 91, apparently approved in *A.G. Can. v. Law Society of B.C.*, 37 B.C.L.R. 145 at 162, [1982] 5 W.W.R. 289, 137 D.L.R. (3d) 1, 43 N.R. 451, 19 B.L.R. 234, 66 C.P.R. (2d) 1.

of Canada would appear to have foreclosed the possibility of Parliament precluding all or some jurisdictional review of federal agencies by provincial superior courts. In the *Paul L'Anglais*[90] case the court held that neither s. 18 of the *Federal Court Act* nor s. 122 of the *Canada Labour Code*[91] could validly prevent the Superior Court of Quebec from reviewing on constitutional (that is, distribution of powers) grounds a preliminary decision by the Canada Labour Relations Board that certain employers were federal undertakings within the Board's jurisdiction. The federal statutes referred to would have meant that this decision could only be reviewed by the Federal Court of Canada, but at a later stage when some final decision of the Board had been made. The Supreme Court held that notwithstanding the provisions for judicial review by the Federal Court at a later stage, Parliament could not preclude the provincial superior court from reviewing such a decision at any time, if a distribution of powers issue were involved. This was seen to be part of a constitutionally-assured jurisdiction of the provincial superior courts fundamental to the federal system. The decision of the court in *A.G. Can. v. Law Soc. of B.C.*[92] was much relied on. Later, in *McEvoy v. A.G. N.B. and A.G. Can.*[93] the court held that s. 96 of the *Constitution Act, 1867* prevents Parliament from large-scale removal from provincial superior courts of jurisdiction under federal laws. That case involved a reference as to whether Parliament could transfer all of their criminal law jurisdiction from the federally-appointed provincial superior courts to provincially-appointed courts, and the Supreme Court held that it could not. When combined with the *Paul L'Anglais* decision which held judicial review of federal tribunals on distribution of powers grounds to be an essential function of provincial superior courts, it would appear to mean that Parliament cannot remove that function from those courts even if it has ensured the availability of such review at a later stage in the Federal Court.[94]

There may, however, be another more important principle which does in some cases guarantee the right of access to both provincial and federal courts for the review of administrative action. Implicit in the constitution is the principle that neither Parliament nor the Legislatures can exercise their jurisdiction with respect to the "Constitution, Maintenance, and Organization" of the courts in a colourable way so as to defeat the other limitations placed on their authority by the *Constitution*

---

[90]*Supra*, note 73.

[91]R.S.C. 1970, c. L-1.

[92]*Supra*, note 89.

[93][1983] 1 S.C.R. 704.

[94]This result is not without anomalies. See *Brink's Canada Ltd. v. Canada Labour Relations Board et al.*, [1985] 1 F.C. 898 (T.D.).

Act, 1867. Where this would be the effect of the privative clause, it can be ignored to the extent required to give effect to this principle.

This principle has been asserted in modern times in other contexts. In *British Columbia Power Corp. v. British Columbia Electric Co.* the Supreme Court rejected a claim of Crown immunity advanced by the Attorney General of British Columbia. Immunity was claimed to preclude the issuing by a court of an interim receivership order with respect to property, the Crown claim to which depended on legislation that was the subject of an action pending in the British Columbia courts. In the Supreme Court of Canada Chief Justice Kerwin stated:

> In a federal system, where legislative authority is divided, as are also the prerogatives of the Crown, as between the Dominion and the Provinces, it is my view that it is not open to the Crown, either in right of Canada or of a Province, to claim a Crown immunity based upon an interest in certain property, where its very interest in that property depends completely and solely on the validity of the legislation which it has itself passed, if there is a reasonable doubt as to whether such legislation is constitutionally valid. To permit it to do so would be to enable it, by the assertion of rights claimed under legislation which is beyond its powers, *to achieve the same results as if the legislation were valid.* In a federal system it appears to me that, in such circumstances, the Court has the same jurisdiction to preserve assets whose title is dependent on the validity of the legislation as it has to determine the validity of the legislation itself.[95] [Emphasis added.]

Similarly in *Amax Potash Ltd. v. Govt. of Sask.* the provincial Government denied liability for repayment of moneys collected under a statute alleged to be invalid. It relied on a specific statutory provision that purported to deny any right of recovery even where the money was collected under an invalid law. Writing for the court, Dickson J. said that:

> . . . it is manifest that if either the federal Parliament or a provincial Legislature can tax beyond the limit of its powers, and by prior or *ex post facto* legislation give itself immunity from such illegal act, *it could readily place itself in the same position as if the act had been done within proper constitutional limits.* To allow moneys collected under compulsion, pursuant to an *ultra vires* statute, to be retained would be tantamount to allowing the provincial Legislature to do indirectly what it could not do directly, and by covert means to impose illegal burdens.[96] [Emphasis added.]

---

[95][1962] S.C.R. 642 at 644–45, 38 W.W.R. 701, 34 D.L.R. (2d) 196 at 275–76. Discussed more fully in chapter 4, *infra.*

[96][1977] S.C.R. 576 at 590, 71 D.L.R. (3d) 1 at 10, 11 N.R. 222, [1976] 6 W.W.R. 61. Discussed more fully, *infra*, at pp. 103–06.

The common theme here is that Parliament, Legislatures, and Governments cannot, by asserting their normal powers to govern their own civil liability, thereby achieve, free from judicial control, what the constitution otherwise prohibits. The same principle surely applies to judicial review of administrative action. While it has been argued above that privative clauses should normally be respected where their meaning is plain, this is subject to the undoubted qualification that where constitutional authority of the agency or officer is in question, judicial review should be possible notwithstanding a privative clause. Such clauses cannot, consistently with the reasoning in cases such as *B.C. Power* or *Amax Potash*, be constitutionally permitted to enable invalid exercises of power to proceed unchecked.[97] It now appears, as a result of the *Crevier* case, that in the case of provincial privative clauses the plain meaning rule must also yield to a constitutional requirement that judicial review of decisions of provincially appointed tribunals on all questions of jurisdiction be available. In the case of federally-appointed tribunals, the *Paul L'Anglais* and *McEvoy* cases appear to ensure the right of provincial superior courts to review their decisions on distribution of powers grounds. Beyond this the more general principles of the *B.C. Power* and *Amax* cases may require the availability of judicial review *by some court*, not necessarily provincial superior courts, of federal tribunals on any constitutional issue (whether it involves the distribution of powers or the Charter) notwithstanding any privative clause in federal law.

It may be useful to consider briefly how such review on constitutional grounds operates. Judicial review of tribunals for constitutional enforcement is required to prevent a federal tribunal from exercising jurisdiction in a provincial field or *vice versa*. To take a common situation: labour relations boards occasionally have to determine whether certain persons are in the employ of an industry within provincial or within federal jurisdiction.[98] Where there is no dispute over the identity of the employer or the contract of employment the decision whether the enterprise is within provincial or federal jurisdiction would almost certainly be one of con-

---

[97]The cases are consistent with this position. See, *e.g. Canard, supra*, note 89 at 216 S.C.R., 583 D.L.R.; *British Columbia Packers Ltd. v. Canada Labour Relations Bd.*, [1974] 2 F.C. 913 at 921–22, (*sub nom. Re British Columbia Packers Ltd. and B.C. Council U.F.A.W.*) 50 D.L.R. (3d) 602 at 609–10 (T.D.).

[98]See *e.g., Pronto Uranium Mines Ltd. v. Ontario Labour Relations Bd.; Algoma Uranium Mines Ltd. v. Ontario Labour Relations Bd.*, [1956] O.R. 862, 5 D.L.R. (2d) 342 (H.C.); *R. v. Ontario Labour Relations Bd.; Ex p. Dunn*, [1963] 2 O.R. 301, 39 D.L.R. 346 (H.C.); *Re Armstrong Transport and Ontario Labour Relations Bd.*, [1964] 1 O.R. 358, 42 D.L.R. 217 (H.C.); *Re British Columbia Packers Ltd., supra; Re Transportaide Inc. and Canada Labour Relations Bd.*, [1978] 2 F.C. 660, 86 D.L.R. (3d) 24 (T.D.); *Northern Telecom Ltd. v. Communications Workers of Canada*, [1980] 1 S.C.R. 115, 98 D.L.R. (3d) 1, 28 N.R. 107; *Paul L'Anglais case, supra*, note 73.

stitutional law. If the board makes a wrong decision in favour of its own jurisdiction and then attempts to exercise that jurisdiction, the courts should be able to intervene at some stage. Otherwise, it would be allowed to exercise an authority which constitutionally it could not be given.

If judicial review of federal tribunals is subject to statutory limitation on questions of jurisdiction other than constitutional jurisdiction, where does one draw the line between purely constitutional decisions, subject to judicial review, and other non-reviewable decisions, which may nevertheless have consequences of constitutional significance? For example, suppose the hypothetical labour relations board must decide whether certain persons who seek certification are employed by a parent company which is admittedly engaged in interprovincial transport or a subsidiary company which is admittedly engaged in intraprovincial transport. The Supreme Court of Canada has said that the power to decide who is the employer may be conferred exclusively on a provincial board, because "employment is a question of fact and depends upon contract".[99] If a federal board decides that the applicants are employed by the parent company, it will proceed to apply the federal statute to them. Suppose also that the subsidiary company asserts that the employees are actually in its employ, and that the federal statute cannot validly apply to it or to its employees. Suppose further that the statute purports to protect the board's decisions from review on any grounds, including jurisdictional grounds. How far should a court go in these circumstances in overriding the privative clause in order to preserve the constitutional limitations on the power of Parliament and its tribunals?

The Supreme Court has given some recognition to the distinction between those jurisdictional issues which involve the application of constitutional limitations and those which involve the application of statutory or common law standards to determine what the court called "administrative jurisdiction". Although the case, *Northern Telecom Ltd. v. Communications Workers of Canada*,[100] did not involve a privative clause that might have made necessary such distinctions, there were evidentiary reasons for considering the difference. The Canada Labour Relations Board had certified the supervisors of previously unionized installers as "employees" within the meaning of the *Canada Labour Code*.[101] There had been some discussion before the board as to whether the matter was within the jurisdiction of the board, apparently because of the nature of the employer Northern Telecom, but the latter did not challenge the

---

[99]*Labour Relations Bd. v. Traders Service Ltd.*, [1958] S.C.R. 672 at 678, 15 D.L.R. (2d) 305 at 321.

[100][1980] 1 S.C.R. 115, 98 D.L.R. (3d) 1, 28 N.R. 107, affg [1977] 2 F.C. 406, 14 N.R. 489.

[101]R.S.C. 1970, c. L-1.

jurisdiction of the board nor did it present any evidence for this purpose. The board in the course of its decision found that Northern Telecom's work and undertaking were within federal jurisdiction. The board also found that the management functions of the supervisors were not such as to disqualify them as "employees" within the meaning of the Code. The company then sought judicial review under s. 28 of the *Federal Court Act* in the Federal Court of Appeal, and the application was dismissed. An appeal to the Supreme Court was then taken on the question of the constitutional jurisdiction of the board. Dickson J. on behalf of the court rejected certain arguments of both parties, that of the union upholding the certification on the basis that the court should not upset the board's finding of "jurisdictional fact" if there was "substantial evidence for its decision of fact and a rational basis for its decision of law", and that of the employer that a "double presumption" should operate against the board's jurisdiction (because it is an inferior tribunal and because labour relations are normally within provincial jurisdiction) so as to put the burden of proving jurisdiction on the union which had not met that burden. Dickson J. regarded these as questions of "administrative or subject-matter jurisdiction" which, he said, was not in issue. The real issue, he said, was that of whether Parliament constitutionally had jurisdiction over Northern Telecom. To determine that would require evidence, among other things, of the relationship between this company and Bell Canada which clearly was a federal undertaking. No such evidence had been introduced. The onus was on the employer attacking the certification order to lead such evidence and this had not been done. Therefore the court could not give an answer to the constitutional question and dismissed the appeal.

The case is instructive in distinguishing between administrative jurisdiction, presumably involving statutory questions such as whether the supervisors were employed by Northern Telecom and whether they were managerial or non-managerial personnel, and constitutional jurisdiction which required an examination of the nature of the employer's enterprise in accordance with constitutional criteria. It is submitted that it is the latter kind of judicial review which is implicitly guaranteed by the constitution with respect to federal tribunals. The former kind, while normally available, is not guaranteed and could conceivably be barred by a sufficiently broad privative clause.

A new range of constitutional problems for privative clauses is presented by the *Canadian Charter of Rights and Freedoms*. Much of the Charter will be irrelevant for this purpose since many of its rights or freedoms will not be in issue before tribunals or agencies likely to be protected by a privative clause. But s. 7 is particularly relevant in this respect. It provides that:

7. Everyone has the right to life, liberty and security of the person

and the right not to be deprived thereof except in accordance with the principles of fundamental justice.

While no one can yet be entirely certain what "the principles of fundamental justice" may entail, they do at least include fairness, procedural due process and, in a proper case, natural justice. Nor is it yet clear what action will be regarded as deprivations of "life, liberty and security of the person". Thus far, it seems clearly established that certain administrative decisions pertaining to parole, prison administration and immigration can be so regarded. Where an agency has taken such a decision, it could be argued that the courts are constitutionally entitled to ensure that the person has been dealt with in a procedurally fair manner, even if the governing statute purports to preclude judicial review by a privative clause. If this position is adopted, it may well be difficult to sustain privative clauses under s. 1 of the Charter as "reasonable limits" on access to "principles of fundamental justice"[102] unless, perhaps, the privative clause only limits the time or forum of judicial review but does not bar it altogether. It should be noted, however, that in the United States where there are constitutional safeguards for both the judicial role and for due process it is not clear that judicial review of administrative action is thereby guaranteed.[103]

In summary, it may be said that Parliament and Legislatures may not exclude judicial review of administrative decisions where review is necessary to prevent a colourable overstepping of constitutional limitations. Further, provincial Legislatures may not exclude judicial review of provincial tribunals on any question of jurisdiction, constitutional or otherwise. Where legislative bodies may limit judicial review, they must be very explicit, more explicit in fact than the courts have found most Canadian statutes to be.

D. EXCLUSION OF JUDICIAL REVIEW THROUGH PROVINCIAL STATUTORY DENIAL OF A RIGHT OF ACTION

Other attempts have been made occasionally to prevent judicial review of legislation, through limiting or abolishing the right of action in which the constitutional point might have been raised. Such attempts involve the same issue as privative clauses, and, where challenged, have

---

[102]See Janisch, "Beyond Jurisdiction: Judicial Review and the Charter of Rights" (1983), 43 *Rev. du B*. 401 at 406–07.
[103]See Tribe, *American Constitutional Law* (1978), at 43, 559, 1121; Hogg, "Is Judicial Review of Administrative Action Guaranteed by the British North America Act?" (1976), 54 *Can. Bar Rev.* 716.

universally failed. The provinces, through purported exercise of their jurisdiction over "Administration of Justice in the Province, including the Constitution, Maintenance, and Organization of Provincial Courts . . . including Procedure in Civil Matters", and over "Property and Civil Rights in the Province" have interfered with substantive rights not within their jurisdiction and then have proceeded to bar the enforcement of those rights in provincial courts. If such legislation had been given full effect, the courts might have been prevented from determining whether these substantive rights had been validly abrogated by the provincial legislation. The courts have refused to give such scope to provincial power under these heads of jurisdiction.

The most wide-sweeping formulation of the judicial position may be seen in *Ottawa Valley Power Co. v. Hydro-Electric Power Comn.*[104] The Ontario *Power Commission Act*[105] of 1927 provided, in s. 6(4) that:

> (4) Without the consent of the Attorney General, no action shall be brought against the Commission or against any member thereof for anything done or omitted in the exercise of his office.

By the *Power Commission Act, 1935,*[106] s. 2, it was declared that certain contracts between the defendant commission and the plaintiff company were illegal, void, and unenforceable against the commission. This statute went on to state:

> 3. No action or other proceeding shall be brought, maintained or proceeded with against the said Commission founded upon any contract by this Act declared to be void and unenforceable, or arising out of the performance or non-performance of any of the terms of the said contracts.

The company brought action against the commission and other defendants asking *inter alia* for a declaration that the 1935 Act was *ultra vires* as interfering with civil rights outside the province, for a declaration that the contracts were valid and binding, and for the payment of money by the commission under one of the contracts. The commission relied on s. 6(4) of the 1927 Act because no consent had been given by the Attorney General thereunder, and on s. 3 of the 1935 Act. At trial the action was dismissed by Rose C.J.H.C. on the basis of s. 6(4) of the 1927 Act.

The Court of Appeal split three to two in favour of allowing the appeal. The majority judges, by reasoning which is far from satisfying,

---

[104][1937] O.R. 265, [1936] 4 D.L.R. 594 (C.A.), revg [1937] O.R. at 266, [1936] 3 D.L.R. 468 (H.C.).

[105]R.S.O. 1927, c. 57.

[106]S.O. 1935, c. 53.

held s. 6(4) to be inapplicable. They then proceeded to hold this section and ss. 2 and 3 of the 1935 Act to be *ultra vires*. It was at this point that Mr. Justice Masten, speaking for himself and Mr. Justice Middleton, made the classic statement which has since found favour elsewhere.[107]

> The conclusion at which I have arrived is as follows:
> (1) The general rule is clear that the administration of justice being by The British North America Act committed to the Provinces, the jurisdiction of the several Courts set up by the Legislature to administer justice is that which is prescribed by the Legislature. Generally speaking any statute passed by a Provincial Legislature limiting the jurisdiction of the Provincial Court is binding on it.
> (2) But to that general rule I think there is this exception, namely, that the Legislature cannot destroy, usurp, or derogate from substantive rights over which it has, by the Canadian constitution, no jurisdiction and then protect its action in that regard by enacting that no action can be brought in the Courts of the Province to inquire into the validity of its legislation, thus indirectly destroying the division of powers set forth in The British North America Act. In other words, it cannot by such indirect means destroy the constitution under which it was created and now exists.

The other majority judge held s. 2 of the 1935 Act to be invalid because it interfered, *inter alia*, with civil rights outside the province and thus could not be justified under s. 92(13) of the B.N.A. Act. It then followed that the provisions designed to prevent these rights from being enforced were also invalid.

The authority of the *Ottawa Valley* decision was weakened by the two strong dissents of Latchford C.J. and Riddell J.A. Both judges thought that s. 6(4) of the 1927 Act clearly applied, and was valid. Mr. Justice Riddell took the view that " 'the right to bring an action is a civil right'; and, of course, the right to bring an action in an Ontario Court is a 'Civil Right in the Province' ".[108]

The principles stated by Masten and Middleton JJ.A. in the *Ottawa Valley* decision have nevertheless been confirmed in several other cases. At about the same time as the *Ottawa Valley* case there was a dispute in Alberta over the validity of legislative attempts to reduce the amount of interest payable on certain provincially guaranteed securities. The first statute[109] for this purpose reduced the interest rate thereon from six per cent to three per cent and then denied a right of action for the recovery of any higher rate in any provincial court. In *Independent Order of*

---

[107]*Supra*, note 104 at 309 O.R., p. 603 [1936] 4 D.L.R.
[108]*Supra*, note 104 at p. 340 O.R., p. 598 [1936] 4 D.L.R.
[109]*Provincial Securities Interest Act*, S.A. 1936, 2nd sess., c. 11.

Foresters v. Bd. of Trustees of Lethbridge Northern Irrigation District[110] this legislation was struck down as interfering with "interest", a federal matter, and with property and civil rights outside the province. New legislation was then passed, similarly reducing interest,[111] accompanied by another statute which provided that "no action . . . shall be commenced . . . in respect of any guaranteed security . . . without the consent of the Lieutenant Governor in Council."[112] This legislation was held invalid for similar reasons. With respect to the various attempts to deny the right of action, Ives J., at the first trial, said that a province could not prevent access to the courts to challenge the validity of a provincial statute, because to permit this result "is most repugnant to one's instinctive sense of justice".[113] At the second trial Ewing J. cited the *Ottawa Valley* decision with approval, and said that if the province could prevent its courts from declaring provincial laws *ultra vires* "then the division of powers as contained in the *B.N.A. Act, 1867*, is a futility".[114] On appeal[115] from the second trial, three concurring judges (Harvey C.J.A., Lunney and Shepherd JJ.A.) confined their decision to holding that the restriction on access to the courts was in this case an attempt to accomplish indirectly what could not be done directly, that is, to reduce enforceable rates of interest. Only McGillivray J.A. sought broader grounds for holding invalid the denial of right of action. He relied on the *Ottawa Valley* decision and declared that if a province could avoid judicial review of its legislation in this way "then the whole scheme of Confederation may be set at naught at the will of any provincial Legislature".[116] When the case reached the Privy Council that body declined to go beyond a finding that the whole scheme was an indirect attempt to invade the federal field of "interest" and thus invalid.[117]

In one further case members of the Alberta Court of Appeal had the opportunity to state the broader principle of the inherent right of judicial review. In *Reference re the Validity of the Legal Proceedings Suspension Act, 1942*,[118] the court held invalid a statute which purported to stay all actions involving the validity of the *Debt Adjustment Act, 1937*, until the

---

[110][1937] 1 W.W.R. 414, [1937] 2 D.L.R. 109 (Alta. S.C.).

[111]*Provincial Guaranteed Securities Interest Act*, S.A. 1937, c. 12.

[112]*Provincially Guaranteed Securities Proceedings Act*, S.A. 1937, c. 11, s. 3.

[113]*Supra*, note 110 at p. 416 W.W.R., p. 110 D.L.R.

[114]*Independent Order of Foresters v. Lethbridge Northern Irrigation District (No. 2)*, [1937] 3 W.W.R. 424 at 429, [1937] 4 D.L.R. 398 (Alta. S.C.).

[115][1938] 2 W.W.R. 194, [1938] 3 D.L.R. 89 (Alta. C.A.).

[116]*Supra*, at p. 211 W.W.R., p. 102 D.L.R.

[117][1940] A.C. 513, [1940] 2 All E.R. 220, [1940] 1 W.W.R. 502, [1940] 2 D.L.R. 273 (P.C.).

[118][1942] 2 W.W.R. 536, [1942] 3 D.L.R. 318 (Alta. C.A.).

Privy Council had disposed of an appeal then pending from the Supreme Court of Canada on this issue. In a 3-to-2 split decision, a majority of the court said that the Legislature might not "determine . . . its own legislative authority" even for a short time. They found that "it is of the essence of our constitution which assigns definite and limited powers of legislation to the Legislatures that the Courts should determine whether the Legislature has exceeded these limits".[119] They also held that the effect of the legislation, if valid, would be to ignore the *Winstanley* case,[120] a previous Supreme Court of Canada decision wherein certain aspects of the *Debt Adjustment Act, 1937*, had already been held invalid.

From the foregoing it may be seen that two possible principles emerge for the setting aside of provincial legislation of this nature. The broader principle is based on some inherent right of the provincial courts to pass on the validity of provincial legislation. The narrower principle is that a province cannot indirectly deny rights arising under federal law or within federal jurisdiction where it could not accomplish this purpose directly. Parliament is given jurisdiction to create certain rights, for example, with respect to "interest". If Parliament can create such rights, it can provide directly or indirectly for their enforcement. It has long been held that where a right existed under federal law and no other means of enforcement was provided, a provincial superior court was deemed to have jurisdiction to enforce it.[121] It has also long been recognized that Parliament could confer judicial duties and powers on provincial courts.[122] It would not necessarily follow that provincial courts would have an obligation to hear such cases where they were expressly prohibited from doing so by provincial law and where there was no express federal law requiring them to do so.[123] But where federal law expressly so required, it should prevail over provincial law. Here, as elsewhere, the "trenching" doctrine would permit federal law to prevail so that Parliament, in conferring certain rights pursuant to s. 91 of the *Constitution Act, 1867*, could incidentally make provision for their enforcement. To the extent necessary to accomplish this purpose Parliament "trenches" on the jurisdiction otherwise conferred on the provinces by s. 92(14). If the provincial Legislature were permitted to prevent this, the federal system might be upset because the province would be barring the effective exercise of federal jurisdiction. This would be a colourable use of provincial power over the administration of justice.

Again we come back to the fundamental rule stated by Chief Justice

---

[119]*Supra*, at p. 540 W.W.R., p. 321 D.L.R.

[120]*Atlas Lumber Co. v. Winstanley*, [1941] S.C.R. 87, [1941] 1 D.L.R. 625.

[121]*Board v. Board*, [1919] A.C. 956, [1919] 2 W.W.R. 940, 48 D.L.R. 13 (P.C.).

[122]*Valin v. Langlois* (1879), 5 App. Cas. 115 (P.C.).

[123]"Case and Comment" (1940), 18 *Can. Bar Rev.* 725.

Kerwin in the *B.C. Power*[124] case that the province may not, by barring access to the courts, "achieve the same results as if the legislation were valid". In a federal system this must mean that a province must not be permitted by such means to interfere with or exercise authority over persons, businesses, or things not otherwise within the jurisdiction permitted to them under the *Constitution Act, 1867*. It must be admitted at once that this rule will invalidate most legislative attempts under s. 92(13) or (14) to bar actions involving constitutional questions. But some jurisdiction in this regard must surely remain. A Legislature may be able to prevent certain lower provincial courts from deciding constitutional questions, as long as some provincial court may do so. It probably cannot prevent provincial superior courts from determining the constitutional validity of provincial laws, given the recent trend toward recognition of a constitutionally guaranteed core of judicial review jurisdiction in those courts.[125] It may surely impose procedural limitations and other conditions precedent, even in superior courts, at least so long as compliance with these is not impossible.

A more difficult problem arises where rights normally within a Legislature's power are interfered with by legislation which is invalid for reasons seemingly not directly related to the constitutional protection of those rights. For example, suppose property is confiscated under a provincial anti-gambling law which is subsequently held to be *ultra vires* because it is characterized as criminal law legislation. Could the province subsequently retain the property pursuant to a new statute which simply provided that any such property in the hands of the Crown would be considered Crown property? If there is no extra-provincial element involved, the question of title seems on its face to be a matter of "Property and Civil Rights in the Province". It is arguable that legislation giving title to the Crown in such a case would be in essence an exercise of the property and civil rights power, and not a continuation of the wrongful exercise of the criminal law power which is denied to the provinces.

Support for this approach may be found in *Vancouver Growers Ltd. v. McLenan*,[126] a decision of the British Columbia Court of Appeal. While the case involved an invalid federal, rather than provincial, statute, ar-

---

[124][1962] S.C.R. 642, 38 W.W.R. 701, 34 D.L.R. (2d) 196.
[125]*Crevier v. A.G. Que.*, [1981] 2 S.C.R. 220, 127 D.L.R. (3d) 1, 38 N.R. 541; *A.G. Can. v. Law Society of B.C.*, 37 B.C.L.R. 145, [1982] 5 W.W.R. 289, 137 D.L.R. (3d) 1, 43 N.R. 451, 19 B.L.R. 234, 66 C.P.R. (2d) 1; *Paul L'Anglais* case, *supra*, note 73.
[126]*Vancouver Growers Ltd. v. McLenan*, 52 B.C.R. 42, [1937] 3 W.W.R. 119, [1937] 4 D.L.R. 143 (C.A.). See also *Royal Trust Co. v. A.G. Alta.*, [1936] 2 W.W.R. 337, [1936] 4 D.L.R. 98 (Alta. S.C.); *Re Bergethaler Waisenamt*, [1949] 1 W.W.R. 323 at 328, [1949] 1 D.L.R. 769 at 773, 29 C.B.R. 189 (Man. C.A.).

guably the same principle would apply. Under the federal *Natural Products Marketing Act, 1934*,[127] boards were appointed to regulate the marketing of certain natural products. The defendants in the *Vancouver Growers* case were members of such a board responsible for the marketing of vegetables grown in a certain area of British Columbia. The board had required the plaintiff to market its vegetables through the board, the vegetables being then sold interprovincially by the board. The plaintiff sued for money paid and received by the board for the use of the plaintiff. It was contended that the board had no valid existence and that it held the money (or such portion as it had retained) illegally. In 1936, while the *Vancouver Growers* case was pending, the British Columbia Legislature enacted that

> No action shall be brought against any person who . . . has acted or purported to act . . . as a member of any board appointed under or pursuant to the provisions of "The Natural Products Marketing Act, 1934," of the Dominion . . . for anything done by him in good faith in the performance . . . of his duties under either of the said Acts, and every action now pending which if it were brought hereafter would be within the scope of this section is hereby stayed.[128]

Before judgment was entered the Privy Council held, in an appeal from a reference to the Supreme Court of Canada, that the *Natural Products Marketing Act, 1934*, was *ultra vires* the Dominion.[129] The British Columbia courts followed this decision and treated the federal Act as invalid. The Court of Appeal nevertheless upheld the 1936 provincial statute as a valid defence to the plaintiff's action. The court apparently distinguished between two issues: the validity of the statute on one hand, and the right of redress for things done under the invalid statute on the other hand.

As a general proposition this approach creates difficulty and probably is not good law today. More recently the Supreme Court of Canada has had the opportunity to address the problem in *Amax Potash Ltd. v. Govt. of Sask.*[130] In this case, the plaintiff had brought an action to seek a declaration that certain provisions of a taxing statute and regulations were *ultra vires* the province. Pending the trial they sought an interim order under the Rules of Court for the preservation of property, that is, the tax moneys paid to the Government under protest. The order sought was to be in terms of requiring repayment if the taxes were found to have been

---

[127]S.C. 1934, c. 57.

[128]*Natural Products Marketing (British Columbia) Act Amendment Act 1936*, S.B.C. 1936, 2nd Sess., c. 30, s. 5.

[129]*A.G. B.C. v. A.G. Can.*, [1937] A.C. 377, 156 L.T. 311, [1937] 1 W.W.R. 328, [1937] 1 D.L.R. 691, 67 C.C.C. 337 (P.C.).

[130][1977] 2 S.C.R. 576, [1976] 6 W.W.R. 61, 71 D.L.R. (3d) 1, 11 N.R. 222.

invalid. In its response to this application for interim relief the provincial Government relied on s. 5(7) of the *Proceedings Against the Crown Act*[131] which provided:

> 5(7) No proceedings lie against the Crown under this or any other section of this Act in respect of anything heretofore or hereafter done or omitted and purporting to have been done or omitted in the exercise of a power or authority under a statute or a statutory provision purporting to confer or to have conferred on the Crown such power or authority, which statute or statutory provision is or was or may be beyond the legislative jurisdiction of the Legislature; and no action shall be brought against any person for any act or thing heretofore or hereafter done or omitted by him under the supposed authority of such statute or statutory provision, or of any proclamation, order in council or regulation made thereunder, provided such action would not lie against him if the said statute, statutory provision, proclamation, order in council or regulation is or had been or may be within the jurisdiction of the Legislature enacting or the Lieutenant Governor making the same.

(This subsection was described by the Supreme Court as "unique among provincial Crown liability Acts".) The Government argued that even if the taxing laws were ultimately held invalid this provision would prevent recovery of moneys already paid and therefore there should be no interim order requiring repayment. The plaintiff argued in response that s. 5(7) was also *ultra vires* if it would have the effect of barring recovery of taxes invalidly imposed.

The motion for an interim order was dismissed in both the Court of Queen's Bench and the Court of Appeal, both relying in part on the *Proceedings Against the Crown Act*, s. 5(7), thus treating it as valid. An appeal to the Supreme Court of Canada succeeded, however. On behalf of the court, Dickson J., said that only the first half of the subsection was in issue (that is, the part dealing with the liability of the Crown rather than of individuals), and found that part to be invalid to the extent that it purported to bar recovery of taxes paid under an invalid law. The most important aspect of the judgment is, perhaps, that the court refused to treat the validity of the law protecting the Crown from liability as a separate issue from the validity of the taxing legislation. Dickson J. said of s. 5(7) that it "has much broader implications than mere Crown immunity. In the present context, it directly concerns the right to tax".[132] Later he summarized the principle that the court saw.

    . . . if a statute is found to be *ultra vires* the legislature which enacted

---

[131]R.S.S. 1965, c. 87. See now R.S.S. 1978, c. P-27, s. 5(7).
[132]*Supra*, note 130 at p. 590 S.C.R., p. 10 D.L.R.

it, legislation which would have the effect of attaching legal consequences to acts done pursuant to that invalid law must equally be *ultra vires* because it relates to the same subject-matter as that which was involved in the prior legislation. If a state cannot take by unconstitutional means it cannot retain by unconstitutional means.[133]

The court therefore rejected the argument by the province that s. 5(7) was simply legislation in relation to the immunity of the Crown in right of the province and thus justifiable under heads 1, 13, 14, and 16, of s. 92 of the B.N.A. Act.

The court distinguished the *Vancouver Growers*[134] case although without fully explaining how it did so. The court is seemingly making a distinction between a taxing statute, whose whole purpose is the collection of money, and other kinds of legislation where the collection or expenditure of money is only incidental to a scheme which has been operating under an invalid law. The problem seems to be one of characterisation, with an immunity statute being seen as an extension of the invalid taxing statute in the former case, but as property legislation in the latter.

In support of its conclusion the court relied on a fairly direct precedent from a Privy Council decision in an Australian case, *Commr. for Motor Transport v. Antill Ranger & Co. Pty. Ltd.; State of New South Wales v. Edmund T. Lennon Pty Ltd.*[135] and found general support in the court's own earlier decision in the *B.C. Power*[136] case that Crown immunity should not be allowed to enable a Legislature to achieve ends not permitted it by the constitution.

While the *Amax* decision has since been applied in other cases[137] its full implications are not yet clear. It is notable that the Saskatchewan immunity legislation is not specifically directed to retaining this particular tax, or even just to retaining any invalid tax. It is general in scope, applying to any action against the Crown or any person for acts done under an invalid statute. Yet the court only dealt with immunity of the Crown, not that of individuals, and stressed the fact that a tax was involved in this case. It specifically found the subsection invalid "in so far as it purports to bar the recovery of taxes paid under a statute . . . which is beyond the legislative jurisdiction of the Legislature of Saskatchewan".[138]

---

[133]*Supra*, note 130 at p. 592 S.C.R., p. 12 D.L.R.
[134]*Supra*, note 126.
[135][1956] A.C. 527, [1956] 3 All E.R. 106.
[136][1962] S.C.R. 642, 38 W.W.R. 701, 34 D.L.R. (2d) 196.
[137]See *e.g. Re the Coloured Gasoline Tax Act*, [1977] 4 W.W.R. 436 (B.C. S.C.); *Société Asbestos Ltée v. Société Nationale de l'Amiante*, [1979] C.A. 342; *Lavigne v. P.G. du Québec*, [1980] C.S. 318.
[138]*Supra*, note 130 at p. 594 S.C.R., p. 13 D.L.R.

This leaves open the possibility that this subsection or its equivalent could be valid in other contexts.

There may be a legitimate place for some kinds of legislation preventing redress for acts done under invalid statutes. For example, there are some federal and provincial laws which would protect a public officer from personal liability with respect to acts done by him in good faith pursuant to a statute that subsequently is found to be invalid.[139] Such laws can be characterized as related to the efficient functioning of the public service and of the courts. They are not primarily designed to further projects which are constitutionally invalid or to retain ill-gotten gains for the Government. They simply represent a legislative judgment that it is more important for the morale and proper functioning of public officers that they should be prepared to act under statutes they believe to be valid, without fear of personal liability should the statute subsequently prove to be invalid. It may be that such laws are viewed as acceptable and genuinely related to the public service rather than to the furtherance of an invalid law because they correspond to common law principles of immunity. In this they may be contrasted to the statute in question in *Amax* which did not correspond to the common law position of liability for the return of money paid under compulsion pursuant to an error of law.[140]

In considering the validity of such protective legislation in particular cases, it will be necessary to make distinctions. Legislation which protects public officers in a general way (without reference to a particular scheme the validity of which may be obviously in doubt) should normally be valid as a law in relation to the public service. However, such laws should give protection only where the public officer has acted in good faith: that is, in an honest belief in the validity of his authority. They should not be allowed to protect officers who knowingly exceed their constitutional authority. Protective laws which make Governments generally immune from suit are far less justifiable. The Government should be able to bear the financial risk of the invalidity of its legislation, and laws prohibiting the recovery of damages or money wrongfully collected do not seem in the normal case to be justifiable. Such legislation, if worded generally, might have more chance of success than the kind of legislation in the *Antill Ranger* case, for example, which pertained to particular sums collected on criteria related to interstate trade and thus appeared to be an

---

[139]See *e.g. Criminal Code*, R.S.C. 1970, c. C-34, s. 717, *Public Authorities Protection Act*, R.S.O. 1980, c. 406, s. 13, *Proceedings Against the Crown Act*, R.S.S. 1978, c. P-27, s. 5(7), *Magistrate's Privilege Act*, R.S.Q. 1977, c. P-24, s. 1, am. S.Q. 1982, c. 32, s. 117.

[140]See *e.g. Crown Trust Co. et al. v. The Queen in Right of Ont. et al.* (1986), 26 D.L.R. (4th) 41 (Ont. Div. Ct.).

extension of the legislation previously held invalid. The *Amax* case would suggest, however, that even a generally worded immunity clause will not be effective to allow a Government to retain illegally collected money if its collection is the principal object of the law found to be invalid. (The problem of governmental immunities in constitutional litigation will be discussed more fully in the next chapter.)

It is submitted, therefore, that provincial power over the jurisdiction of, or rights of action in, provincial courts is not entirely excluded where constitutional issues are involved. But the provincial Legislature cannot restrict jurisdiction in such a way as to permit it colourably to accomplish ends otherwise denied it by the constitution.

E. EXCLUSION OF JUDICIAL REVIEW THROUGH FEDERAL STATUTORY DENIAL OF A RIGHT OF ACTION

Any federal measures of this type are potentially limited because Parliament's power in s. 101 of the *Constitution Act* is restricted to "the Constitution, Maintenance, and Organization of a General Court of Appeal for Canada, and for the Establishment of any additional Courts for the better Administration of the Laws of Canada." Parliament could attempt to restrict judicial review in the Supreme Court of Canada, perhaps, and could also attempt to deprive the Federal Court or any other federally created court of power to consider constitutional issues. The results might not be as serious as the results of some of the provincial measures already discussed. In a case appealed to the Supreme Court, for example, the constitutional issues would already have been canvassed in the provincial courts. In the Federal Court only rights arising under federal statutory law are enforceable, unlike the situation in provincial courts which normally deal with cases under both federal and provincial law. Thus the possibility of Parliament invalidly barring provincially created rights of action by means of the *Federal Court Act*[141] could not arise. If, however, in proceedings under the *Income Tax Act*[142] in the Federal Court, for example, the taxpayer was precluded from attacking the Act's validity, this might violate the principles heretofore advanced. That is, Parliament, like the Legislatures, is precluded from limiting the jurisdiction of its courts to the extent that it is thereby enabled to evade effectively the constitutional limitations on its own jurisdiction. This exception to its power under s. 101 is necessarily implied in the existence of a federal division of legislative power.

Another form of federal limitation has been experienced and con-

---

[141]R.S.C. 1970 (2nd Supp.), c. 10.
[142]S.C. 1970–71–72, c. 63.

tested as a result of the *Federal Court Act* of 1971 which purports to give exclusive jurisdiction to the Federal Court in certain matters that might otherwise fall within the residual jurisdiction of the provincial superior courts. Subsection 17(1) provides that the Trial Division of the Federal Court has exclusive original jurisdiction "in all cases where relief is claimed against the Crown" except where otherwise provided. Section 18 gives the Trial Division exclusive jurisdiction over prerogative writs, and declarations, and similar relief against federal tribunals or officers including proceedings against the Attorney General. The purpose and effect of this section is to exclude provincial superior courts from a review jurisdiction which they formerly exercised over federal agencies.[143] Within the Federal Court system, however, the Act does provide for sharing of first-instance judicial review between the Trial Division and the Court of Appeal. By s. 18 the former can review decisions of an administrative nature and by s. 28 the latter can hear applications to review final quasi-judicial decisions of federal agencies on grounds of want of jurisdiction, denial of natural justice, error of law or errors of fact based on findings "made in a perverse or capricious manner or without regard for the material before it".

These provisions in federal law obviously have a major impact on the right of provincial superior courts to consider constitutional issues as they relate to federal Government activity. Questions have arisen, however, as to their interpretation and validity.

In the Ontario courts s. 17 has been interpreted to be an effective bar to an action for a declaration in a provincial superior court that a federal Act was *ultra vires*[144] and s. 18 was similarly held to bar an action against a federal board for a declaration with respect to a constitutional issue.[145] On the other hand, there have been decisions in other contexts not involving the *Federal Court Act* that an action for a declaration concerning the validity of a statute is not an action "against the Crown" or its agencies and only affects the crown indirectly.[146] Distinctions have been drawn between this kind of action and one which seeks a declaration concerning a specific personal or property right contested between the Crown and the individual where Crown property or financial interests

---

[143]See *e.g. Commonwealth of Puerto Rico v. Hernandez*, [1975] 1 S.C.R. 228 at 233–37.

[144]*Denison Mines Ltd. v. A.G. Can.*, [1973] 1 O.R. 797, 32 D.L.R. (3d) 419 (H.C.).

[145]*Hamilton v. Hamilton Harbour Commrs.*, [1972] 3 O.R. 61, 27 D.L.R. (3d) 385 (C.A.).

[146]*McNeil v. N.S. Bd. of Censors* (1975), 9 N.S.R. (2d) 483, 53 D.L.R. (3d) 259, affd [1976] 2 S.C.R. 265, 12 N.S.R. (2d) 85, 55 D.L.R. (3d) 632, 5 N.R. 43, 32 C.R.N.S. 376; *Canex Placer Ltd. v. A.G. B.C.*, [1976] 1 W.W.R. 24, 58 D.L.R. (3d) 241 (B.C.C.A.).

would be affected. This distinction has been applied by other provincial courts to enable them to hold that ss. 17 and 18 of the *Federal Court Act* do not prevent actions in provincial courts for declarations as to the validity of federal laws.[147]

The Supreme Court, on appeals involving such rulings, has recently put this distinction aside, however, in favour of a more direct and fundamental approach to the interpretation of ss. 17 and 18. In *A.G. Can. v. Law Society of B.C.* the court held that Parliament does not have, in providing courts under s. 101 of the *Constitution Act, 1867* for the better administration of its laws, the power to prevent provincial superior courts from determining the constitutional validity of those laws. Mr. Justice Estey, writing for the court, declined to decide the matter simply on a narrow interpretation of the scope of ss. 17 and 18, but instead said that they could not validly prevent such judicial review even if that were their intended meaning. In a rhetorical flourish he pronounced that Parliament could not so provide because:[148]

> To do so would strip the basic constitutional concepts of judicature of this country, namely the superior courts of the provinces, of a judicial power fundamental to a federal system as described in the *Constitution Act*.

As this passage would have it, those superior courts are "basic constitutional concepts of judicature". These "concepts", it appears, must be taken to have the power of judicial review over federal laws because this is "fundamental to a federal system". This suggests that the jurisdiction of these "concepts" in such matters is implicitly guaranteed for the preservation of the distribution of powers between the two orders of government. This does not necessarily mean that such "concepts" must always have jurisdiction over Charter issues arising under federal law. Here only the guarantee of judicial review provided in s. 24 of the Charter (which is to be available only in a "court of competent jurisdiction" otherwise having jurisdiction over the person, the subject-matter, and the remedy[149]) and that implied by s. 52 of the *Constitution Act, 1982*, are applicable. Neither of these seemingly dictate a mandatory jurisdiction for the superior courts of the provinces in Charter cases in the face of an

---

[147]*Law Society of B.C. v. A.G. Can.*, 18 B.C.L.R., 181, [1980] 4 W.W.R. 6, 108 D.L.R. (3d) 753, 15 C.P.C. 195, 50 C.P.R. (2d) 87 (C.A.), affd [1982] 2 S.C.R. 307, [1982] 5 W.W.R. 289, 137 D.L.R. (3d) 1, 43 N.R. 451, 66 C.P.R. (2d) 1 (S.C.C.); *Borowski v. Minister of Justice*, 6 Sask. R. 218, [1981] 1 W.W.R. 1, affd [1981] 2 S.C.R. 578, 12 Sask. R. 420, [1982] 1 W.W.R. 97, 130 D.L.R. (3d) 588, 39 N.R. 331, 64 C.C.C. (2d) 97, 24 C.P.C. 62, 24 C.R. (3d) 352. See also *Zutphen Brothers Const. Ltd. v. Dywidag Systems International et al.* (1987), 35 D.L.R. (4th) 433 (N.S.C.A.).

[148]*Supra*. at p. 328. See now also *Paul L'Anglais* case, *supra*, note 73.

[149]See *supra*, at pp. 70–73.

exclusive assignment to the Federal Court, by federal law, of jurisdiction over the person, matter, and remedy in question.[150]

F. LEGISLATIVE PRE-DETERMINATION OF JUDICIAL FINDINGS

Where the courts are permitted to embark on judicial review of legislation, it is clear that the Legislature cannot dictate the conclusion which they must reach on the constitutional question. The highest courts have apparently not yet had occasion to deal with such legislative attempts. When they do, they can hardly escape the conclusion that the Legislature could not be permitted to exceed its jurisdiction merely by requiring a court to make findings of fact or law in its favour.

Perhaps the strongest decision to this effect in the provincial courts is *Home Oil Distributors v. A.G. B.C.*[151] A provincial royal commission had investigated the fuel industry, apparently in part because of the competition being given local coal producers by the sale of imported fuel oil at less than cost price. The report and recommendations were submitted to the Legislature. Later the *Coal and Petroleum Products Control Board Act, 1937*[152] was passed. The plaintiff sued for a declaration and an injunction contending that the Act interfered with interprovincial or international trade, matters within federal jurisdiction with respect to "the regulation of trade and commerce". It was also contended that the Royal Commission report should be admitted as evidence and that the report indicated that a purpose was to be achieved which was *ultra vires* the Legislature. On an appeal from an order granting an interlocutory injunction, the British Columbia Court of Appeal held the report to be admissible "in so far only as it finds facts which are relevant to the ascertainment of the said alleged purpose and the effect of the enactment".[153]

Four days later, while further proceedings were pending, the Legislature amended the impugned statute as follows:[154]

---

[150]*Cf.* Mullan, "Annotation" (1983), 3 *Admin. L.R.* 114; *Eleveurs de Volailles de l'Est de l'Ontario et al. v. Canadian Chicken Marketing Agency*, [1985] 1 F.C. 280 at 301–302 (T.D.).

[151]53 B.C.R. 355, [1939] 1 W.W.R. 49, [1939] 1 D.L.R. 573 (C.A.).

[152]S.B.C. 1937, c. 8.

[153]*Supra*, note 151 at 51 W.W.R., p. 574 D.L.R. This view of admissibility of such material was taken more recently by the Supreme Court of Canada in *Reference re Residential Tenancies Act*, [1981] S.C.R. 714 at 720–27, 123 D.L.R. (3d) 554 at 560–66, 37 N.R. 158. See generally, *infra*, at pp. 283–86.

[154]*Coal and Petroleum Products Control Board Act Amendment Act*, S.B.C. 1938, c. 5, s. 4.

> This Act is not intended to implement or carry into effect the recommendations or findings of any report made or to be made by the Commissioner appointed by the Lieutenant-Governor in Council under the *"Public Inquiries Act"* . . . and in construing this Act and in ascertaining its purpose, intention, scope and effect no reference shall be made to any such reports . . .

Nevertheless, at the trial Mr. Justice Manson proceeded to look at the report. He noted that the report indicated that the petroleum industry had an international aspect, and that the Legislature had apparently thought that by its declaration it could prevent the court from looking at the report or finding the true purpose of the statute. "It need scarcely be said that if the legislation encroaches upon the legislative jurisdiction of the Dominion with respect to trade and commerce the declaration will not save the situation. As I have already said, mere assertion does not change facts".[155]

On appeal, the Court of Appeal reversed the decision and held the statute to be *intra vires*. While the judges did not consider the international aspects of the petroleum industry as revealed by the report to be decisive, they did not hesitate to look at the report itself. Speaking for the court, Chief Justice Martin said that "we have not given effect to the amending statute . . . because we regard that interlocutory enactment as ineffective to curtail the unassailable jurisdiction of the Courts of Canada to adjudicate upon constitutional questions under the *British North America Act*".[156] On appeal to the Supreme Court of Canada[157] only Kerwin J. (Rinfret J. concurring) held the report to be admissible. The other judges either ignored the report or declined to make a decision as to its admissibility.

The principle stated by the Court of Appeal, on the ineffectiveness of the amendment purporting to direct the court in characterizing the impugned legislation, is probably unassailable. That is, the Legislature cannot preclude a court, where the constitutional issue is properly before it, from reaching certain conclusions as to the effect of legislation.

At least one judge of the Supreme Court of Canada has expressed this view. In the *Reference re s. 5(a) of the Dairy Industry Act*[158] (the Margarine Case) the court was asked to answer certain questions concerning a section of a federal statute which prohibited the manufacture and sale of margarine in Canada. Those seeking to uphold the validity

---

[155]*Home Oil Distributors v. A.G. B.C. (No. 2)*, 53 B.C.R. 355, [1939] 1 W.W.R. 666 at 681 (B.C. S.C.). For a somewhat similar view see *United States v. Klein*, 80 U.S. 128 (1872).

[156][1939] 2 W.W.R. 418 at 419–20, [1939] 3 D.L.R. 397 at 398–99 (B.C. C.A.).

[157][1940] S.C.R. 444, [1940] 2 D.L.R. 609.

[158][1949] S.C.R. 1, [1949] 1 D.L.R. 433, affd [1951] A.C. 179 (*sub nom. Can. Fed. of Agriculture v. A.G. Que.*), [1950] 4 D.L.R. 689.

of the Act argued, *inter alia*, that it was valid "criminal law" enacted under s. 91, head 27 of the B.N.A. Act. To support the argument that Parliament had thereby intended to prohibit a public evil, they quoted the preamble to the original Act which began:[159]

> Whereas the use of certain substitutes for butter, heretofore manufactured and exposed for sale in Canada is injurious to health, and it is expedient to prohibit the manufacture and sale thereof. . . .

In subsequent general revisions the preamble had been deleted, in accordance with legislative practice. Mr. Justice Rand commented that:[160]

> Ordinarily a preamble indicates the purpose of the statute and it may be a guide to the meaning and scope of the language where that is doubtful or ambiguous. But when the question is the real character of the legislation for the purposes of jurisdiction between two legislatures under a federal constitution, different considerations arise. A legislation [*sic*] cannot conclude the question by a declaration in a preamble: at most it is a fact to be taken into account, the weight to be given to it depending on all circumstances . . .

It is important to note here that Rand J. distinguished between normal interpretation of a statute and interpretation for the purpose of determining constitutional validity.[161] Ordinary statutory interpretation is carried out to ascertain the real intention of the Legislature. Any clear assertion by the Legislature as to its intention is therefore the best evidence and in most cases will be conclusive. Where a constitutional issue is involved, however, it is necessary to ascertain whether the effect of the legislation is within the jurisdiction of the enacting Legislature. A Legislature cannot be allowed to legislate colourably and thereby achieve an effect not within its power merely by asserting that it intends to achieve some effect within its powers.[162]

This distinction may have been lost sight of in the case of *Beauharnois Light, Heat & Power Co. Ltd. v. Hydro-Electric Power Comn.*[163] Just as in the *Ottawa Valley*[164] case, the Power Commission relied on s. 6(4) of the *Power Commission Act* of 1927 as a defence to Beauharnois' action. Section 6(4), it will be recalled, seemed to require the consent

---

[159]S.C. 1886, c. 42.

[160]*Supra*, note 158 at pp. 47–48 S.C.R.

[161]The same distinction is carefully drawn by Dickson J. in *Reference re Residential Tenancies Act*, [1981] S.C.R. 714 at 723, 123 D.L.R. (3d) 554 at 562–63.

[162]See *A.G. Alta. v. A.G. Can.*, [1943] A.C. 356 at 376, [1943] 1 All E.R. 240.

[163][1937] O.R. 796, [1937] 3 D.L.R. 458 (C.A.).

[164][1937] O.R. 265, [1936] 4 D.L.R. 594 and see accompanying text at note 104.

of the Attorney General before action could be commenced against the commission. In the *Ottawa Valley* case the section had been held inapplicable to that type of action and this decision was followed at trial in the *Beauharnois* case. After trial the Ontario Legislature enacted a declaration[165] as to what "the meaning and effect" of the subsection "is and always has been". This declaration very specifically set out the meaning so that the subsection would clearly be a bar to the *Beauharnois* type of action.

The Court of Appeal nevertheless held the declaration to be inapplicable. Speaking for the court, Mr. Justice Middleton stated that:[166]

> The Legislature, in matters within its competence, is unquestionably supreme, but it falls to the Courts to determine the meaning of the language used. If the Courts do not determine in accordance with the true intention of the Legislature, the Legislature cannot arrogate to itself the jurisdiction of a further appellate Court and enact that the language used in its earlier enactment means something other than the Court has determined. It can, if it so pleases, use other language expressing its meaning more clearly. It transcends its true function when it undertakes to say that the language used has a different meaning and effect to that given it by the Courts, and that it always has meant something other than the Courts have declared it to mean.

With respect, it is submitted that this states the power of the Legislature too narrowly. The Legislature can, when a statute is first passed, expressly state how it is to be construed (in the absence of any constitutional problem). Similarly if the effect is not the creation of an offence or the increasing of penalties for acts already committed (which would violate s. 11 of the Charter of Rights and Freedoms), the Legislature may make such a declaration later and make it retroactively, as there is nothing in the Canadian constitution to prevent the enactment of civil laws *ex post facto*. Even though a trial court has pronounced on rights under a statute, that statute may subsequently be altered retroactively to remove the basis for the earlier judgment, and an appellate court should take cognizance of this alteration. Thus, the statement by Mr. Justice Middleton in the *Beauharnois* case must be confined to situations where the legislative declaration could preclude a judicial finding of constitutional invalidity. Otherwise the statement would be too broad in its implications.[167] The distinction must be remembered at all times as between statutory inter-

---

[165]*Power Commission Declaratory Act, 1937*, S.O. 1937, c. 58.

[166]*Supra* note 163 at pp. 822–23 O.R., pp. 462–63 D.L.R.

[167]See comments on this case by Cartwright J. in *Western Minerals Ltd. v. Gaumont*, [1953] 1 S.C.R. 345 at 372, [1953] 3 D.L.R. 245 at 269. But *cf. Liyanage v. R.*, [1967] A.C. 259, [1966] 1 All E.R. 650 (P.C.).

pretation and characterisation of statutes for constitutional purposes. Legislative power to direct the courts in their findings is limited only as required to prevent the Legislature achieving a constitutionally invalid result.

G. CONCLUSION

The discussion in chapter 2 indicated that the right of judicial review is not absolute, that it must be considered qualified by other factors. One of these is the express legislative power conferred on Parliament and the Legislatures by the *Constitution Act, 1867*. By s. 92(14) the provincial Legislatures, and by s. 101 Parliament, are given jurisdiction to regulate the "Constitution, Maintenance, and Organization" of the courts. They are also given jurisdiction to create, alter, or abolish substantive rights in their respective spheres.

In the legislative attempts to limit judicial review, as herein examined, we have seen the complexities involved in balancing the forces of judicial review and legislative power. Legislatures have been permitted to impose procedural requirements as long as they do not thereby create an absolute bar to judicial review. They have been permitted to delegate to non-curial bodies the power to determine certain issues relevant to the application of constitutional norms, provided that the courts can ultimately define the constitutional limits of jurisdiction of such bodies. Legislatures may not use their control over the courts to prevent the enforcement of rights not within their legislative jurisdiction. But whether they can confirm rights vested under invalid legislation may depend on whether the protecting legislation is seen as having a separate and valid constitutional purpose, or whether it is seen as simply serving the same purpose as the other legislation found to be invalid. Legislatures may also dictate to the courts the meaning of legislation, but not its constitutional effect.

These examples are sufficient to demonstrate the impossibility of thinking in absolute terms when considering legislative restrictions on judicial review. Lawyers and judges who assert an absolute parliamentary sovereignty or an absolute right of judicial review will fail to cope with the more important issues. Instead we should start with the premise that Legislatures can normally regulate the work of the courts, and then concentrate on determining in each case whether the legislative attempt at regulation has gone as far as to threaten the maintenance of the constitution. Will it really effect an alteration in the constitution by allowing the Legislature to prevent an adjudication as to validity of laws, or limitations on guaranteed rights, or will it merely impose a special procedure, alter the available remedies, or change the available judicial forum? These are the kinds of questions the courts should ask in examining the substance, not merely the form, of legislative limitations on judicial review.

For their part, the Legislatures should eschew any exercise of their jurisdiction over the courts and over substantive rights which might amount to a colourable invasion of the ultimate power of judicial review required for the maintenance of the federal structure and the protection of constitutionally guaranteed rights and freedoms.

Chapter 4

Crown Prerogative and the Power of Judicial Review

A. GENERAL PRINCIPLES OF CROWN IMMUNITY

At common law the citizen had no right to sue the Crown. In spite of a steady development away from this position in favour of Crown liability, problems still arise when an action is brought against the Crown or its representatives. In a federal state such as Canada, with a written constitution limiting legislative and executive powers, these problems take on a special significance where the complaint against the Crown is that it acts or has acted unconstitutionally. In such circumstances the question arises of the extent to which traditional Crown immunity can prevent the courts from entertaining an action to determine the validity of legislation or governmental action.

In England the Crown was immune from suit because the central courts were the King's courts, and like any feudal lord he was not subject to the jurisdiction of his own courts. From about 1300 onwards, the petition of right procedure was available to permit many actions. By this procedure a claim was submitted to the King and if he in his unfettered discretion saw fit he could by his fiat refer it to the courts for adjudication in the normal way. This procedure was regularized and simplified by statute in 1860.[1] However, it was never available for actions in tort, at least those which were not real actions. Tort actions were denied because the Crown was not considered capable of committing a tort: "the King can do no wrong". Petition of right was thus used mainly in actions for the recovery of money or property in the hands of the Crown or for the enforcement of contracts. Where no such relief was sought it was not available.[2]

In Canada the same rules applied to proceedings against the Crown, both federal and provincial. The federal authority and some provinces

---

[1] *Petition of Right Act*, 1860, 23 & 24 Vict., c. 34 (U.K.).

[2] See Holdsworth, "The History of Remedies Against the Crown" (1922), 38 *L.Q. Rev.* 141; Morgan, "Introductory Chapter", in Robinson, *Public Authorities and Legal Liability* (1925), at xviii–liii; Street, *Governmental Liability* (1953), at 1–6; 11 Halsbury, *Laws of England,* 4th ed. (1976), at 747–50.

had legislation pertaining to petition of right, while other provinces apparently left unaltered the uncertainties of the common law which had obtained in England prior to 1860.[3] Parliament did, at an early stage, extend the scope of petition of right by permitting actions for tort in some cases.[4] But it was clear in Canada that the Crown's representative, either the Governor General or the Lieutenant Governor, had an unlimited discretion in this matter. A refusal to grant a fiat could not be questioned in the courts, even where the proceedings were to be used to test the validity of legislation.[5] If an action could be framed so that the Crown was not a necessary party, the problem of Crown immunity did not arise. But wherever Crown title or interests in property would be affected, the Crown had to be made a party.[6] Petition of right was the proper procedure where such rights could be directly affected by a request for relief which would deprive the Crown of its property or money.[7]

Even in its most extended application the principle of Crown immunity was only a limited obstacle to constitutional litigation. If the action were so framed as to constitute a claim for damages against a person or company acting under an invalid statute, this was permissible without petition of right so long as Crown property interests were not directly attacked. One could always maintain an action against a fellow subject of the Crown under such circumstances.[8] A public officer could be sued for damages for unauthorized acts committed by him,[9] or could be restrained by injunction from committing such acts.[10] In none of these cases was petition

---

[3]For a survey of Canadian law prior to more recent statutory modifications see "The Crown as Litigant: Report of Committee on Comparative Provincial Legislation and Law Reform, 1936" (1936), 14 *Can. Bar Rev.* 606.

[4]See *Exchequer Court Act*, R.S.C. 1952, c. 98, s. 18 and its predecessors. See also, *infra*, note 38, and accompanying text.

[5]*Orpen v. A.G. Ont.*, 56 O.L.R. 327, [1925] 2 D.L.R. 366 (H.C.), affd 56 O.L.R. 530, [1925] 3 D.L.R. 301 (C.A.); *Lovibond v. Gov. Gen. Can.*, [1930] A.C. 717, 144 L.T. 47 (P.C.).

[6]*Esquimalt & Nanaimo Ry. v. Wilson*, [1920] A.C. 358 at 369, [1919] 3 W.W.R. 961, 50 D.L.R. 371 (P.C.); *Trawnik et al. v. Lennox et al.*, [1985] 2 All E.R. 368 (C.A.).

[7]*A.G. Ont. v. McLean Gold Mines Ltd.*, [1927] A.C. 185, [1926] 3 W.W.R. 193, [1926] 4 D.L.R. 213 (P.C.); *Lovibond v. Grand Trunk Ry.*, [1936] 2 All E.R. 495, [1936] 2 W.W.R. 298, [1936] 3 D.L.R. 449, 45 C.R.C. 162 (P.C.); *Contact Mining & Development Co. v. Craigmont Mines Ltd.* (1961), 35 W.W.R. 480, 29 D.L.R. (2d) 592 (S.C.C.), affg 35 W.W.R. 214, 26 D.L.R. (2d) 35 (B.C. C.A.); *Calder v. A.G. B.C.*, [1973] S.C.R. 313 at 424–26, [1973] 4 W.W.R. 1 at 89–90, 34 D.L.R. (3d) 145.

[8]*Lovibond* case, *supra*, note 7, at pp. 311–12 W.W.R., pp. 460–61 D.L.R.

[9]*Musgrave v. Pulido* (1879), 5 App. Cas. 102, 41 L.T. 629 (P.C.); *Roncarelli v. Duplessis*, [1959] S.C.R. 121, 16 D.L.R. (2d) 689.

[10]See Strayer, "Injunctions Against Crown Officers" (1964), 42 *Can. Bar Rev.* 1.

of right required to question the validity of the authority under which the person, officer, or agency had acted or intended to act.

The Crown itself could apparently be sued without petition of right by means of an action for a declaratory judgment where the citizen sought a clarification of his rights, and Crown property or money interests were not directly at stake. The leading English case on this point is still *Dyson v. Attorney General*[11] decided in 1911. The plaintiff had received a notice (some eight million such notices had been sent out) from the Commissioners of Inland Revenue requiring him to make certain returns with respect to his property. Failure to deliver the returns would make him liable to a penalty recoverable at the suit of the Attorney General. The plaintiff commenced action for a declaration that the notice and other requirement were not in accordance with the statute and were *ultra vires* of the commissioners. The Attorney General moved to strike out this pleading on the grounds that such action could be maintained only by petition of right because the rights of the Crown would be directly affected. The Court of Appeal held that the action would lie and that a petition of right was not necessary.

The *Dyson* decision is far from clear on the question of whether petition of right would be required where the Crown's rights were directly affected. Cozens-Hardy M.R. seems to treat it as a case directly affecting Crown rights but cites authority from the Court of Exchequer to show that a declaration could be made in such circumstances.[12] Farwell L.J. appears to hold that Crown rights were only indirectly affected, and for that reason the action would be maintainable.[13] Fletcher Moulton L.J. objected to the point being dealt with on a motion to strike out pleadings and simply held that it should be left for decision at the trial. It would appear, however, that Crown rights would not be affected very directly if at all in this action. No existing property of the Crown was involved. At most the decision could only affect possible future revenues. The issue of the ultimate liability of the plaintiff to pay taxes were not raised, although the decision could have an adverse effect on the right of the Crown to enforce the penalty. One of the counsel in the case, later elevated to the bench, interpreted the *Dyson* action as one which affected Crown

---

[11][1911] 1 K.B. 410, 103 L.T. 707. See also Edwards, *The Law Officers of the Crown* (1964), at 293–95.

[12]*Supra*, note 11 at pp. 415–17 K.B. For a criticism of this reliance on Exchequer decisions see Street, *supra*, note 2, at pp. 132–34. The arguments there stated are probably not relevant in many Canadian jurisdictions where the superior courts were given the same jurisdiction as all of the royal courts in England had enjoyed.

[13]*Supra*, note 11 at pp. 421–22.

rights only indirectly.[14] The Privy Council similarly regarded the decision,[15] and it refused to allow declaratory actions which would directly affect Crown rights in the absence of petition of right.[16] The Supreme Court of Canada distinguished between the petition of right, properly used only where some relief was sought against the Crown involving its interest in property, and a declaration against the Attorney General which did not deal with such rights.[17] This is consistent with the traditional principles of Crown immunity which would prohibit a court from depriving the Crown of its property. The modern constitutional justification for this is more clearly attributable to parliamentary supremacy. If the court could, without consent of the Legislature (granted only under petition of right legislation), order the payment of public funds or the transfer of Crown property, then the Legislature's primary jurisdiction over these matters would be denied. But where the court order in the form of a declaratory judgment would not involve interference with public property, the court may proceed without infringing on Crown or Legislature.

The declaratory action without petition of right had particular significance in a federal system such as Canada's. It provided a means for raising constitutional issues in situations where it was not necessary to attack Crown title to property or seek recovery of money from the Crown. As in England, legislation in most Canadian jurisdictions permits the grant of a declaration though no other relief is sought.[18] The constitutional validity of governmental action could thus be attacked without Government consent. It was in fact held that the declaration was the proper method of attacking legislative validity where Crown rights were not directly involved,[19] and that petition of right was not an appropriate procedure in such cases.[20]

---

[14]Rowlatt J. in *Bombay & Persia Steam Navigation Co. v. MacLay*, [1920] 3 K.B. 402 at 408, 124 L.T. 602.

[15]*A.G. Ont. v. McLean Gold Mines Ltd.*, *supra*, note 7 at p. 191 A.C. See also *Esquimalt & Nanaimo Ry. v. Wilson*, *supra*, note 6.

[16]*McLean* case, *supra*, *Lovibond v. Grand Trunk Ry.*, *supra*, note 7.

[17]*R. v. Bradley*, [1941] S.C.R. 270 at 276, [1941] 2 D.L.R. 737, 1 C.P.R. 1, 1 Fox Pat. C. 131.

[18]See e.g. *Judicature Act*, R.S.A. 1980, c. J-1, s. 11; *Courts of Justice Act, 1984*, S.O. 1984, c. 11, s. 110; *Queen's Bench Act*, R.S.S. 1978, c. Q-1, s. 45(17); *Code of Civil Procedure*, R.S.Q. 1977, c. C-25, arts. 55, 453 discussed, *infra*, at pp. 151–53. For a history of this aspect of the declaratory action see Zamir, *The Declaratory Judgment* (1962), at 7–17.

[19]*Esquimalt & Nanaimo Ry. v. Wilson*, *supra*, note 6 at p. 364 A.C.

[20]*C.P.R. v. A.G. Sask.*, 1 W.W.R. 193, [1951] 3 D.L.R. 362 (Sask. K.B.) revd in part 2 W.W.R. 424, [1951] 4 D.L.R. 21 (Sask. C.A.), restored, [1952] 2 S.C.R. 231, [1952] 4 D.L.R. 11, without reference to this point. See also *Tiny Separate School Trustees v. The King*, [1927] S.C.R. 637 at 706–07, 713, [1927] 4 D.L.R. 857, at 906, 911, affd [1928] A.C. 363, [1928] 2 W.W.R. 641, [1928] 3 D.L.R. 753.

The dominant modern view in Canada of the *Dyson*-type action for a declaration of constitutional invalidity is that it never was an action against the Crown and therefore is not now governed either by provincial legislation permitting actions against the Crown[21] nor by s. 17 of the *Federal Court Act* which gives exclusive jurisdiction to that court "in all cases where relief is claimed against the Crown" in right of Canada.[22]

B. STATUTORY MODIFICATION

The foregoing common law rules with respect to Crown immunity from suit have undergone changes through both legislative and judicial action. Important legislative reform came in England with the passage of the *Crown Proceedings Act, 1947*.[23] Section 1 of that Act provided that, in all cases where a person had a claim against the Crown which previously would have been enforceable only by petition of right, the claim could now be enforced as of right and without fiat. Section 21 provided that the court could make such orders against the Crown as it could against a subject, except that instead of making an order for delivery of property by the Crown the court was confined to making a declaratory order.[24]

In Canada the use of declaratory judgments against a representative of the Crown was facilitated by statute in some jurisdictions many years ago. Typical of these statutory provisions is s. 26 of the *Judicature Act*[25] of Alberta which confers jurisdiction on the Supreme Court of the province as follows:

---

[21]*McNeil v. N.S. Board of Censors* (1975), 9 N.S.R. (2d) 483, 53 D.L.R. (3d) 259 (C.A.); *Canex Placer Ltd. v. A.G. B.C.*, [1976] 1 W.W.R. 24, 58 D.L.R. (3d) 241 (B.C. C.A.). But cf. *N.B. Telephone Co. v. Minister of Municipal Affairs* (1979), 34 N.B.R. (2d) 63, 107 D.L.R. (3d) 208 (C.A.).

[22]*Law Society of B.C. v. A.G. Can.*, 18 B.C.L.R. 181, [1980] 4 W.W.R. 6, 108 D.L.R. (3d) 753, 15 C.P.C. 195, 50 C.P.R. (2d) 87 (B.C. C.A.); *Borowski v. Minister of Justice*, 6 Sask. R. 218, [1981] 1 W.W.R. 1 (C.A.); *Waddell v. Governor in Council*, 30 B.C. L.R. 127, [1981] 5 W.W.R. 662, 126 D.L.R. (3d) 431 (*sub nom. Waddell v. Schreyer*) (S.C.), affd [1983] 1 W.W.R. 762, 142 D.L.R. (3d) 177 (C.A.), leave to appeal to S.C.C. refused [1983] 1 W.W.R. lii. This view of s. 17 was questioned but seemingly not decided by the Supreme Court on appeal in the *B.C. Law Society* case, 37 B.C.L.R. 145 at 158, [1982] 5 W.W.R. 289, 137 D.L.R. (3d) 1, 43 N.R. 451, 19 B.L.R. 234, 66 C.P.R. (2d) 1.

[23]1947, 10 & 11 Geo. VI, c. 44 (U.K.).

[24]For details of practice with respect to declaratory actions under the Act see Zamir, *supra*, note 18, at pp. 289–97.

[25]R.S.A. 1980, c. J-1.

26(1) The Court has jurisdiction to entertain an action at the instance of either

(a) the Attorney General for Canada, or

(b) the Attorney General for Alberta,

for a declaration as to the validity of an enactment of the Legislature though no further relief is prayed or sought.

(2) An action under this section for a declaration as to the validity of an enactment shall be deemed sufficiently constituted if the 2 Attorneys General are parties to it.

(3) A judgment in an action under this section may be appealed against as other judgments of the Court.

This procedure was provided in Ontario as early as 1886 and is now also found in Manitoba, British Columbia, and New Brunswick.[26] The Ontario provision,[27] though cast somewhat differently, seems to be similar in effect, except that it also provides for the questioning of the validity of federal legislation. Where such provisions are in force it would seem that no problem of Crown immunity would arise in the grant of a declaratory judgment against the Attorney General of the province. Whereas by the common law no such judgment could be given without petition of right if the Crown's rights were directly affected, by this statutory innovation the Attorney General is made subject to suit regardless of the effect on Crown rights. The effect of such procedure, while no doubt beneficial in situations where it applies,[28] is nonetheless very limited. It is of no use to private litigants because the action must be instituted by an Attorney General, almost certainly the Attorney General of Canada who would probably be most reluctant to institute such proceedings. It is useful only as against provincial legislation, except in Ontario. It is not available in many provinces, and not at all in the federal courts except through appeal to the Supreme Court of Canada.

More significant in Canada have been the general statutory modifications of Crown immunity which have facilitated private actions, including those challenging legislative validity, against the Crown. There had been discussion in Canada for years as to the need for reform of the Crown prerogative of immunity from suit.[29] Passage of the *Crown Pro-*

---

[26]*Queen's Bench Act*, R.S.M. 1970, c. C280, s. 62; *Constitutional Question Act*, R.S.B.C. 1979, c. 63, s. 9; *Judicature Act*, R.S.N.B. 1973, c. J-2, s. 22, am. 1980, c. 28, s. 5; 1982, c. 3, s. 39(1); 1983, c. 43, s. 6.

[27]*Courts of Justice Act, 1984*, S.O. 1984, c. 11, s. 110.

[28]See Grant, "Judicial Review in Canada: Procedural Aspects" (1964), 42 *Can. Bar Rev.* 195 at 202–03.

[29]See *e.g.* Kennedy, "Suits by and Against the Crown" (1928), 6 *Can. Bar Rev.* 329; "Report" *supra*, note 3. Some progress had been made in establishing the liability to suit of some Crown agencies incorporated with capacity to sue and be sued. See Smith, "Liability to Suit of an Agent of the Crown" (1950), 8 *U. Tor. L.J.* 218; *Yeats v.*

ceedings Act, 1947,[30] in England gave the necessary impetus to action, and in 1948 the Conference of Commissioners on Uniformity of Legislation in Canada undertook a study of the problem. In 1950 a model Act[31] was adopted, patterned very closely after the English Act. This statute has been adopted in similar terms by all common law provinces.[32] Section 4 of the Uniform Proceedings against the Crown Act, which is similar to s. 1 of the English Act, provided that: "Subject to this Act, a claim against the Crown, that, if this Act had not been passed, might be enforced by petition of right, subject to the grant of a fiat by the Lieutenant Governor, may be enforced as of right by proceedings against the Crown in accordance with this Act, without the grant of a fiat by the Lieutenant Governor." Section 5(1) abolished the rule that "the King can do no wrong" by making the Crown liable as an ordinary person would be in tort, including vicarious liability for torts of Crown servants, liability of a master to his servants, liability "in respect of any breach of the duties attaching to the ownership, occupation, possession or control of property" and liability imposed by or under any statute. Section 5(3) made clear that the Crown would be liable even if the Crown servant had acted in an unauthorized fashion while carrying out the duties assigned to him. "Where a function is conferred or imposed upon an officer of the Crown as such, either by any rule of the common law or by statute, and that officer commits a tort in the course of performing or purporting to perform that function, the liability of the Crown in respect of the tort is such as it would have been if that function had been conferred or imposed solely by virtue of instructions lawfully given by the Crown." Subject to certain limitations stated therein, ss. 4 and 5 of the Uniform Act eliminated Crown immunity from suit. Where action could previously be initiated only by petition of right, that is, where Crown property was directly involved, no petition would be required. Where the Crown could not be sued at all, that is, for liability in tort, it could now be sued in an ordinary action.

Central Mortgage & Housing Corp., [1950] S.C.R. 513, [1950] 3 D.L.R. 801; *Government Companies Operation Act*, S.C. 1946, c. 24, am. 1950, c. 51, s. 13 [now R.S.C. 1970, c. G-7].

[30]*Supra*, note 23.

[31][1950] *Proceedings of Conference of Commissioners on Uniformity of Legislation in Canada* (hereinafter cited as Uniform Act), at 76. See also 1962 Consolidation, p. 244.

[32]*Proceedings Against the Crown Act*, R.S.A. 1980, c. P-18; *Crown Proceeding Act*, R.S.B.C. 1979, c. 86 as amended; *Proceedings Against the Crown Act*, R.S.M. 1970, c. P-140 as amended; *Proceedings Against the Crown Act*, R.S.N.B. 1973, c. P-18 as amended; *Proceedings Against the Crown Act*, S.N. 1973, c. 59 as amended; *Proceedings Against the Crown Act*, R.S.N.S. 1967, c. 239; *Proceedings Against the Crown Act*, R.S.O. 1980, c. 393 as amended; *Crown Proceedings Act*, R.S.P.E.I. 1974, c. C-31 as amended; *Proceedings Against the Crown Act*, R.S.S. 1978, c. P-27 as amended.

These changes effected by the Uniform Act are of considerable importance for constitutional litigation. A citizen wishing to sue the Crown in right of a province for recovery of property or for damages in tort may well allege that Crown title is defective because it is based on an *ultra vires* statute, or that acts by Crown officers causing damage to him were committed under invalid legislation. Courts were sometimes precluded in such cases from dealing with the constitutional point because of the immunity of the Crown from the action itself. No such situation need now arise due to the adoption by the provinces of the Uniform Act. The Act does in certain cases limit particular remedies against the provincial Crown. No injunction may be given against the Crown[33] or an officer of the Crown,[34] nor may an order for the recovery of land or the delivery of property be made against the Crown or its officers.[35] In each case, however, the court is permitted in lieu of such orders to make a declaratory order as to respective rights. Rights, including constitutional rights, may thus be adjudicated though certain remedies are precluded.

Quebec achieved a similar result in its revised *Code of Civil Procedure*.[36] Article 94, as amended, provides that

> 94. Any person having a claim to exercise against the Crown, whether it be a revendication of moveable or immoveable property, or a claim for the payment of moneys on an alleged contract, or for damages, or otherwise, may exercise it in the same manner as if it were a claim against a person of full age and capacity, subject only to the provisions of this chapter.

Article 94.2 provides that:

> 94.2 No extraordinary recourse or provisional remedy lies against the Crown.

But, unlike the position in the common law provinces adopting the Uniform Act where the injunction is not available against the Crown, this apparently does not prevent such an injunction where the Crown would allegedly be acting contrary to the constitution.[37] Article 94.9 makes execution procedures inapplicable to the Crown.

---

[33]Section 16(2).

[34]Section 16(4). The "Crown" referred to in the provincial statutes is of course the Crown in right of the respective province.

[35]Section 16(3) and (4). See s. 21 of the *Crown Proceedings Act, 1947, supra*, note 23, for comparable provisions in England.

[36]R.S.Q. 1977, c. C-25 as amended.

[37]*Société Asbestos Ltée v. Société Nationale de l'amiante*, [1979] C.A. 342; folld in *Lavigne v. P.G. du Québec*, [1980] C.S. 318; distd in *P.G. du Québec v. Laurendeau*, [1985] C.A. 494 at 498.

At the federal level the immunity of the Crown in right of Canada has been similarly reduced. The first federal *Petition of Right Act* passed in 1875 in effect adopted the same rules as those obtaining in England under the *Petition of Right Act* of 1860 and the common law.[38] Twelve years later a modification of those rules began in Canada with the passage of an amendment to the *Supreme and Exchequer Courts Act* giving the Exchequer Court jurisdiction in certain tort actions against the Crown. While the jurisdiction was at first quite limited, applying only in cases of claims arising out of "death or injury to the person or to property . . . upon any public work" resulting from the negligence of a Crown officer or servant acting within the scope of his employment, it did represent one of the earliest exceptions in the Empire to the rule that "the king can do no wrong". This jurisdiction was gradually widened so that after 1938 the court had jurisdiction over claims arising out of such death or injury through negligence whether or not it occurred in connection with a "public work".[39]

It had been necessary, of course, to use petition of right procedure for such tort actions against the Crown and to obtain the fiat of the Governor General consenting to the action. The Governor General had an unfettered discretion to refuse his fiat.[40] This obstacle was eliminated in 1951 by an amendment to the *Petition of Right Act* abolishing the requirement of the Governor General's fiat, with respect either to a claim or counter claim against the Crown.[41] But the petition of right, without need for a fiat, continued to be the means for commencement of an action until 1971 when this special procedure was also eliminated.[42]

Shortly after the elimination of the procedural need for consent, the substantive liability of the Crown federal was enlarged by the enactment of the *Crown Liability Act*[43] in 1953. The most important provision therein is s. 3 which provides in part:

> 3(1) The Crown is liable in tort for the damages for which, if it were a private person of full age and capacity, it would be liable

---

[38]S.C. 1875, c. 12. See *R. v. McFarlane* (1882), 7 S.C.R. 216; *R. v. McLeod* (1882), 8 S.C.R. 1.

[39]See S.C. 1917, c. 23, s. 2; R.S.C. 1927, c. 34, s. 19(1)(*c*); S.C. 1938, c. 28, s. 1; R.S.C., 1952, c. 98, s. 18(1)(*c*). Another important extension of liability was effected by S.C. 1943–44, c. 25 making members of the armed forces "servants of the Crown" for the purpose of imposing vicarious liability on the Crown in actions under the *Exchequer Court Act.*

[40]*Lovibond v. Gov. Gen. Can.*, [1930] A.C. 717, 144 L.T. 47 (P.C.).

[41]S.C. 1951 (1st Sess.), c. 33, s. 1. See *R. v. Pfinder*, [1959] Ex. C.R. 30.

[42]S.C. 1970–71–72, c. 1, s. 64 [see R.S.C. 1970, c. 10 (2nd Supp.)].

[43]1952–53, c. 30, see now R.S.C. 1970, c. C-38.

(*a*) in respect of a tort committed by a servant of the Crown, or

(*b*) in respect of a breach of duty attaching to the ownership, occupation, possession or control of property.

Paragraph (*b*) of s-s. (1) extended the scope of Crown liability by making the Crown liable as an owner and occupier of property instead of merely vicariously liable for the negligence of its servants, although the practical results of this change may not have been significant.[44] Paragraph (*a*), however, substantially extended Crown liability in tort. The latter had previously been confined by the *Exchequer Court Act*[45] to a "claim against the Crown arising out of any death or injury to the person or to property resulting from the negligence of any officer or servant of the Crown while acting within the scope of his duties or employment". The 1953 Act for the first time made the Crown in right of Canada generally liable in tort.[46] It also enabled a claimant to sue in the provincial courts in tort where small amounts are involved.[47]

The net effect of these developments is that the Crown in right of Canada now enjoys practically no immunity from suit. It would therefore not be possible for the Government of Canada to avoid, as it has on at least one occasion[48] in the past, the judicial review of Parliament's legislation through a refusal to grant a fiat. The citizen now can, without obstruction, sue the Crown in tort, contract, or for the enforcement of property rights and in the process challenge the validity of legislation under which the Crown acts or intends to act.

C. JUDICIAL MODIFICATION

While Crown immunity has thus been eliminated by statute within the federal and provincial jurisdictions, judicial decisions have in the

---

[44]Through its liability for the negligence of Crown servants the Crown had been made answerable for the condition of its property. See *e.g. R. v. Canada Steamship Lines Ltd.*, [1927] S.C.R. 68, [1927] 1 D.L.R. 991; *Johnson v. The King*, [1931] Ex. C.R. 163; *Farthing v. The King*, [1948] Ex. C.R. 134, [1948] 1 D.L.R. 385; *Grossman v. The Queen*, [1952] 1 S.C.R. 571, [1952] 2 D.L.R. 241.

[45]R.S.C. 1952, c. 98, s. 18(1)(*c*).

[46]For the significance of this change see *Magda v. The Queen*, [1964] S.C.R. 72 at 76–78, 42 D.L.R. (2d) 330 at 334–35.

[47]R.S.C. 1970, c. C-38, ss. 8 [re-en. 1981, c. 47, s. 11], 9, 10, 11 [re-en. R.S.C. 1970, c 10 (2nd Supp.), s. 65], 12, 13, 14.

[48]See *Lovibond v. Gov. Gen. Can.*, [1930] A.C. 717, 144 L.T. 47 (P.C.) and *Lovibond v. Grand Trunk Ry.*, [1936] 2 All E.R. 495, [1936] 2 W.W.R. 298, [1936] 3 D.L.R. 449, 45 C.R.C. 162 (P.C.).

meantime also virtually eliminated its effects on judicial review. A review of a few leading Canadian authorities will indicate the extent of this judicial development.

In the first of these cases, *Lovibond v. Grand Trunk Ry.*,[49] the Judicial Committee of the Privy Council in 1936 held Crown immunity to be an obstacle to claims based on the alleged invalidity of federal statutes. By means of various federal statutes and orders in council passed thereunder the Minister of Finance had become owner in trust for the Crown of certain stock in the Grand Trunk Railway. This stock had been taken compulsorily from its former holders in 1923 and the Grand Trunk had been merged with another line to form the new Canadian National Railway. In 1929 the plaintiff, Lovibond, who as a stockholder had been deprived of his stock in this manner, presented a petition of right to seek a declaration that the stock was still legally vested in the previous holders on the grounds that the various Acts of Parliament and orders in council were *ultra vires*. The Governor General's fiat was refused and the Privy Council refused to review the Governor General's decision.[50] Lovibond then obtained transfers of certain Grand Trunk shares from some of the previous stockholders and sought to be registered as the new holder. The Grand Trunk and Canadian National officers refused to so register him. He then commenced action against the Grand Trunk, the Canadian National, and the Attorney General of Canada seeking three types of relief. First, he sought declarations that the various statutes, together with the orders in council and agreements made thereunder, were *ultra vires* the Parliament and Government of Canada. Secondly, he sought other declarations that his old stock had not been validly transferred to the minister and an order against the railways requiring them to rectify the stock register of the Grand Trunk so as to show him as owner of this stock and of the new stock recently transferred to him. Thirdly, he sought damages against the railways, as an alternative remedy, for failure to restore his name as stockholder or to register him as owner of the stock newly transferred to him.

The Privy Council held that the second type of relief could not be had without petition of right.[51] The effect of such declarations and orders would be to take stock away from the Minister of Finance, who was trustee for the Crown. The Crown would thus be deprived of its beneficial interest in property and this could only be done by petition of right. With respect to the declarations sought, it was held that these were "sought as foundations upon which to base the claims to have the names of the old holders of the junior stock restored as such to the register of the

---

[49]*Lovibond v. Gov. Gen. of Canada, supra*, note 48.

[50]*Lovibond v. Gov. Gen. of Canada, supra*, note 48.

[51]*Supra*, note 48 at pp. 310–11 W.W.R., pp. 459–60 D.L.R.

Grand Trunk: in other words they are ancillary to the claims which can only be the subject of a petition of right. The action cannot be allowed to proceed in regard to them''.[52] As the Attorney General was sued only with respect to these declarations, it was held that he was no longer a party. The Privy Council did find, however, that the action for damages could proceed without petition of right. This claim was against the railway companies, not the Crown. Lord Russell of Killowen said that it could proceed because the relief sought would not involve the Crown as a party nor would the Crown be deprived of its interest in property by an award of damages against the railway companies. It was immaterial that the basis for claiming damages might be the alleged invalidity of various statutes and orders in council.[53]

This decision made Crown immunity from suit a formidable obstacle to judicial supervision of constitutional limitations. From his earlier experience it was clear to the plaintiff here that a fiat would probably not be granted to him in a petition of right procedure. He was thus effectively barred from asserting against the Crown, the new beneficial owner of his property, a claim to that property based on the unconstitutionality of the Crown's title. In this case he might have obtained some relief through the recovery of damages from the railway companies, but one can imagine situations where there might not be any such convenient defendants against whom the constitutional claim could be urged. If, for example, the Crown had, under similar legislation, seized real property from him directly without intervention or assistance of other agencies, he might well be barred from all action. Even in the circumstances of the *Lovibond* case, of course, the plaintiff could never recover his property no matter how invalid the Crown title. He would have to settle for damages instead.

The *Lovibond* case was criticized at the time by Mr. F.A. Brewin, writing in the *Canadian Bar Review*.[54] He suggested that the principles of Crown immunity should be modified in a federal state where both legislative and executive powers are limited by the constitution. In his view, the Crown prerogative to refuse to permit actions involving Crown title to property ought not to extend to cases where that title was being attacked on constitutional grounds. The decision has, however, been followed in Canada in a constitutional dispute[55] and has never been expressly repudiated by any Canadian court.

---

[52]*Supra*, note 48 at p. 312 W.W.R., p. 461 D.L.R.

[53]*Supra*, note 48 at pp. 311–12 W.W.R., pp. 460–61 D.L.R. The damage action subsequently failed on substantive grounds, *sub nom. Lovibond v. Grand Trunk Ry. Co.*, [1939] O.R. 305, [1939] 2 D.L.R. 562, 50 C.R.T.C. 124 (C.A.).

[54]"Comment'' (1936), 14 *Can. Bar Rev.* 621.

[55]*Royal Trust Co. v. A.G. Alta.*, [1936] 2 W.W.R. 337, [1936] 4 D.L.R. 98 (Alta. S.C.).

Before leaving the *Lovibond* case it is interesting to note that the trial judge whose decision[56] the Privy Council affirmed in part was Mr. Justice Kerwin of the Ontario High Court. He had held that no part of the action, not even the claims for damages against the railways, could proceed without petition of right. The Privy Council agreed in part but felt that he had defined Crown immunity too broadly. Mr. Justice Kerwin was appointed in 1935 to the Supreme Court of Canada and was an important figure in the next leading case on this subject now to be discussed.

In *British Columbia Power Corp. v. British Columbia Electric Co.*[57] the Supreme Court of Canada was faced with a similar problem with respect to the effect of Crown immunity on actions challenging constitutional validity of legislation. B.C. Electric was a provincially incorporated company the shares of which were wholly owned by B.C. Power, a federally incorporated company. The British Columbia Legislature passed the *Power Development Act, 1961,*[58] which purported to vest all of the shares of B.C. Electric in the Crown in right of the province. The company was also declared to be an agent of the Crown. Compensation was fixed in a manner unsatisfactory to B.C. Power. At that time and for some years after, the immunity of the Crown provincial had not been abolished in British Columbia. B.C. Power attempted to commence action against the Crown in September 1961 by petition of right to claim additional compensation. A fiat was refused.

In November 1961, B.C. Power commenced an action without petition of right against B.C. Electric, the Attorney General of British Columbia, and others. As later amended, the claim of the plaintiff sought, *inter alia*, various declarations as to the invalidity of the *Power Development Act*. The legislation was attacked on the grounds that it ''sterilized'' a federally incorporated company, that B.C. Electric was an undertaking connecting the province with other provinces and with the United States and thus beyond provincial jurisdiction, that there was a denial of ''due process of law'', and that it would frustrate the Columbia River Treaty, a matter of federal concern.

At the end of March 1962 the Legislature passed two further acts with respect to the B.C. Electric takeover. The *Power Development Act, 1961*, was amended[59] to increase the compensation for B.C. Electric shares, which compensation was not to be open to question in any court. Section 5 of the amending Act provided that the meaning or effect of the Act as amended should not be reviewable by a court except through

---

[56][1933] O.R. at 741, [1933] 1 D.L.R. 798, 40 C.R.C. 337 (H.C.).
[57][1962] S.C.R. 642, 38 W.W.R. 701, 34 D.L.R. (2d) 196.
[58]S.B.C. 1961, 2nd Sess., c. 4.
[59]S.B.C. 1962, c. 50.

petition of right proceedings. The other statute enacted at this time was the *British Columbia Hydro and Power Authority Act, 1962.*[60] It created the Authority by merger of B.C. Electric and the British Columbia Power Commission. The new Authority was made the owner of all the assets of B.C. Electric and was declared to be an agent of the Crown in right of the province.

Meanwhile, in interlocutory proceedings in its action, the plaintiff B.C. Power Corporation applied for and obtained an order appointing a receiver and manager of the undertaking, property, and interests of the B.C. Electric Company pending the trial of the action. This order was appealed and was set aside by the Court of Appeal. B.C. Power appealed the latter decision and in this manner brought the case before the Supreme Court of Canada.

While the Attorney General of British Columbia did not contend that a court could not review the validity of these Acts in some proceeding, he took the position that a receivership order could not be made pending determination of the constitutional issue. It was argued that such an order would directly affect the estate of the Crown. If the court appointed a receiver of the assets, the Crown would be barred from exercising its rights as sole shareholder to bring about a merger of these assets into the new Hydro Authority. The *Power Development Act* had also made B.C. Electric an agent of the Crown, and it was contended that B.C. Electric's assets were those of the Crown held by its agent. Thus no such order could be made except through petition of right procedure.[61] The respondent Hydro and Power Authority took much the same position, citing, *inter alia*, the *Dyson* and *Lovibond* cases.[62]

The appellant B.C. Power put forward four main arguments on this aspect of the jurisdiction of the court to make the order appointing a receiver. First, it was asserted that whatever the position of the Crown prerogative of immunity from suit might be in England, the prerogative was necessarily limited in Canada. The Privy Council decision of *Bonanza Creek Gold Mining Co. v. The King*[63] was cited wherein it was held that the Crown prerogative had by implication been divided among the federal and provincial executives in a manner correlative to the distribution of legislative powers.[64] Secondly, on the assumption that the court had jurisdiction to decide as to the constitutional validity of the statutes in question, the order appointing a receiver was said to be necessarily incidental

---

[60]S.B.C. 1962, c. 8.

[61]Factum of the Attorney General of B.C., at pp. 3–5.

[62]Factum of the B.C. Hydro & Power Authority, at pp. 6–7.

[63][1916] 1 A.C. 566 at 579–80, 586–87, [1916–17] All E.R. Rep. 999, 26 D.L.R. 273, 10 W.W.R. 391, 34 W.L.R. 177, 25 Que. K.B. 170 (P.C.).

[64]Appellant's factum, at p. 10.

to jurisdiction. It was suggested that otherwise a declaration of invalidity could "be meaningless if in the meantime the Legislature has been able to achieve by indirect means its illegal object".[65] An analogy was drawn with cases where an interim injunction had been granted against Crown officers pending trial of a constitutional dispute. Thirdly, it was argued that the order would not directly affect the rights of the Crown and therefore, on an analogy with the *Dyson* case, the court could make such an order without petition of right. It was contended that the only right of the Crown here was the right to appoint directors of B.C. Electric, which right was not interfered with even though effective power of the directors might be curtailed by the appointment of a receiver.[66] Fourthly, and in the alternative, it was urged that even if the order would directly affect the rights of the Crown, these were rights arising under a statute the validity of which was under attack. Further reference was made to the limited nature of the Crown prerogative in a federal state as interpreted by the *Bonanza* case, and to cases where interim injunctions had been issued against Crown officers pending the trial of actions involving constitutional issues.[67]

Chief Justice Kerwin, on behalf of the majority, disposed of these detailed and substantial arguments in summary fashion. After referring very briefly to the contentions of the Attorney General, he made this pronouncement.

In a federal system, where legislative authority is divided, as are also the prerogatives of the Crown, as between the Dominion and Provinces, it is my view that it is not open to the Crown, either in right of Canada or of a Province, to claim a Crown immunity based upon an interest in certain property, where its very interest in that property depends completely and solely on the validity of the legislation which it has itself passed, if there is a reasonable doubt as to whether such legislation is constitutionally valid. To permit it to do so would be to enable it, by the assertion of rights claimed under legislation which is beyond its powers, to achieve the same results as if the legislation were valid. In a federal system it appears to me that, in such circumstances, the Court has the same jurisdiction to preserve assets whose title is dependent on the validity of the legislation as it has to determine the validity of the legislation itself.[68]

No other reference was made to the arguments or to the cases cited. Five judges concurred with the Chief Justice, and Mr. Justice Abbott alone dissented.

---

[65]*Ibid.*, at p. 11.
[66]*Ibid.*, at pp. 13–14.
[67]*Ibid.*, at pp. 14–16.
[68]*Supra*, note 57, at pp. 644–45 S.C.R., pp. 275–76 D.L.R.

This decision is remarkable more for what it omits than what it says. How did the court avoid the inhibiting influence of the Privy Council's *Lovibond* decision, or the whole line of authority starting with *Dyson* which distinguished between orders directly and indirectly affecting the Crown? Were these decisions repudiated or were they distinguished on the grounds that the receiver order would not directly affect Crown property? Unless the latter represents the true decision it is hard to see how the *Lovibond* cases could be other than a strong precedent against the grant of such relief. It is clear from the factums that *Lovibond* and associated cases were brought to the attention of the court. And one must assume that Chief Justice Kerwin, who had been the trial judge in the *Lovibond* case, must have been fully aware of its implications with respect to the order sought by B.C. Power.

It might be argued that the Supreme Court's decision was of limited scope and not an abandonment of common law principles of Crown immunity. While the court did not say so, the order appointing a receiver need not necessarily have been construed as an interference with Crown property in the sense that the Crown would be permanently divested of its interest or title. An order made *pendente lite* for the preservation of the *status quo* would be much less serious in its effects than a declaration as sought in the *Lovibond* case that the Crown never had, and should no longer assert, an interest as *cestui que trust* in the shares of a railway company.

Given its later applications, however, it now appears that the implications of the *B.C. Power* case were much wider than this. It should first be noted that Chief Justice Kerwin stated his opinion very broadly when he said that "it is not open to the Crown, either in right of Canada or of a Province, to claim a Crown immunity based upon an interest in certain property" where the existence of that interest depends on the validity of impugned legislation. This is the clearest and broadest possible denial of Crown immunity from property actions. From this it would appear that in such circumstances even a direct attack on Crown title could be entertained by a court without petition of right. Apart from this, while the order in question in the *B.C. Power* case was of limited effect it was still a direct interference with Crown property interests. By the *Power Development Act, 1961*, B.C. Electric had been made an agent of the Crown and by the *British Columbia Hydro and Power Authority Act* its assets were transferred to the authority which was in turn declared to be an agent of the Crown. As a result, the assets of B.C. Electric, itself an agent of the Crown, transferred to another agent of the Crown, were surely Crown assets being held for the Crown by its agent. The interference with Crown property interests was at least as clear here as in the *Lovibond* case where shares were by statute vested in the name of the Minister of Finance as trustee for the Crown. While the Crown would not be permanently deprived of title to its property by an order appointing a receiver of that property, it would certainly be deprived of many of the incidents of title, such as the exclusive right of use, possession, and disposition, for a substantial period of time.[69]

A later decision of the Supreme Court, *Amax Potash Ltd. v. Govt. of Sask.*[70] cited with approval the *B.C. Power* case and further limited the applicability of Crown immunity as a barrier to enforcement of the constitution. This case, which has been discussed at length earlier,[71] involved the validity of s-s. 5(7) of the *Proceedings Against the Crown Act* of Saskatchewan[72] which, it will be recalled, provides as follows.

> 5(7) No proceedings lie against the Crown under this or any other section of this Act in respect of anything heretofore or hereafter done or omitted and purporting to have been done or omitted in the exercise of a power or authority under a statute or a statutory provision purporting to confer or to have conferred on the Crown such power or authority, which statute or statutory provision is or was or may be beyond the legislative jurisdiction of the Legislature; and no action shall be brought against any person for any act or thing heretofore or hereafter done or omitted by him under the supposed authority of such statute or statutory provision, or of any proclamation, order in council or regulation made thereunder, provided such action would not lie against him if the said statute, statutory provision, proclamation, order in council or regulation is or had been or may be within the jurisdiction of the Legislature enacting or the Lieutenant Governor making the same.

The action in question was for a declaration that a tax imposed by the provincial Legislature was constitutionally invalid and for recovery of money paid in payment of such tax. The Government of Saskatchewan relied on s-s. 5(7) as a defence to the claim for repayment and to any interim order with respect to the money pending trial of the action. The province argued that this subsection dealt with a form of Crown immunity and therefore was within the legislative authority of the province as being in relation to the amendment of the provincial constitution, property and civil rights, administration of justice, or matters of a local or private nature.[73]

The Supreme Court was not willing, however, to characterize

---

[69]The order appointing a receiver was made on March 22, 1962. The decision of the trial judge in the action was not handed down until July 29, 1963, reported in 44 W.W.R. 65 (B.C. S.C.).

[70][1977] 2 S.C.R. 576, [1976] 6 W.W.R. 61, 71 D.L.R. (3d) 1, 11 N.R. 222.

[71]*Supra*, at pp. 103–05.

[72]R.S.S. 1978, c. P-27.

[73]B.N.A. Act, s. 92(1), (13), (14) and (16).

s-s. 5(7) of the *Proceedings Against the Crown Act* as legislation in respect of Crown immunity, but instead regarded it in these circumstances as legislation in relation to taxation: that is, as applied to the recovery of a tax invalidly imposed, it would take on the constitutional colouration of the tax and not be validly operative to bar recovery.

The decision then is of more interest in the present context not for its setting aside of Crown immunity but rather for its view of what is or is not genuine Crown immunity legislation. It is perhaps significant that there was no such subsection in the original Uniform Proceedings against the Crown Act now adopted in substance by all the provinces;[74] this subsection was added by Saskatchewan to its Act in 1956.[75] Dickson J., in his judgment on behalf of the court specifically observed that the subsection "is unique among provincial Crown liability Acts".[76] The importance of this is that such a purported immunity was not perceived as being part of the traditional common law protection from suit for the Crown. The Uniform Act, and the *Proceedings Against the Crown Act* of Saskatchewan based on it, generally abolished other forms of immunity, but in this respect Saskatchewan was trying to create an immunity which it was not certain would otherwise be found to exist. These factors probably influenced the court in characterizing the subsection as being in relation to the attempted validation of an otherwise possibly invalid tax, rather than as being in relation to Crown immunity.

The result of the *Amax* case closely parallels the *B.C. Power* case even though its rationale is different. That is, it prevented the concept of Crown immunity from being applied to prevent an action for enforcement of the constitution. And its articulation of the basic right of judicial review echoes that of the earlier case.

> . . . if either the federal Parliament or a provincial Legislature can tax beyond the limit of its powers, and by prior or *ex post facto* legislation give itself immunity from such illegal act, it could readily place itself in the same position as if the act had been done within proper constitutional limits.[77]

While the *Amax* case appeared to leave open the possibility of some limitation of judicial review through legislative or administrative decisions genuinely made in protection of traditional Crown immunities, that possibility seems to have been eliminated also in the Supreme Court decision

---

[74]Discussed, *supra*, notes 31–37 and accompanying text.
[75]S.S. 1956, c. 15.
[76]*Supra*, note 70 at p. 582 S.C.R., p. 4 D.L.R.
[77]*Supra*, note 70 at p. 590 S.C.R., p. 10 D.L.R.

in *Air Canada v. A.G. B.C.*[78] There the Lieutenant Governor of British Columbia had refused, on the advice of the Executive Council, to grant a fiat allowing Air Canada to sue the provincial government for the recovery of certain allegedly invalid taxes paid prior to August 1, 1974. (It was on this date that the need for a petition of right was abolished in British Columbia, the last province to do so). In a short statement of reasons issued on behalf of the court by LaForest J., reference was made to the *B.C. Power* and the *Amax* cases. Relying on these, the court went further in saying that where the issue was alleged invalidity of a tax law, a refusal by the Lieutenant Governor to issue a fiat was not constitutionally permissible. To remedy the situation the court ordered the provincial Attorney General to advise the Lieutenant Governor to issue the fiat. It thus avoided the difficult question of whether the personal representative of the Crown could be ordered to exercise his prerogative in a certain way. But it did not attempt to distinguish or explain away earlier cases such as *Orpen*[79] or *Lovibond v. Gov. Gen. of Canada*[80] which had long since held that the refusal of the Crown and its advisers to issue a fiat could not be reviewed by the courts.

Together these decisions present a formidable obstacle to any future use of Crown immunities, whether revived from their present state of legislative supression or extended legislatively beyond their traditional scope, to prevent enforcement of the constitution.[81] Although they all involved distribution of powers issues, they probably apply equally to any attempted use of Crown immunity to escape judicial enforcement of Charter guarantees as well. In *Amax* the Supreme Court prefaced its conclusions with the affirmation that

> it is the high duty of this Court to insure that the Legislatures do not transgress the limits of their constitutional mandate and engage in the illegal exercise of power.[82]

This provides an equally valid rationale for characterising attempts similarly to preclude judicial review of Charter infringements as direct abridgement of the rights or freedoms in question and thus invalid.

---

[78][1986] 2 S.C.R. 539.
[79]*Supra*, note 5.
[80]*Supra*, note 48.
[81]See, *e.g.*, *Société Asbestos Ltée v. Société National de l'Amiante*, [1979] C.A. 342; *Lavigne v. P.G. du Québec*, [1980] C.S. 318; *Ominayak et al. v. Norcen Energy Resources Ltd. et al.* (1982), 23 Alta. L.R. (2d) 284 (Q.B.).
[82]*Supra*, note 70, at 590.

D. CONCLUSION

It might be thought that, with the adoption during the last decade of legislation abolishing Crown immunity in those remaining jurisdictions where it had still survived, its relevance to judicial review had vanished. It must be kept in mind, however, that some vestiges of immunity do continue in the kind of remedies that may be sought against the Crown. Moreover, it is always open to the Legislature which abolished Crown immunities to re-enact them in their original or perhaps an extended form.

It is therefore important that the Supreme Court has firmly established constitutional limits for the application of Crown immunities, existing or future: namely that they cannot be invoked in such a way as to allow Legislatures or Governments to achieve results otherwise denied to them by the constitution. This is an eminently sensible result in a country with a written constitution imposing limits on the powers of Governments and Legislatures.

It may be noted in passing that the immunity rule was an anomaly even in England. It had been accepted there for over three centuries that the courts were in other cases entitled to review the legality of the exercise of the prerogative, though not the manner in which it was exercised. That is, the courts could ascertain whether the Crown was acting within the legal limits of prerogative power.[83] Unlike the legislative power of Parliament, the prerogative power was limited by statute and by judicial decision so that there were grounds for the exercise of judicial review in the maintenance of these limitations.[84] But immunity from suit where the Crown's claim to property was directly attacked precluded review of the exercise of the prerogative in such cases. It is little wonder that the rule was abolished in England by the *Crown Proceedings Act, 1947*. The decisions of the Supreme Court of Canada modifying the rule in a country of divided legislative powers were long overdue.

Where Crown immunity was formerly a bar to suit, it could constitute an obstacle to effective judicial review of the validity of governmental action. That obstacle has now been eliminated, by statute in all jurisdictions and by authoritative judicial decisions which preclude its revival. Thus neither Government nor Legislature can prevent judicial scrutiny by raising the shield of Crown immunity. In the struggle between judicial review and the prerogative of Crown immunity, judicial review emerged supreme.

---

[83]See Heuston, *Essays in Constitutional Law*, 2nd ed. (1964), at 58–81.

[84]More recent developments indicate that even decisions under the prerogative can be reviewed for Charter purposes not only as to jurisdiction but also, in certain respects, as to content or procedure: see, *e.g., Operation Dismantle Inc. et al. v. The Queen et al.*, [1985] 1 S.C.R. 441.

Chapter 5

Judicial Review and the Separation of Powers

In considering the propriety or the legality of Canadian courts giving decisions on questions of constitutional validity, it is essential to keep in mind that they are not restricted by any concept of separation of powers. Canadian courts have not been confined to a purely "judicial" role in such a manner as to prevent them from exercising, even with legislative sanction, a non-judicial function in the rendering of constitutional opinions. In this respect their position differs from that of the courts of the United States and Australia.

It has been held that there is no constitutional separation of powers at either the provincial or the federal level in Canada. Thus the delegation by Legislature[1] or Parliament[2] of part of its law-making power to executive or other agencies has been upheld.[3] It is also apparent that the executive branch of Government can exercise judicial functions on occasion, subject to the requirement that the members of any agency exercising functions analogous to a Superior, District, or County Court must, by virtue of s. 96 of the B.N.A. 1867, be appointed by the Governor General.[4]

It has also been held that the courts may perform non-judicial as well as judicial functions. The leading decisions in this field arose out of disputes over the use of the power given to the Governor in Council or the Lieutenant Governor in Council to refer constitutional questions to federal and provincial courts respectively. In *A.G. Ont. v. A.G. Can.*,[5]

---

[1] *Hodge v. The Queen* (1883), 9 App. Cas. 117, 50 L.T. 301 (P.C.).
[2] *Re Gray*, 57 S.C.R. 150, [1918] 3 W.W.R. 111, 42 D.L.R. 1; *Reference re Regulations in Relation to Chemicals*, [1943] S.C.R. 1, [1943] 1 D.L.R. 248, 79 C.C.C. 1.
[3] The opposite has been held in the United States on occasion. See, *e.g.*, *Panama Refining Co. v. Ryan*, 293 U.S. 388 (1935); *Schechter Poultry Corp. v. U.S.*, 295 U.S. 495 (1935).
[4] *Labour Relations Board for Sask. v. John East Iron Works Ltd.*, [1949] A.C. 134, [1948] 2 W.W.R. 1055, [1948] 4 D.L.R. 673 (P.C.); *Farrell v. Workmen's Compensation Board*, [1962] S.C.R. 48 at 52, 37 W.W.R. 39, 31 D.L.R. (2d) 177 at 180–81, *Brooks v. Pavlick*, [1964] S.C.R. 108, 42 D.L.R. (2d) 572, *Reference re Residential Tenancies Act*, [1981] 1 S.C.R. 714, 123 D.L.R. (3d) 554, 37 N.R. 158; *Crevier v. A.G. Qué. et al.*, [1981] 2 S.C.R. 220, 127 D.L.R. (3d) 1. See also, *supra*, at pp. 89–92.
[5] [1912] A.C. 571, 3 D.L.R. 509 (P.C.).

the Governor General, acting pursuant to the *Supreme Court Act*,[6] had referred to the Supreme Court of Canada some questions of law involving the extent of the provincial power with respect to the incorporation of companies. Several provinces intervened to object to such a reference, asserting that the provision for references in the Supreme Court Act was *ultra vires*. The Supreme Court, in a split decision, rejected this contention. When the matter came on appeal to the Privy Council the provinces argued, *inter alia*, that Parliament had no power to require the Supreme Court to perform non-judicial functions. It was said that s. 101 of the B.N.A. Act, in empowering Parliament to create a "Court of Appeal", required the court so established to be a truly judicial body. The giving of opinions on questions of law was characterized as an executive function not suitable for a genuine court.

Earl Loreburn L.C., in his judgment for the Judicial Committee, started with the premise that collectively the powers given to the dominion and the provinces "cover the whole area of self-government within the whole area of Canada".[7] The implication was clear that, except for the limitations imposed by the division of powers between dominion and province, and except for any other clear limitations in the B.N.A. Act on legislative power, it was open to Parliament and the Legislatures to distribute governmental power within their own spheres in such manner as they chose. The question then remaining was, did s. 101, with its reference to a "Court of Appeal", constitute such a clear limitation as to preclude the creation of a body which might be obliged to perform an advisory function? Lord Loreburn felt that it did not. He seems to have been particularly impressed by the fact that other courts more familiar to him had been required to perform the same function. The Judicial Committee of the Privy Council was itself given this duty in its original Act.[8] It was also noted that the judges of the superior courts in England had in some cases answered questions referred to them by the House of Lords,[9] though Lord Loreburn felt that practice to be somewhat distinguishable as in that situation the questions arose out of pending litigation. But he

---

[6]R.S.C. 1906, c. 139, s. 60, which provided in part: "Important questions of law or fact touching (*a*) the interpretation of the British North America Acts, 1867 to 1886; or (*b*) the constitutionality or interpretation of any Dominion or provincial legislation . . . may be referred by the Governor in Council to the Supreme Court for hearing and consideration".

[7]*Supra*, note 5 at 581 A.C.

[8]*Judicial Committee Act*, 1833, 3 & 4 Wm. IV, c. 41, s. 4 (U.K.). For an example of the use of the power see *Re Cape Breton* (1846), 5 Moo. P.C.C. 259, 13 E.R. 489; *Re Parliamentary Privilege Act, 1770*, [1958] A.C. 331, [1958] 2 All E.R. 329 (P.C.). The provision in the *Supreme Court Act* seems originally to have been based on this section. *A.G. Ont. v. A.G. Can., supra*, note 5, at pp. 577 and 585 A.C.

[9]See, *e.g.*, *Re Westminster Bank* (1834), 2 Cl. & F. 191, 6 E.R. 1127, *M'Naghten's Case* (1843), 10 Cl. & F. 200, 8 E.R. 718.

thought it significant that the Privy Council had in numerous appeals from Canada dealt with reference cases, and this without any suggestion that such a procedure was subversive of the judicial function. Even many of the provinces which now argued against the validity of references by the federal Government had themselves provided for such references to be made by the provincial Government to a provincial superior court. This also reinforced the view that such a function was not generally considered to make the tribunal exercising it something other than a court.

While the Privy Council thus held that a "court" could be required by statute to answer questions referred to it, the decision indicated that this was definitely not a judicial function. According to Lord Loreburn, "the answers are only advisory and will have no more effect than the opinions of the law officers". The distinction between the adjudicatory function and the advisory function, and the constitutional validity of the latter, were both affirmed again by the Privy Council two years later. Viscount Haldane made some general comments on the reference procedure.[10]

> It is at times attended with inconveniences, and it is not surprising that the Supreme Court of the United States should have steadily refused to adopt a similar procedure, and should have confined itself to adjudication on the legal rights of litigants in actual controversies. But this refusal is based on the position of that Court in the Constitution of the United States, a position which is different from that of any Canadian Court, or of the Judicial Committee under the statute of William IV. The business of the Supreme Court of Canada is to do what is laid down as its duty by the Dominion Parliament, and the duty of the Judicial Committee, although not bound by any Canadian statute, is to give to it as a Court of review such assistance as is within its power.

With respect to similar powers of reference by provincial Governments to provincial courts, Canadian decisions have been the same. The Supreme Court of Canada originally refused to entertain appeals from provincial courts where the original decision took the form of an opinion on a reference. It was held that the relevant provincial statute itself, by stating that such a decision "shall be deemed a judgment" was an admission that it was not a judgment. In the view of the Supreme Court, "There is no judgment to be appealed from . . . . There is no action, no parties, no controversy perhaps". The Supreme Court had jurisdiction only to entertain appeals from "judgments".[11] It required an amendment[12]

---

[10]*A.G. B.C. v. A.G. Can.*, [1914] A.C. 153 at 162, 5 W.W.R. 878, 15 D.L.R. 308 (P.C.).
[11]*Union Colliery Co. of B.C. v. A.G. B.C.* (1897), 27 S.C.R. 637 at 639.
[12]S.C. 1922, c. 48, s. 1.

to the *Supreme Court Act* before the court would hear appeals from decisions in reference cases. In spite of this clear recognition that the reference procedure was not judicial in nature, the provincial courts nevertheless accepted the obligation to render advisory opinions when asked to do so by the Lieutenant Governor in Council.[13]

It is apparent, therefore, that in the matter of giving advisory opinions the provincial courts and the Supreme Court of Canada do not perform strictly judicial functions. It is equally apparent that there is no constitutional bar to their making decisions on issues not arising out of litigation. They may be required by statute to make such decisions. It is also arguable that, even in the absence of clear statutory direction, they have more discretionary power to accept or reject disputes for decision than have the courts of countries where the separation of powers prevails.

The contrast is quite sharp between the Canadian situation and the situation prevailing in countries such as the United States or Australia.[14] In the United States the constitutional limitation on the federal judicial role is illustrated in *Muskrat v. United States*.[15] Congress, in 1904 and 1906, by statute increased the size of the class entitled to share in the final distribution of lands and funds of the Cherokees. As there were complaints about such legislation from those who had been previously entitled, Congress passed a statute in 1907 permitting certain named persons to bring a class action in the Court of Claims to determine the validity of the 1904 and 1906 legislation. It was specified that the United States should be the defendant, that the Attorney General should defend the suits, and that there should be a right of appeal to the Supreme Court. An action was brought pursuant to the statute and was dismissed in the Court of Claims on the basis that the 1904 and 1906 legislation was valid. On appeal to the Supreme Court, that body held the 1907 statute and the proceedings taken thereunder to be invalid. The court referred to Article III of the Constitution, which in s. 1 confers the "judicial power" on the federal courts established by Congress and in s. 2 defines the "judicial power" as extending to the "cases" and "controversies" specified therein. Relying on various precedents[16] the Supreme Court held that the duty which the 1907 statute purported to cast on the federal courts was not a

---

[13]*Re Order in Council; Re Crop Payments Act*, 36 Man. R. 34, [1926] 2 W.W.R. 844, [1927] 2 D.L.R. 50 (C.A.).

[14]See generally Laskin, "Comparative Constitutional Law — Common Problems: Australia, Canada, United States of America" (1977), 51 *A.L.J.R.* 450.

[15]219 U.S. 346 (1911).

[16]*Hayburn's Case*, 2 Dall. 408 (1792, Cir. Ct.); *U.S. v. Ferreria*, 13 How. 39 (1851, S.C.); *Gordon v. U.S.*, 117 U.S. 697 (1864). Reference was also made to Chief Justice Jay's celebrated answer to President Washington in 1793 in which he stated that it would not be proper for the judges of the Supreme Court to advise the executive branch on legal questions.

judicial duty because it did not involve a case or controversy. "That judicial power, as we have seen, is the right to determine actual controversies arising between adverse litigants, duly instituted in courts of proper jurisdiction".[17] But, under the 1907 statute the purpose of the action "is not to assert a property right as against the Government, or to demand compensation for alleged wrongs. . . . The whole purpose of the law is to determine the constitutional validity of this class of legislation".[18] In other words, the United States had no interest adverse to the plaintiffs, and was a party only to facilitate the determination of the Act's validity. Hence there was no case or controversy. Congress, it was held, could not validly confer on the Court of Claims or the Supreme Court the duty to entertain this type of proceeding.

It is therefore apparent that in the United States the federal courts which are established under Article III of the Constitution must confine themselves to deciding matters which they are prepared to regard as involving a "case" or "controversy".[19] Congress cannot require them to deal with other matters such as the giving of opinions, because to do so would be to force them into non-judicial functions.

Nor, consistently with the separation of powers, can Congress confer certain judicial powers on tribunals not established under Article III.[20]

In Australia the situation is similar. The *Commonwealth of Australia Constitution Act*, s. 71, vests the "judicial power" of the Commonwealth in the High Court and other federal courts created by Parliament. Section 73 sets out the High Court's appellate power, and ss. 75 and 76 confer on it original jurisdiction with respect to certain "matters" therein specified.[21] Parliament in the early part of this century attempted in s. 88 of the *Judiciary Act*[22] to give to the High Court "jurisdiction to hear and determine . . . any question of law as to the validity of any Act or

---

[17]*Supra*, note 15 at p. 361.

[18]*Supra*. See also *Warth v. Seldin*, 422 U.S. 490 (1975).

[19]This is also true in respect of the courts in many states, but not in the courts of those states where the state constitution permits advisory opinions to be given. For the classic criticism of the advisory opinion system, see Frankfurter, "A Note on Advisory Opinions" (1924), 37 *Harv. L. Rev.* 1002. It is arguable that where the state courts are prepared to entertain an action involving the federal law or constitution, the U.S. Supreme Court should be able to treat an appeal from that decision as a "case or controversy" even though a similar action, if commenced in a federal court, would not be regarded as a "case or controversy". See *e.g.* Scharpf, "Judicial Review and the Political Question: A Functional Analysis" (1966), 75 *Yale L.J.* 517 at 521.

[20]See, *e.g.*, *Northern Pipeline Const. Co. v. Marathon Pipe Line Co. and United States* (1982), 458 U.S. 50.

[21]1900, 63 & 64 Vict., c. 12. See generally Lane, *The Australian Federal System*, 2nd ed. (1979), at 1145–47; Howard, *Australian Federal Constitutional Law*, 3rd ed. (Sydney, N.S.W.: Law Book Co., 1985), at 230–82.

[22]*Judiciary Act*, Austl. C. Acts, 1910, c. 10, s. 3.

enactment of the Parliament'' which the Governor General might refer to it. In *Re the Judiciary Act*[23] the High Court rejected this jurisdiction in a case referred to it under the *Judiciary Act* with respect to the validity of the *Navigation Act*, a federal statute. The majority of the court took the view that Parliament was seeking, through this device, to obtain authoritative declarations of the law. They believed that the making of such declarations would be a judicial function. While thus coming to a different conclusion than that of the Canadian and United States courts about the judicial nature of advisory opinions, they nevertheless held that the giving of such opinions would be unconstitutional.[24] The scope of the judicial power of the federal courts was that spelled out in the constitution. As this was an original jurisdiction which the *Judiciary Act* purported to confer, it would have to be brought under s. 75 or s. 76 of the constitution. Section 75 being inapplicable, they considered and rejected s. 76 as a possible source of power. ''[W]e do not think that the word ''matter'' in Section 76 means a legal proceeding, but rather the subject-matter for determination in a legal proceeding. In our opinion there can be no matter within the meaning of the section unless there is some immediate right, duty or liability to be established by the determination of the Court''.[25] They were unable to find anything in the constitution which would authorize Parliament to confer power on the High Court ''to determine abstract questions of law without the right or duty of any body or person being involved.''[26]

While a committee of the Australian Constitutional Convention has recently recommended a constitutional amendment to permit references to the High Court by the Governor-General in Council in certain cases and by the Houses of Parliament in other cases, no such amendment has yet been made.[27]

The contrasting situation in the United States and Australia points up the comparative freedom of the judiciary in Canada. Where it is so provided by the Legislature, Canadian courts have both a right and a duty to exercise the function of deciding issues, even those not raised in the

---

[23](1921), 29 C.L.R. 257.

[24]The assumption that this was a judicial power has since been criticized. It is also now clear that judicial and non-judicial functions may not be given to the same tribunal: *R. v. Kirby, ex parte Boilermakers' Society* (1956), 94 C.L.R. 254. See also Wynes, *Legislative, Executive and Judicial Powers In Australia*, 3rd ed. (1962), at 545–82.

[25]*Supra*, note 23 at p. 265.

[26]*Supra*, note 23 at p. 267.

[27]Australian Constitutional Convention, Standing Committee ''D'' (*Fourth Report to Executive Committee*, Aug. 27, 1982, vol. 1.); discussed in Lumb, ''The Judiciary, the Interpretation of the Constitution and the Australian Constitutional Convention'' (1983), 57 *Aust. L.J.* 229.

course of a real dispute between two or more adverse parties. In the light of this freedom from constitutional restraint, it may be open to Canadian courts to entertain proceedings of various kinds (even in the absence of express legislative sanction) in situations where the United States federal courts would not find a "case" or "controversy" or the Australian federal courts would not be able to identify a "matter" suitable for litigation.

The freedom from textual limitations to a traditional "judicial" function is particularly relevant to the problems of standing and justiciability which will be explored in the two succeeding chapters. These limitations in the United States and Australia have shaped, and been shaped by, the way the courts in those countries view the role of judicial review. This perception is very much affected by rules as to what parties should be allowed to raise constitutional issues and what issues are really appropriate for judicial, as opposed to political, determination. Canadian courts have also had to address these questions but within a different constitutional and statutory framework which has seemingly left them with a wider latitude to enlarge the judicial role; a latitude of which they have increasingly made use in recent times. If this trend continues it could begin to raise questions as to whether there may be good functional, if not constitutional, reasons for a basic separation of powers.

Chapter 6

The Proper Parties to a Constitutional Case

A. STANDING TO RAISE THE CONSTITUTIONAL ISSUE

Where the validity of legislation or administrative action is attacked in ordinary litigation between citizens or between the citizen and the state, such citizens clearly have standing to raise a constitutional issue. In such cases the individual is seeking to assert some right for himself. In the process of establishing this right he contends that legislation or an administrative act which would interfere with it is invalid. This is an incidental and collateral attack on the legislation or act in the process of claiming a right peculiar to the claimant. For present purposes this type of action may be referred to as a "private" action because the constitutional issue is raised solely to assert one's own interests. It might embrace a diversity of proceedings such as an action for damages,[1] for recovery of money,[2] for enforcement of a contract,[3] a prosecution,[4] an

[1] E.g., Murphy v. C.P.R., [1958] S.C.R. 626, 15 D.L.R. (2d) 145, 77 C.R.T.C. 322; Transport Oil Co. v. Imperial Oil Co., [1935] O.R. 215, [1935] 2 D.L.R. 500, 63 C.C.C. 108 (C.A.); Central Canada Potash Co. v. Sask., [1979] 1 S.C.R. 42, [1978] 6 W.W.R. 400, 88 D.L.R. (3d) 609, 23 N.R. 481, 6 C.C.L.T. 265.

[2] E.g., Cairns Const. Ltd. v. Sask., [1960] S.C.R. 619, 35 W.W.R. 241, 24 D.L.R. (2d) 1; Fort Frances Pulp & Paper v. Manitoba Free Press Co., [1923] A.C. 695, [1923] 3 D.L.R. 629 (P.C.); Amax Potash Ltd. v. Sask., [1977] 2 S.C.R. 576, [1976] 6 W.W.R. 61, 71 D.L.R. (3d) 1, 11 N.R. 222.

[3] E.g., John Deere Plow Co. v. Wharton, [1915] A.C. 330, 7 W.W.R. 706, 29 W.L.R. 917, 18 D.L.R. 353 (P.C.); Beauharnois Light, Heat & Power Co. v. Hydro-Electric Power Comm., [1937] O.R. 796, [1937] 3 D.L.R. 458 (C.A.); McNamara Const. (Western) Ltd. v. The Queen, [1977] 2 S.C.R. 654, 75 D.L.R. (3d) 273, 13 N.R. 181 (sub nom. Canada v. McNamara Const. (Western) Ltd.; Canada v. J. Stevenson & Assoc.).

[4] E.g., R. v. Pee-Kay Smallwares Ltd., [1947] O.R. 1019, [1948] 1 D.L.R. 235, 90 C.C.C. 129, 6 C.R. 28 (C.A.); R. v. Campbell, [1964] 2 O.R. 487, 46 D.L.R. (2d) 83, [1964] 3 C.C.C. 112 (C.A.); R. v. Hauser, [1979] 1 S.C.R. 984, 16 A.R. 91, [1979] 5 W.W.R. 1, 98 D.L.R. (3d) 193, 26 N.R. 541, 46 C.C.C. (2d) 481, 8 C.R. (3d) 89; Jack v. The Queen, [1980] 1 S.C.R. 294, [1975] 5 W.W.R. 364, 100 D.L.R. (3d) 193, 28 N.R. 162, 48 C.C.C. (2d) 246; R. v. Big M Drug Mart Ltd., [1985] 1 S.C.R. 295 at 312–14.

action for enforcement of taxes,[5] or a proceeding to review an order of an inferior tribunal.[6] The challenge to validity might be raised as a ground for the claim or as a defence. The feature which these "private" actions have in common is that they involve a matter of particular concern to the party raising the constitutional issue, a right which is peculiar to him and which he can establish only by showing the statute or administrative decision to be of no effect. "Private" actions of this nature create no particular problem for the court because they involve real disputes over rights pertaining to the actual parties.

At the other end of the spectrum are those situations in which an individual challenges legislation or official action on behalf of the public at large. In such cases he does not claim a right peculiar to himself. At best his position is that of a member of the public seeking to have the court enforce the requirements of the constitution. Such proceedings may perhaps best be described as "public" actions.[7]

Between the two polar situations represented by purely "private" actions and purely "public" actions there is a variety of possibilities. There may be situations, for example, in which the person seeking to raise a constitutional point may assert the interest of a class constituting only a portion of the public. Or he may assert some interest which the courts do not recognize as a matter of "right" or "duty", the type of matters with which courts normally deal. In such cases the problem of standing to sue arises just as in the purely "public" action. Attention must therefore be given to all situations involving proceedings other than "private" actions. This is the real problem area with respect to standing in constitutional disputes.

In the United States the federal courts are in principle reluctant to entertain attacks on the validity of legislation or of administrative acts where the plaintiff's claim does not give rise to a "case or controversy". In earlier times, this requirement was quite strictly applied by Article III courts which insisted that the plaintiff be asserting a legal right, rather than some other interest no matter how important, in order to recognize his standing.[8] The more modern formulation is that the plaintiff must

---

[5]*E.g., R. v. Caledonian Collieries Ltd.*, [1928] A.C. 358, [1928] 2 W.W.R. 417, [1928] 3 D.L.R. 657 (P.C.).

[6]*E.g., Labour Relations Bd. for Sask. v. John East Iron Works Ltd.*, [1949] A.C. 134, [1948] 2 W.W.R. 1055, [1948] 4 D.L.R. 673 (P.C.), *Northern Telecom Ltd. v. Communications Workers of Canada*, [1980] 1 S.C.R. 115, 98 D.L.R. (3d) 1, 28 N.R. 107; *Singh et al. v. Min. of Employment and Immigration*, [1985] 1 S.C.R. 177.

[7]See Jaffe, "Standing to Secure Judicial Review: Public Actions" (1961), 74 *Harv. L. Rev.* 1265; Pepin, "L'intérêt à poursuivre en Droit public canadien" (1975), 6 *R. de D.* 4; *Gouriet v. Union of Post Office Workers*, [1978] A.C. 435 at 477, [1977] 3 All E.R. 70 (H.L.).

[8]*E.g., Tennessee Electric Power Co. v. T.V.A.*, 306 U.S. 118 (1939); *Frothingham v. Mellon*, 262 U.S. 447 (1923).

have suffered, or be threatened by, "injury in fact". This has been generally interpreted to include injury to interests such as that of a federal taxpayer in preventing expenditures expressly prohibited by the constitution[9] or of environmentalists in areas used or inhabited by them.[10] It is still believed, however, that Article III of the Constitution does impose some limits on standing, and precludes the federal courts from hearing cases where the plaintiff's only interest is that of the general population in having government act in accordance with the constitution.[11] A further, perhaps discretionary, self-limitation involves the "nexus" requirement, namely that at least in taxpayer's actions the plaintiff's interest must be protected by the constitutional provision sought to be enforced.[12] This test may be based more generally on the separation of powers and the view which the federal courts take of their role *vis-à-vis* the political branches of government. The requirements of Article III and of the general separation of powers explicit in the U.S. Constitution are not necessarily relevant to the Canadian situation.

In Canada the issue of standing has been seen more in functional, rather than constitutional, terms, because the judicial role is not confined by a constitutional separation of powers. There are no general rules of standing applicable to all kinds of proceedings, but instead there are special rules applicable to particular remedies. While the rules for some remedies impose limitations on the right to such judicial review, these limitations have become of much less importance in recent years with the general relaxation by the Supreme Court of Canada of standing requirements in actions for declarations as to constitutional validity. As will be seen, the court has in those actions virtually eliminated any need for an "interest" in the traditional sense, and thus has provided an avenue for judicial review which will probably cause litigants to avoid the use of other remedies where standing might be a problem.

In the past, standing requirements seemed to have served two main

---

[9]*E.g., Flast v. Cohen*, 392 U.S. 83 (1968); and see generally Blake, "Standing to Litigate Constitutional Rights and Freedoms in Canada and the United States" (1984), 16 *Ottawa L. Rev.* 66 at 73–75.

[10]*E.g., United States v. SCRAP*, 412 U.S. 669 (1973); *Duke Power Co. v. Carolina Environmental Study Group, Inc.*, 438 U.S. 59 (1978). *Cf. Islands Protection Soc. v. The Queen in right of B.C.*, 11 B.C.L.R. 372, [1979] 4 W.W.R. 1, 98 D.L.R. (3d) 504 (S.C.).

[11]*E.g., United States v. Richardson*, 418 U.S. 166 (1974); *Schlesinger v. Reservists Committee to Stop the War*, 94 S. Ct. 2925, 418 U.S. 208 (1974); *Simon v. Eastern Kentucky Welfare Rights Organization*, 426 U.S. 26 (1976); *Valley Forge Christian College v. Americans United for Separation of Church and State Inc. et al.*, 454 U.S. 464 (1982); Tribe, *Constitutional Choices* (Cambridge, Mass: Harvard University Press, 1985), at pp. 108–14.

[12]See *Richardson* case, *supra; Duke Power* case, *supra*, note 10.

functional purposes. First, they have been seen by the courts as a safeguard against being overwhelmed by officious litigants. Second, they have been believed to help avoid the raising of issues that are not suitable for determination by a court because not sufficiently precise, given the fact that no actual injury has yet occurred to anyone, or at least to anyone before the court who would be in a position to demonstrate the true impact of the law or administrative action in question. These considerations have seemingly been given less importance as the courts have come to attach more importance to providing access to judicial review. It will be necessary to look at particular remedies to see how standing rules have evolved.[13]

1. Requirements for Particular Remedies

(a) Declarations

By its very nature the declaration states the law without changing anything. By its terms, it neither prevents illegal action, redresses injuries, provides compensation, nor nullifies decisions. For these reasons, it is more commonly resorted to by those who have no claim to other remedies because their person or property is not in immediate jeopardy. We must consider to what extent the courts will allow them to use the declaratory action to assert rights on behalf of the public.

Where the plaintiff who seeks a declaration does in fact have private rights to vindicate in this way, it is no objection that many others similarly placed could seek the same kind of declaration. In the leading common law case on the use of the declaratory action in public law, *Dyson v. Attorney General*,[14] the plaintiff was the recipient of one of some eight million similar notices sent out by the Commissioners of Inland Revenue requiring the making of certain tax returns. Failure to make the returns would subject the recipient to penalties. Dyson, while occupying a position similar to that of millions of others, nevertheless could show that he would suffer injury to specific private rights of his own, and he was therefore allowed to seek a declaration that the notice was *ultra vires* of the commissioners.

While the *Dyson* case involved an attack on public officers for exceeding

---

[13]For a comprehensive treatment of standing, see Cromwell, *Locus Standi: A Commentary on the Law of Standing in Canada* (Toronto: Carswell, 1986).

[14][1911] 1 K.B. 410, 103 L.T. 707. See *supra*, at pp. 107–09. For a modern example of this type of situation see *King v. Liquor Control Bd. of Ontario* (1981), 33 O.R. (2d) 816, 125 D.L.R. (3d) 661 (H.C.).

their powers,[15] the same principles have been applied where the plaintiff attacks the constitutional validity of a statute under which officers act,[16] or even where the statute is attacked without reference to any particular steps taken or threatened to be taken under it.[17]

The more debatable use of the declaration arises where the plaintiff seemingly cannot demonstrate that he has an interest, in the traditional sense of personal or property rights which are affected by the allegedly invalid law or administrative action. It is in this area where the law has evolved dramatically.

The more restrictive traditional view and its rationale was demonstrated in two cases in the Supreme Court of Canada: *Smith v. A.G. Ont.*[18] in 1924 and *Saumur v. A.G. Que.*[19] in 1964.

In the *Smith* case, the plaintiff was a resident of Ontario who wished to attack the validity of the *Canada Temperance Act* as applied in his province. Part IV of the Act prohibited interprovincial movement of liquor into provinces which had adopted suitable local prohibition legislation and had passed a legislative resolution making the federal Act apply. In 1920 the Ontario Legislature passed such a resolution and the federal cabinet passed an order in council declaring Part IV to be in force in the province. Smith subsequently ordered from a dealer in Montreal some whisky, ale, and beer. The dealer declined to accept the order because the *Canada Temperance Act* prohibited such importation into Ontario. No attention was ever paid to this exchange by any government official.

Smith then sued the Attorney General of Ontario for a declaration that the *Canada Temperance Act* did not validly apply in Ontario. He contended that existing provincial legislation was not of the type required to make the *Canada Temperance Act* validly applicable. On the question of standing, he argued that he was illegally prevented from exercising his right to import liquor into the province, except under intolerable conditions, that is, the subjection of himself and his employees to possible criminal proceedings. He relied on the *Dyson* case to justify the form in which the action was brought.

---

[15]For other examples see, *e.g.*, *Gruen Watch Co. v. A.G. Can.*, [1950] O.R. 429, [1950] 4 D.L.R. 156, [1950] C.T.C. 440, revd in part (*sub nom. Bulova Watch Co. Ltd. v. A.G. Can.*) [1951] O.R. 360, [1951] 3 D.L.R. 18, [1951] C.T.C. 94 (H.C.); *King v. Liquor Control Bd.*, *supra*, note 14.

[16]*E.g.*, *Law Society of B.C. v. A.G. Can.*, 18 B.C.L.R. 181, [1980] 4 W.W.R. 6, 108 D.L.R. (3d) 753, 15 C.P.C. 195, 50 C.P.R. (2d) 87 (C.A.), affd [1982] 2 S.C.R. 307, 37 B.C.L.R. 145, [1982] 5 W.W.R. 289, 137 D.L.R. (3d) 1, 43 N.R. 451, 19 B.L.R. 234.

[17]*Canex Placer Ltd. v. A.G. B.C.*, [1976] 1 W.W.R. 24, 58 D.L.R. (3d) 241 (B.C.C.A.).

[18][1924] S.C.R. 331, [1924] 3 D.L.R. 189, 42 C.C.C. 215.

[19][1964] S.C.R. 252, 45 D.L.R. (2d) 627.

The court,[20] in a series of separate judgments, held that Smith had no standing to bring an action for a declaration under these circumstances. Idington J. distinguished the *Dyson* case on the grounds that there the Crown had actually made a claim against Dyson. By sending him the tax return, they had put him in the position where, if he did not act by completing the return, the Attorney General could proceed against him for penalties. In the *Smith* case, however, there was no similar foundation laid for such proceedings by the Crown against Smith. The possibility of such action was purely speculative. It could not arise until Smith had actually imported some liquor. Idington J. took the view that the plaintiff was merely trying to elicit an opinion from the court and that such an attempt should be rejected "unless we are quite prepared to assent to such like requests on any point of law puzzling any private citizen on any question".[21]

Duff J. (Maclean J. concurring) took a similar view. The *Smith* case was unlike *Dyson* because it involved only a hypothetical state of facts. "[O]nly if the liquor ordered were actually shipped, that is to say, only in a contingency which has not happened, could the appellant be put in jeopardy."[22] Smith had argued that the existence of the *Canada Temperance Act*, the resolution of the Ontario Legislature, and the order in council constituted an implied threat to many people including himself, a threat that if they carried on their lawful business they would be prosecuted. Mr. Justice Duff had some sympathy for the point of view that one ought not to have to subject himself to prosecution in order to raise the constitutional point.

> We think, however, that to accede to appellant's contention upon this point would involve the consequence that virtually every resident of Ontario could maintain a similar action; and we can discover no firm ground on which the appellant's claim can be supported which would not be equally available to sustain the right of any citizen of a province to initiate proceedings impeaching the constitutional validity of any legislation directly affecting him, along with other citizens, in a similar way in his business or in his personal life.
>
> We think the recognition of such a principle would lead to grave inconvenience and analogy is against it. An individual, for example, has no status to maintain an action restraining a wrongful violation of a public right unless he is exceptionally prejudiced by the wrongful act.[23]

Mignault J. in agreeing with Duff J. stated that the position of this

---

[20]Davies C.J., Idington, Duff, Mignault, and Maclean JJ.; Sir Louis Davies died before judgment was delivered. Maclean J. was sitting only *ad hoc*.

[21]*Supra*, note 18 at pp. 333–34 S.C.R., p. 190 D.L.R.

[22]*Supra*, note 18 at p. 336 S.C.R., p. 192 D.L.R.

[23]*Supra*, note 18 at p. 337 S.C.R., pp. 193–94 D.L.R.

plaintiff did not differ materially from that of hundreds of other citizens who might be opposed to prohibition. Smith was not in jeopardy at the time he commenced the action. It would be a great inconvenience to allow actions to be brought by those not showing any special interest.

All of the judges thus held that Smith had no right to a declaration. As long as he had not received any liquor from outside the province he was not in any danger of prosecution. In their view he was not being required by the impugned law to take any action or to give up his property. Thus he had no private right to assert or protect. He was in the same position as any other person who might like to import liquor but who would not be prepared to do so as long as there was a prohibitory law on the statute books.

Curiously, three of the judges, after coming to the conclusion that Smith had no standing to raise the issue as to the validity of the *Canada Temperance Act* in Ontario, proceeded to decide against him on the substantive issue as well. Duff J. (Maclean J. concurring) had indicated that to decide such an issue at the suit of such a party would lead to "grave inconvenience". Having established this principle he indicated that the judges were "loath to give a judgment against the appellant solely based upon a fairly disputable point of procedure". He then analyzed the means by which the Act had been applied to Ontario and held them to be adequate. Mignault J. similarly found the procedural objection suffi-cient to dispose of the matter but in addition held the Act to be validly in force. One cannot fail to note the contrast here with the practice of United States federal courts. It is most improbable that one of those courts would find that a plaintiff had no standing to bring the action in question and then proceed to decide a constitutional or quasi-constitutional issue such as this. The difference in treatment must reflect to some extent the comparative lack of constitutional restraint imposed on Canadian courts. As they are not strictly limited to the exercise of "judicial" functions alone, Canadian courts are free to render a decision with respect to an issue raised by a person not properly a party before the court. In this case it seems to have been a matter of discretion for the Supreme Court of Canada whether they dealt with the substantive issue. Though all the judges had decided that to entertain actions of this type would, as a general rule, lead to "inconvenience", three of them could not bring themselves to dismiss this particular action. They were "loath" to do so on a "disputable point of procedure". Apparently they considered that the power was in their hands to deal with the substantive question of validity if they chose to do so. This may have influenced the more generous approach to standing taken by the Supreme Court in later years.

The 1964 *Saumur* decision saw another attempt to obtain a decla-ration of invalidity rejected by the Supreme Court. Earlier efforts by the City of Quebec to regulate by by-law the distribution of religious pamphlets on city streets had been successfully attacked in 1953 by Saumur, a minister and missionary of the Jehovah's Witnesses.[24] On January 28, 1954, there came into effect an amendment to the provincial *Freedom of Worship Act*. This amendment[25] prohibited the distribution of any pamphlets containing abusive attacks on the religion of any portion of the population. Speeches and broadcasts containing attacks of this nature were also prohibited. On the next day, January 29, 1954, the plaintiffs commenced this action for a declaration that the amendment was *ultra vires* of the Quebec Legislature. They also asked for injunctions against the police and the Attorney General to prevent enforcement of the new law. The plaintiffs alleged that they carried on their proselytizing by activities such as distribution of pamphlets, and preaching. They asserted that their actions did not violate the prohibitions of the amendment, but that they believed that it was the immediate intention of the City of Quebec and its officers to use the provincial law to stop the activities of the Jehovah's Witnesses. They attempted to introduce evidence at the trial to the effect that the Premier and Attorney General had made statements in the Legislature indicating that the Act was to be used against the Witnesses. This evidence was held to be inadmissible and the action was dismissed.

The Attorney General had contended, *inter alia*, that in Quebec there was no action for a declaration such as that used in the *Dyson* case. It was also contended that the plaintiffs did not have the "interest" which is required to bring an action in Quebec.[26] On appeal[27] to the Court of Queen's Bench, appeal side, two of the judges held that Quebec law did not recognize the action for a declaration of invalidity of a statute. One held that the plaintiffs lacked the "interest" required under art. 77 of the *Code of Civil Procedure*, and another held that a declaration could not be given where the plaintiffs had not yet been prosecuted or their property yet affected by the impugned statute.

The appeal to the Supreme Court was dismissed, although it is not entirely clear on which grounds. On behalf of the court Taschereau C.J. said that in Quebec "l'action déclaratoire n'existe pas". But he also went on to say that Quebec courts "ne donnent pas des consultations légales. . . .

---

[24]*Saumur v. Quebec City*, [1953] 2 S.C.R. 299, [1953] 4 D.L.R. 641, 106 C.C.C. 289. Here the plaintiff in seeking a declaration could show that he had already been prosecuted under the impugned by-law.

[25]S.Q. 1953–54, c. 15, amending R.S.Q. 1941, c. 307.

[26]*Code of Civil Procedure*, 1897, Art. 77: "No person can bring an action at law unless he has an interest therein. Such interest, except where it is otherwise provided, may be merely eventual". See now *Code of Civil Procedure*, R.S.Q. 1977, c. C-25, Art. 55 to a similar effect.

[27][1963] Que Q.B. 116, 37 D.L.R. (2d) 703.

La seule crainte que peut avoir un citoyen qu'un jour une action possible peut être instituée contre lui ne justifie pas *per se* un recours en justice''.[28] This could mean that under Quebec law a declaration could not be given under any circumstances, or it could mean that the court considered the action here to be premature because no interest of the plaintiffs was yet being affected. The latter rationale would in the circumstances appear to be quite justifiable, since the plaintiffs while seeking a declaration that a statute was *ultra vires* were also arguing that their own practices were not in violation of that statute. The former rationale did apparently leave the status of the declaratory action in Quebec in a state of some uncertainty, a situation which was subsequently addressed by the Office of Revision of the Civil Code. The resulting art. 453 of the new *Code of Civil Procedure* has been held to confirm the availability of the declaration in Quebec, but subject to the plaintiff being able to show a sufficient "interest".[29] The interest requirement means, *inter alia*, that he must, unlike the *Saumur* plaintiffs, show that he is within the ambit of the statute he attacks.[30]

The *Smith* and *Saumur* cases are today perhaps more of historic interest. If they can be reconciled it is on the basis that both assume the requirement of an interest, and while a declaration was given in neither case because of lack of interest, the court in *Smith* was prepared to discuss the constitutional issues raised because the plaintiff was asserting that he had been and would be affected by the Act whereas in *Saumur* the plaintiffs asserted that the Act could not by its terms apply to their activities.

Standing continued to be an important factor in many lower court decisions in actions for declarations to assert "public" rights.[31] This traditional requirement of the plaintiff having an interest, in the sense of protecting personal or property rights immediately threatened, has largely been done away with by the Supreme Court of Canada in recent years in a series of decisions which have progressively lowered the standing barrier almost to the vanishing point. The common theme running through

---

[28][1964] S.C.R. 252 at 257, 45 D.L.R. (2d) 627 at 630.

[29]*Protestant School Bd. of Montreal v. Minister of Education*, [1976] C.S. 358 at 363–65; applied in *Blaikie v. A.G. Que.*, [1978] C.S. 37, 85 D.L.R. (3d) 252 (the issue of standing was dropped before subsequent appeals).

[30]*Protestant School Bd.*, *ibid.*

[31]*Cowan v. C.B.C.*, [1966] 2 O.R. 309, 56 D.L.R. (2d) 578 (C.A.) and Strayer, "Comment" (1967), 45 Can. Bar Rev. 154; *Jamieson v. A.G. B.C.*, [1971] 5 W.W.R. 600, 21 D.L.R. (3d) 313 (B.C. S.C.); *Burnham v. A.G. Can.* (1970), 74 W.W.R. 427, 15 D.L.R. (3d) 6; *Mercer v. A.G. Can.* [1972] 3 W.W.R. 701, 24 D.L.R. (3d) 758 (Alta. C.A.); *Moose Jaw School Dist. Bd. of Education v. A.G. Sask.*, [1974] 2 W.W.R. 27, 41 D.L.R. (3d) 732, vard [1975] 6 W.W.R. 133, 57 D.L.R. (3d) 315.

these cases appears to be that a constitutional or other public rights issue, if it is genuinely justiciable, ought not to fail of judicial consideration for want of standing.

The breakthrough first came with *Thorson v. A.G. Can.*[32] in 1975. The plaintiff sued as a federal taxpayer seeking a declaration that the *Official Languages Act*[33] was invalid, as were the appropriations made for its implementation. This Act contained various provisions for the use of both official languages in the federal executive departments and agencies and in federally created courts. In the Ontario courts the Attorney-General for Canada successfully challenged the plaintiff's right to sue for lack of standing. On appeal the Supreme Court split 6 to 3 in favour of the plaintiff-appellant. Against the plaintiff was argued the precedent of the *Smith* case on the basis that he was in no way specifically affected by the *Official Languages Act*. While he contended that all taxpayers were prejudiced by these allegedly illegal expenditures, he did not demonstrate that he was specifically affected or prejudiced in comparison to other taxpayers.

The three dissenting judges agreed with the lower courts that the plaintiff did not have sufficient standing, and based themselves mainly on the *Smith* case. They did not regard this case as falling within the principle of the *Dyson* case, distinguishing between that sort of declaratory action with respect to the validity of administrative action and the present case involving the validity of a statute.

The majority of the court, in a judgment by Laskin J., obviously approached the issue with a different premise: namely, that if there is a justiciable constitutional issue, then it is open to the court to exercise its discretion in favour of recognizing standing. A passage near the end of the judgment demonstrates their rationale. In putting aside as "unreal" the question of whether there is a recognizable financial interest in a federal taxpayer as such, they said that:

> It is not the alleged waste of public funds alone that will support standing but rather the right of the citizenry to constitutional behaviour by Parliament where the issue in such behaviour is justiciable as a legal question.[34]

Proceeding on this view, they distinguished the *Smith* case on the basis that it involved a "regulatory" statute which created offences and imposed penalties. Therefore there could be people able to attack it because, once genuinely threatened with enforcement of the Act against them, they could resist prosecution by attacking its validity. By contrast the *Official Languages Act* creates no offences or penalties. It was said to be "dec-

---

[32][1975] 1 S.C.R. 138, 43 D.L.R. (3d) 1, 1 N.R. 225.
[33]R.S.C. 1970, c. 0–2.
[34]*Supra*, note 32 at p. 163 S.C.R., p. 19 D.L.R.

laratory and directory''. No duties are laid upon members of the public and while members of the public service may incur certain duties and responsibilities under it this was apparently regarded as of no consequence. Thus, in the view of the court, it would not be possible for individual members of the public to challenge the law because of its application to them. Nor could the court envisage any other forms of ''public'' action being available short of a constitutional reference to test validity. On the assumption, then, that there must be a possibility of judicial review because of ''the right of the citizenry to constitutional behaviour by Parliament'', and emphasizing that this was a matter of discretion, the court granted the plaintiff standing.[35] In doing so it treated municipal taxpayer actions[36] as a species of public action useable where standing was not otherwise available because no one was specially affected by the law, and regarded the federal taxpayer's action before it as another species of the same genus, the basic rationale being the same for both.

This emphasis in *Thorson* on the availability of standing to a member of the public because the statute was declaratory rather than regulatory gave rise to further debate in the case of *Nova Scotia Board of Censors v. McNeil*[37] which followed soon after. Here the plaintiff, a resident and taxpayer of Nova Scotia, had ascertained that the provincial Board of Censors had prohibited the exhibition of the film "Last Tango in Paris". After being denied standing in an administrative appeal of that decision, and having unsuccessfully requested the provincial Attorney General to refer to the courts the constitutionality of the *Theatres and Amusements Act*[38] under which the board acted, he sought a declaration that the Act was invalid. He was granted standing to do so in the Nova Scotia courts. On appeal to the Supreme Court on the question of standing it was argued by the appellants that standing should not be recognized here because, by the criteria defined in the *Thorson* case, this was a regulatory statute. There were businesses or people who would be directly controlled by it, namely film exchanges, cinema owners and operators, who would be subject to prosecution or possibly loss of license if they distributed or exhibited a prohibited film. The plaintiff was not one of these and therefore

---

[35]Before this action was completed the *Official Languages Act* was upheld by the Supreme Court in another case, *Jones v. A.G. N.B.*, [1975] 2 S.C.R. 182, 45 D.L.R. (3d) 583 (*sub nom. Jones v. A.G. Can.*), 1 N.R. 582 (*sub nom. Reference re Official Language Act*), 16 C.C.C. (2d) 297, 7 N.B.R. (2d) 526.

[36]See *infra* at pp. 179–83.

[37][1976] 2 S.C.R. 265, 12 N.S.R. (2d) 85, 55 D.L.R. (3d) 632, 5 N.R. 43, 32 C.N.R.S. 376; folld in *Dybikowski v. The Queen in right of B.C.*, [1979] 2 W.W.R. 631 at 637–38 (B.C. S.C.).

[38]R.S.N.S. 1967, c. 304.

did not fall within the distinction which *Thorson* represented from the principle applied in the earlier *Smith* case.

By putting the emphasis again on the necessity for there to be some way to litigate constitutionality, however, the court, in a judgment by Laskin C.J., confirmed the standing of the plaintiff-respondent. While the merits were not before the court in these proceedings, it noted that all sides appeared to accept that a substantial constitutional issue had been raised. It also noted the unsuccessful efforts of the plaintiff to have the issue raised otherwise. As to the argument based on the distinction in *Thorson* between regulatory and declaratory statutes, the court recognized that those engaged in film distribution and exhibition would be "directly regulated" by the Act and thus, presumably, would thereby have standing to challenge it, but nevertheless held that standing was not confined to them because the Act also enabled the board indirectly "to determine what members of the public may view in theatres or other places of public entertainment". The implication appears to be that this creates some kind of interest in members of the public to attack the law. Also implicit is the assumption that the industry is not likely to initiate such action, since the court concludes that "there appears to be no other way, practically speaking, to subject the challenged Act to judicial review" and this justified the court in exercising its discretion to give standing.

What principle is to be gleaned from the *McNeil* decision? Perhaps it means that even if the impugned statute is regulatory, standing is not confined to the people regulated if they are not likely to challenge it (although nowhere is this made explicit in the judgment nor does there appear to have been any evidence on the question of such likelihood). Perhaps it means that a member of the public who is actually denied a freedom he might otherwise have enjoyed, if it were not for the impugned law, may be given standing to attack that law, no matter who else may be more immediately regulated by it. This rationale would be more compelling if the plaintiff had been asserting a constitutionally guaranteed freedom for the protection of the public rather than having to rely, as he did, on the constitutional distribution of powers and its limitations on provincial legislative authority. Also, this rationale is at least hard to reconcile with the *Smith* case: on the principle of *McNeil* any thirsty Ontarian should have had standing to attack the prohibition law, and *a fortiori* Smith as a would-be importer of liquor surely should have had standing.

The consistent thread that runs through *Thorson* and *McNeil* is that, where the issue is a justiciable one, want of standing should not prevent judicial review by way of an action for a declaration. This interpretation is further strengthened by *Minister of Justice v. Borowski*.[39] While this

---

[39][1981] 2 S.C.R. 575, 12 Sask. R. 420, [1982] 1 W.W.R. 97, 130 D.L.R. (3d) 588,

did not involve the constitutional validity of any law, but rather the issue of alleged conflict between the *Criminal Code* and the *Canadian Bill of Rights*, the court treated the rules of standing as being entirely the same. Here the plaintiff, who sued as a citizen and federal taxpayer, was a former member of the Manitoba Legislature and former provincial cabinet minister. He sought a declaration that s-ss. 251(4), (5) and (6) of the *Criminal Code*,[40] which permit therapeutic abortions under certain conditions as an exception to the general criminal prohibition against abortion, abridge "the right of the individual to life . . . and the right not to be deprived thereof except by due process of law" as recognized and declared in para. 1(*a*) of the *Canadian Bill of Rights*. Some preliminary questions of jurisdiction had been argued in the Saskatchewan courts and appealed to the Supreme Court where the standing question was raised and determined in favour of the plaintiff. The majority judgment written by Martland J. was expressly based on the *Thorson* and *McNeil* decisions. He found that the legislation here was neither regulatory nor declaratory, but instead "exculpatory" because it provides a defence to what would otherwise be a crime, and thus was not directly parallel to the statutes in question in the two earlier cases. Nevertheless, he found it quite consistent to grant standing. Referring to *Thorson* and *McNeil*, Martland J. said:

> I interpret these cases as deciding that to establish status as a plaintiff in a suit seeking a declaration that legislation is invalid, if there is a serious issue as to its invalidity, a person need only show that he is affected by it directly or that he has a genuine interest as a citizen in the validity of the legislation and that there is no other reasonable and effective manner in which the issue may be brought before the court. In my opinion, the respondent has met this test, and should be permitted to proceed with his action.[41]

In this case the plaintiff alleged that he had tried to raise the issue by various forms of protest, and by unsuccessfully requesting various federal and provincial ministers and officials to initiate appropriate legal action "to protect the rights of individual human foetuses". The majority of the court did not think anyone directly affected by these exculpatory provisions could be expected, as a practical matter, to attack them. Doctors performing abortions, protected by the sections, would not. Doctors not performing them would have no reason to do so. The same would apply respectively to hospitals permitting or not permitting abortions. Women obtaining abortions would have no reason to challenge the law.

---

[39] N.R. 331, 64 C.C.C. (2d) 97, 24 C.P.C. 62, 24 C.R. (3d) 352. See also *Forest v. A.G. Man.*, [1979] 4 W.W.R. 229, 98 D.L.R. (3d) 405 at 411, 47 C.C.C. (2d) 417 (Man. C.A.).

[40] R.S.C. 1970, c. C-34.

[41] *Supra*, note 39 at p. 117 W.W.R.

Nor, thought the court, would a husband wanting to prevent an abortion be able to bring proceedings in time, since the events of abortive move more rapidly than do the legal processes. Therefore, it was open to a citizen whose only interest was, apparently, social, moral, or philosophical, to challenge the application of the law because, "There is no reasonable way in which that issue can be brought into court unless proceedings are launched by some interested citizen".[42] The plaintiff was obviously regarded as an "interested citizen" in this sense.

The dissenting judgment by Laskin C.J., concurred in by Lamer J., appears to be a belated effort to put some limits on the grant of standing. A general rule is stated, that no one has a right to such a ruling on the validity or meaning of a statute unless he is directly affected. "Mere distaste has never been a ground upon which to seek the assistance of a court." This rationale "is based on the purpose served by courts. They are dispute-resolving tribunals".[43] Only Governments have authority to refer hypothetical questions to the courts. Two exceptions are noted: that of the right of action of municipal taxpayers with respect to illegal expenditures, and the exercise of discretion in cases such as *Thorson* where there was a justiciable issue and no other way to test validity in court. *McNeil* was distinguished from the present case on the basis that the plaintiff there was actually deprived of the right to view a film, whereas in *Borowski* the plaintiff was not affected personally by the fact that *Criminal Code* provisions saved certain other people from criminal liability. An important element of this dissenting judgment appears to be the view that this is not a situation for exercising discretion as in *Thorson* because, in the opinion of the dissenting judges, there were real possibilities that doctors, hospitals, or husbands of pregnant wives might seek judicial review.

The latter conclusion appears to be the main point of difference between the majority and minority, notwithstanding the principles involved. It is clear the plaintiff was not subject to direct regulation, nor did he allege that as a member of the public he was, like *McNeil*, personally being denied some privilege such as seeing a film. Instead, both the majority and minority accepted that where no one is affected in either of these ways the court may still, as a matter of discretion, grant him standing if necessary to serve the overriding need that there be some means of achieving judicial review. The majority thought there were no reasonably probable alternative means, whereas the minority thought there were.

It is true that the dissenters mentioned another reason, in effect, lack of ripeness or "concreteness", for exercising discretion against granting standing. But this seems to be another aspect of the same concern that

---

[42]*Ibid.*, at p. 116.
[43]*Ibid.*, at p. 100.

the plaintiff is not alleging a particular injury to himself that would provide the specific facts that would enable the court to make a meaningful determination.

The combined result of these three cases appears to leave the door open for standing to seek a declaration of invalidity of a statute for anyone who can show either: (1) that he has been, or is imminently threatened under the statute with legal consequences of a regulatory or enforcement nature; (2) that he has suffered or will suffer, like all members of the public, some denial by the statute of a benefit or privilege or freedom that would otherwise be available to him, even if there may be certain other people potentially within category (1) who have not chosen to attack it; or (3) even if he cannot bring himself within categories (1) or (2), that there is no one else who would have standing for other reasons or, having standing, would be likely to attack the statute. The ultimate rationale appears to be that questions of constitutional validity, or of quasi-constitutional interpretation under the *Canadian Bill of Rights*, must be ultimately susceptible of judicial review. This would imply that the broadened rules of standing required to achieve this need not be available where the issue in a "public action" is not constitutional or quasi-constitutional.[44]

These three cases were considered by the Supreme Court recently in *Operation Dismantle Inc. et al. v. The Queen et al.*[45] In that case the plaintiffs had sought, *inter alia*, a declaration that testing of cruise missiles by the United States in Canadian territory was contrary to s. 7 of the *Canadian Charter of Rights and Freedoms*. The Federal Court of Appeal had ordered the statement of claim struck out as not disclosing a reasonable cause of action. The plaintiffs contended that they did not have to allege the violation or threatened violation of a right, because they were raising a "serious constitutional issue" which, according to the above trilogy of standing cases, gave them standing. In a separate judgment Wilson J. considered the possibilities of the plaintiffs obtaining a declaration based on s-s. 24(1) of the Charter, s-s. 52(1) of the *Constitution Act, 1982*, or on common law principles applicable to the granting of declarations.[46] It

---

[44]See, *e.g.*, *Rosenberg v. Grand River Conservation Authority* (1976), 12 O.R. (2d) 496, 69 D.L.R. (3d) 384, 1 C.P.C. 1 (C.A.); *Islands Protection Soc. v. The Queen in right of B.C.*, 11 B.C.L.R. 372, [1979] 4 W.W.R. 1, 98 D.L.R. (3d) 504 (S.C.); *Greenpeace Foundation of B.C. v. Min. of Environment*, [1981] 4 W.W.R. 587, 122 D.L.R. (3d) 179 (B.C. S.C.); *Waddell v. Governor in Council*, 30 B.C.L.R. 127, [1981] 5 W.W.R. 662, 126 D.L.R. (3d) 431 (*sub nom. Waddell v. Schreyer*) (S.C.), affd 41 B.C.L.R. 317, [1983] 1 W.W.R. 762, 142 D.L.R. (3d) 177 (C.A.), leave to appeal to S.C.C. refused [1983] 1 W.W.R. lii. But see *Finlay* case, *infra*, note 50 and accompanying text.

[45][1985] 1 S.C.R. 441.

[46]*Ibid.*, at pp. 479–87.

seemed to be assumed that a declaration could not be based on s-s. 24(1) because no right had as yet been allegedly infringed and that subsection applies to "anyone whose rights or freedoms . . . have been infringed or denied . . . ." Wilson J. held that, to make out a claim for a declaration based on s-s. 52(1) or the common law, the plaintiffs would have to show that the testing of the cruise missile would infringe *their* rights to "life, liberty and security of the person". Although there are frequent references to standing in this passage it is not clear that this is a conclusion that for standing to seek a declaration of Charter violations one must allege infringement or threatened infringement of his own rights. It would instead appear to be an observation that, as a matter of substantive law, there is no constitutional violation of the Charter unless the right or freedom of *someone* is alleged. This interpretation would appear to be most consistent with her discussion of the *Borowski* case, which she explains on the basis that infringement of the rights of foetuses, even though not those of the plaintiff, was being alleged and this was sufficient "[w]here . . . the unconstitutionality of a law or an act is founded upon its conflict with a right".[47] Dickson C.J., writing for the majority, in concurring with Wilson J. on this matter simply observed that the plaintiffs to[48]

> . . . advance this claim for declaratory relief . . . must at least be able to establish a threat of violation, if not an actual violation, of *their* rights under the *Charter*. (Emphasis added.)

It was held by the court in effect that the allegations in the Statement of Claim did not and could not disclose an infringement of the rights of anyone under s. 7 of the Charter. Thus the question of standing does not appear to have been determinative of the issue. The suggestions in the judgments that plaintiffs seeking a declaration must show a violation, real or apprehended, of their own rights may not be of much significance in the context of a case where the perceived menace — nuclear war — would be assumed to threaten all members of the public equally, including the plaintiffs.

It would appear, then, that the Supreme Court has in the *Operation Dismantle* case confirmed that the declaratory action is available in Charter cases whether s-s. 24(1) is applicable or not, and that standing for it will be recognized in persons who seek to vindicate the constitutional rights of the members of the public generally. There have been several examples of the use of declaratory proceedings for such purposes.[49]

---

[47]*Ibid.*, at p. 481.

[48]*Ibid.*, at p. 450.

[49]See, *e.g., Nat. Citizens' Coalition Inc., Coalition Nat. des Citoyens Inc. et al. v. A.G. Can.* (1984), 11 D.L.R. (4th) 481 (Alta. Q.B.); *Re Scott and A.G. B.C. et al.*, [1986] 5 W.W.R. 207 (B.C. S.C.).

The scope of availability of the action for a declaration to vindicate essentially public interests has been extended even to non-constitutional cases in the Supreme Court decision in *Min. of Finance of Can. et al. v. Finlay*.[50] In that case the plaintiff, a resident of Manitoba and recipient of a social allowance provided under a provincial program cost-shared with the federal government, sought a declaration that the federal payments were invalid because the provincial program did not comply with the conditions imposed by federal law for cost-sharing. On a motion brought by the defendant Minister to strike out the statement of claim, the court held that while the plaintiff had no sufficient direct personal interest to bring him within general requirements for standing, he could as a matter of discretion be given "public interest standing". The court expressly extended the principles of *Thorson*, *McNeil* and *Borowski* to cover a non-constitutional case involving a challenge as to whether governmental action was in fact authorized by the relevant statute. It was noted that there were serious, justiciable, issues and there was no other way in which the issues could be brought before a court.

A further word on the *Thorson*, *McNeil* and *Borowski* trilogy is required on the question of exhaustion of remedies. In each of these cases some emphasis was put by the plaintiff and the court on the fact that he had first sought unsuccessfully to get the relevant Attorney General of the jurisdiction whose law was questioned to initiate action to test its validity in court. It appears, however, that the Supreme Court has not adopted this as an automatic precondition to granting standing. In the *Thorson* case, Laskin J. noted that while there might be some justification in England for requiring in a public action that the plaintiff first have ascertained that the Attorney General would neither commence action himself nor give his consent to a relator action by the plaintiff in the name of the Attorney General,[51] the same could not be assumed in Canada. In England such actions were to challenge the authority of subordinate agencies, not of Parliament, and the Attorney General could be reasonably expected to initiate action. In a federal state such as Canada it was not realistic to expect the Attorney General to attack the legislation which as law officer he is obliged to enforce.[52] It appears in the *Thorson* and subsequent cases, however, that an unsuccessful attempt to get the Attorney General to initiate action could be a factor in the exercise of discretion in favour of standing, in that it contributes to the conclusion that there is no reasonable possibility of the constitutional issue otherwise being submitted to judicial review.

---

[50] [1986] 2 S.C.R. 607.

[51] See *A.G. ex rel. McWhirter v. Independent Broadcasting Authority*, [1973] Q.B. 629, [1973] 1 All E.R. 689 (C.A.).

[52] *Thorson v. A.G. Can.*, [1975] 1 S.C.R. 138 at 146–47, 43 D.L.R. (3d) 1 at 7–8, 1 N.R. 225.

This does lead, however, to a more general question as to the possible role of the Attorney General in initiating actions in the public interest to challenge constitutionally invalid laws or actions. Traditionally, only the Attorney General could sue for a declaration that a public body is exceeding its powers.[53] Presumably this could include situations where it is alleged that the public body acts without jurisdiction because the statute under which it purports to act is itself *ultra vires*. While the Attorney General has a right of action only if the public as a whole is affected,[54] it would seem that the question of whether a statute of the Legislature is valid or not would be of concern to the public as a whole.

The application of these common law principles within a federal system causes considerable difficulty. Could a provincial Attorney General commence action in this way to challenge the authority of a federal agency on the grounds that its Act of Parliament was *ultra vires*? Could the Attorney General of Canada challenge a provincial statute in a similar manner? These questions have not been fully answered in Canada.

We have seen that in four provinces (Manitoba, British Columbia, Alberta, and Ontario) there is a statutory right for either the federal or the provincial Attorney General to seek a declaration of invalidity of a provincial statute, and the Ontario law also permits an action by either such officer with respect to the validity of a federal law.[55] There is some precedent for the Attorney General of Canada being admitted as an additional plaintiff in an action commenced by a private party for a declaration of invalidity of a provincial law and regulation where it was alleged that the provincial provisions interfered with a field of federal jurisdiction.[56] There is some logic to this in that in such a case the Attorney General of Canada is the only law officer with the responsibility of protecting the jurisdiction of Parliament which was alleged to be affected. There is also some authority that the Attorney General of Canada now has a sufficient interest, as required in Quebec, in order to intervene in a case involving the *Canadian Charter of Rights and Freedoms* and its possible effect on a provincial law.[57] On the other hand, doubt has been expressed by the Supreme Court that a provincial Attorney General would by the general rules have standing to seek a declaration against the validity of federal

---

[53]*Robertson v. Montreal* (1915), 52 S.C.R. 30, 26 D.L.R. 228; *Loggie v. Town of Chatham*, 54 N.B.R. 230, [1928] 2 D.L.R. 583 (C.A.); *Jenkins v. Winnipeg*, 48 Man. R. 233, [1941] 1 W.W.R. 37, [1941] 1 D.L.R. 477 (Man. K.B.) and see Zamir, *The Declaratory Judgment* (1962), at 254–70.

[54]*Livingstone v. Edmonton* (1915), 8 W.W.R. 976, 31 W.L.R. 609, 24 D.L.R. 191 (Alta. S.C.), vard 9 Alta. L.R. 343, 9 W.W.R. 794, 33 W.L.R. 164, 25 D.L.R. 313 (C.A.).

[55]*Supra*, at pp. 121, 122.

[56]*Central Canada Potash Ltd. v. Sask.*, [1975] 5 W.W.R. 193, 57 D.L.R. (3d) 7 (Sask.Q.B.).

[57]*Que. Assn. of Protestant School Bds. v. A.G. Que. (No. 1)* (1982), 140 D.L.R. (3d) 19, 3 C.R.R. 97 (Que. Sup. Ct.).

legislation, because he would not be in a different position from other provincial Attorneys General.[58]

In Australia the High Court has held that a state Attorney General had a sufficient title to challenge the validity of the federal *Pharmaceutical Benefits Act* as it operated within his state.[59] This view may be open to question. It may be that each Attorney General should on principle be entitled to commence an action by himself only with respect to the laws of the jurisdiction to which he belongs. The right of the Attorney General in these cases probably stems from the Crown's prerogative rights as *parens patriae*. It has been held in other situations that the extent of the prerogative in right of Canada or of a province corresponds to the distribution of legislative power under the *Constitution Act*.[60]

If this constitutional distribution does apply to declaratory actions by Attorneys General, it is unlikely that they will ever be a means of bringing a public action to challenge directly the validity of legislation. This action has the virtue of simplicity in that the Attorney General need prove no interest in the matter to commence action. But in bringing action he must challenge the validity of acts of his own legislature. He is a member of the Government responsible to that legislature and if he has formed the opinion that the legislation is invalid he should advise that it be repealed. If the Government rejects his advice he must either accept the majority decision or resign. If he merely has doubts about the validity of the law or if outright repeal is impolitic, then the easier course is for him to advise the cabinet to refer the matter to the courts for an opinion. Or, put another way as Laskin J. did for the Supreme Court in the *Thorson* case, it is doubtful if a requirement as a condition of standing that the Attorney General first be requested to attack his own legislation "can have any application in a federal system where the Attorney General is the legal officer of a Government obliged to enforce legislation enacted by Parliament and a challenge is made to the validity of the legislation."[61]

It is possible for a private citizen to initiate such proceedings by way of a relator action. In such cases he must obtain the consent of the Attorney General to commence the action in the latter's name.[62] Presumably the same principles which would inhibit the Attorney General from

---

[58]*Thorson v. A.G. Can.*, [1975] 1 S.C.R. 138 at 152, 43 D.L.R. (3d) 1 at 11–12, 1 N.R. 225.

[59]*A.G. Vict. v. Commonwealth* (1945), 71 C.L.R. 237 (H.C.). But see *South Carolina v. Katzenbach*, 383 U.S. 301 (1966), at p. 324. Also questioned in *Thorson* case, *supra*, note 58.

[60]*Bonanza Creek Gold Mining Co. Ltd. v. The King*, [1916] 1 A.C. 566, [1916–17] All E.R. Rep. 999, 25 Que. K.B. 170, 26 D.L.R. 273, 10 W.W.R. 391, 34 W.L.R. (P.C.); *A.G. Can. v. A.G. Ont.*, [1898] A.C. 247, 77 L.T. 539 (P.C.).

[61]*Thorson* case, *supra*, note 58 at p. 146 S.C.R., p. 7 D.L.R.

[62]See Zamir, *supra*, note 53 at pp. 262–66.

suing by himself would deter him from granting his consent to a private citizen to bring this unique public action.

The Attorney General's action against public bodies to prevent an excess of jurisdiction might be used in a quasi-constitutional manner. This could arise where the allegation was that the public body was wrongly exercising valid statutory powers, in a manner which would apply the statute unconstitutionally in contravention of the distribution of powers or of the Charter of Rights and Freedoms. Thus a provincial Attorney General might seek a declaration that a municipality had exercised its power to make bylaws for the preservation of order on municipal streets in a way which conflicted with the *Criminal Code*.[63] This would not involve an attack on the provincial statute under which the municipality purported to make its by-law, but only an attack on the by-law itself as being outside the contemplation of that statute.

Apart from the apparent discretion which courts have in recognizing *locus standi* in declaratory actions (as emphasized in the *Thorson, McNeil* and *Borowski* cases) it is also clear that they have a discretion to refuse the declaration even where the action is properly instituted. Even if the plaintiff has standing, considerations of utility may deter the court from granting the declaration. The importance of the issue to the parties, the usefulness of a declaration in the dispute, the existence of sufficient facts on which to base a decision, the question of whether matters of public importance may also be conveniently settled at the same time, the balance of convenience to the parties, and similar criteria will influence the court in the exercise of its discretion.[64] The Supreme Court of Canada has subsumed these factors under two rubrics: reality of the dispute, and utility of the remedy.[65]

It is clear then that discretion plays a major part in a court's decision, first, to entertain a declaratory action, and second, to grant or refuse a declaration. It is submitted that in constitutional cases there are special factors which should be of importance in the exercise of that discretion. What those factors are will be discussed subsequently.[66]

It may also be noted that declarations can be obtained in some jurisdictions by means of an application rather than requiring the commencement of an action. This seems to be the case where the relevant rules of procedure are silent on the point and the court considers that the matter may be adequately dealt with on the facts already available without

---

[63]See *Kent District v. Storgoff* (1962), 40 W.W.R. 278 (B.C. S.C.).
[64]See Zamir, *supra*, note 53 at pp. 191–201.
[65]*Solosky v. The Queen*, [1980] 1 S.C.R. 821 at 832–33, applied in *Operation Dismantle*, *supra*, note 45, at pp. 481–82.
[66]See *infra*, at pp. 187–91.

the need for pleadings, discovery, and a trial.[67] In some courts, however, no discretion is allowed in this respect and an action is required to obtain a declaration.[68]

(b) Injunctions

To seek an injunction in a private action the plaintiff must allege that he has an "interest".[69] Normally the injunction is sought as incidental relief in association with some other remedy. Where the claim for the principal remedy is barred, the incidental relief by injunction falls with it.[70] There are some additional requirements peculiar to interlocutory injunctions which would probably prevent their use except in the clearest case of imminent violation of the plaintiff's property or personal interest. A court would refuse to issue an injunction where damages would be an adequate remedy, or where the plaintiff did not have "clean hands", for example. The grant is normally also subject to an equitable discretion.[71]

Given all these constraints on the remedy of injunction, it has been thought not very useful as a public law remedy for use by private parties. Past jurisprudence has held to the effect that a purely public right unconnected to any personal interests could not be asserted by an individual by means of an injunction.[72] The recent Supreme Court of Canada decision in *Min. of Finance of Can. v. Finlay*[73] held, however, that even where a plaintiff

---

[67]*Re Danson and A.G. Ont.* (1985), 20 D.L.R. (4th) 288 (Ont. H.C.); affd 27 D.L.R. (4th) 758 (Div. Ct.), and cases referred to therein.

[68]*Le Groupe des éleveurs de volailles de l'est de l'Ontario et al. v. Can. Chicken Marketing Agency*, [1985] 1 F.C. 280 at 291–92, and cases referred to therein.

[69]24 Halsbury *Laws of England*, 4th ed. (London: Butterworths, 1979) at 580–81. But see Cromwell, *supra*, note 13 at 148–49.

[70]See, *e.g.*, *Loggie v. Town of Chatham*, 54 N.B.R. 230, [1928] 2 D.L.R. 583 (C.A.) and *Jenkins v. Winnipeg*, 48 Man. R. 233, [1941] 1 W.W.R. 37, [1941] 1 D.L.R. 477 (K.B.).

[71]See *Snell's Principles of Equity*, 28th ed. (London: Sweet & Maxwell, 1982); Sharpe *Injunctions and Specific Performance* (Toronto: Canada Law Book, 1983), at pp. 59–89.

[72]See, *e.g.*, *MacCormick v. Lord Advocate*, [1953] Sess. Cas. 396 (Scot. Ct. of Sess.); *Grant v. St. Lawrence Seaway Authority*, [1960] O.R. 298, 23 D.L.R. (2d) 252 (C.A.), leave to appeal to S.C.C. refused June 6, 1960; *Gouriet v. Union of Post Office Wkrs.*, [1978] A.C. 435 (H.L.); *Greenpeace Foundation of B.C. et al. v. Min. of Environment*, [1981] 4 W.W.R. 587, 122 D.L.R. (3d) 179 (B.C. S.C.); *League for Life in Man. Inc. et al. v. Morgentaler et al.* (1985), 19 D.L.R. (4th) 703 (Man. Q.B.); *Carruthers et al. v. Langley et al.* (1984), 13 D.L.R. (4th) 528 (B.C.S.C.), affd 23 D.L.R. (4th) 623, leave to appeal to S.C.C. refused 67 N.R. 239n.

[73]*Supra*, note 50.

lacked ordinary standing for a declaration or an injunction, he could as a matter of discretion be given "public interest standing". That reasoning, applied in a non-constitutional public interest case, would presumably apply *a fortiori* in a constitutional case.

Even if standing is granted, as a matter of discretion, to seek an injunction in a constitutional case, there will remain other special difficulties for the applicant. In such cases the balance of convenience will often tend to favour treating the law as valid and permitting its enforcement until it is determined to be invalid. Court intervention by way of an interlocutory injunction is for the purpose of maintaining the *status quo*, and in most cases this will be better achieved by not dispensing with observance of the law.[74] It may be easier, however, in Charter cases to obtain an interlocutory injunction as it appears that the normal presumption of constitutionality may have little or no weight in the granting or refusal of interlocutory injunctions in such cases.[75]

An injunction may be sought by the Attorney General in a purely "public" action to enforce the law. In such cases the injunction may be granted even though other sanctions or remedies are provided by statute and even though there is no invasion of property rights actual or apprehended.[76] However, as noted before, the probability of an Attorney General seeking such a remedy to restrain the enforcement of an *ultra vires* statute of his own Legislature is not very great. It is perhaps more likely that he would do so to prevent violations of the Charter by an independent agency of his Government.

(c) Certiorari

It appears that there is no absolute requirement that an applicant for *certiorari* have an "interest" at stake in order to achieve standing. Standing is a matter of discretion but if the applicant is a "person aggrieved" he is normally entitled to the issue of the writ, and even if he is a

---

[74]*Morgentaler et al. v. Ackroyd et al.* (1983), 150 D.L.R. (3d) 59 (Ont. H.C.); *Gould v. A.G. Can. et al.*, [1984] 1 F.C. 1133 (C.A.), affirmed on appeal [1984] 2 S.C.R. 124; *Marchand v. Simcoe County Bd. of Educ. et al.* (1984), 10 C.R.R. 169 (Ont. H.C.). And see, *infra*, at pp. 305–07.

[75]*A.G. Man. v. Metro. Stores (MTS) Ltd. et al.*, [1987] 1 S.C.R. 110.

[76]*A.G. B.C. v. Cowen*, 53 B.C.R. 50, [1938] 2 W.W.R. 497, [1938] 4 D.L.R. 17 (C.A.), affd [1939] S.C.R. 20, [1939] 1 D.L.R. 288, without reference to this point. See also *Winner v. S.M.T. (Eastern) Ltd.*, [1951] S.C.R. 887, [1951] 4 D.L.R. 529, vard [1954] A.C. 541 (*sub nom. A.G. v. Winner*), 13 W.W.R. 657, 71 C.R.T.C. 225, where it was noted that the Attorney General of New Brunswick, originally an intervenant in a private action for an injunction, had been made a party in a newly constituted relator action; *United Nurses of Alta. v. A.G. Alta.* (1980), 25 A.R. 69, 124 D.L.R. (3d) 64, 61 C.C.C. (2d) 561, 82 CLLC 14,007 (Q.B.); *Gouriet v. Union of Post Office Workers*, [1978] A.C. 453, [1977] 3 All E.R. 70 (H.L.).

"stranger" to the proceedings for which he wishes judicial review by *certiorari* the court may exercise a discretion to grant him standing.[77]

Some examples of cases where the court has found the applicant to be a "person aggrieved" will illustrate the rather tenuous nature of the connection required with the decision to be attacked. In *Re Surrey Municipal By-Law*[78] the applicant was a resident of a town seeking *certiorari* to quash a decision of the municipal planning board which had permitted a club to reconstruct its building, allegedly without adequate parking space. In *Beaton v. P.E.I. Land Use Comm.*[79] the respondent commission had granted a permit for commercial development for an area which was allegedly larger than allowed by the regulations under which it operated. The applicant for *certiorari* to attack this decision on the basis of excess of jurisdiction owned land adjacent to the proposed development. He was apparently regarded as a "person aggrieved" for the purpose of seeking *certiorari* even though the court also indicated he would in any event be a person in whose favour judicial discretion could be exercised to grant standing. In *W.A.W. Holdings Ltd. v. Summer Village of Sundance Beach*[80] an adjacent landowner was held to have standing to seek *certiorari* against a decision of the village which had rejected the applicant's request for a pedestrian right-of-way through the village's road allowances.[81]

Apart from these situations where the applicant has been found to be a "person aggrieved" even though it may be hard to find interference with a legal right in the strict sense, it is open to the courts to exercise a discretion in favour of a "stranger".[82] There seems to be a particular willingness to do this where there is an issue of jurisdiction involved.[83] Therefore, where *certiorari* is an appropriate remedy, it should be avail-

---

[77]*De Smith's Judicial Review of Administrative Action*, 4th ed, Evans, ed. (London: Stevens, 1980), at 418–21; Mullan, *Administrative Law*, 2nd ed. (1979), at 157; but see Cromwell, *supra*, note 13, at pp. 103–09. In Quebec *certiorari* and prohibition have been replaced with the writ of evocation (C.C.P. Art. 846). As elsewhere, an applicant must have the interest required by C.C.P. Art. 55: *Turcotte v. Régie des eaux du Québec*, [1972] C.A. 623.

[78](1956), 6 D.L.R. (2d) 768 (B.C. S.C.).

[79](1979) 20 Nfld. & P.E.I.R. 140, 101 D.L.R. (3d) 404 (P.E.I. C.A.).

[80][1980] 1 W.W.R. 97, 105 D.L.R. (3d) 403 (Alta. Q.B.), revd [1981] 1 W.W.R. 581, 117 D.L.R. (3d) 351, 14 M.P.L.R. 68 (Alta. C.A.).

[81]See also *Re MacKenzie and MacArthur* (1980), 25 B.C.L.R. 303, 119 D.L.R. (3d) 529, 57 C.C.C. (2d) 130 (S.C.), distinguishing an earlier case where standing had been denied, *Young v. A.G. Man.* (1960), 33 W.W.R. 3, 25 D.L.R. (2d) 352, 129 C.C.C. 110 (Man. C.A.).

[82]*Energy Probe v. Atomic Energy Control Bd. et al.*, [1984] 2 F.C. 227 affd on other grounds [1985] 1 F.C. 563 (C.A.), application for leave to appeal to S.C.C. refused. Jan. 31, 1985.

[83]See, *e.g.*, *Re Thomas' Certiorari Application* (1969), 72 W.W.R. 54 (B.C. S.C.); *Beaton* case, *supra*, note 79.

able as a matter of discretion in a "public action" to challenge the constitutional validity of the decision in question. The considerations relevant to the exercise of such discretion will be discussed further.[84]

(d) Prohibition

While the rules for standing in prohibition proceedings are basically similar to those for *certiorari*, there is one situation where a "stranger" has a clear right to prohibition. Where he alleges a defect of jurisdiction which is patent on the face of the proceedings in question the court must grant his application for prohibition.[85] Otherwise, the court has a discretion to grant or refuse the application of a stranger.[86]

How do these rules apply where the excess of jurisdiction alleged is of a constitutional nature? When could it be said that the constitutional invalidity of a statute would be patent, rendering the attempted proceedings thereunder invalid so as to require the issue of a writ of prohibition? In almost every case where a statute is impugned there is serious doubt as to how it ought to be characterized in order to decide whether it genuinely comes within the jurisdiction of the enacting Legislature. In other cases there will be doubt whether the statute can be validly applied to the facts in question, or whether pending administrative acts will violate *Charter* rights.

Thus, in *R. v. Ontario Labour Relations Board; Ex p. Dunn*[87] prohibition was sought by a stranger to proceedings before the board, in order to stop the board from taking a vote among employees of a certain company. The applicant asserted that the company and its employees came under federal jurisdiction because it was a subsidiary of a company operating an undertaking which was within federal jurisdiction. Various factual issues concerning the nature of the relationship between the two companies were involved. Because of this complex legal and factual question the invalidity of the board's proceedings was far from "patent". The judge, as a result, admitted to having some doubt as to the standing of the applicants but proceeded to deal with the application on its merits. In this he appeared to be exercising his discretion in favour of allowing standing to a stranger.

---

[84]See, *infra*, at pp. 187–91.

[85]*Lott v. Cameron* (1897), 29 O.R. 70 (C.A.); *Re Holman and Rea* (1912), 27 O.L.R. 432, 9 D.L.R. 234, 21 C.C.C. 11 (C.A.); see also De Smith, *supra*, note 77 at pp. 416–18.

[86]*Re Board of Manhood Suffrage Registrars* (1901), 13 Man. R. 345 (K.B.); *Re I.U.O.E., Local No. 968 and Michelin Tires Mfg. Co.* (1973), 43 D.L.R. (3d) 602 (N.S. S.C.).

[87][1963] 2 O.R. 301, 39 D.L.R. (2d) 346 (H.C.).

It is suggested that most prohibition applications raising questions of constitutional validity will involve similarly difficult questions. As a result, it will be rare indeed that the constitutional defect will be so patent that the court will be bound to allow a "stranger" to apply. Instead it will have to exercise its discretion.[88]

(e) Mandamus

The requirements for standing in mandamus applications appear to be somewhat more stringent than those applying to *certiorari* and prohibition.[89] It has been suggested that here an applicant has no *locus standi* unless he has a specific legal right to performance of the official act with respect to which he seeks mandamus.[90] While a legal right will give an applicant the required standing, so apparently will some other special interest which the applicant has which is greater than the interest of the public generally.[91] Or he may sue on behalf of a class where that class has a special interest, even though it is not a legal interest. For example, a municipal taxpayer can apply for mandamus to require proper tax enforcement if he sues on behalf of all taxpayers. But he cannot apply on his own behalf alone because he has no interest greater than the taxpayers generally in the proper administration of municipal finances.[92] Nor, apparently, can a provincial voter require the issue of an election writ because he has no extraordinary interest in the holding of an election.[93]

Whereas the court may exercise a discretion in favour of granting standing to any applicant for *certiorari* or prohibition, the same is not true of mandamus. But the court may take a generous view of what constitutes a "special interest" sufficient to set the applicant apart from the general public. He need not show that in the absence of mandamus

---

[88]See, *infra*, at pp. 187–91.

[89]See generally Jaffe, *supra*, note 7, at pp. 1269–73.

[90]*E.g. Hughes v. Henderson* (1963), 46 W.W.R. 202, 42 D.L.R. (2d) 743 (Man. Q.B.); see also *Canadians for the Abolition of the Seal Hunt v. Min. of Fisheries and the Environment*, [1981] 1 F.C. 733, 111 D.L.R. (3d) 333 (T.D.).

[91]*R. v. Publicover* (1940), 15 M.P.R. 187 at 193, [1940] 4 D.L.R. 43 at 45 (N.S. C.A.); *W.A.W. Holdings Ltd.* case, *supra*, note 80; De Smith, *supra*, note 77 at pp. 550–51; Kavanagh, *A Guide to Judicial Review*, 2nd ed. (Toronto: Carswell, 1984), at p. 158.

[92]*Re Leahy and Garvey*, [1935] O.W.N. 41 (C.A.); *Cf. Re Simpson and Henderson* (1977), 13 O.R. (2d) 322, 71 D.L.R. (3d) 24 (H.C.).

[93]According to the Ontario Court of Appeal, in *Temple v. Bulmer*, whose decision is reported in [1943] S.C.R. 265 at 267, [1943] 3 D.L.R. 649 at 650, affd on other grounds by the Supreme Court of Canada. But see *Saskatchewan Human Rights Code*, S.S. 1979, c. S-24.1, s. 8, which recognizes the right of the voter to require that a legislative assembly shall not continue for more than five years.

he would be entitled to sue for damages for the failure to perform the duty in question.[94]

How useful could mandamus be in judicial review of legislation? To use this remedy an applicant would have to show that a public officer had refused to perform a constitutional duty or that he was prevented from performance by an invalid statute. The possibility of finding a constitutional duty of this sort cast on a particular official would be rather small. It might be more useful in enforcing individual or group rights under the Charter such as legal rights, equality rights, or minority language education rights. However, mandamus would not be an appropriate remedy where the official is primarily responsible to the Crown[95] or to the Legislature[96] for the way in which he exercises his functions.

(f) References

By legislation in each of the provinces the Lieutenant Governor in Council is empowered to refer constitutional questions to a provincial superior court (usually the court of last resort) for an opinion. Similarly, the *Supreme Court Act* permits the Governor in Council to refer to that court "important questions of law or fact" touching, *inter alia*, the constitutionality of legislation.[97]

The requirements of standing appear to be largely irrelevant where a constitutional issue is referred to the courts. In the first place, the court is obliged to consider such questions and to answer them if possible, even if there is no actual controversy between interested parties.[98] The court would seemingly have to perform this function even if no one appeared to argue for or against the validity of legislation.

Statutes or rules in respect of references recognize or assume a leading role of Attorneys General in the argument of such cases. Notice requirements in constitutional cases generally enable provincial Attorneys General and the Attorney General of Canada to be heard where appropriate

---

[94]De Smith, *supra*, note 77 at pp. 550–51.

[95]*R. v. Treasury Lords Commrs.* (1872), 7 L.R. Q.B. 387, 26 L.T. 64.

[96]*Temple v. Bulmer, supra,* note 93; see also *Canadians for the Abolition of the Seal Hunt, supra,* note 90.

[97]See c. 9, *infra*.

[98]*A.G. Ont. v. A.G. Can.*, [1912] A.C. 571, 3 D.L.R. 509 (P.C.); *A.G. B.C. v. A.G. Can.*, [1914] A.C. 153, 5 W.W.R. 878, 15 D.L.R. 308 (P.C.). *Re Order in Council; Re Crop Payments Act*, 36 Man. R. 34, [1926] 2 W.W.R. 844, [1927] 2 D.L.R. 50 (C.A.); *Re Resolution to Amend the Constitution*, [1981] 1 S.C.R. 753 at 884–85, 125 D.L.R. (3d) 1 at 87–88, 11 Man. R. (2d) 1, 34 Nfld. & P.E.I.R. 1, [1981] 6 W.W.R. 1 (*sub nom. A.G. Man. v. A.G. Can.*), 39 N.R. 1, 1 C.R.R. 59.

in provincial courts.[99] Rule 32 of the Supreme Court of Canada requires notice to all Attorneys General of any issue as to the constitutional validity or constitutional applicability of any federal or provincial statute or regulation. (This does not apply where the issue is simply the possible administrative infringement of a Charter right.) In such cases, the Attorneys General when notified are entitled as of right to intervene. Thus they are entitled to intervene in appeals to the Supreme Court of decisions on references taken to, and decided initially by, the court of any province. Reference statutes also make provision for the presentation of argument by other interested persons. A typical provincial statute states: "The court may direct that any person interested, or where there is a class of persons interested, any one or more persons as representatives of that class, shall be notified of the hearing, and those persons shall be entitled to be heard."[100] Similar provisions can be found in all of the provinces and in the *Supreme Court Act*.[101] While there appears to be a requirement that a person to be heard must be "interested", this is interpreted very loosely in practice. In examining reports of decisions in constitutional references one may sometimes wonder what recognizable "interest" some of the "parties" would have had. It was clearly not a legal "interest" of the type required to bring an action for damages. For example, in *Reference re Wartime Leasehold Regulations*[102] concerning the validity of certain federal rent controls, the following organizations were heard by the Supreme Court: "Tenants within Canada", the Canadian Legion of the British Empire Service League, the Canadian Federation of Property Owners Association, and the Canadian Congress of Labour. In *Reference re Anti-Inflation Act*,[103] among those represented were: the Canadian Labour Congress; the Ontario Teachers' Federation; Renfrew County Division, District 25, Ontario Secondary School Teachers' Federation; Ontario Public Service Employees' Union; Canadian Union of Public Employees; and Canadian Union of Public Employees, Local 1230. In *Reference re Residential Tenancies Act*[104], the Federation of Metro Tenants Associations and the London Property Management Association were repre-

---

[99]See, *supra*, at pp. 74–77.

[100]*Constitutional Questions Act*, R.S.S. 1978, c. C-29, s. 5.

[101]*Judicature Act*, R.S.A. 1980, c. J-1, s. 27(4); *Constitutional Question Act*, R.S.B.C. 1979, c. 63, s. 5; *The Constitutional Questions Act*, C.C.S.M., c. C180, s. 4(1); *Judicature Act*, R.S.N.B. 1973, c. J-2, s. 23(4); *Judicature Act, 1986*, S.N. 1986, c. 42, s. 17; *Constitutional Questions Act*, R.S.N.S. 1967, c. 51, s. 5; *Courts of Justice Act, 1984*, S.O. 1984, c. 11, s. 19(5); *Judicature Act*, R.S.P.E.I. 1974, c. J-3, s. 38(4); *Court of Appeal Reference Act*, R.S.Q. 1977, c. R-23, s. 4; *Supreme Court Act*, R.S.C. 1970, c. S-19, s. 55(4).

[102][1950] S.C.R. 124, [1950] 2 D.L.R. 1.

[103][1976] 2 S.C.R. 373, 68 D.L.R. (3d) 452, 9 N.R. 541.

[104][1981] 1 S.C.R. 714, 123 D.L.R. (3d) 554, 37 N.R. 158.

sented. In *Re Resolution to Amend the Constitution*;[105] the Four Nations Confederacy, Inc., a native organization, was represented.

In *Reference re Language Rights in Manitoba*[106] there were 11 non-governmental interveners allowed, 7 of whom were individuals (6 represented together), and 4 of whom were interest groups including "Alliance Québec" and the "Freedom of Choice Movement". In *Reference re an Act to amend the Education Act*[107] in the Ontario Court of Appeal there were over 30 intervenants represented, including a variety of separate school boards, public school boards, private schools, teachers' associations, public interest groups and individuals.

If persons concerned with the legislation do not come forward to participate, provision is made in most jurisdictions for presentation of argument on behalf of unrepresented interests. The Saskatchewan *Constitutional Questions Act* states:

> 6. Where any interest affected is not represented by counsel the court may request counsel to argue the case in that interest, and reasonable expenses thereof shall be paid out of the consolidated fund.[108]

Comparable provisions may be found in six other provinces[109] and in the *Supreme Court Act*.[110] This clearly indicates that a "dispute" may be simulated by the court where no genuine conflict of interest between individuals has emerged.

The foregoing rules all relate to the hearing at first instance in the court to which a question is initially referred. What of provincial references which are appealed from the court of last resort in the province to the Supreme Court? The *Supreme Court Act* now specifically permits appeals in such cases where an appeal is so authorized by provincial law.[111]

As noted earlier, all Attorneys General are entitled to intervene in such appeals of constitutional reference decisions. While the Supreme Court briefly provided by its rules that anyone who had intervened in the courts below was entitled to intervene on the appeal, this provision has

---

[105]*Supra*, note 98.
[106][1985] 1 S.C.R. 721, [1985] 4 W.W.R. 385.
[107](1986), 25 D.L.R. (4th) 1.
[108]R.S.S. 1978, c. C-29.
[109]*Judicature Act*, R.S.A. 1980, c. J-1, s. 27(5); *The Constitutional Questions Act,*, C.C.S.M., c. C180, s. 5; *Judicature Act, 1986*, S.N. 1986, c. 42, s. 18; *Constitutional Questions Act*, R.S.N.S. 1967, c. 51, s. 6; *Courts of Justice Act, 1984*, S.O. 1984, c. 11, s. 19(6); *Judicature Act*, R.S.P.E.I. 1974, c. J-3, s. 38(5).
[110]R.S.C. 1970, c. S-19, s. 55(5).
[111]*Ibid.*, s. 37. Quebec has no general authorization for such appeals.

been repealed.[112] All interveners other than Attorneys General are obliged to apply pursuant to Rule 18 for leave to intervene at the Supreme Court stage. While there has been a certain tendency of late for the Supreme Court to restrict interventions in a constitutional case, this has been less noticeable in references and reference appeals.[113] Perhaps to meet some of the concerns expressed as to the desirability of such interventions, while enabling the court to control the length of its hearings, it has recently amended Rule 18 to require those seeking leave to intervene to define their position, to outline their submissions, and to show how their submissions "will be different and useful", all before leave is granted. Further, the amendment provides that such interveners shall not present oral argument unless the court otherwise orders.[114] (This will be discussed more fully later in connection with the role of interveners).[115] The court can, of course, give leave for additional persons to intervene at the appeal stage even if they had not been heard in the provincial courts.[116]

The reference system does provide a means whereby constitutional issues may be fought in the courts by persons with no legal interest at stake. This has the advantage of permitting judicial review in some situations where it would not otherwise be available because no one would have standing to raise the issue. For example, in the absence of a clear denial of his established right to vote in a given election, it is uncertain that a citizen has sufficient standing to go to court over the way in which the election machinery is operated[117] (although since the *Thorson, McNeil*, and *Borowski* cases it is less clear that a voter could not raise such an issue in an action for a declaration).[118] A voter might not be able to prevent a reapportionment of constituencies which would wrongly reduce the number of members which his province was entitled to in the House of Commons. Yet, in the reference *A.G. P.E.I. v. A.G. Can.; A.G. N.B. v. A.G. Can.*,[119] the Supreme Court and Judicial Committee of the Privy Council were enabled to consider the validity of such a reapportionment. A judicial interpretation was given to the provisions of the B.N.A. Act, upholding the reduction in the number of members of Parliament from

---

[112]Supreme Court Act Rules, SOR/83–74, Rule 18(2), repealed by SOR/83–930.

[113]Welch, "No Room at the Top: Interest Group Intervenors and *Charter* Litigation in the Supreme Court of Canada" (1985), 43 *U.T. Fac. L. Rev.* 204 at 227–28.

[114]SOR/87–292.

[115]*Infra.* pp. 195–97.

[116]See, *e.g., Re A.G. Que. and A.G. Can.* (1982), 140 D.L.R. (3d) 385, 45 N.R. 317 (*sub nom. Quebec Constitutional Amendment Reference (No. 2)*).

[117]See, *infra*, at pp. 175–79.

[118]See, *e.g., Nat. Citizens' Coalition Inc.—Coalition Nat. des Citoyens Inc. v. A.G. Can.* (1984), 11 D.L.R. (4th) 481 (Alta. Q.B.).

[119][1905] A.C. 37, 91 L.T. 636 (P.C.).

Prince Edward Island and New Brunswick. Here there was an issue suitable for judicial action, that is, the interpretation of the meaning of a formula laid down by statute. It was an issue which might well have gone without judicial solution had it not been for the reference system.

(g) Appeals by an Attorney General as Intervenant

In most provinces and in the Supreme Court of Canada the provincial or federal Attorney General must be given notice and allowed to appear in cases where someone has attacked the validity of legislation.[120] Normally, of course, the Attorney General would appear in a position analogous to defendant and the standing problem would not arise. Suppose, however, that the lower court fails to uphold his argument in favour of validity. Suppose further that other parties of like interest wish to drop the matter at this stage but the Attorney General as intervenant wishes to appeal the constitutional point. Can he maintain an appeal in his own right where he would have to appear as appellant and not merely as intervenant?

In those provinces where the Attorney General is given the status of an intervenant only, he cannot maintain an appeal in the absence of another party of like interest. In those provinces where by statute he is made a party or put in the same position as a party he can apparently maintain the appeal by himself.[121] The same would, of course, be true where he has actually been added as a party in the original court.

As a result of the recent revision of the Rules of the Supreme Court of Canada, it appears that if an Attorney General, though not a party, has intervened in the courts below, he has some recognized status in an appeal brought by one of the parties. He can apply to the court for the purpose of stating a constitutional question.[122]

This provides other examples of a person being allowed to bring a constitutional issue before the courts where he has no legal interest at stake.

(h) Statutory Rights of Action

At least two obvious examples may be noted of actions specially authorized by law where a legal interest may be lacking in the person instituting the action.

---

[120]See, *supra*, at pp. 74–86.

[121]See, *supra*, at pp. 81–83. This could be particularly useful where the original action was collusive. *Cf. U.S. v. Johnson*, 319 U.S. 302 (1943).

[122]SOR/83–74, subrule 32(8).

Provincial statutes governing municipalities usually permit an action to be brought to quash municipal by-laws. Often the action is allowed to persons not having a legal interest in the narrow sense.[123] The grounds of attack might be that the provincial Legislature had no jurisdiction to confer power on the municipality to pass such a by-law.[124]

Another special action is that permitted to Attorneys General in some of the provinces for a declaration as to the validity or invalidity of statutes. Four of the provinces, Alberta, British Columbia, Manitoba and New Brunswick, permit such actions, at the instance of either the Attorney General of Canada or the Attorney General of the province, with respect to the validity of provincial legislation. Ontario legislation goes farther in allowing a similar action with respect to federal legislation.[125] It has been held that such provisions authorize an action to be brought by an Attorney General even where no rights of his Government are at stake.[126]

2. Interests Recognized in Particular Classes of Persons

(a) Voters

The common law since *Ashby v. White* has recognized that a qualified voter has a right to his vote in the nature of a property interest. In the absence of some valid statute denying that right, he would have an action for damages against those who prevented him from exercising it.[127] If legislation purported to deny the franchise to a person otherwise entitled by law to vote he would apparently have sufficient standing, in attacking the constitutional validity of that legislation, to employ any remedy for which an ''interest'' is required.[128] As well, some electoral laws permit an appeal to the courts from the decision of election officials with respect to the right of a person to vote. In such cases there appears to be no

---

[123]See Rogers, *The Law of Canadian Municipal Corporations*, 2nd ed. (Toronto: Carswell, 1971), at 989–90.

[124]*Ibid.*, at pp. 1017–18. And see, *e.g., City of Winnipeg v. Barrett; City of Winnipeg v. Logan*, [1892] A.C. 445, 67 L.T. 429.

[125]For particulars of these actions see, *supra*, at pp. 121, 122.

[126]*A.G. Ont. v. A.G. Can.*, [1931] O.R. 5, [1931] 2 D.L.R. 297, 55 C.C.C. 346 (H.C.).

[127]*Ashby v. White* (1704), 2 Raym. Ld. 938, 92 E.R. 126 (H.L.); *Crawford v. St. John* (1898), 34 N.B.R. 560 (C.A.). In some jurisdictions the right to damages as against election officials is limited or abolished by legislation. Even where the right to damages is abolished, there would presumably still be a right of action against other persons interfering with the franchise, and there should still be a recognition that the citizen has a legal ''interest'' in his franchise. The civil law in Quebec has apparently also recognized such an interest: see, *e.g.*, Mignault, 5 *Droit civil canadien* (1901), at 363.

[128]See *Collins v. Min. of Interior*, [1957] 1 So. Afr. L.R. 552 (C.A.).

difficulty in the appellant challenging the validity of legislation or administrative action which has deprived him of his vote.[129]

This position at common law has been reinforced by the provisions of ss. 3 and 24 of the *Canadian Charter of Rights and Freedoms*.[130] Section 3 constitutionally guarantees the right to vote in federal and provincial elections to "every citizen of Canada". (This is, of course, a right subject to "reasonable limits" prescribed by law under s. 1.) Section 24 assures that anyone "whose rights or freedoms, as guaranteed by this Charter, have been infringed or denied" has standing to sue and it gives the court a complete discretion to grant such remedy as it "considers appropriate and just in the circumstances". So anyone suffering or threatened with an actual denial of a right to vote is now constitutionally regarded as having sufficient standing for any remedy.[131]

Short of an absolute loss of his vote, of what other abuses of the electoral system can a voter complain? In Canada such common law authority as can be found seems to indicate that the voter has few if any other rights in relation to the way in which the electoral machinery is operated. He cannot require that an election be held because the election officials are responsible only to the Legislature; the voter has no right to have an election held unless some statute specifically confers that right upon him.[132] Thus it is arguable that a voter would have no special interest to enforce s. 4 of the Charter which requires in effect that elections for the House of Commons and legislative assemblies be held at least once every five years. Yet a statute which purported to delay the election beyond this period would, under ordinary circumstances, be invalid. The life of these legislative bodies can only be extended "in time of real or apprehended war, invasion or insurrection" and then only if less than one-third of the members of the chamber in question object. No voter would have standing to challenge the validity of a wrongful extension, at least if he employed a remedy which required him to have an "interest". Perhaps, with relaxed rules of standing, he could seek a declaration but this might be all.

The position of the voter at common law with respect to redistribution

---

[129]*Cunningham v. Tomey Homma*, [1903] A.C. 151, 87 L.T. 572 (P.C.).

[130]Schedule B of *Canada Act, 1982*, c. 11 (U.K.).

[131]This appears to have been taken for granted in cases under s. 3 of the Charter such as *Re Maltby et al. and A.G. Sask. et al.* (1982), 143 D.L.R. (3d) 649 (Sask. Q.B.), revd on other grounds 10 D.L.R. (4th) 745 (Sask. C.A.); *Re Reynolds and A.G. B.C.* (1984), 11 D.L.R. (4th) 380 (B.C. C.A.) leave to appeal to S.C.C. granted 57 N.R. 158n; and *Re Hoogbruin et al. and A.G. B.C. et al.* (1985), 24 D.L.R. (4th) 718 (B.C. C.A.).

[132]*Temple v. Bulmer*, [1943] S.C.R. 265, [1943] 3 D.L.R. 649. But see the *Saskatchewan Human Rights Code*, S.S. 1979, c. S-24.1, s. 8.

or reapportionment of constituencies is even less certain. While there seems to be no decision on the precise point, he appears to have no interest in any election matter not actually constituting a deprivation of his vote. He has no standing to complain about how the voter's list is prepared, as long as he cannot show that his name will be wrongfully left off the list.[133] Apart from special statutory provisions, he has no right to insist on a recount of votes being held, even if he is both a voter and a defeated candidate.[134] In neither case can he complain that he has been denied a vote, and thus the principles of *Ashby v. White*[135] do not apply. It is therefore doubtful that a Canadian court would under the common law recognize an interest vested in any voter to cast his vote in a constituency of any particular size. Thus, for example, no voter would have such an interest to enable him to enforce the constitutional formula for periodic redistribution of seats in the House of Commons. Section 51 of the *Constitution Act, 1867* requires a redistribution after each decennial census, to be effected (with several exceptions) on the basis of representation by population. If Parliament should fail to effect a redistribution prior to the election following the decennial census, which frequently occurs, it is doubtful if a voter could attack the validity of the existing distribution. Nor, if a redistribution is carried out, would he have a sufficient interest to challenge the legislation effecting it. He would have to employ some remedy for which he would not have to show an interest. Alternatively the courts could be called on for an opinion by means of a governmental reference.[136]

It must nevertheless be recognized that in other common law jurisdictions voters have been allowed status in court to attack redistribution schemes where constitutional issues were involved. In the State of Victoria, Australia, such an issue was involved in the case of *McDonald v. Cain*.[137] The state Legislature had passed a statute establishing a commission to redistribute the electoral districts. The plaintiffs were members, and also voters, in constituencies which would probably disappear if the scheme of the Act were applied. They sought a declaration that the Act was invalid because it had not received the special majority of the vote in each house of the Legislature which they claimed the constitution required. With respect to the question of their status to seek such a declaration, the court held that the plaintiffs as voters had a sufficient interest. They appear to have treated the abolition of a constituency as tantamount to a denial of the right to vote. Reliance was placed on the

---

[133]*Re Bd. of Manhood Suffrage Registrars* (1901), 13 Man. R. 345 (K.B.).
[134]*McLeod v. Noble* (1897), 28 O.R. 528 (Div. Ct.).
[135]*Supra*, note 127.
[136]As was done, *e.g.*, in *A.G. P.E.I. v. A.G. Can.*, *supra*, note 119.
[137][1953] Vict. L.R. 411 (S.C.).

decision in *Ashby v. White* by Gavan Duffy J., and the other judgments seemed to proceed on a similar basis. The case does appear to be unique in recognizing a right in the voter to continue to vote in the same constituency, going beyond the recognition of a simple right to vote in some constituency. It may be noted that the declaration was in fact refused on substantive grounds.

More recently in Australia the High Court entertained an action to challenge two Commonwealth laws under which federal voters were apportioned among constituencies, on the basis that these laws did not adequately meet the implicit requirements of the constitution for equality of representation. There were several plaintiffs, including a voter suing as such and a state Attorney General suing as *parens patriae*. While Barwick C.J. thought the individual citizen would not have standing[138] (although the other plaintiffs would) the general approach of the court was to accept the standing of all plaintiffs. The substantive issues were therefore dealt with.

In the United States it has been clear since the decision in *Baker v. Carr*[139] that a state voter has standing to bring an action to challenge the apportionment of electoral districts in a state Legislature. Standing in such cases appears to turn on the existence of constitutional standards such as the guarantee of the ''equal protection of the laws'' in the Fourteenth Amendment to the federal Constitution. A voter is thereby deemed to have an interest in being able to vote in a district containing approximately the same number of voters as other districts in the state.

In the past in Canada it would have been hard to find any entrenched constitutional standards for apportionment in provincial Legislatures, and there were only limited requirements for Parliament related to distribution, as among provinces and the territories, of seats in the House of Commons without reference to distribution within a given province.[140] Moreover, the past jurisprudence, particularly before the *Thorson* and subsequent cases on standing for declarations, would not likely have sustained the right of an individual voter to attack any redistribution scheme for the House of Commons that failed to meet these constitutional requirements. But with the adoption of the *Canadian Charter of Rights and Freedoms* the position may have changed. Apart from the right of the citizen to complain under s. 3 with respect to an actual denial of his right to vote, any ''individual'' may be able to complain under s-s. 15(1), because of a dilution or distortion of this right through malapportionment of constituencies.[141] Subsection 15(1), it will be remembered, states that

---

[138]*A.G. ex rel. McKinlay v. Commonwealth of Australia* (1975), 135 C.L.R. 1 at 26.
[139]369 U.S. 186 (1962).
[140]*Constitution Act, 1867*, c. 3 (U.K.), ss. 51, 51A, 52.
[141]In *Re Election Act (B.C.); Scott v. A.G. B.C. et al.*, [1986] 5 W.W.R. 207 (B.C.

> Every individual is equal before and under the law and has the right
> to the equal protection and equal benefit of the law without discrimination
> and, in particular, without discrimination based on race, national or ethnic
> origin, colour, religion, sex, age or mental or physical disability.

If Canadian courts take the same route as United States courts, they may
regard alleged malapportionment[142] or overly broad restriction of the franchise on particular issues[143] as denying equal protection of the law. Discrimination in apportionment or conditions for exercise of voting rights
that appear, for example, to be related to race, colour, or sex, some of
which have been found to fall within the Fifteenth Amendment of the
United States Constitution[144] instead of or as well as the equal protection
clause of the Fourteenth Amendment, might also be embraced by the
more broad provisions of s. 15 of the Charter. As the rights stated in
s. 15 attach to the "individual", the voter or would-be voter should be
entitled to commence action because it is his own legal right that has
been denied; he asserts not only the right to vote (as already recognized
by *Ashby v. White* as a legal right which confers standing to sue on its
holder) but also the constitutional right to vote on an equal basis with
other individuals. By definition his claim is not the same as every other
voter, although there may be a large number of other voters similarly
situated.

Standing now exists, by virtue of the Charter, for a citizen to raise
other election-related issues concerning laws governing contributions for
political purposes on the basis of possible interference with freedom of
expression.[145] And, as has been noted elsewhere, once he demonstrates
a denial of a right guaranteed under the Charter, he can invoke s-s. 24(1)
to request any appropriate remedy.

(b) Taxpayers

Apart from their special statutory rights of action previously discussed,[146] municipal ratepayers are allowed standing by the common law

---

S.C.), an individual voter was granted standing to seek a declaration based on ss. 3
and 15 of the Charter, although malapportionment was not the issue.

[142]*E.g., Baker v. Carr, supra*, note 139 and accompanying text.

[143]*E.g., Kramer v. Union Free School Dist.* 395 U.S. 621 (1969); *Cipriano v. City of
Houma*, 395 U.S. 701 (1968).

[144]*E.g., Gomillion v. Lightfoot*, 364 U.S. 339 (1960).

[145]*Nat. Citizens' Coalition* case, *supra*, note 118; *Re Lavigne and Ont. Pub. Service
Employees Union* (1986), 55 O.R. (2d) 449, 29 D.L.R. (4th) 321 (H.C.).

[146]See *supra*, notes 123, 124 and accompanying text. See also Cromwell, *supra*, note 13,
at pp. 48–50.

to challenge the validity of by-laws in certain other cases. These actions appear to be "public" actions because the ratepayer is permitted to sue even though he can show no special injury to himself or no special interest different from that of the ratepayers generally.

This right of action arises where the municipal Government has made or is about to make an expenditure which is alleged by a ratepayer to be *ultra vires*.[147] The rationale of this action is that all municipal ratepayers are threatened with financial loss if an illegal expenditure is made, because the treasury will have to be replenished from additional or unnecessary taxes imposed on them. Thus if there is no threatened financial loss of this nature the ratepayer has no standing to challenge the validity of the municipal Government's decisions. The Attorney General is the only one who can commence an action to restrain *ultra vires* activity in such cases.[148] If the financial aspect affects not only the municipality but the province generally, then the ratepayer does not have standing.[149] The object of the action is to require the municipality to take appropriate measures to correct its error, not to raise abstract issues. Where the municipality has performed its duty and repudiated *ultra vires* measures, the ratepayer loses his standing.[150]

In these ratepayers' actions of a public nature, the ratepayer must sue on behalf of himself and all other ratepayers in a class action. The theory of the class action is that where there is a common interest and a common grievance, all persons sharing that interest and grievance can be represented in such a suit if the relief sought would be appropriate for all those represented.[151] Thus the relief most commonly available in ratepayers' actions is the declaration of invalidity, sometimes combined with an injunction. Damages are not available in such class actions.

It is obvious that where the ratepayer's action is available, it could be used on occasion to challenge the validity of legislation under which the municipality purported to act. Assume, for example, that provincial legislation required municipalities to spend money on defence by mount-

---

[147]*MacIlreith v. Hart* (1908), 39 S.C.R. 657, 4 E.L.R. 468; folld in *Affleck v. City of Nelson* (1957), 23 W.W.R. 386, 10 D.L.R. (2d) 442 (B.C. S.C.); *Vladicka v. Calgary Bd. of School Trustees*, [1974] 4 W.W.R. 159, 45 D.L.R. (3d) 442 (Alta. S.C.); *Maguire v. City of Calgary*, [1981] 2 W.W.R. 154 (Alta. Q.B.). For the earlier English authority see *Boyce v. Paddington B.C.*, [1903] 1 Ch. 109. But see *Ottawa Separate Schools Trustees v. Mackell*, [1917] A.C. 62 (P.C.).

[148]*Robertson v. Montreal* (1915), 52 S.C.R. 30, 26 D.L.R. 228; *S.M.T. (Eastern) Ltd. v. St. John*, 18 M.P.R. 374, [1946] 4 D.L.R. 209, 60 C.R.T.C. 186, affd 19 M.P.R. 103, [1947] 1 D.L.R. 842 (N.B.C.A.); *Fransden v. Lethbridge* (1965), 52 W.W.R. 620 (Alta. S.C.).

[149]*Loggie v. Town of Chatham* (1927), 54 N.B.R. 230, [1928] 2 D.L.R. 583 (C.A.).

[150]*Dilworth v. Town of Bala*, [1955] S.C.R. 284, [1955] 2 D.L.R. 353.

[151]*Bedford (Duke) v. Ellis*, [1901] A.C. 1, [1900–03] All E.R. Rep. 694 (H.L.); *Tiny R.C. Separate Schools Trustees v. The King*, 59 O.L.R. 96 at 152–53 (H.C.).

ing air-raid warning sirens. A ratepayer might sue in a class action for a declaration that such expenditures by the municipality would be *ultra vires* because defence is not a matter on which a province can legislate.[152] Or, suppose that a provincial enactment is alleged to violate the guarantees for denominational schools, by interfering with the right to give religious education during school hours. Those persons assessed for taxes for such schools might challenge the constitutional right of the local authority to implement such a law if its implementation would throw additional financial burdens on them.[153]

If the municipal taxpayer has a standing to restrain illegal expenditures, including those which are without constitutional authorization, what of the provincial or federal taxpayer? In the United States a distinction was made at one time between standing in federal courts for municipal taxpayers and those of senior Governments.[154] More recently, however, standing has been recognized in federal taxpayers to challenge unauthorized expenditures,[155] provided that a specific constitutional limitation on expenditures is sought to be enforced.[156]

In Canada the Supreme Court appears, with the *Thorson*,[157] *McNeil*[158] and *Borowski*[159] cases, to have merged the municipal taxpayer's action into a broader basis for standing which allows anyone to challenge governmental action for validity, constitutional or otherwise, simply because in its view there must be a way to bring before the courts for resolution any question of governmental illegality.

The early consideration of the applicability of *MacIlreith v. Hart*,[160] the leading Supreme Court decision of 1908 on the municipal taxpayer's action, to provincial taxpayers, had not been promising. In *Smith v. A.G. Ont.*[161] the majority treated the *MacIlreith* principle as an exception and were unwilling to extend it to allow standing for provincial taxpayers as

---

[152]See *Constitution Act, 1867*, c. 3, s. 91(7), (U.K.).

[153]For an example of the converse situation see *Ottawa Separate Schools Trustees v. Mackell, supra,* note 147.

[154]*Frothingham v. Mellon*, 262 U.S. 447 (1923).

[155]*Flast v. Cohen*, 392 U.S. 83 (1968).

[156]*E.g., United States v. Richardson*, 418 U.S. 166 (1974); *Schlesinger v. Reservists Committee to Stop the War*, 94 S.Ct. 2925, 418 U.S. 208 (1974).

[157]*Thorson v. A.G. Can.*, [1975] 1 S.C.R. 138, 43 D.L.R. (3d) 1, 1 N.R. 225.

[158]*McNeil v. N.S. Bd. of Censors*, [1976] 2 S.C.R. 265, 12 N.S.R. (2d) 85, 55 D.L.R. (3d) 632, 5 N.R. 43, 32 C.R.N.S. 376.

[159]*Borowski v. Min. of Justice of Canada*, [1981] 2 S.C.R. 575, 12 Sask. R. 420, [1982] 1 W.W.R. 97, 130 D.L.R. (3d) 588, 39 N.R. 331, 64 C.C.C. (2d) 97, 24 C.P.C. 62, 24 C.R. (3d) 352. See now also *Min. of Finance of Can. et al. v. Finlay* [1986] 2 S.C.R. 607.

[160]*Supra*, note 147.

[161][1924] S.C.R. 331, [1924] 3 D.L.R. 189, 42 C.C.C. 215, discussed, *supra*, notes 18, 20–23 and accompanying text.

they thought it would "lead to grave inconvenience".[162] This view was also approved by the dissenting minority 50 years later in the *Thorson*[163] case where the plaintiff sued as a federal taxpayer.

It is clear, however, from the majority judgment in *Thorson* that while the plaintiff taxpayer was granted standing in an action to attack the validity of a federal law and the expenditures in connection with its implementation, this was not really dependent on his taxpayer status. First, Laskin J. for the majority explains the refusal of the Supreme Court to apply the principle of *MacIlreith* in the *Smith* case on the basis that the latter involved an attack on a regulatory statute where the plaintiff had not yet been directly regulated. But the salient feature of *MacIlreith* was, seemingly, that *ultra vires* activity was involved and, as a general principle, the court had been prepared to deal with that issue where it would otherwise go without remedy.[164] The recognition of standing for a federal taxpayer therefore is treated as a matter for judicial discretion which should turn on such considerations as justiciability of the issue, and the nature of the legislation whether regulatory or declaratory. (If declaratory there might be no one specifically injured so someone should be granted standing to challenge it.)[165]

In conclusion, the majority judgment by Laskin J., virtually discards the concept of the federal, and, by implication, the provincial, taxpayer's action.

> I recognize that any attempt to place standing in a federal taxpayer suit on the likely tax burden or debt resulting from an illegal expenditure, by analogy to one of the reasons given for allowing municipal taxpayers' suits, is as unreal as it is in the municipal taxpayer cases. Certainly, a federal taxpayer's interest may be no less than that of a municipal taxpayer in that respect. It is not the alleged waste of public funds alone that will support standing but rather the right of the citizenry to constitutional behaviour by Parliament where the issue in such behaviour is justiciable as a legal question.[166]

Apart from this express dismissal of federal taxpayer status as the justification *per se* for standing, it is apparent from the judgment that such status was irrelevant to the conclusion reached. There was no analysis of the constitutional limitations on expenditures, if any, that might be invoked by the plaintiff to establish the connection between his status as a taxpayer and the constitutional illegality he was alleging. The majority

---

[162]*Ibid.*, at pp. 337–38 S.C.R.
[163]*Supra*, note 157 at pp. 141–42 S.C.R., p. 4 D.L.R.
[164]*Supra*, note 157 at pp. 157–58, S.C.R. pp. 15–16 D.L.R.
[165]*Supra*, note 157 at p. 161 S.C.R., pp. 17–18 D.L.R.
[166]*Supra*, note 157 at pp. 162–63 S.C.R., p. 19 D.L.R.

judgment in fact recognizes that, unlike municipalities, neither federal nor provincial Governments are limited in the objects for which they can spend money,[167] presumably because they both have a "spending power" that goes beyond their legislative powers.

Little attention was paid to taxpayer status in the subsequent *McNeil* and *Borowski* cases, even though in each case the plaintiff apparently described himself as a provincial and federal taxpayer respectively. This aspect was not addressed in *McNeil* and in *Borowski* the majority quoted the above passage from the *Thorson* judgment[168] as to the unreality of taxpayers' interests. While it later referred to the plaintiff as "a concerned citizen and a taxpayer" nothing appeared to turn on the latter characteristic. Again, no attention was paid to the question of what expenditures were illegal nor to the constitutional limitation which would allegedly make them illegal.

It would therefore appear that little weight is added to a claim for standing, in a challenge to federal or provincial laws or actions, by an allegation that the plaintiff is a taxpayer of the jurisdiction in question. It is possible that if the alleged illegality were that of an expenditure contrary to specific spending limitations in the constitution (though none such come to mind) then this would be an important factor in the exercise of discretion in favour of granting standing. But the result of the case law on standing in declaratory actions is now such that it appears almost certainly to be available wherever constitutionally unauthorized activity can be alleged, without resort to comparatively limiting factors such as taxpayer status. Presumably the municipal taxpayer's action can still be resorted to, even for unconstitutional expenditures by municipalities, but the concerned ratepayer would seemingly also have available to him the action for a declaration on the virtually unlimited basis laid down by the *Thorson, McNeil* and *Borowski* decisions whether the complaint involves an illegal expenditure or not.[169]

(c) Shareholders

The right of a shareholder to sue his company with respect to *ultra vires* acts is also in the nature of a public remedy which could be used for raising a constitutional issue. Again the plaintiff may not be able to show any special interest in himself distinct from similar interests in many others.

---

[167]*Supra*, note 157 at p. 159 S.C.R., p. 16 D.L.R.
[168]*Supra*, note 166.
[169]See *Stein v. City of Winnipeg*, [1974] 5 W.W.R. 484, 48 D.L.R. (3d) 223 (Man. C.A.).

The shareholder's action is available wherever it is alleged that the company has done or is about to do something which is *ultra vires*.[170] It is apparently not necessary that some illegal expenditure be involved. Nor is it necessary that the shareholder sue as a representative of a class. He may sue on his own behalf alone,[171] unless the court otherwise requires.

Shareholders' actions have been used in several cases as a means of challenging the validity of legislation before the courts. The device usually employed has been an action by a shareholder against the company to restrain it from carrying on business without complying with certain legislation. The company then defends on the basis that the legislation is itself *ultra vires*.[172] The converse method could be used as readily, with the plaintiff seeking to restrain the company from obeying a law which he alleged to be invalid.[173]

There seems to be little reason for giving company shareholders any special privileges with respect to standing in constitutional cases. Why should a shareholder through his membership in the company be able to raise the question of validity, regardless of financial prejudice to himself or to the company, when a provincial taxpayer as such cannot challenge the validity of a law which materially increases his taxes? There is also the possibility, in shareholders' actions of this kind, that the litigants are not always of adverse interest. Suspicions of collusion have been voiced by the courts in some cases. In *Union Colliery v. Bryden* Lord Watson remarked that the Attorney General of British Columbia had suspected collusion and had intervened.[174]

In *Great West Saddlery Co. v. The King; John Deere Plow Co. v. The King; A. MacDonald Co. v. Harmer*, Idington J., in the Supreme Court of Canada, said:[175]

> I am strongly impressed with a suspicion begotten of circumstances coming under my observation in these proceedings and the needless frame of the questions submitted that these actions are collusive and used as a

---

[170]*Burland v. Earle*, [1902] A.C. 83, [1900–03] All E.R. Rep. Ext. 1452 (P.C.); *Dominion Cotton Mills Co. Ltd. v. Amyot*, [1912] A.C. 546, 4 D.L.R. 306 (P.C.).

[171]*Theatre Amusement Co. v. Stone* (1914), 50 S.C.R. 32, 6 W.W.R. 1438, 16 D.L.R. 855; *Scott v. Sask. Co-operative Wheat Producers Ltd.*, [1933] 1 W.W.R. 726 (Sask. K.B.).

[172]*E.g.*, *Union Colliery Co. of B.C., Ltd. v. Bryden*, [1899] A.C. 580, 81 L.T. 277 (P.C.); *John Deere Plow Co. v. Wharton*, [1915] A.C. 330, 7 W.W.R. 706, 29 W.L.R. 917, 18 D.L.R. 353 (P.C.); *Great West Saddlery Co. v. The King*, [1921] 2 A.C. 91, [1921] All E.R. Rep. 605, [1921] 1 W.W.R. 1034, 58 D.L.R. 1 (P.C.).

[173]See, *e.g.*, *Carter v. Carter Coal Co.*, 298 U.S. 238 (1936).

[174]*Supra*, note 172 at 584 A.C.

[175]59 S.C.R. 19 at 33, [1919] 2 W.W.R. 561, 48 D.L.R. 386 at 396, revd. *supra*, note 172 without reference to this point.

means of interrogating this court in a way it should not submit to at the mere whim of any private individuals desiring to know how far their companies can go.

The possibility certainly exists in such litigation that the parties will not argue the issues fully and that the side which has the burden of defending the validity of legislation will do it less than enthusiastically. The statutory right of intervention by the Attorney General in such cases is usually resorted to, no doubt wisely.

(d) Persons Claiming Under the Canadian Charter of Rights and Freedoms

Subsection 24(1) of the Charter provides:

> Anyone whose rights or freedoms, as guaranteed by this Charter, have been infringed or denied may apply to a court of competent jurisdiction to obtain such remedy as the court considers appropriate and just in the circumstances.

The question arises as to whether this extends or limits standing in respect of alleged violations of Charter rights or freedoms.

It can be argued that this restricts standing because it apparently requires that to invoke judicial remedies the plaintiff must show that it is his own rights or freedoms which are at stake and that they have already been infringed. On this line of interpretation the subsection could be much more demanding than the tests for discretionary grants of standing as developed in *Thorson, McNeil* and *Borowski* where there is seemingly no requirement that the claimant's own personal rights or freedoms be affected, either in the past or even in contemplation.

The other possible interpretation, and the one that seems most compatible with the nature and purpose of the Charter, is that this subsection merely recognizes that standing exists as a right rather than as a discretionary privilege (as granted in the *Thorson* and subsequent decisions) where one is challenging actual violations of his own rights and freedoms under the Charter, and extends the discretion of the courts as to what remedies they can grant. While it was probably never in doubt that such a person would have standing where his rights or freedoms had been affected differently from those of the public generally, this subsection may clarify his standing as of right even in situations where his interests were affected similarly to the interests of the public at large: for example, by denial of the equal protection of the law in voting such as through gerrymandering of constituencies.

But such an interpretation need not detract from the wide discretion given by the *Thorson* line of jurisprudence for the grant of standing to those who allege the denial of the rights of others, or the anticipated future denial of rights. One should assume that the purpose of s-s. 24(1) was to expand, not detract from, the exercise and enforcement of rights, as the whole purpose of the Charter may be seen to be the enhancement of protection of rights and freedoms. Considering that in the *Borowski* case the Supreme Court was prepared, in a claim based on the *Canadian Bill of Rights*, to exercise its discretion in favour of granting standing in the most extensive manner yet, recognizing the status to sue where the law was not "declaratory" (as in *Thorson*) nor limiting of the privileges of the public at large including the plaintiff (as in *McNeil*), it seems almost certain that the court will be at least as generous in public actions for declarations alleging inconsistencies with the Charter.

The interpretations given to date of s. 24 have tended to confirm that it is not as restrictive as first supposed by some. First, there is at least some authority for the proposition that s-s. 24(1) can be resorted to even where the infringement of rights is only anticipated but has not yet occurred.[176] It also appears that s. 24 in no way inhibits the courts from dealing with claims, based on s. 52 of the *Constitution Act, 1982*, that a law is invalid as being in conflict with the Charter. The courts can deal with such cases on the same tests of standing as applied before the Charter to actions attacking the validity of laws on distribution of powers grounds.[177] Declarations can, in a proper case, be given on the principles of the *Thorson* line of cases, as to possible invalidity of a law for being inconsistent with a part of the Constitution (*i.e.*, the Charter).[178] In such cases it may therefore not be necessary for the plaintiff or applicant to show that it is his own Charter right which has been infringed or is in danger of being infringed, if the remedy he invokes does not require that kind of an interest.

It also appears that rights recognized by the Charter which depend on the existence of a group to exercise them, such as minority language or religion education rights, can be asserted as individual rights, by individuals, as long as they can show they belong to the protected group.[179]

---

[176]*Que. Assn. of Protestant School Bds. et al. (No. 2) v. A.G. Que. et al. (No. 2)* (1982), 140 D.L.R. (3d) 33 (Que. S.C.); this point was not dealt with in the subsequent appeals. *Nat. Citizens' Coalition* case, *supra*, note 118; *Kravets v. Min. of Employment and Immigration*, [1985] 1 F.C. 434 (T.D.). See also Gibson, *The Law of the Charter: General Principles* (Toronto: Carswell, 1986), at pp. 195–98.

[177]*R. v. Big M Drug Mart Ltd.*, [1985] 1 S.C.R. 295 at 312–13.

[178]See *e.g.*, *Re Allman et al. and Commr. of N.W.T.* (1983), 144 D.L.R. (3d) 467, affd 8 D.L.R. (4th) 230 (N.W.T.C.A.), leave to appeal to S.C.C. refused 55 N.R. 394n.

[179]*Reference re an Act to Amend the Education Act* (1986), 25 D.L.R. (4th) 1 at 54–55 (Ont. C.A.), affd S.C.C. June 25, 1987.

Such individuals should thus be able to invoke s. 24 of the Charter to assert what some might regard as group rights.

3. The Role and Test of Standing in Constitutional Cases: An Overview

As we have seen, the Canadian legal system did not start from any general principle in evolving rules for standing in constitutional cases. Instead, we have moved gradually from the common law requirements for standing for particular remedies.

As a result we still have a number of anomalies with respect to the entitlement of an individual to commence an action or proceeding to litigate a constitutional issue. There are some kinds of parties who have a special claim to standing even though their interests are the same as much or all of the public, such as voters with respect to the loss of right to vote, municipal taxpayers with respect to challenging unlawful expenditures of their municipal corporations, or shareholders alleging *ultra vires* conduct by their company. Yet there is seemingly no such automatic right to standing for the same voter complaining of a distortion or dilution of his vote through gerrymandering, a provincial or federal taxpayer with respect to unlawful expenditures at those levels, or even a municipal taxpayer complaining of unlawful municipal activity other than expenditures. There are other remedies potentially useful for challenging constitutional validity but for which the recognition of standing is purely a matter of discretion, even though the issues may be equally or more important. Among these are the declaration, *certiorari*, and prohibition. Mandamus is an even more difficult remedy for which to establish standing, although it too could serve a public law purpose of enforcing the constitution.

While our law of standing continues to present certain anomalies, important developments have taken place in recent years which have greatly extended the availability of standing in constitutional cases and considerably systematized the law on that subject.

One of these developments is the coming into force of the *Canadian Charter of Rights and Freedoms*. Whereas previously there had been few if any individual rights guaranteed by the constitution, there are now numerous personal rights and freedoms defined in the Charter. Therefore there will be many more litigants who can assert a personal interest, namely a denial or threatened denial of any of these rights or freedoms, in seeking a remedy involving enforcement of the constitution.

The other important development has been the lowering of standing requirements for the declaratory action as represented by the *Thorson, McNeil* and *Borowski* cases, together with the articulation in those cases of a more general principle which will probably pervade future developments in this field. That principle is that if a litigant raises a genuinely justiciable issue, the lack of any special interest in the matter different from that of the public at large should not necessarily bar him from having his claim for a declaration of invalidity considered by the court: the interest which he or any other member of the public is entitled to vindicate is "the right of the citizenry to constitutional behaviour"[180] by public bodies. If he cannot otherwise show that he has a special interest or is one of the category of parties which has a recognized right to commence a public action, then he can seek a declaration and in such case it will be within the discretionary power of the court to grant him standing. This approach, then, attaches considerable importance to justiciability, at least in theory, and very little to standing, in the total process of managing the judicial role.

In adopting it, the court appears to be stressing its role as the guardian of the constitution and downplaying its more traditional function as a forum for settling disputes between two parties with conflicting interests.

With respect to standing, it is clear that for remedies such as the declaration, *certiorari*, and prohibition, the grant of standing is discretionary. But it is not clear what the criteria are for the exercise of discretion. Some pattern seemed to be emerging with the *Thorson* case,[181] namely that the court should grant standing to litigants with no special interest where the legislation was not regulatory and therefore not subject to attack by anyone directly controlled by it. But this test was attenuated in the *McNeil* case where standing was granted to a member of the public indirectly regulated by the law even though there were people directly regulated by it. And the *Borowski* decision went further yet in its discretionary recognition of standing where the plaintiff was not alleging a direct or indirect regulation of himself.

It is therefore difficult to know what would be seen as grounds for a negative exercise of this discretionary power. In attempting to suggest such criteria it is desirable first to identify a legitimate continuing role for standing. As we have seen earlier, there are no limitations in the Canadian constitution which restrict the capacity of Canadian courts to undertake judicial review such as the "case or controversy" requirement or the separation of powers. Yet there are functional reasons for judicial self-restraint which may in part be recognized by the discretionary refusal of standing. Two principal reasons are suggested here: the protection of the courts from an excessive and frivolous workload, and the ensuring of a meaningful issue suitable for determination by a court. It will probably

---

[180]*Thorson v. A.G. Can.*, [1975] 1 S.C.R. 138 at 163, 43 D.L.R. (3d) 1 at 19, 1 N.R. 225.

[181]See, *e.g.*, Johnson, *"Locus Standi* in Constitutional Cases after Thorson", [1975] *Public Law* 137.

be a rare instance where these reasons will need to be invoked to justify a refusal of standing, but they are both worthy of brief consideration.

First, it is at least hypothetically possible that courts could be besieged by officious litigants seeking to assert arguments of constitutional principle, if such litigants are not required to show any special interest in the matter in order to achieve standing. This was asserted in the *Smith* case as a sufficient reason for not recognizing standing when the court referred to the "inconvenience" that would otherwise result, and it has since commended itself to some other judges.[182] The majority in the *Thorson* case rejected this rationale as a basis for an absolute bar to granting standing to a person without a special interest different from that of the public at large, but seemingly recognized it as a basis for the negative exercise of discretion in a proper case. Laskin J. for the court said:

> I do not think that anything is added to the reasons for denying standing, if otherwise cogent, by reference to grave inconvenience and public disorder. . . . The Courts are quite able to control declaratory actions, both through discretion, by directing a stay, and by imposing costs; and as a matter of experience, *MacIlreith v. Hart*, to which I will return, does not seem to have spawned any inordinate number of ratepayers' actions to challenge the legality of municipal expenditures.[183]

In other words, the fear of excessive demands on the judicial system are probably exaggerated and is not adequate reason for a blanket denial of standing, but if such demands ever materialized they could be a reason for refusing standing as a matter of discretion.[184] This appears to be a sensible approach to the problem and thus represents one possible criterion for the negative exercise of discretion.

Second, it is important that courts not try to deal with questions which are so general or abstract that they cannot be meaningfully answered. While this need may more commonly be met through tests of justiciability,[185] one of the implicit values of standing requirements is that they eliminate the plaintiff who really cannot point to a specific application of the law to himself so as to enable the court to see just what is its effect. This may be particularly important in actions for a declaration

---

[182]*Smith v. A.G. Ont.*, [1924] S.C.R. 331 at 337–47, [1924] 3 D.L.R. 189 at 193–201; cited with approval in *Saumur v. A.G. Que.*, [1963] Que. Q.B. 116 at 138–39, 37 D.L.R. (2d) 703 at 724, affd [1964] S.C.R. 252, 45 D.L.R. (2d) 627, and by the dissenting judgment of Judson J., (Fauteux C.J. and Abbott J. concurring) in the *Thorson* case, [1975] 1 S.C.R. 138 at 140–42, 43 D.L.R. (3d) 1 at 4, 1 N.R. 225.

[183]*Supra*, note 180, at p. 145 S.C.R., pp. 6–7 D.L.R.

[184]See also Roman, "Locus standi: A Cure in Search of a Disease?" in *Environmental Rights in Canada*, Swaigen ed. (1981), at 17–25.

[185]See, *infra*, at pp. 216–36.

where the plaintiff does not seek an effective cure for his problem but only a statement by the court of the law.[186] The point was well stated in the dissenting judgment of Laskin C.J. (Lamer J., concurring) in the *Borowski* case. He pointed out that courts are "dispute-resolving tribunals" which "do not normally deal with purely hypothetical matters where no concrete legal issues are involved, where there is no lis that engages their processes or where they are asked to answer questions in the abstract merely to satisfy a person's curiosity".[187] He went on to conclude that the case lacked "concreteness" and that "to permit the issue to be litigated in as abstract a manner . . . would hardly do justice to it". Therefore the court's discretion should have been exercised to deny the plaintiff standing.[188] While the majority did not share this view of the case in question, it is submitted that the principle stated by the minority is correct and should be the basis for the exercise of discretion in other cases where the court concludes that the plaintiff's lack of special interest would result in an excessively general or abstract issue being put to it for determination. As will be argued later,[189] we have had problems in Canadian constitutional jurisprudence with abstract decisions, mostly as a result of our system of constitutional references.

It is important that various self-limitations, including discretionary control of standing, be employed by the courts in the interests of a more realistic jurisprudence devoted to the assessment of actual, not imagined, effects of impugned legislation and actual, not hypothetical, official action. This need has become more acute with the adoption of the Charter with a whole new range of constitutional norms which may attract officious litigants self-chosen to vindicate human rights and freedoms on behalf of their fellow man. There are many issues, of course, which are sufficiently clear notwithstanding the lack of special interest of the plaintiff, but the courts should scrutinize the nature of the question raised in deciding how to exercise its discretion in granting standing.

Connected with the second criterion, namely the concreteness of the issue absent a plaintiff with a special interest, is the possible consideration that there may be other parties better placed to commence proceedings and raise the essential issues in a more effective way[190]. This should also be weighed in the exercise of discretion. For example, a court might reject standing to a civil liberties group to attack censorship legislation

---

[186]See Kerr, Comment, "Blaikie and Forest: The Declaratory Actions as a Remedy against Unconstitutional Legislation" (1980), 26 *McGill L.J.* 97.

[187]*Supra*, note 159 at p. 100 W.W.R.

[188]*Ibid.*, at p. 107.

[189]See, *infra*, c. 9, *passim*.

[190]For U.S. jurisprudence which appears to take this factor into account, see Blake, *supra*, note 9, at pp. 75-76.

on the basis of s. 2 of the Charter if it were very probable that a newspaper publisher would soon attack an actual exercise of those censorship powers under the law in respect to his paper.

We have seen, then, a large reduction in the barriers to standing. While this is generally desirable in support of judicial review where there are issues with which the court should deal, there are functional reasons for some limitations on standing that will strengthen, not weaken, the effectiveness of judicial review.

B. OTHER PARTIES

Assuming that someone is allowed to challenge the constitutional validity of a statute, who else must be joined in the proceedings? The general approach taken by the courts is that parties should be joined so that as far as possible all matters in controversy in the litigation may be finally settled and a multiplicity of proceedings may be avoided.[191] It is necessary to inquire what parties, if any, are essential to the final determination of constitutional questions.

There appears to be no basis on which any private person may be considered an essential party in constitutional litigation. He may of course be a necessary party to litigation where a constitutional issue is incidentally involved, but only if he seeks to justify his personal actions or assert personal rights by reliance on the constitution or on an impugned statute.[192] His relationship to the proceedings stems from his personal interests: he has no personal interest in the upholding of the constitution.

The only person who may have a special interest in constitutional litigation is the Attorney General. It is doubtful, however, that at common law even he would be an essential party where no Crown or public interest were otherwise involved.

We have seen that most of the provinces and the Supreme Court of Canada have made specific provision for notice to be given to the relevant Attorney General where the validity of a statute is being questioned. While some of the legislative provisions specifically make the intervening Attorney General a party for certain purposes, it appears that in the absence of such provisions, or of a special order, he is not a party.[193] Apparently these provisions were introduced to assure that the Attorney General would have an opportunity to appear in such cases. There is no

---

[191]*Ottawa Separate School Trustees v. Quebec Bank* (1917), 39 O.L.R. 118, 35 D.L.R. 134 (H.C.).

[192]See *Turner's Dairy Ltd. v. Williams*, 55 B.C.R. 81, [1940] 2 W.W.R. 193, [1940] 3 D.L.R. 214 (B.C. C.A.).

[193]See, *supra*, at pp. 81–83.

evidence to indicate that prior to such enactments the Attorney General was normally made a party in such cases, nor does this appear to be the situation in those provinces which have never adopted the notice requirement.

An example of the recognition of a broader interest of the Attorney General of Canada, which may justify his being a party in Charter cases, arose in *Que. Assn. of Protestant School Bds. et al. v. A.G. Qué. et al.* where provincial legislation was being challenged as inconsistent with s. 23 of the Charter. Article 95 of the Québec *Code of Civil Procedure* does not require that notice be given to the Attorney General of Canada in constitutional cases. While the latter was brought in by the parties as *mis-en-cause*, he sought leave to intervene so as to be able to ask for certain declarations of invalidity himself. This was obviously an "intervention" more in the nature of making him a party. The provincial Attorney General objected on the basis that the Government of Canada had no interest in the matter, as there was no issue of distribution of powers, potentially affecting federal power, involved. Deschênes C.J.S.C., nevertheless allowed the intervention on the grounds that minority language education had, by s. 23 of the Charter, been

> elevated to the status of a fundamental right entrenched in the Constitution for the general benefit of the whole of Canada . . . the interest of the Attorney-General of Canada is obvious with respect to a sound administration of the Charter throughout the whole of the country . . .[194]

This case may support a broadened role for the Attorney General of Canada, both as intervener and as party, in Charter cases regardless of notice requirements.

It is suggested that there are two different concepts which must be distinguished in considering the role of the Attorney General. The joinder of parties is related to the rules of *res judicata inter partes*. If a person, including the Crown or its representative, is joined as a party, then any decision about law or fact made in the proceedings will be binding on him or it in future in relation to the same parties.[195] On the other hand, the intervention of the Attorney General subsequent to notice being given him in constitutional cases is related to the rules of *stare decisis*. It was deemed advisable to allow the Attorney General to be heard in such cases so that the Government would not be prejudiced by a decision against statutory validity, reached in a proceeding in which the views of the Government had not been expressed.

It is submitted that in the absence of other factors which will be

---

[194](1982), 140 D.L.R. (3d) 19 at 24 (Qué. S.C.).

[195]Mundell, "The Crown and Res Judicata" in *Legal Essays in Hour of Arthur Moxon*, Corry, Cronkite, and Whitmore eds. (1953), at 208, *passim*.

referred to below, the Attorney General is not an essential party in constitutional cases. Where statutes or rules of court give him the opportunity to intervene, he may do so. If he declines to do so, he cannot be brought into the proceedings compulsorily. In jurisdictions with no such provisions, he may, but need not, be admitted to the proceedings, nor can he be required to participate.

Other factors may of course involve the Crown or the Attorney General as parties in constitutional cases. It may be alleged by a claimant that the Crown is acting or holding property under an invalid statute. Any such claim directly[196] or indirectly[197] affecting Crown interests would necessarily involve the Crown or the Attorney General as a party. It would seem also that if there were a constitutional problem involved in an action with respect to some public right, the Attorney General might have to be a party on behalf of the Crown as *parens patriae*. His addition as a party would be required in order that the matter would become *res judicata* binding on the public as well as on others.[198] The possible conflict between the role of the Attorney General in such a situation and his role as adviser to, and as a member of, the Government has been previously noted.[199]

These proceedings in which the Attorney General or the Crown must be made parties result in judgments *inter partes* deemed *res judicata* only between the parties to the action. If the court declares a statute to be invalid, and, for example, enjoins the officers of the Crown from enforcing it against the plaintiff, it would seem that such a decision would bind the Crown only with respect to future proceedings with this particular party.[200] It may be noted in passing, however, that it could be argued that a decision about the validity or invalidity of a statute is a judgment *in rem*, binding not only upon the parties but as against the whole world.[201] Halsbury gives a generally accepted definition of a judgment *in rem* as one "determining the status or the disposition of a thing, as distinct from the particular interest in it of a party to the litigation".[202] Could it be said

---

[196]*E.g. Lovibond v. Grand Trunk Ry.*, [1936] 2 All E.R. 495, [1936] 2 W.W.R. 298, [1936] 3 D.L.R. 449, 45 C.R.C. 162 (P.C.).

[197]*E.g. Esquimalt & Nanaimo Ry. v. Wilson*, [1920] A.C. 358, [1919] 3 W.W.R. 961, 50 D.L.R. 371 (P.C.). And see generally chapter 4, *supra*.

[198]See *Tuxedo Holding Co. v. Univ. of Man.*, 38 Man. R. 506, [1930] 1 W.W.R. 464, [1930] 3 D.L.R. 250 (C.A.). *Williams & Wilson Ltd. v. Toronto*, [1946] O.R. 309, [1946] 4 D.L.R. 278 (H.C.), *McNeil v. N.S. Bd. of Censors* (1974), 46 D.L.R. (3d) 259 (N.S. S.C.).

[199]*Supra*, at pp. 161–63.

[200]Zamir, *The Declaratory Judgment* (1962), at 251.

[201]See Mundell, *supra*, note 195.

[202]26 Halsbury *Laws of England*, 4th ed. (1979), at p. 238. See also Bower, *The Doctrine of Res Judicata*, 2nd ed. by Turner (1969), at pp. 213–36.

that a decision that a statute is invalid is a judgment as to the status of a "thing" binding on parties and non-parties alike? With one possible exception,[203] there would seem to be no judicial authority to this effect. It is submitted that on principle a decision as to statutory invalidity, made in ordinary litigation, other than a declaratory action, should not lead to a judgment *in rem*. Such proceedings involve a collateral attack on the legislation, not a direct attack. That is, the issue before the court may involve for example a claim for damages, a criminal prosecution, or an application to quash the order of an inferior tribunal. The relief requested is not a declaration of invalidity of a statute *per se*, though it may be necessary for the court to make some finding in this regard where statutory invalidity is alleged, as a ground for the granting of the relief requested. Strictly speaking, the court is entitled to deal with statutory validity only as it is material to the main issue before the court, that is, the right to the relief requested. In principle this does not constitute a determination of the status of the statute, "as distinct from the particular interest in it of a party to the litigation". As a practical matter, of course, it may well be determinative, depending on the level of the court deciding the matter.

Are there proceedings involving a direct attack on statutory validity, capable of producing a judgment *in rem*? In constitutional references the principle issue is that of validity. It has been held that a decision in a reference does not bind non-parties.[204] On principle, such a decision should be regarded as an opinion only, and not a judgment.[205] Perhaps the one procedure which may result in a judgment *in rem* is the action for a declaration as to legislative validity. Five provinces provide by statute for such a right of action.[206] Here the action must be brought by the federal Attorney General against a provincial Attorney General, or vice versa. The declaration to be sought is "as to the validity of a statute". This clearly constitutes a direct attack on a statute, where validity is the sole issue involved. The judgment determines the "status" of the statute and may be considered a judgment *in rem*. No common law problem arises as to parties, however, because by the terms of the statutes the

---

[203]In John Hampden's famous case (*R. v. Hampden* (1637), 3 State Tr. 826), the Exchequer Court held that the ship-money levy imposed by the King without Parliament's approval was valid. Subsequently in *Lord Say's Case* (1639), Cro. Car. 524, 79 E.R. 1053 (K.B.), the plaintiff tried to argue that the levy was invalid. The Attorney General argued that this matter could not be reopened as it was decided in *Hampden's Case*. The Court of King's Bench upheld this objection, apparently treating the earlier decision as a judgment *in rem*.

[204]*C.P.R. v. Estevan*, [1957] S.C.R. 365 at 368–69, 7 D.L.R. (2d) 657, 75 C.R.T.C. 185.

[205]*Supra*, at pp. 139, 140.

[206]*Supra*, at pp. 121, 122.

respective Attorneys General must be parties and such actions will be considered sufficiently constituted if they and they alone are the parties.

Another form of this action is the common law procedure descended from *Dyson*[207] exemplified by cases such as *Thorson* and *McNeil*, where a declaration may be sought against the Attorney General with respect to the validity of a law of his jurisdiction. Here again the Attorney General is, by definition, a party. Once a declaration is made in such an action, the Attorney General participating should be bound by the judgment *in rem* in relation to all other persons. This may present some difficulties, however. If an Ontario court, for example, decides in such a case that a section of the federal *Criminal Code* is invalid, should this decision bind the Attorney General of Canada in all other provinces? It is suggested that it should not bind him except with respect to matters in the Ontario courts, even if confirmed by the Supreme Court. But the force of *stare decisis* will in most cases produce the same results outside Ontario, once the Supreme Court has made its decision.

In general it may be said that there are few requirements with respect to the persons who must be joined in an action in response to an attack on statutory validity. The usual need for adding parties in litigation stems from the concept of *res judicata*. In constitutional cases *res judicata* will play a very small part and, where it is relevant, statutes or common law require the appropriate Attorney General to be added as a party. Otherwise the concept of *stare decisis* is more important in determining where the Attorney General ought to participate in such litigation.

C. NON-GOVERNMENTAL INTERVENERS

This chapter and chapter 4 have examined in detail the role of parties to constitutional litigation and the special position of governments as represented by their Attorneys General. The right to participate of actual parties to causes in which constitutional issues are raised is obvious. The importance of the participation of Attorneys General has been underlined. Some consideration has been given to the procedural position of other individuals or groups in reference cases. It remains to consider the role of such interveners generally, both in references and in ordinary litigation.

As noted earlier,[208] statutes providing for references permit the court to allow, at its discretion, interventions by ''interested'' persons. Similarly, it appears that courts have implicit authority, where not expressly granted in their general rules of procedure, to allow interventions in

---

[207]*Dyson v. A.G.*, [1911] 1 K.B. 410, 103 L.T. 707 (C.A.).
[208]*Supra*, pp. 170–72.

constitutional or other cases.[209] As yet, however, no very clear criteria have been developed as to when such interventions should be allowed in constitutional cases. The advent of the Charter gives rise to new questions in this respect.

Where the only constitutional issues flowed from the distribution of powers, the Attorneys General could quite plausibly be relied on to present to the courts the respective claims to jurisdiction of two orders of government. As has been pointed out since the adoption of the Charter,[210] its guarantees in effect pit the individual against governments generally, not one order of government against another. For this reason it is not enough to rely on Attorneys General to present to the court all major points of view as to the proper interpretation and application of the Charter. Individuals or interest groups may well have useful contributions to make. They are all able to argue as to the impact of laws or administrative actions on particular segments of society, whereas an Attorney General may have to take a position more acceptable to current majority opinion. To the extent that the Charter is intended to protect unpopular minorities or dissidents, it may not be well defended by governments.

The perceived disadvantage of such interventions is that they may be duplicative, or of marginal relevance (reflecting particular concerns not directly involved in the case before the court). They may also have the effect of unnecessarily prolonging cases, thus imposing burdens of time and expense on the parties and the courts. These concerns are most acute in respect of interventions in litigation involving private parties. Particularly in civil cases, the conduct of the case is normally a matter for determination by the parties who can largely control the issues to be contested and the length of the process. Admittedly, once a constitutional issue is raised the case ceases to be solely of concern to the parties and they must countenance interventions by others, at the very least by governments with concerns related to *stare decisis* as discussed above. But how much farther must the parties be obliged to go in accepting the intrusion of self-appointed guardians of self-defined "public interests"? As for the court, in private litigation it must have particular regard to the resolution of the immediate dispute and the avoidance of unfairness to any or all of the parties. Where the constitutional issue arises in a criminal prosecution, the court must be particularly careful to avoid any unfairness to the accused in making his defence.

These concerns are not nearly as compelling, of course, in the hearing

---

[209]*Fishing Vessel Owners' Assn. of B.C. et al. v. Can.* (1985), 57 N.R. 376 (Fed. C.A.); *Re Can. Labour Congress and Bhindi et al.* (1985), 17 D.L.R. (4th) 193 (B.C. C.A.).

[210]See, *e.g.*, Welch, *supra*, note 113, at pp. 224–26; Swan, "Intervention and Amicus Curiae Status in Charter Litigation" in Sharpe, ed., *Charter Litigation* (Toronto: Butterworths, 1987), p. 27.

of references. In such cases there is normally no private interest directly at stake and there are no parties who are there involuntarily. Most of the participants will normally be participating at the expense of the state. The court is engaged much more in its constitutional guardian role and not in the resolution of conflicts *inter partes* in the normal sense. In such a role it can profit more from a variety of submissions without imposing undue burdens on private parties. Nevertheless, the court may still have concerns about controlling its agenda, about avoiding repetition and irrelevancy and the waste of court time.

It appears that the Supreme Court of Canada has taken a somewhat more restrictive view in recent years on applications for leave to intervene in appeals. Among these, it has been more strict with respect to criminal appeals and less strict with respect to references.[211] It has also modified its rules: it eliminated an automatic right that briefly existed under subrule 18(2) for interveners in the courts below to intervene on appeal to the Supreme Court; and it also repealed another short-lived provision in Rule 32 which required notice to Attorneys General (with an ensuing automatic right to intervene) in cases where only an infringement of Charter rights (not involving invalidity of a law based on conflict with the Charter) was involved.[212] A further set of amendments to Rule 18 have, however, possibly facilitated interventions by providing for the possibility of Attorney General interveners, and the probability of other interveners, submitting written arguments without being heard.[213] This could broaden the scope of submissions before the court while facilitating control of the time and expense of hearings. These developments will not be without influence on the attitudes taken to interventions by other courts, although special considerations will always apply in trial courts. There the role of interveners will require particular attention as to how it may help or hinder the establishment of the facts.

---

[211]Welch, ibid., at pp. 213–23.
[212]SOR/83–74, as amended by SOR/83-930, SOR/84-821, and SOR/87-60.
[213]SOR/87-292. See, *supra*, note 114, and accompanying text.

Chapter 7

The Proper Issues for Decision in a Constitutional Case

This chapter will consider when the courts should determine constitutional issues and the nature of those issues. While the courts cannot control the timing or nature of the issues submitted to them, it is often a matter of discretion as to which issues they actually decide. The approach which the courts take to the exercise of this discretion depends on the view which they take of their role in the total governmental system. The more that they willingly decide constitutional issues the less they are prepared to defer to the judgment of other governmental institutions, legislative or executive. Given the enlarged scope of standing which the courts have extended to litigants in essentially "public actions", as surveyed in the last chapter, it is not surprising to find that they have also been relatively uninhibited about taking on for decision almost any constitutional issue that has managed to find its way into the judicial tent.

A. REAL ISSUES

1. Necessary Issues

If proceedings are properly commenced and the opportunity arises for the court to make a decision as to the validity of a statute, or administrative act, should it do so if the matter can be disposed of on other grounds? Or if the constitutional impact of the act complained of is purely speculative? In the United States the Supreme Court has generally refused to deal with constitutional issues under such circumstances.[1] If the Canadian courts and the Privy Council have failed to display consistently an equal restraint it may be because of the lack of comparable constitutional limitations on the judicial role in Canada[2] and the generous view which our courts take of their role in the protection of the constitution.

It is a general principle of the Anglo-Canadian judicial system that

---

[1]See *e.g. Coffman v. Breeze Corp.*, 323 U.S. 316 (1945); *Rescue Army v. Mun. Ct. of Los Angeles*, 331 U.S. 549 (1947); *Socialist Labor Party v. Gilligan*, 406 U.S. 583 (1972).

[2]*Supra*, c. 5, *passim*.

the courts in the course of ordinary litigation ought not to answer purely hypothetical questions.[3] The courts have piously asserted this principle in constitutional cases as well, refusing on occasion to decide constitutional issues if another ground for decision existed, or refusing to explore the constitutional implications more fully than necessary to decide the case in hand or than the facts would fairly permit. A few examples of this attitude may be noted.

The leading declaration of judicial self-denial appeared in the 1881 decision of *Citizens Ins. Co. v. Parsons; Queens Ins. Co. v. Parsons.*[4] The Privy Council was faced with the problem of deciding, *inter alia*, whether the regulation of insurance contracts was a federal matter of "regulation of trade and commerce" or a provincial matter of "property and civil rights in the province". Sir Montague Smith noted that the various heads of ss. 91 and 92 of the B.N.A. Act must be read together in order to understand the scope of each in relation to particular problems. He added that "in performing this difficult duty, it will be a wise course for those on whom it is thrown, to decide each case which arises as best they can, without entering more largely upon an interpretation of the statute than is necessary for the decision of the particular question in hand".[5] This statement was quoted with approval 12 years later in *Hodge v. The Queen*,[6] where the Privy Council confined itself to holding that a province could regulate the conduct of taverns. It declined to lay down any broader definition of the respective scope of provincial and federal power over the liquor traffic. The statement in *Citizens Ins. Co.* was also approved in *John Deere Plow Co. v. Wharton*. Viscount Haldane added some reasons of his own for judicial caution.

> The wisdom of adhering to this rule appears to their Lordships to be of especial importance when putting a construction on the scope of the words "civil rights" in particular cases. An abstract logical definition of their scope is not only, having regard to the context of ss. 91 and 92 of the Act, impracticable, but is certain, if attempted, to cause embarrassment and possible injustice in future cases. It must be borne in mind in construing the two sections that matters which in a special aspect and for a particular purpose may fall within one of them may in a different aspect and for a different purpose fall within the other. In such cases the nature and scope of the legislative attempt of the Dominion or the Province, as the case may be, have to be examined with reference to the actual facts if it is to be possible to determine under which set of powers it falls in substance

---

[3]*Glasgow Navigation Co. v. Iron Ore Co.*, [1910] A.C. 293, 102 L.T. 435 (H.L.).
[4](1881), 7 App. Cas. 96, 45 L.T. 721 (P.C.).
[5]*Ibid.*, at p. 109 App. Cas. In spite of this caveat, the judgment proceeded, at p. 113, to lay down gratuitously a general definition of "regulation of trade and commerce" which has been followed ever since.
[6](1883), 9 App. Cas. 117, at 128, 50 L.T. 301 (P.C.).

and in reality. This may not be difficult to determine in actual and concrete cases. But it may well be impossible to give abstract answers to general questions as to the meaning of the words, or to lay down any interpretation based on their literal scope apart from their context.[7]

Consistently with this view, Viscount Haldane refrained in his judgment from dealing with the wider issues raised in argument as to the possible scope of provincial power to legislate in a manner affecting the operations of dominion-incorporated companies. He confined himself to the specific sections of the provincial statute in issue in that case and found them to be *ultra vires*.

A later decision showing similar judicial restraint is *A.G. Ont. v. Winner*.[8] The proceedings started in the form of an action by S.M.T. (Eastern) Ltd., a New Brunswick transportation company, which sought to enjoin Winner from operating his bus line through New Brunswick in a manner inconsistent with the licence issued to him by the provincial Motor Carrier Board. That licence had permitted Winner to operate his buses through the province but forbade him "to embus or debus passengers" in the province. Winner continued to embus and debus passengers, apparently taking the view that the province had no constitutional power to impose such a limitation on an interprovincial or international undertaking which he alleged his to be. The trial judge referred to the provincial Supreme Court (Appellate Division) various points of law for determination before the case proceeded. As finally settled, these questions raised several broad issues, including that of the general validity of a statute part of which was not otherwise involved in this proceeding. When the matter reached the Supreme Court of Canada, a majority of the judges pointed out that this was not a constitutional reference and thus the questions were too broad. They declined to answer the questions except to the extent necessary to decide whether as a matter of law the defendant had a good constitutional defence to the action for an injunction.[9] Issues of legislative validity not germane to the operations of the defendant were not dealt with. When the case reached the Privy Council, it too declined to deal with the broader issues raised by the questions. Lord Porter avoided defining for all purposes the limits on the power of the provinces to legislate in a manner affecting interprovincial undertakings. He confined his examination to the particular regulation and the particular undertaking in question.[10]

---

[7][1915] A.C. 330 at 339, 7 W.W.R. 706, 29 W.L.R. 917, 18 D.L.R. 353 (P.C.).

[8][1954] A.C. 541, 13 W.W.R. 657, 71 C.R.T.C. 225 (P.C.).

[9]*Winner v. S.M.T. (Eastern) Ltd.*, [1951] S.C.R. 887 at 911, 915, 931, 937, 942, 946, [1951] 4 D.L.R. 529 at 550, 555, 563, 569, 574, 579, 583.

[10]*Supra*, note 8, *e.g.*, at pp. 576–77, 579–80, 583 A.C.

Similar reluctance has sometimes been shown, since the adoption of the Charter, to decide Charter issues where ordinary litigation can be disposed of on other grounds. For example, in *Skoke-Graham et al. v. The Queen*[11] the Supreme Court of Canada was able to acquit the appellant charged under the *Criminal Code* on the basis of its interpretation of s-s. 172(3). It therefore found it unnecessary to decide the constitutional questions stated for the purpose of the appeal, invoking issues of distribution of powers and the possible application of the Charter and of the *Canadian Bill of Rights*. A number of other courts have similarly declined to make Charter decisions when the case could be disposed of otherwise.[12] Consistently with this, in the *Skapinker* case the Supreme Court, having once decided that a provincial law did not abridge the rights in para. 6(2)(*b*) of the Charter, declined to decide whether any such abridgment would in any event be permitted by s-s. 6(3) or s. 1 of the Charter. On behalf of the Court, Estey J. held that[13]

> The development of the *Charter*, as it takes its place in our constitutional law, must necessarily be a careful process. Where issues do not compel commentary on these new *Charter* provisions, none should be undertaken.

He made it clear, however, that there is no absolute bar to pronouncements which are not strictly speaking necessary to the decision of the case in hand.

> There will be occasion when guidance by *obiter* or anticipation of issues will serve the Canadian community, and particularly the evolving constitutional process. On such occasions, the Court might well enlarge its reasons for judgment beyond that required to dispose of the issue raised. Such an instance might, in a small way, arise here.

He then proceeded to comment on the limitations of the brief which had been filed in respect of s. 1, "in the cause of being helpful to those who

---

[11][1985] 1 S.C.R. 106, 16 D.L.R. (4th) 321.

[12]See, *e.g.*, *R. v. Christiansen* (1983), 150 D.L.R. (3d) 340 (N.S. C.A.); *Re Joseph et al. v. M.N.R.* (1985), 20 D.L.R. (4th) 577 (Ont. H.C.), *Re Sherwood Park Restaurant Inc. et al. and Town of Markham et al.* (1984), 9 D.L.R. (4th) 708 (Ont. H.C.), revd (1984), 14 D.L.R. (4th) 287, leave to appeal to S.C.C. refused February 21, 1985, 14 D.L.R. (4th) 287n; *Royal Trust Corp. of Can. et al. v. Law Soc. of Alta.* (1985), 19 D.L.R. (4th) 159 (Alta. Q.B.), affd 24 D.L.R. (4th) 633 (C.A.); *Re Koumoudouros et al. and Mun. of Metro. Toronto* (1985), 52 O.R. (2d) 442 (C.A.); *Re Information Retailers Assn. of Metro. Toronto Inc. and Mun. of Metro. Toronto* (1984), 13 D.L.R. (4th) 251 (Ont. Div. Ct.), revd in part (1985), 22 D.L.R. (4th) 161 (C.A.).

[13]*Law Soc. of Upper Canada v. Skapinker*, [1984] 1 S.C.R. 357 at 383.

come forward in similar proceedings . . . ''.[14] This suggests that the test as to how much will be decided in Charter cases may be more functional than absolute.

Other examples of judicial self-restraint may be found.[15] Nevertheless it must be recognized that the courts have been inconsistent in their practice. Various decisions have dealt with constitutional issues where there were grounds for declining to do so.[16] A particularly notable example is *Prov. Secretary P.E.I. v. Egan*[17] where the respondent Egan had unsuccessfully attempted to obtain a driver's licence from the provincial secretary. He appealed the alleged refusal of the provincial secretary to a County Court judge who allowed the appeal and ordered the provincial secretary to issue the licence. The latter appealed to the Supreme Court of Prince Edward Island, contending, *inter alia*, that there had been no right of appeal to the County Court judge because the provincial secretary had not refused to issue a licence; that the applicant was simply barred

---

[14]*Ibid.*, at p. 384.

[15]*E.g., Reference re Alberta Statutes*, [1938] S.C.R. 100, [1938] 2 D.L.R. 81, where with reference to the Press Bill three of the six judges declined to deal with the issue of which legislative body has power to regulate freedom of the press. They merely held *ultra vires* the particular statute before them. In *A.G. Alta. v. A.G. Can.*, [1939] A.C. 117 at 128, [1938] 3 W.W.R. 337, [1938] 4 D.L.R. 433, (Bank Tax Reference) the Privy Council declined to consider the validity of statutes which could no longer be brought into effective operation because of the repeal of related legislation. In *Ref. re Anti-Inflation Act*, [1976] 2 S.C.R. 373, 68 D.L.R. (3d) 452, 9 N.R. 451, the majority upheld the legislation essentially on the basis of the federal "emergency" power, and avoided dealing specifically with the other main justification urged, namely that inflation was a matter of "national concern" and that this justified action by Parliament. In *C.N.R. v. Williams*, [1978] 1 S.C.R. 1092, the court declined to deal with a preliminary constitutional issue once the plaintiffs indicated they would discontinue the action. In *A.G. Que. v. Que. Assn. of Protestant School Bds.*, [1984] 2 S.C.R. 66, the Supreme Court at pp. 90–91 declined to deal with issues not dealt with in the courts below. In *Edwards Books & Art Ltd. v. The Queen*, [1986] 2 S.C.R. 713, three judges declined to consider the position of persons who observed neither Saturday nor Sunday, because they lacked evidence to do so.

[16]*E.g., Smith v. A.G. Ont.*, [1924] S.C.R. 331, [1924] 3 D.L.R. 189, 42 C.C.C. 215; *Calder v. A.G. B.C.*, [1973] S.C.R. 313, [1973] 4 W.W.R. 1, 34 D.L.R. (3d) 145, judgment of Judson J. (Martland, Ritchie JJ. concurring); *Denison Mines Ltd. v. A.G. Can.*, [1973] 1 O.R. 797, 32 D.L.R. (3d) 419 (H.C.); *Labatt Breweries Ltd. v. A.G. Can.*, [1980] 1 S.C.R. 914, 110 D.L.R. (3d) 594, judgment of Ritchie J., at p. 952 S.C.R., p. 603 D.L.R. See also Laskin, "Tests for the Validity of Legislation: What's the Matter?" (1955), 11 *U. Tor. L.J.* 114 at 116–17, for a criticism of the judiciary for premature generalizing in constitutional cases; MacPherson "Developments in Constitutional Law: The 1979–80 Term" (1981), 2 *Supreme Court L.R.* 49 at 50 and cases cited there.

[17][1941] S.C.R. 396, [1941] 3 D.L.R. 305, 76 C.C.C. 227.

by statute from eligibility for a licence during the period in question. The provincial Supreme Court not only rejected this attack on the jurisdiction and decision of the County Court judge, but also proceeded quite gratuitously to hold the provincial *Highway Traffic Act ultra vires*. This brought the Attorneys General of Prince Edward Island and of Ontario into the controversy when an appeal was taken to the Supreme Court of Canada.

Mr. Justice Rinfret, writing for three of the six judges, held that there had been no right of appeal to the County Court judge and that the provincial Supreme Court ought to have found for the provincial secretary on that basis. It was unnecessary for the provincial Supreme Court to deal with the constitutional issue. What then should the Supreme Court of Canada do? "The reasons already stated are sufficient to dispose of the appeal; and, following a wise and well defined tradition, this Court should, no doubt, refrain from expressing an opinion upon any other point not necessary for the decision of the case." Referring to the constitutional decision of the court below, he continued:[18]

> It is because of the declaration on that point that the Attorney General of Prince Edward Island has carried his appeal to this Court and that the Attorney General of Canada and the Attorney General for Ontario have been allowed to intervene. It was represented to us that this declaration has an important and wide consequence and that, while only an obiter dictum, it might affect the jurisprudence not only in Prince Edward Island but also in other provinces. It appears desirable, therefore, that this Court should express its opinion upon the matter.

He then proceeded to explore fully the constitutional issue and held the provincial statute to be *intra vires*. Of the judges writing separate opinions, Taschereau J. recognized that a constitutional decision was unnecessary but proceeded to give one; Duff C.J. and Hudson J. both proceeded to deal with the constitutional issue without hesitation.

Can one reconcile the approach exemplified by the *Egan* case with those decisions previously discussed? If, as was suggested in the *Winner* case, a court in ordinary litigation ought not to make any decision not strictly required to dispose of the contest before it, then the Supreme Court seriously erred in *Egan*. It is submitted that the fundamental principle lies elsewhere: that a court cannot in many cases make a competent judgment on the validity of legislation in the absence of specific fact-situations to which the legislation might apply. It was observed in chapter 5 that Canadian courts are relatively free of constitutional restraint in the matter of deciding hypothetical questions. But this does not free them

---

[18]*Supra*, note 17 at pp. 411–12 S.C.R., pp. 318–19 D.L.R.

from the practical necessity of having a factual context in which to test legislation for validity. Some statutes may bear on their face ample evidence of a legislative intent to invade prohibited areas of jurisdiction. But other statutes, or proposed statutes, though seemingly unobjectionable in the abstract, may when applied to a given situation render an invalid result. With respect to the latter it may be impossible for a court to render any precise opinion in advance of a specific problem arising. To do so would also be to state general propositions which could have all sorts of unintended effects when applied to situations not within the knowledge of the court or perhaps not foreseen by any of the parties at the time of this litigation.

Thus the *Egan* case involved a specific factual situation, arising out of specific sections of the *Criminal Code* and the provincial *Highway Traffic Act*. The court could determine whether the province had in the challenged section sought to invade a federal field, or whether this section conflicted with the relevant section of the *Criminal Code*. But in cases such as *Winner* the questions about the general validity of the provincial statutes could not be answered except in relation to the way in which these statutes affected the particular interprovincial undertaking there involved. How they might affect other carriers, existing or future, could not be foreseen by the court with any degree of precision. It therefore declined to answer fully the questions referred by the trial judge.

That judicial self-restraint is based on practical rather than theoretical grounds may be seen in the field of constitutional references. Here the courts are not only free of constitutional restraint in the matter of answering hypothetical questions, but are positively required by statute to give an answer to whatever questions the Government sees fit to refer.[19] Yet in the very case where the Privy Council most clearly acknowledged the judicial obligation to answer, it maintained that in some cases answers could not be given.

Nevertheless, under this procedure questions may be put of a kind which it is impossible to answer satisfactorily. Not only may the question of future litigants be prejudiced by the Court laying down principles in an abstract form without any reference or relation to actual facts, but it may turn out to be practically impossible to define a principle adequately and safely without previous ascertainment of the exact facts to which it is to be applied.[20]

---

[19]*Supra*, at pp. 137–40. The court may refuse to deal with questions logically related but not referred: *Reference re An Act Respecting the Jurisdiction of Quebec Magistrate's Court*, [1965] S.C.R. 722, 55 D.L.R. (2d) 701.

[20]*A.G. B.C. v. A.G. Can.*, [1914] A.C. 153 at 162, 5 W.W.R. 878, 15 D.L.R. 308 (P.C.).

While the Privy Council did not have to refuse an answer in this particular case, it has done so in several references. For example, in *A.G. Ont. v. Hamilton Street Ry.*[21] the provincial cabinet had referred to the Ontario Court of Appeal certain questions concerning the validity, and the proper interpretation, of various provisions in the provincial *Profanation of the Lord's Day Act*. The Privy Council held the Act to be invalid as an invasion of the criminal law power of Parliament. It refused to answer the other questions. While technically the reference procedure would require the answering of all questions put, the Privy Council felt that "it would be extremely unwise for any judicial tribunal to attempt before hand to exhaust all possible cases and facts which might occur to qualify, cut down, and override the operation of particular words when the concrete case is not before it".[22] What statutory phrases such as "work of necessity" might mean would have to be determined if and when they were applied in specific situations. Again, in *A.G. Ont. v. A.G. Can.*[23] a number of abstract questions were raised in a federal reference concerning the powers of provinces to incorporate companies and to regulate dominion companies. The Privy Council in its decision simply referred to previous decisions, most of them involving actual specific disputes, and said that in their opinion the questions were answered as fully as possible in those cases. The questions not answered by the previous decisions referred to were considered best left because of their "highly abstract character".

More recently the Supreme Court has chosen similar restraint in a reference. In 1978, the Government of Canada tabled in Parliament, for purposes of discussion but not for enactment in that session, a comprehensive Bill (C-60) to revise the constitution to the extent that this was within the jurisdiction of Parliament.[24] After the Bill had been considered extensively by two parliamentary committees and a number of suggestions for change had been made, it was decided, in response to requests to that effect, to refer to the Supreme Court certain questions as to the power of the Parliament of Canada, without the assistance of the United Kingdom Parliament, to legislate Senate reform. Because the specifics of such reform were by this time under discussion with the provinces, with consequential changes anticipated in the scheme proposed in Bill C-60, the Bill itself was not referred but instead a series of questions were posed encompassing in fairly broad terms possible approaches to reform. The Supreme Court[25] answered categorically, against Parliament's power, on

---

[21][1903] A.C. 524, 2 O.W.R. 672, 7 C.C.C. 326 (P.C.).

[22]*Ibid.*, at p. 529 A.C.

[23][1916] 1 A.C. 598, 10 W.W.R. 410, 34 W.L.R. 197, 26 D.L.R. 293 (P.C.).

[24]*Constitutional Amendment Bill*, Bill C-60, 3rd Sess., 30th Parliament 1978.

[25]*Re Authority of Parliament in Relation to the Upper House*, [1980] 1 S.C.R. 54, 102 D.L.R. (3d) 1, 30 N.R. 271 (*sub nom. Re B.N.A. Act and the Federal Senate*).

the questions concerning total abolition, changes in distribution of Senate seats among provinces, and possible changes to provide for direct election of Senators or to reduce the Senate's power to that of a suspensive veto only. But it declined to answer other questions which it said "in the absence of a factual background, cannot be answered categorically".[26] These included questions such as whether Parliament could change the name of the Senate, the new name not being specified, whether it could change the qualifications or the tenure of its members, particulars not supplied, or whether it could allow a provincial role in the selection of Senators, the procedure here being fairly specifically described. This reluctance to answer was apparently related to the court's conclusion that "it is not open to Parliament to make alterations which would affect the fundamental features, or essential characteristics, given to the Senate as a means of ensuring regional and provincial representation in the federal legislative process".[27] Until they knew specifically what changes were contemplated, it was not appropriate to speculate as to whether these would "affect the fundamental features" of the Senate.

A less clear example of restraint is found in the several provincial references on the constitutional proposals of the federal Government in 1980–81. Both Manitoba[28] and Newfoundland[29] referred to their respective Courts of Appeal several questions, including an identical Question 1 which asked about the effect of enactment by Westminster of the federal proposals in the following words:

> . . . would federal-provincial relationships or the powers, rights or privileges granted or secured by the Constitution of Canada to the provinces, their legislatures or governments be affected and if so, in what respect or respects?[30]

In these courts the Attorney General of Canada argued that this question was premature and speculative, not suitable for judicial answer. The "proposed resolution" for a Joint Address to the Queen to request the legislation for patriation, the adoption of a Charter and an amending formula, was under consideration by a Joint Parliamentary Committee and was expected to undergo many changes before being submitted to the Parliament of Canada for approval and submission to London. More-

---

[26]*Ibid.*, at p. 78 S.C.R., p. 18 D.L.R.

[27]*Ibid.*

[28]*Reference re Amendment of the Constitution of Canada*, 7 Man. R. (2d) 269, [1981] 2 W.W.R. 193, 117 D.L.R. (3d) 1 (C.A.).

[29]*Reference re Amendment of the Constitution of Canada (No. 2)* (1981), 29 Nfld. & P.E.I.R. 503, 118 D.L.R. (3d) 1 (C.A.).

[30]See *Re Resolution to Amend the Constitution*, [1981] 1 S.C.R. 753 at 762, 11 Man. R. (2d) 1, 34 Nfld. & P.E.I.R. 1, [1981] 6 W.W.R. 1 (*sub nom. A.G. Man. v. A.G. Can.*), 125 D.L.R. (3d) 1 at 12, 39 N.R. 1, 1 C.R.R. 59.

over, the question as posed appeared to require a very elaborate analysis of an infinite variety of potential conflicts between, for example, the proposed Charter and a host of provincial legislative powers. This seemed particularly required by the final words of the question: "in what respect or respects". Some of the phraseology of the question appeared very broad: "federal-provincial relationships" had no previously defined meaning, for example.

The two provincial courts responded differently on this issue. In the Manitoba Court of Appeal, a majority, three of five, refused to answer Question 1 on the basis that it was speculative and premature, while the other two judges answered it affirmatively, but generally. In the Newfoundland Court of Appeal all the judges answered affirmatively in a general way.

The Government of Quebec referred slightly different questions to its Court of Appeal[31] but Question A was basically the same as the first question in the other provinces, asking whether the federal proposals would affect the legislative competence of the provincial Legislatures or "the status or role of the provincial legislatures or governments within the Canadian Federation". While the Attorney General of Canada once again argued that this question was premature and speculative, the court unanimously answered it "yes" without going into details.

By the time these appeals reached the Supreme Court of Canada in April, 1981, the Joint Parliamentary Committee had reported recommending the text of a substantially altered resolution and an actual resolution had been extensively debated in Parliament. It was in virtually final form with all other expected amendments agreed to when the debate was adjourned pending the arguments and decision in the Supreme Court. As a result the Attorney General of Canada conceded in the Supreme Court that the question was answerable, in the affirmative, and the Supreme Court agreed. It limited itself to a simple "yes" and did not undertake to answer "in what respect or respects" provincial interests would be affected.[32]

The provincial courts were thus divided as to whether the first question should be answered. Although the Attorney General of Canada conceded before the Supreme Court that the questions were answerable, it seems likely that the court would in any event have so found. But it is important to see that all the courts which did answer the question did so on a very limited basis only, seemingly because that was all that was possible to do with assurance, and all that the circumstances required. As to the lack of certainty, it would be impossible to foresee all the

---

[31]*Reference re Amendment of the Constitution of Canada (No. 3)*, [1981] C.A. 80, 120 D.L.R. (3d) 385.

[32]*Supra*, note 30 at p. 773 S.C.R., p. 20 D.L.R.

potential applications of the proposed new constitutional provisions to provincial laws and institutions, and idle speculation could create unforeseen problems in future. If for example a court found that the Charter guarantee of freedom of expression would conflict with provincial jurisdiction over property and civil rights, would that dictate a future finding that an ordinary provincial law on libel and slander would be invalid? Also in order to respond adequately to the question, it was not essential, in dealing with whether it was open to the Parliament of Canada to seek these amendments either in terms of law or constitutional convention, to specify in what respect provincial interests would be affected. It was sufficient to know that they would in some way be affected.

Some examples may now be found of provincial courts of appeal declining to answer referred questions raising Charter issues. In *Reference re Pub. Service Employee Relations Act, Labour Relations Act and Police Officers Collective Bargaining Act*[33] the Alberta Court of Appeal answered the first three of seven questions by finding that the legislation in question was not inconsistent with the Charter guarantees of freedom of association. That being decided, it declined to deal with questions 4 to 6 because these questions assumed that freedom of association had been limited and raised issues under s. 1 of the Charter. It was therefore unnecessary to decide them. Question 7 was not answered because it again involved s. 1 issues which, in the view of the majority, required more facts for determination than were available to the court.[34] In *Reference re an Act to Amend the Education Act*[35] the Ontario Court of Appeal, having found that the legislation extending funding to Roman Catholic high schools was saved from conflict with the Charter by virtue of s. 29 of the Charter, declined to consider how particular aspects of separate school legislation might in future go beyond the protection of s. 29. Noting that there could conceivably be conflicts arise with para. 2(a) or s. 15 of the Charter where legislation, or things done pursuant thereto by separate schools, went beyond what was genuinely pertinent to the protection of their "essential Catholic nature", the court said it could not deal with such issues "without a clear and precise factual background". The reference question having only submitted the funding bill in general terms for an opinion as to its constitutionality, the court was able to answer only in general terms.

Consistently with the position of restraint it has been held that a referred constitutional question ought not to be answered in its entirety

---

[33](1984), 16 D.L.R. (4th) 359, especially at 363, 370, 380–81.
[34]On appeal the Supreme Court also declined to answer question 7: [1987] 1 S.C.R. 313 at 389, 422.
[35](1985), 25 D.L.R. (4th) 1, especially at pp. 64–66, decision of S.C.C. June 25, 1987, not yet reported,

if the issues raised by it have not been fully argued.[36] There are no pleadings and often no specific definition of the issues in a constitutional reference. If issues are not made specific through the course of argument, the court is again faced with abstract questions which may be impossible to answer.

The judicial objection to answering fully in constitutional references is sometimes based on an expressed concern for private rights unrepresented before the court. It sometimes is suggested that if the questions are to be fully answered, private individuals would possibly be prejudiced in future proceedings where the same issues might be raised.[37] This apprehension would appear to be misplaced. What justification can this provide for the courts refusing to do the very thing which under the reference procedure they are required by statute to do? Some references may involve questions the answers to which may be relevant in future litigation over private rights. But if this creates problems for future litigants who were not represented on the reference, it is a difficulty familiar to the common law system.[38] A decision in one motor vehicle accident case may create a precedent for a later case of a similar nature, but that is no reason for the court refusing to decide the first case. Technically the rules of *stare decisis* do not even apply to reference decisions, though as a practical matter such decisions are treated as binding. If the reference involves a specific question as to the rights of particular individuals, the court should if possible order that those individuals be given notice and be permitted to participate in the argument. If "private rights" are affected only in the sense that a decision on a general question may have implications for particular individuals in the future, there would appear to be no special need for consideration of their position. In any event, reference legislation requires that answers be given, and if an answer is otherwise possible the court ought not to hesitate through solicitude for private rights.

The involvement of "private rights" may legitimately preclude decision on a reference, however, where the necessary facts are not available to the court. For example, if the questions referred involved the effect of legislation on particular individuals or a class of individuals, it may be impossible for the court to express any opinion in the absence of specific

---

[36]*Crawford and Hillside Farm Dairy Ltd. v. A.G. B.C.*, [1960] S.C.R. 346 at 359, 22 D.L.R. (2d) 321 at 332.

[37]See, *e.g., Re Order in Council: Re Crop Payments Act,* 36 Man. R. 34, [1926] 2 W.W.R. 844 at 854, [1927] 2 D.L.R. 50 at 60 (C.A.); *A.G. Can. v. A.G. Ont.,* [1898] A.C. 700 at 717 (P.C.); *A.G. Can. v. C.P.R.,* [1958] S.C.R. 285 at 294, 12 D.L.R. (2d) 625 at 630, 76 C.R.T.C. 241.

[38]See Grant, "Judicial Review in Canada: Procedural Aspects" (1964), 42 *Can. Bar Rev.* 194 at 210–11.

facts concerning these individuals.[39] In such cases an answer may be impossible, again because the question is too indefinite or ambiguous.

2. Ripeness and Mootness

A concern for avoiding impossibly abstract issues may also be seen in Canadian judicial treatment of the problem of "ripeness". Federal courts in the United States have usually insisted that they should not deal with issues not ripe for review. In effect this means that until a person, whose interests would clearly be affected if the statute were applied to him, is actually being subjected to an impugned statute, the issue of its validity is not ripe for determination at his request.[40] Similarly, if the situation or subject matter giving rise to the controversy has since ceased to exist, the court will not decide that which has become an academic question.[41] Canadian courts have seemingly not concerned themselves unduly with the need for an actual and continuing dispute. They have generally exercised a discretion whether to decide an issue which is not yet ripe or is already moot. While the decisions are far from conclusive they seem to indicate once again a willingness to decide a speculative issue as long as it is a precise issue.

Thus, in *Smith v. A.G. Ont.*[42] the plaintiff unsuccessfully attempted to import liquor into Ontario. Until he did import it he could not be subject to prosecution under the *Canada Temperance Act*. When he brought an action for a declaration that the Act was not validly put into force in Ontario, the judges of the Supreme Court all agreed that the question was purely speculative because he was not yet faced with prosecution. Yet the majority proceeded to give an opinion on the validity of the Act as applied in Ontario. Here the nature of the dispute was clearly defined. It involved questions of law which the court was in a position to decide even in the absence of an actual prosecution.

Similarly, an action for a declaration that a law not yet in force would conflict with Charter rights has been allowed, where the effect of the legislation was amply clear.[43] As has been noted earlier, there is some

---

[39] *E.g., A.G. Can. v. C.P.R., supra*, note 37; *Pub. Service Employee Act reference, supra*, note 33; *Education Act, reference, supra*, note 35.

[40] *Rescue Army v. Mun. Ct. of Los Angeles*, 331 U.S. 549 (1947); *South Carolina v. Katzenbach*, 383 U.S. 301 at 317 (1966).

[41] *Doremus v. Bd. of Educ.*, 342 U.S. 429 (1952); *Hall v. Beals*, 396 U.S. 45 (1969).

[42] [1924] S.C.R. 331, [1924] 3 D.L.R. 189, 42 C.C.C. 215. See *supra*, at pp. 149–51 for a full discussion of this case.

[43] *Nat. Citizens' Coalition Inc.–Coalition Nat. des Citoyens Inc. et al. v. A.G. Can.* (1984), 11 D.L.R. (4th) 481 (Alta. Q.B.).

authority that remedies under s-s. 24(1) of the Charter may be obtained in anticipation of a denial or abridgment of guaranteed rights.[44]

By contrast one may note *Saumur v. A.G. Que.*,[45] where the impugned legislation prohibited the distribution of pamphlets containing abusive attacks on the religion of any portion of the provincial populace. The day after the Act came into effect the plaintiffs sought declarations that the statute was *ultra vires*, and that in any event it did not apply to their activities. The Supreme Court of Canada agreed that this was not a proper case for adjudication. It said that the courts could not give a decision as to constitutional validity merely on the basis of some citizen's fear that the Act might some day be applied to him. In the circumstances, this seems quite sound. How the Act would apply to any individual would depend on what kind of activities he might be carrying on. In the absence of specific facts it would be impossible to say that the Act would abridge freedom of religion as alleged by the plaintiff. Less easy to understand is a recent decision[46] of the Alberta Court of Appeal, involving an appeal by an accused from a conviction under the provincial *School Act*[47] based on the failure of his children to attend school. The children were being instructed at home. Under the Act, children could be excused from regular school attendance if the appropriate authority issued a certificate to the effect that they were "under efficient instruction" at home. The accused had never applied for such a certificate. At trial he contended that the relevant sections of the *School Act*, including the requirement even to apply for a certificate, abridged his freedom of conscience and religion guaranteed under para. 2(a) of the Charter, and his rights under s. 7 of the Charter. The trial judge held that he had not established a factual basis for his claim of denial of his freedom of religion but acquitted him on the basis that his s. 7 rights were violated. On appeal the Court of Appeal refused to consider the Charter arguments because he had never applied for a certificate, saying that it declined, except in references or certain declaratory actions, "to consider questions in the abstract". It indicated that the accused would not be able to raise these issues unless he applied for a certificate and was refused it. The rationale of this decision is not entirely clear. It appears that the contention of the accused was that it was a violation of his Charter rights to be forced to apply for a licence. That being so, his refusal to apply and the subsequent prosecution surely gave him the standing to challenge the validity of the requirement

---

[44]*Ibid.*, and see, *supra*, at pp. 159, 160, 186.

[45][1964] S.C.R. 252, 45 D.L.R. (2d) 627. See *supra*, at pp. 151–53 for a full discussion of this case. For a somewhat similar decision see *A.G. Can. v. A.G. Ont.* (1894), 23 S.C.R. 458 at 470.

[46]*R. v. Jones* (1984), 10 D.L.R. (4th) 765, revd on other grounds [1986] 2 S.C.R. 284.

[47]R.S.A. 1980, c. S–3, ss. 142, 143, 180.

of a certificate. It is hard to see what was "abstract" about the issue once he was prosecuted. It may be that the real problem was, as indicated by the trial judge, that the facts were not adequate to enable a court to determine whether the impugned Act really conflicted with his particular religious beliefs. But the Court of Appeal did not discuss the issue in those terms. On appeal, however, the Supreme Court of Canada dealt with the Charter issues, apparently without hesitation.

A particular problem of "ripeness" of Charter issues arises from the provisions of s-s. 24(2) which provides that where a court concludes that evidence was obtained in a manner that infringed Charter rights, it

> shall be excluded if it is established that, having regard to all the circumstances, the admission of it in the proceedings would bring the administration of justice into disrepute.

The better view would appear to be that normally questions of admissibility of evidence should be determined by the trier of fact in the proceeding where it is sought to introduce such evidence, rather than through some preliminary proceeding seeking a decision in advance as to admissibility. This again reflects the need for a complete factual context in which to determine whether admission of the evidence would bring the administration of justice into disrepute.[48]

Decisions on constitutional issues have also been made after the termination of the situation giving rise to the dispute, i.e., after it was moot. In *A.G. Can. v. Cain; A.G. Can. v. Gilhula*[49] the respondent had been arrested for the purposes of deportation. He was subsequently released by *habeas corpus* proceedings in which it was held that the statute under which he was arrested was *ultra vires*. By the time the appeal was heard in the Privy Council, the statutory period during which he could be re-arrested had expired. Thus the decision could have no effect on his position. While Lord Atkinson noted that "the question has in this instance become more or less an academic one" he proceeded to decide the constitutional issue, holding the Act to be *ultra vires*. Here the issue was sufficiently clear: would the Act as applied to the respondent have an extra-territorial effect? This was a question which the court could effectively answer because the judges had a factual context to which they could refer.

In other constitutional cases the courts have proceeded to a decision even where there was no longer a *lis* in the conventional sense. When

---

[48]*Re Blackwoods Beverages Ltd. et al. and The Queen et al.* (1984), 15 D.L.R. (4th) 231 (Man. C.A.), leave to appeal to S.C.C. refused March 14, 1985. See also *Re Siegel and the Queen* (1982), 142 D.L.R. (3d) 426 (Ont. H.C.).

[49][1906] A.C. 542, [1904–07] All E.R. Rep. 582 (P.C.).

private parties have raised constitutional issues in ordinary litigation and then subsequently dropped out of the proceedings, courts have heard appeals where the only adverse interest was that of an intervening Attorney General.[50] In such cases the original subject matter of the controversy has disappeared and there is no real necessity for a decision. Yet because the issues have been clearly defined in terms of the original situation the court feels able to express an opinion on the validity of the impugned statute. When, however, the litigation is initiated by individuals who have since ceased to be controlled by a system of detention which they attack under the Charter, and the evidence is not sufficient to allow an appellate court to determine such issues, the court will exercise its discretion not to determine such moot questions.[51]

Another factor which is now recognized as justifying a decision of a moot issue is that of its intrinsic importance. This was perhaps most clearly demonstrated by the Supreme Court of Canada decision of 1982 in *A.G. Que. v. A.G. Can.*,[52] a reference involving the question of whether the consent of the government or legislature of Quebec was required for the constitutional amendments of 1982. By the time the appeal from the decision of the Quebec Court of Appeal was heard, the amendments were already in operation. With respect to objections of the respondent that the matter had become moot and the reference question should not be answered, the Supreme Court agreed that the constitutional question was moot. It held, however, that it had a discretion to exercise and could take into consideration the importance of the issue already determined by the Court of Appeal which would otherwise remain unreviewed. It accordingly decided to deal with that question.[53] In ordinary litigation under the Charter, the Supreme Court has similarly continued with an appeal that had become moot in relation to the party originally bringing it, emphasizing however that it was doing so because of the "important and novel issues" involved.[54]

The ability and willingness of the court to consider speculative issues

---

[50]*E.g. Switzman v. Elbling*, [1957] S.C.R. 285, 7 D.L.R. (2d) 337, 117 C.C.C. 129.

[51]*Re Maltby et al. and A.G. of Saskatchewan* (1984), 10 D.L.R. (4th) 745 (Sask. C.A.). But see *Re Marshall and the Queen* (1984), 13 C.C.C. (2d) 73 (Ont. H.C.).

[52][1982] 2 S.C.R. 793.

[53]*Ibid.*, at pp. 805–06. Folld in *Re Maltby, supra*, note 51. See, to similar effect, *Howard v. Presiding Officer of Inmate Disciplinary Ct. of Stony Mt. Institution*, [1984] 2 F.C. 642 (C.A.); leave to appeal to S.C.C. granted June 13, 1985.

[54]*Law Soc. of Upper Can. v. Skapinker*, [1984] 1 S.C.R. 357 at 360–61. But see *Re Cadeddu and The Queen* (1983), 146 D.L.R. (3d) 653 (Ont. C.A.) where the court refused to consider an appeal on a *habeus corpus* application based on s. 7 of the Charter where the applicant-respondent had died the day after the argument of the appeal. The court appeared to distinguish the case of *A.G. Que. v. A.G. Can. supra*, note 52, on the basis that where a party to an appeal dies that is the end of the matter.

will of course vary, depending on the nature of the remedy being employed. For example, mandamus will not be issued unless the applicant can show that he has made a specific demand that a certain act be done and that there has been a refusal to act. In equitable remedies the lack of necessity may be a good reason for the exercise of judicial discretion against deciding the issue.

3. An Overview

If there is a common thread running through most of the choices made by Canadian courts as to whether to decide those constitutional issues which it is not strictly speaking necessary to decide, it is that of a strong reluctance to determine issues where the factual context is not adequately before the court. This tendency has been exhibited even in references where the law actually requires an answer to be given to the questions referred by the government. What appears to be an additional criterion for the choice of issues is that of importance. It is probable, however, that even the importance of an issue will not induce a court to decide it if the facts are not sufficiently well defined.

It may be argued that Canadian courts in the past have been too willing to make constitutional decisions. Opposition in the United States to speculative constitutional litigation is fundamental and of long standing.[55] It is submitted, however, that much of the objection to "judicial activism" stems from the fear that unwarranted conclusions will be reached because the issues have not been clearly defined. Canadian courts should therefore exercise care on functional grounds in their choice of cases for decision. They should accept only those in which the factual context is either not important, or, if important, is well defined. United States practice should be of increased interest, because of the adoption of the *Canadian Charter of Rights and Freedoms*. We now have in our constitution many broad phrases like those which have inspired so much litigation in the United States. Our courts may well be more reluctant to interpret such constitutional phrases in the abstract, and in the absence of a particular individual complaining of a specific, real or threatened, interference with a Charter right. There seems to be no shortage of parties willing to invite judicial consideration of Charter issues, but those issues are often received prematurely and hypothetically. To avoid too rapid a crystallization of interpretation, which may be inappropriate in later cases, it would be preferable to deal with the issues which must be decided for the case in hand, and then only when the facts adequately demonstrate an impact of

---

[55] A strong expression of this viewpoint may be seen in Frankfurter, "A Note on Advisory Opinions" (1924), 37 *Harv. L. Rev.* 1002.

the impugned law or administrative practice on the persons invoking the Charter.

B. JUSTICIABLE ISSUES

Even where there is a party with standing and the issue is sufficiently well defined and ripe for decision, a court may conclude that the questions raised are not suitable for judicial determination. We have never had a clear doctrine of justiciable and non-justiciable issues. While the latter have often been thought to include "political questions", there has been little express reliance on this concept as a major definition of non-justiciable issues. In Canada, as discussed in chapter 5, we have no separation of powers which might rigidly exclude courts from decision-making of a kind normally assigned to other branches of government. Yet there is a certain functional value in the distinction between justiciable and non-justiciable issues. At one end of the decision-making spectrum courts more typically deal with certain kinds of issues: fact-finding and the application of statutes, precedents, and fundamental legal principles. Such a process is predominantly objective in nature. At the other end of the spectrum, political decision-making is typically based on only general facts or impressions gained in an informal or random manner, and is supposedly directed to producing a result that will do the greatest good for the greatest number. This often sacrifices the interest of some for the benefit of others. Such decision-making is arbitrary in the sense that it is based neither on fully demonstrable facts nor on applying pre-existing rules. It is highly subjective, although in no way less important or less essential in a democratic society because of that.

This functional distinction in decision-making has institutional bases in the constitution which assigns certain functions to each branch of government. As will be discussed below, courts pay deference to other branches of government in many areas of decision-making because of their respective mandates. Yet these distinctions in function are not always well-defined in the Canadian constitution. And the advent of the Charter has without doubt imposed on the courts the necessity for making certain decisions which, on the same spectrum of decision-making referred to above, come much closer to the political end.

In the United States decisions made on such bases are often said to involve "political questions" and to be beyond judicial review. This terminology has been rejected by the Supreme Court of Canada in *Operation Dismantle Inc. et al. v. The Queen et al.*[56] Indeed, the majority of the court virtually dismissed the concept of justiciability, while at the same

---

[56][1985] 1 S.C.R. 441.

time deciding the case on what could readily be characterized as a test of non-justiciability. In that case the plaintiffs, a coalition of interest groups, commenced an action for a declaration that the Canadian government's decision to permit the testing of cruise missiles in Canada was an infringement of their rights under s. 7 of the Charter in that it would increase the risk to their life, liberty, and security of the person. An injunction was also sought to prevent the testing. A motion to strike out the statement of claim was dismissed by the Trial Division of the Federal Court but granted by the Court of Appeal.[57] Separate opinions were given by each of the five judges of the Court of Appeal who heard the case, and of these two judges, Ryan and LeDain JJ. held that the effect of the testing of cruise missiles in Canada over the ultimate security of Canadians was an issue that was not "triable" (Ryan J.) or was "non-justiciable" (LeDain J.). While the appeal from this decision was dismissed by the Supreme Court, both the majority judgment (by Dickson C.J., Estey, McIntyre, Chouinard and Lamer JJ. concurring) and the concurring judgment (by Wilson J.) made clear that the court was not precluded from deciding political questions. As for the majority, Dickson C.J. stated:[58]

Justiciability

The approach which I have taken is not based on the concept of justiciability. I agree in substance with Madame Justice Wilson's discussion of justiciability and her conclusion that the doctrine is founded upon a concern with the appropriate role of the courts as the forum for the resolution of different types of disputes. I have no doubt that disputes of a political or foreign policy nature may be properly cognizable by the courts. My concerns in the present case focus on the impossibility of the Court finding, on the basis of evidence, the connection, alleged by the appellants, between the duty of the government to act in accordance with the *Charter of Rights and Freedoms* and the violation of their rights under s. 7. As stated above, I do not believe the alleged violation—namely, the increased threat of nuclear war—could ever be sufficiently linked as a factual matter to the acknowledged duty of the government to respect s. 7 of the *Charter*.

Wilson J., after considering various theories in the United States on the concept of political questions, adopted the view that[59]

courts should not be too eager to relinquish their judicial review function simply because they are called upon to exercise it in relation to weighty matters of state.

---

[57][1983] 1 F.C. 745.
[58]*Supra*, note 56, at p. 459.
[59]*Ibid.*, at p. 471.

She then found that[60]

> The question before us is not whether the government's defence policy is
> sound but whether or not it violates the appellants' rights under s. 7 of
> the *Charter of Rights and Freedoms*. This is a totally different question.
> I do not think there can be any doubt that this is a question for the courts.

The court, she said, could not relinquish its jurisdiction on the basis that
such an issue is a political question or non-justiciable. She then proceeded
to determine that as a matter of law the guarantees of s. 7 could not be
interpreted so broadly as to affect every action of the state which might
incidentally have the effect of decreasing or increasing risks to its citizens.[61]

> The concept of "right" as used in the *Charter* must also, I believe,
> recognize and take account of the political reality of the modern state.

Two observations can be made on these decisions. First, the passages
quoted confirm, if it were necessary to do so, that not every question that
has political importance is non-justiciable. It is unlikely that the concept
of "political question" had ever been contemplated that broadly. And a
majority of this court had already held, in the *Patriation Reference*,[62] that
it could define rules of political conduct such as constitutional conventions
and determine if they had been violated. It is therefore not surprising that
it was undeterred by the political importance of the issues in the *Operation
Dismantle* case.

Second, while the Supreme Court may have put aside familiar labels,
it would appear that it has reinforced the functional validity of the concept
of justiciability. That basic concept is that courts cannot exercise judicial
review on constitutional grounds unless the constitution has provided
norms which are capable of application by courts. There is of course no
clear line of demarcation between those decisions suitable for a court and
those suitable for one of the political branches of government. But within
loose limits it is possible to identify questions suitable for the court: those
questions of fact capable of proof by admissible evidence to a reasonable
degree of certainty; and those questions of law which may be determined
on the basis of enacted law or by analogy and deduction from already
established principles. Viewed in this way, both the majority and concurring opinions in *Operation Dismantle* recognize such limitations on
the judicial role. Dickson C.J. concludes that a finding of fact as to
whether there was indeed a risk to life or security resulting from the

---

[60]*Ibid.*, at p. 472.
[61]*Ibid.*, at p. 488.
[62][1981] 1 S.C.R. 753. Discussed, *infra*, at pp. 230–32.

testing would involve so many imponderables and the weighing of so many probabilities as to be impossible of judicial determination. The reasons of Wilson J. recognize that the constitution has provided no norm applicable to the testing of cruise missiles. Therefore there is no existing law which a court can apply to the situation.

While the *Operation Dismantle* decision is a useful reminder that there is no magic in terms such as justiciability or "political questions" (the latter being a U.S. concept more relevant to a rigid system of separation of powers), it also demonstrates some of the intrinsic functional limits of judicial review. These limits may still usefully be described as tests of justiciability for ease of reference. It will be convenient to examine these limits in two aspects: the role of other branches of government, and the intrinsic nature of the decisions to be made. Though part of one continuum, these two aspects are often emphasized separately in the cases.

1. Deference to other Branches of Government

While the Canadian constitution, as we have seen, does not impose a rigid separation of powers or specifically limit courts to a judicial function,[63] courts do accept that in certain fields they cannot "second guess" the other branches of government.

First, there is a vast area of governmental decision-making which has been reserved for the executive branch of government. The courts may examine executive decisions to ascertain whether they are within the scope of the authority of the officer or agency concerned, and perhaps to see whether they were reached by a proper procedure and in accordance with law including now the requirements of the *Canadian Charter of Rights and Freedoms*.[64] But to the extent that the executive power being exercised is purely discretionary the court may not substitute its discretion for that of the officer or agency on whom the power has been conferred.[65]

Second, the legislative branch, so long as it observes the constitutional norms prescribed by the *Constitution Act* may exercise its legislative power in any manner it chooses. The courts may review legislation in relation to constitutional limitations on legislative power, but may not review it to test its intrinsic merit. The courts will not concern themselves

---

[63]*Supra*, c. 5, *passim*.

[64]*Operation Dismantle* case, *supra*, note 56; *A.G. Can. v. Inuit Tapirisat of Can. et al.*, [1980] 2 S.C.R. 735; *Council of Civil Service Unions et al. v. Min. for the Civil Service*, [1984] 3 W.L.R. 1174 (H.L.).

[65]See the discussion of privative clauses, *supra*, pp. 86–97; *Chandler v. D.P.P.*, [1962] 3 All E.R. 142 (H.L.); *Operation Dismantle* case, *supra*, note 56, at p. 472.

with the wisdom of legislation[66] or the possibility of abuse of legislative power.[67]

But can every constitutional norm be enforced by the courts? It would appear that most can, but that in some cases the judicial branch of government recognizes an exclusive or at least initial jurisdiction in the legislative branch to decide certain questions, some of which may involve the application of constitutional standards.

For example, the *Constitution Act, 1867* lays down certain requirements as to the method of conducting elections for the House of Commons. Section 51[68] specifies the method of apportionment of seats and requires a reapportionment every decade. Could a court be called upon to decide whether the requirements had been met and the House duly elected in accordance with s. 51? While there is no direct authority on this point, related decisions would suggest that it could not. There is ample authority to the effect that the validity or propriety of an election cannot be questioned in the courts except to the extent that Parliament or the Legislature has delegated this function.[69] Admittedly, these cases deal with alleged violations of statutory, not constitutional, rules for the conduct of elections. It could be argued that, whatever the exclusive power of the Legislature might be with respect to judging the propriety of elections, that power could not be exclusive with respect to the application of constitutional norms. Indeed, the Privy Council in *A.G. P.E.I. v. A.G. Can.; A.G. N.B. v. A.G. Can.*[70] on a reference was able to apply the existing constitutional rules for distribution in order to determine to how many members of Parliament certain provinces were entitled. That is, the judicial body could reach a decision because there were constitutional norms capable of application. It might be argued that the real problem

---

[66]*A.G. Can. v. A.G. Ont.*, [1898] A.C. 700 (P.C.); *A.G. Ont. v. A.G. Can.*, [1912] A.C. 571, 3 D.L.R. 509 (P.C.); *Royal Bank v. The King*, [1913] A.C. 283, [1911–13] All E.R. Rep. 846, 3 W.W.R. 994, 9 D.L.R. 337 (P.C.); *Co-operative Committee on Japanese Canadians v. A.G. Can.*, [1947] A.C. 87, [1947] 1 D.L.R. 577 (P.C.); *Morgentaler v. The Queen*, [1976] 1 S.C.R. 616 at 671, 53 D.L.R. (3d) 161 at 203, 4 N.R. 277, 20 C.C.C. (2d) 449, 30 C.R.N.S. 209; *Reference re Anti-Inflation Act*, [1976] 2 S.C.R. 373 at 425, 68 D.L.R. (3d) 452 at 497, 9 N.R. 541; *Reference re s. 94(2) of the Motor Vehicle Act, R.S.B.C. 1979, c. 288*, [1985] 2 S.C.R. 486 at 496–99.

[67]*Bank of Toronto v. Lambe* (1887), 12 App. Cas. 575 (P.C.), at p. 587; *Reference re Adoption Act*, [1938] S.C.R. 398, [1938] 3 D.L.R. 497, 71 C.C.C. 110.

[68]Am. S.C. 1974–75–76, c. 13, s. 2; c. 28, s. 2.

[69]*Valin v. Langlois* (1879), 5 App. Cas. 115 (P.C.); *McLeod v. Noble* (1897), 28 O.R. 528 (H.C.); *Lamb v. McLeod*, [1932] 1 W.W.R. 206 (Sask. C.A.); *Sideleau v. Davidson*, [1942] S.C.R. 318, [1943] 1 D.L.R. 59.

[70][1905] A.C. 37, 91 L.T. 636 (P.C.).

of justiciability in the matter of distribution arises out of a lack of a plaintiff with sufficient standing,[71] or the lack of an appropriate remedy.

Closely associated with the problem of testing electoral validity is that of testing the right of members to sit in the Legislature or Parliament. The *Constitution Act, 1867* lays down certain requirements for eligibility of legislators.[72] Could a court by declaration or otherwise enforce these requirements? The traditional view of the common law has been that each legislative body has exclusive jurisdiction to determine the right of its members to take or retain their seats.[73] Only where the Legislature has clearly delegated such powers to the courts will they attempt to decide these matters. Since there would not appear to be anything in these constitutional requirements which has particular significance for the maintenance of the federal structure or fundamental rights and freedoms, we can probably assume that the courts would not try to enforce the criteria for legislators imposed by the *Constitution Act, 1867*. In any event, if the appropriate legislative body chose to alter the qualifications for its members, this would appear to be within its powers under ss. 44 or 45 of the *Constitution Act, 1982*, subject to the protections for the Senate in s. 42.

What of the requirement for periodic elections? Section 4 of the *Canadian Charter of Rights and Freedoms* (replacing s. 50 of the former B.N.A. Act) requires that no House of Commons, and no legislative assembly shall continue more than five years, and s. 5 (replacing s. 20 of the former B.N.A. Act) requires a session of Parliament and of each Legislature at least once every twelve months. Therefore there is a clear requirement that elections be held at least once every five years.[74] An interval of six or more years would contravene the Charter. Would the court order an election? The Supreme Court has refused to enforce comparable time restrictions in provincial legislative provisions.[75] But that was decided before the adoption in the Charter of these constitutional requirements for the provinces. It is submitted that a court might, assuming that the issue were properly before it, declare invalid any statutory provision which purported to lengthen the life of Parliament or a Leg-

---

[71]See *supra*, at pp. 176–79.

[72]See, *e.g.*, ss. 23 (am. S.C. 1974–75–76, c. 53, s. 2), 31, 39, 83.

[73]*R. ex rel Tolfree v. Clarke*, [1943] O.R. 501, [1943] 3 D.L.R. 684 (C.A.), leave to appeal refused [1944] S.C.R. 69, [1944] 1 D.L.R. 495, folld in *R. ex rel Stubbs v. Steinkopf* (1964), 49 W.W.R. 759, 47 D.L.R. 105 (Man. Q.B.) (set aside on other grounds, 50 W.W.R. 643, 49 D.L.R. (2d) 671 (Man. C.A.)); *Chamberlist v. Collins* (1962), 39 W.W.R. 65, 34 D.L.R. (2d) 414 (Yukon C.A.).

[74]Subject to the exception in s-s. 4(2) with respect to times of emergency.

[75]*Temple v. Bulmer*, [1943] S.C.R. 265, [1943] 3 D.L.R. 649.

islature in violation of s. 4. The criteria are clear and there is a distinct public interest to be protected.

The courts might be effective in ensuring the observance of procedural requirements imposed by the constitution with respect to the enactment of legislation. For example, s. 48 of the *Constitution Act, 1867*, specifies the quorum required in the House of Commons, s. 49 the nature of the majority required to decide questions, ss. 53 and 54 the procedure for the introduction of money bills, and s. 55 the necessity for royal assent. Section 90 makes several of these provisions equally applicable in provincial Legislatures. It was at one time thought to be an element of parliamentary sovereignty that statutes could not be judicially challenged on procedural grounds. Any judicial investigation of such matters was thought to be an invasion of parliamentary privilege.[76] The better view would now appear to be that a court can refuse to give effect to legislation enacted by an improper procedure, that is, not in accordance with predetermined procedural requirements.[77] Courts in other parts of the Commonwealth have been prepared to review legislation on such grounds,[78] and in Canada the Supreme Court has recently attached the consequence of invalidity in a most dramatic way to laws not adopted in conformity with a manner and form requirement. In *Reference re Language Rights in Manitoba*[79] the court had to consider the effect, on virtually all laws of Manitoba passed since it joined Confederation, of the failure to comply with the requirements of s. 23 of the *Manitoba Act, 1870*[80] — that both English and French "shall" be used in the records and journals of the Legislature and that all Acts "shall be printed and published in both languages". The court held all such laws to be invalid because of the failure to use the French language in records, journals, and enactments. This decision was rendered in a reference. It would appear that an in-

---

[76]*R. v. Irwin*, [1926] Ex. C.R. 127; *British Railways Bd. v. Pickin*, [1974] A.C. 765, [1974] 1 All E.R. 609 (H.L.).

[77]See, *e.g.,* Heuston, *Essays in Constitutional Law*, 2nd ed. (1964), at 16–31; W. Tarnopolsky, *The Canadian Bill of Rights*, 2nd ed. (Toronto: McClelland & Stewart, 1975), at 92–112; Conklin, "Pickin and its Applicability to Canada" (1975), 25 *U. Tor. L.J.* 193; Winterton, "The British Grundnorm: Parliamentary Supremacy Re-examined" (1976), 92 *L.Q.R.* 591; Swinton, "Challenging the Validity of an Act of Parliament: the Effect of Enrolment and Parliamentary Privilege" (1976), 14 *Osgoode Hall L.J.* 345. But see H.W.R. Wade, *Constitutional Fundamentals* (1980), at 28–29.

[78]*Harris v. Min. of Interior*, [1952] 2 S. Afr. 428, [1952] 1 T.L.R. 1245 (*sub nom. Harris v. Dönges*) (C.A.); *Min. of Interior v. Harris*, [1952] 4 S. Afr. 769 (C.A.); *Collins v. Min. of Interior*, [1957] 1 S. Afr. L.R. 552 (C.A.); *Bribery Commr. v. Ranasinghe*, [1965] A.C. 172, [1964] 2 All E.R. 785 (P.C.); *Namoi Shire Council v. A.G. N.S.W.* (1980), 2 N.S.W.L.R. 639 (S.C.).

[79][1985] 1 S.C.R. 721.

[80]R.S.C. 1970, App. II, confirmed by 34 & 35 Vict., c. 28 (U.K.).

dividual who is proceeded against under such a statute can also raise this question of validity, although other principles such as the *de facto* doctrine may nevertheless render him liable.[81]

Whatever the problem might be of establishing standing in certain cases, following the *Manitoba Language Rights* case the door now seems open to judicial enforcement of other constitutional requirements as to parliamentary procedure. This is consistent with the criterion suggested above — that if there is a constitutional norm which is sufficiently precise, it is potentially justiciable. Reservations that courts may have had in the past about intrusions on the domain of parliamentary procedure seem to be greatly attenuated by that decision.

One new and important possibility for judicial supervision of a manner and form requirement arises out of the "override" provision of the Charter of Rights and Freedoms. Subsection 33(1) provides that:

> Parliament or the legislature of a province may expressly declare in an Act of Parliament or of the legislature, as the case may be, that the Act or a provision thereof shall operate notwithstanding a provision included in section 2 or sections 7 to 15 of this Charter.

By s-s. (2) it is provided that any legislative provision in respect of which such a declaration is made shall operate in spite of conflict with the Charter. The purported use of s. 33 by the National Assembly of Quebec has already been the subject of judicial review. Shortly after the coming into force of the Charter, the provincial Legislature adopted *An Act Respecting the Constitution Act, 1982*[82] which purported to amend all existing enactments and make them override any or all of the guarantees in ss. 2 and 7 to 15 of the Charter. It has been held in *Alliance des Professeurs de Montréal et al. v. A.G. Qué.*[83] that this declaration was not a proper use of s. 33 and was therefore invalid. The court held that to be effective, the declaration must refer specifically to the provision of the Charter to be overridden to ensure the matter is properly considered by the Legislature. In this case there appears to have been no problem raised as to the standing of the plaintiff association to seek a declaration as to the invalidity of the 1982 law. It has been suggested that declarations under s. 33 of the Charter may be open to review on other grounds as well, such as that it must still be justified under s. 1.[84]

---

[81]*Bilodeau v. A.G. Man.*, [1986] 1 S.C.R. 449.

[82]S.Q. 1982, c. 21. For a further discussion of this legislation see, *supra*, at pp. 62, 63.

[83](1985), 21 D.L.R. (4th) 354 (Que. C.A.), leave to appeal to S.C.C. granted Sept. 30, 1985.

[84]Arbess, "Limitations on Legislative Override under the Canadian Charter of Rights and Freedoms: a Matter of Balancing Values" (1983), 21 *Osgoode Hall L.J.* 113.

The courts can probably supervise Parliament in at least one other "internal" aspect. Section 18[85] of the *Constitution Act* provides that Parliament may not confer on itself any greater privileges than those enjoyed at the time by the Parliament of the United Kingdom. With the reception of the common law Canada acquired the guarantees of the *Bill of Rights, 1688,* s. 9 of which provided that "proceedings in Parliament ought not to be impeached or questioned in any court or place out of Parliament".[86] Clearly the courts could not review the manner in which Parliament exercised its privileges, for example, in punishing a person for contempt of Parliament. But it has long been held that the courts can ascertain whether the privilege asserted by Parliament is one recognized by the law.[87] Therefore, the courts could in a proper case test any statute pursuant to s. 18 to determine whether the privilege it created was one which the Canadian Parliament was entitled to claim for itself. Such an issue might be raised by means of a reference or by proceedings such as *habeas corpus,* or by damage actions on behalf of individuals who had suffered at the hand of Parliament in the exercise of its alleged privileges.

The foregoing suggests that the situation is far from clear as to when the courts can and should review questions which have primarily been assigned by the constitution or the law for decision by other instruments of government. It is, of course, clear that actions of both the executive and the legislative branches can be reviewed on jurisdictional grounds. It is also clear that administrative law permits review of executive decisions on a wide range of procedural grounds, but that substantive decisions may not be reviewed where the matter is one clearly left in the discretion of the executive to decide. It is more debatable to what extent Parliament's internal processes, and the exercise of its historic privileges with respect to determining its own composition and the conduct of its members, can be reviewed.[88]

If one may venture some factors for consideration by the courts in determining which constitutional norms in their application give rise to justiciable issues, and which must be left to the decision of others, at least three can be suggested: the nature of the interest being protected by the constitutional norm, the difficulties or embarrassment of judicial

---

[85]Re-en 1875, 38 & 39 Vict., c. 38 (U.K.).

[86]1688, 1 Wm. III and Mary II, 2nd Sess., c. 2, s. 9 (Imp.).

[87]*Stockdale v. Hansard* (1839), 9 Ad. & El. I, 112 E.R. 1112 (Q.B.); *Kielly v. Carson* (1842), 4 Moo. P.C.C. 63, 13 E.R. 225; *Landers v. Woodworth* (1878), 2 S.C.R. 158; *Re Parliamentary Privilege Act, 1770,* [1958] A.C. 331, [1958] 2 All E.R. 329 (P.C.); Swinton, *supra,* note 77.

[88]Mallory, "Beyond 'Manner and Form': Reading Between the Lines in *Operation Dismantle Inc. v. R.*" (1986), 31 *McGill L.J.* 480.

enforcement, and the presence or absence of sufficiently objective criteria to be applied.

On the first question, one can argue that the public interest is adequately protected in other ways with respect to some decisions. For example, the exercise of discretion to prosecute or to exempt a particular product from customs duties can be effectively questioned in Legislature or Parliament. Internal procedures of Parliament or Legislature can be governed by those bodies and the public has no vital interest in the details as long as the majority can ultimately determine the procedure and express their wishes on the substance. If, however, a Parliament or a legislative assembly tries to prolong its life beyond constitutional limits, or to disenfranchise powerless minorities, or to ignore minority language rights, then the public does have a strong and direct interest, otherwise unguarded, that the courts should protect.

The matter of potential embarrassment in judicial enforcement may not often be a determinative factor, but it surely underlies some of the judicial deference which has been and should be shown to the executive and the Legislature. One can imagine the distress which would ensue for both judges and politicians if the former were expected to probe the reasons of the latter for discretionary decisions. What would the effect be, on the pressing and sometimes pragmatic needs of procedural rulings in Parliament, of potential judicial oversight?

The third factor suggested, the presence or absence of adequately objective criteria for judicial application, will be looked at next in the following section.

2. Lack of Objective Criteria for Judicial Application

Obviously one is dealing with relativities rather than absolutes in considering whether adequate criteria exist for a court to treat a question as justiciable, and thus determinable by it. To take an example from another area of law precious to common lawyers, the test of the "reasonable man" in the law of torts, the courts have applied a standard which, while said to be objective *vis-à-vis* the person whose conduct is being retrospectively assessed, has a strong element of subjectivity for the court which *ex post facto* decides what it thinks would have been reasonable conduct.

In the realm of the constitution a court, in similarly deciding *ex post facto* whether legislative or official action was constitutionally permitted, while theoretically applying constitutional norms that existed before the action was taken, must also decide whether the acts in question were rationally related to the permitted ends. Normally this aspect of judicial review has been fairly well obscured and the courts have denied any intention of "second-guessing" legislators on matters such as wisdom or necessity of legislation.[89]

In distribution of powers cases there have been two main exceptions to this approach where the courts are seemingly willing to judge the question of necessity. These include the interpretation of the power of Parliament to legislate with respect to "the peace, order, and good government of Canada" and the interpretation of the scope of Parliament's power to legislate with respect to "the criminal law". The problem arises because in some situations the power to legislate with respect to these matters is dependent on a certain factual situation having existed at the time of the enactment of the legislation.

The federal power with respect to "Peace, Order and good Government", conferred by the opening words of s. 91 of the *Constitution Act, 1867*, is in a large measure a residual power. Thus, where a matter falls entirely outside the scope of provincial powers under s. 92, and is not otherwise protected from legislative interference,[90] it clearly falls within this residual federal power if it cannot be ascribed specifically to one of the enumerated heads of federal jurisdiction in s. 91.[91] But there may be other situations in which federal legislation, purportedly enacted for the peace, order, and good government of Canada, may interfere with or affect certain matters within provincial jurisdiction. In the early judicial interpretation of ss. 91 and 92 this was thought to be permissible,[92] but later decisions imposed more stringent limitations on the exercise of the federal power. It was suggested that "peace, order, and good government" would be justification for an interference with matters otherwise provincial only in those situations where a national emergency existed.[93] While subsequent decisions in the Privy Council suggested a broader scope for this power, including the control of any problem which "must from its inherent nature be the concern of the Dominion as a whole",[94] a later decision in the Supreme Court of Canada has probably put severe limits on that concept.[95]

---

[89]*Supra*, note 66.

[90]*I.e.*, is not the subject of a guarantee such as those found in ss. 121, 125, or 133 of the *Constitution Act, 1867* or in the *Canadian Charter of Rights and Freedoms*.

[91]*John Deere Plow Co. v. Wharton*, [1915] A.C. 330, 7 W.W.R. 706, 29 W.L.R. 917, 18 D.L.R. 353 (P.C.); *Re Regulation and Control of Radio Communication in Canada*, [1932] A.C. 304, [1932] 1 W.W.R. 563 (P.C.).

[92]*Russell v. The Queen* (1882), 7 App. Cas. 829, 46 L.T. 889 (P.C.).

[93]See, *e.g.*, *Re Board of Commerce Act*, [1922] 1 A.C. 191, [1922] 1 W.W.R. 20, 60 D.L.R. 513 (P.C.); *Fort Frances Pulp & Power Co. v. Man. Free Press Co.*, [1923] A.C. 695, [1923] 3 D.L.R. 629 (P.C.).

[94]*A.G. Ont. v. Canada Temperance Fed.*, [1946] A.C. 193 at 205, [1946] 2 W.W.R. 1, [1946] 2 D.L.R. 1, 85 C.C.C. 225, 1 C.R. 229.

[95]See judgment of Beetz J. in *Reference re Anti-Inflation Act*, [1976] 2 S.C.R. 373 at

So a major use of the "peace, order and good government" power appears to be predicated on the existence of an emergency. Yet this is the kind of matter which responsible politicians typically are expected to assess and decide. The decision of Parliament or the federal cabinet that an emergency exists because of wartime or immediate post-war conditions seems to enjoy a very strong presumption in its favour. The courts have not only accepted such decisions without question but have indicated that the opinion of Parliament and the Government must be respected in the absence of very clear evidence that it is wrong.[96] But where Parliament has attempted to legislate in exercise of the "Peace, Order, and good Government" power on matters not directly related to war, the courts have generally examined the facts more fully.[97] In *Reference re Anti Inflation Act*[98] the court examined considerable extrinsic evidence on the question of whether there was an economic emergency caused by inflation. While Ritchie J. on behalf of three of the majority judges upholding the law used the test of requiring "very clear evidence that an emergency had not arisen", and concluded that the evidence presented did not meet this test,[99] Laskin C.J. in his judgment (concurred in by three other of the judges in the majority) suggested a somewhat different test.[100]

In considering such material and assessing its weight, the Court does not look at it in terms of whether it provides proof of the exceptional circumstances as a matter of fact. The matter concerns social and economic policy and hence governmental and legislative judgment. It may be that the existence of exceptional circumstances is so notorious as to enable the Court, of its own motion, to take judicial notice of them without reliance on extrinsic material to inform it. Where this is not so evident, the extrinsic material need go only so far as to persuade the Court that there is a rational basis for the legislation which it is attributing to the head of power invoked in this case in support of its validity.

On this basis he was unable to conclude that Parliament did not have a

---

440–59, 68 D.L.R. (3d) 452 at 510–25, 9 N.R. 541. This aspect of his judgment was apparently concurred in by a majority of the court.

[96]*Fort Frances* case, *supra*, note 93 at p. 706 A.C.; *Co-operative Committee on Japanese Canadians v. A.G. Can.*, [1947] A.C. 87, [1947] 1 D.L.R. 577 (P.C.).

[97]*Pronto Uranium Mines Ltd. v. O.L.R.B.; Algoma Uranium Mines Ltd. v. O.L.R.B.*, [1956] O.R. 862, 5 D.L.R. 342 (S.C.); *Re Bd. of Commerce* case, *supra*, note 93 at pp. 197–98 A.C.; but see *Gagnon v. The Queen*, [1971] C.A. 454 at 460–69, 14 C.R.N.S. 321 at 348–56.

[98][1976] 2 S.C.R. 373, 68 D.L.R. (3d) 452, 9 N.R. 541.

[99]*Ibid.*, at p. 439 S.C.R., p. 509 D.L.R.

[100]*Ibid.*, at p. 423 S.C.R., pp. 495–96 D.L.R.

rational basis for regarding the *Anti Inflation Act* as "temporarily necessary to meet a situation of economic crisis".[101]

This latter approach seems to strike a good balance as between courts and Parliament in defining justiciability. It is important that the courts maintain some presence in this area to prevent the "peace, order, and good government" power from being the completely open-ended authority for federal action that its words would suggest.[102] But there are lacking clear legal criteria as to when an emergency exists or what measures are necessary for its resolution. Thus the court should defer to the judgment of the executive and Parliament as long as their assessment and action is not clearly colourable and unrelated to any rational view of the facts.

A similar situation arises in determining the scope of the federal power to legislate with respect to "The Criminal Law" under s. 91(27). Again, there is a certain area of jurisdiction assured to Parliament. This includes legislation of a sort clearly recognized as criminal at the time when the original B.N.A. Act was passed.[103] But the scope of the criminal law power was not frozen as of 1867. Parliament is free to create new crimes by prohibiting certain forms of activity and attaching penal sanctions.[104] While the concept of "Criminal Law" is thus capable of growth to cope with changing conditions, there obviously must be some limitation on it. Otherwise Parliament could take over almost any provincial field by requiring certain forms of conduct and forbidding others, with penal sanctions attached for failure to comply.[105] A strong indication as to the judicial limitation which will be imposed on the expansion of "Criminal Law" emerged in the Margarine Reference. One of the questions raised in this case was whether a federal prohibition against manufacture and sale of margarine, even where confined to a single province, could be justified as a matter of "Criminal Law". Both the Supreme Court[106] and the Privy Council[107] held that it could not because it was not designed to

---

[101]*Ibid.*, at p. 425 S.C.R., p. 498 D.L.R.

[102]See Marx, "The 'Apprehended Insurrection' of October, 1970 and the Judicial Function" (1972), 7 *U.B.C. L. Rev.* 55.

[103]See *e.g. A.G. Ont. v. Hamilton Street Ry.*, [1903] A.C. 524, 2 O.W.R. 672, 7 C.C.C. 326 (P.C.); *Johnson v. A.G. Alta.*, [1954] S.C.R. 127, [1954] 2 D.L.R. 625, 108 C.C.C. 1, 18 C.R. 173; *Switzman v. Elbling*, [1957] S.C.R. 285, 7 D.L.R. (2d) 337, 117 C.C.C. 129.

[104]*Proprietary Articles Trade Assn. v. A.G. Can.*, [1931] A.C. 310 at 324, [1931] All E.R. Rep. 277, [1931] 1 W.W.R. 552, [1931] 2 D.L.R. 1, 55 C.C.C. 241 (P.C.).

[105]*A.G. Ont. v. Reciprocal Insurers*, [1924] A.C. 328, [1924] 2 W.W.R. 397, [1924] 1 D.L.R. 789, 41 C.C.C. 336 (P.C.); *Can. Fed. of Agriculture v. A.G. Que.*, [1951] A.C. 179, [1950] 4 D.L.R. 689 (P.C.).

[106]*Reference re s. 5(a) of the Dairy Industry Act*, [1949] S.C.R. 1, [1949] 1 D.L.R. 433.

[107]*Can. Fed. of Agriculture* case, *supra*, note 105.

protect the public as such against some evil. It was in essence economic legislation. Mr. Justice Rand in the Supreme Court succinctly described the distinction.

> Is the prohibition then enacted with a view to a public purpose which can support it as being in relation to criminal law? Public peace, order, security, health, morality: these are the ordinary though not exclusive ends served by that law, but they do not appear to be the object of the parliamentary action here. That object, as I must find it, is economic and the legislative purpose, to give trade protection to the dairy industry. . . .[108]

It is obvious that a test of this nature will involve factual opinions and value judgments about whether the activity prohibited by the putative criminal law is one which threatens "public peace, order, security, health, morality". In the Margarine Reference itself it was necessary to decide whether margarine was a harmful substance which could endanger public health. The courts had in the past been reluctant to substitute their opinions on such matters for those of Parliament.[109] But where the evidence clearly showed the lack of any public danger, as it did in the Margarine Reference, the judicial opinion prevailed. That case may be a rarity in that the order in council referring the question of validity to the Supreme Court of Canada itself contained evidence sufficient to defeat the statute. In a reference order of unusual dimensions there was recited, *inter alia*, legislative history indicating that for a period during the First World War the sale of margarine had been legalized, and an article from the Canadian Medical Association Journal which attested to the healthful potential of margarine. With such evidence gratuitously provided to it by the Government of Canada, the Supreme Court had little difficulty in concluding that margarine could not be considered as a serious threat to public health. It may be a rare event for a court to have such weighty evidence before it to contradict the alleged opinion of Parliament. But it would appear that, just as in the case of judicial definition of the "Peace, Order, and good Government" power, there is a point at which the courts will be prepared to question the wisdom of Parliament on such matters.[110] This

---

[108]*Supra*, note 106 at p. 50 S.C.R., p. 473 D.L.R. folld in *Dominion Stores Ltd. v. The Queen*, [1980] 1 S.C.R. 844 at 866, 106 D.L.R. (3d) 581 at 599, 30 N.R. 399, 50 C.C.C. (2d) 277). See also Laskin C.J. in *Morgentaler v. The Queen*, [1976] 1 S.C.R. 616 at 624–28, 53 D.L.R. (3d) 161 at 167–70, 4 N.R. 277, 20 C.C.C. (2d) 449, 30 C.R.N.S. 209.

[109]See, *e.g.*, *Standard Sausage Co. v. Lee* (1934), 47 B.C.R. 411, [1934] 1 W.W.R. 81, [1933] 4 D.L.R. 501 and [1934] 1 D.L.R. 706, 60 C.C.C. 265 and 61 C.C.C. 95 (C.A.); *R. v. Perfection Creameries Ltd.*, 47 Man. R. 150, [1939] 2 W.W.R. 139, [1939] 3 D.L.R. 185, 72 C.C.C. 19 (C.A.).

[110]See also *Labatt Breweries Ltd. v. A.G. Can.*, [1980] 1 S.C.R. 914 at 934, 110 D.L.R. (3d) 594 at 619, 30 N.R. 496, 9 B.L.R. 181, 52 C.C.C. (2d) 433, 14 C.P.C. 170, 49

appears to be acceptable as long as the judicial review is confined to ensuring that the criminal law power is not allowed to be completely open-ended. The "rational basis" test as articulated in the Anti Inflation Reference would be a sound guide for the courts here as well so that they do not become engaged in "second guessing" difficult political judgments about what is a danger to the public requiring protective action and the precise nature of the action warranted.[111]

An area of greater contention over justiciability has been opened by the decision of the Supreme Court in *Re Resolution to Amend the Constitution*.[112] One of the questions referred to the provincial Courts of Appeal of Manitoba, Quebec, and Newfoundland asked those courts whether, as a matter of constitutional convention the "agreement of the provinces" (Manitoba, Newfoundland) or the "consent of the provinces" (translation, Quebec) was required for the federal Parliament to request patriation and the other constitutional changes from the United Kingdom Parliament. What such agreement or consent might be, of how many or of which provinces it might be required, or what institution of government would give the provincial consent or agreement referred to, were not specified. In spite of arguments by the Attorney General of Canada that these were political questions which a court should not answer, each of the provincial courts did answer them, those of Manitoba and Quebec finding against such a convention and Newfoundland's finding that it did exist. In the Supreme Court the federal Government again argued that this was a political question which was not justiciable. After setting out the predominant view of legal writers that conventions are not enforceable by the courts, it said that

> . . . it is clear that not only are conventions unsuitable for judicial determination because they are imprecise and flexible, but also because they are *political* rules of conduct for the exercise of legal powers. And, the courts ought not to be drawn into the determination of political issues.[113]

In other words, it was argued that conventions are developed by political practice and are legitimized by political acceptability: that there are no

---

C.P.R. (2d) 179, where it was said that because beer if properly labelled could be lawfully sold, the labelling standards under the *Food and Drug Act*, R.S.C. 1970, c. F-27, could not be regarded as for the protection of health and thus were not "criminal law".

[111]It was this kind of balancing of risks and other disadvantages in the field of national defence that the courts declined to undertake in the *Operation Dismantle* case, *supra*, notes 56, 57.

[112][1981] 1 S.C.R. 753, 11 Man. R. (2d) 1, 34 Nfld. & P.E.I.R. 1, [1981] 6 W.W.R. 1 (*sub nom. A.G. Man. v. A.G. Can.*), 125 D.L.R. (3d) 1, 39 N.R. 1, 1 C.R.R. 59.

[113]Factum of the Attorney General of Canada at 31.

objective criteria for the testing of conventions beyond the ultimate test of public opinion.

A majority of six judges in the Supreme Court rejected this argument, however: it decided that there was a convention which required "at least a substantial measure of provincial consent", and that the provincial consent as it then stood, that is, of the Governments of Ontario and New Brunswick, was not enough.[114] Nevertheless, the majority recognized that these are not objective criteria of the kind normally defined and applied by courts. Constitutional conventions were said to ensure that "the legal framework of the constitution will be operated in accordance with the prevailing constitutional values or principles of the period", they "are not judge-made rules",[115] "it is because the sanctions of convention rest with institutions of government other than courts . . . with public opinion and ultimately, with the electorate that it is generally said that they are political",[116] and that they "by their nature develop in the political field and it will be for the political actors, not this Court, to determine the degree of provincial consent required".[117] Yet the court was prepared to define in a general way a convention that some provincial consent was required, and to judge that the existing consents were not enough.

The court seems to have distinguished between the creation and enforcement of conventions (said to be political matters), and the definition of conventions (where they saw a role for the courts). This involves a very generous view of justiciability which requires the court to define standards of political acceptability. It is hard to distinguish between enforcement of conventions and their definition: they are "enforced" by political actors and ultimately the public in accordance with their views on the existence, definition, continuing relevance of, or possible need for modification of, the convention in question. How can a court judge, let alone prejudge, these issues?[118]

The activism of the Court on the matter of acceptable practices for constitutional amendment stands in contrast to the approach taken by the U.S. Supreme Court in *Coleman v. Miller*[119] where the Court was asked to determine among other things whether a state had to ratify within a reasonable time a constitutional amendment proposed by Congress and, failing timely action, whether the possibility of ratification would lapse. The Court declined to decide the matter and noted the lack of criteria for a judicial determination.

---

[114]*Supra*, note 112 at p. 905 S.C.R., p. 103 D.L.R.

[115]*Supra*, at p. 880 S.C.R., p. 84 D.L.R.

[116]*Supra*, at pp. 882–83 S.C.R., p. 87 D.L.R.

[117]*Supra*, at p. 905 S.C.R., p. 103 D.L.R.

[118]See Strayer, Book Review (1983), 15 *Ottawa L.R.* 231, for further discussion of these points.

[119]307 U.S. 433 (1939).

It can be argued that the decision of the Supreme Court of Canada is distinguishable because it was in response to questions referred to the courts below by provincial Governments and appealed to the Supreme Court. Arguably, courts are obliged to answer reference questions,[120] and the court referred obliquely to this in mentioning the "broad statutory basis" upon which the references were made so that the provincial Governments "are in our view entitled to an answer to a question of this type."[121] Yet we know that in the past various courts, including this Court as recently as the Senate Reference, have found it impossible to answer certain reference questions and have declined to do so.[122] And in the Patriation Reference itself a different majority, holding the amendment project to be legal, observed that provincial reference legislation

> . . . is wide enough to saddle the respective courts with the determination of questions which may not be justiciable and there is no doubt that those courts, and this Court on appeal, have a discretion to refuse to answer such questions.[123]

If the Patriation Reference proves to be representative of a trend in the Supreme Court on matters of justiciability, it will further and drastically reduce, just as the court's decisions on standing have done, the limitations on judicial review. Conventions govern many aspects of governmental activity and the potential which they create for judicial supervision of the political process seems immense. Will courts be called upon to determine under what circumstances a government can be considered to have the confidence of its Legislature, or when the Queen should act on the advice of her Canadian ministers? Consistently with the majority view in the Patriation Reference it would appear they can, although all of these issues involve what have normally been thought of as political criteria. The apparent rejection by the court of the American "political question" doctrine in the subsequent *Operation Dismantle* case reinforces grounds for belief that the Court will not readily eschew issues of this nature.[124]

Indeed, the advent of the Charter has imposed on all courts the necessity of applying constitutional norms which go beyond traditional Canadian judicial experience. Some of the Charter provisions involve concepts or tests which are familiar: the timeliness of trials; fair and

---

[120]See, *supra*, at pp. 138, 139.

[121]*Supra*, note 112 at p. 884 S.C.R., p. 88 D.L.R.

[122]*Supra*, notes 20–35 and accompanying text. See now also *McEvoy v. A.G. N.B. et al.*, [1983] 1 S.C.R. 704, for a discussion of the court's powers in this respect.

[123]*Supra*, note 112 at p. 768 S.C.R., p. 16 D.L.R.

[124]*Supra*, notes 58–61, and accompanying text.

public hearings; or protection from self-incrimination. But other provisions may require judgments which in the past we have thought of as the sole preserve of legislators.

The most prominent of these is s. 1 with its tests of reasonability and justifiability in a free and democratic society. The Supreme Court has elaborated in *R. v. Oakes*[125] the criteria for determining such questions. They involve a judgment first as to whether the objective of the measure which abridges a Charter right is sufficiently important to warrant overriding that right; and second as to whether the means are appropriate — including proportionality of the measure in relation to the purpose being served and in relation to its effects on Charter rights, a kind of balancing of the interests of society and the individual. These, it is submitted, are all issues which cannot be precisely determined as questions of fact (though evidence will usually be helpful) nor can the answers be adduced from existing law, directly or by analogy.

This can be illustrated by considering two examples of the use of the *Oakes* tests in the application of s. 1 of the Charter. In *Oakes* itself, the court had to consider whether the curbing of drug trafficking was a sufficiently important objective to warrant intrusion on constitutional rights such as the presumption of innocence guaranteed under para. 11(*d*) of the Charter. In reaching a conclusion on this subject the court relied on general information such as a Royal Commission report, international conventions to which Canada is a signatory, and the legislation of other countries. From these it concluded that the suppression of such trafficking was of sufficient importance to justify governmental measures. It went on, however, to consider the suitability of the means employed by Parliament and found s. 8 of the *Narcotic Control Act* to be inappropriate. It reached this conclusion on the basis that the means (the presumption of guilt of trafficking where an accused was found in possession of a narcotic) were not rationally related to the ends because it was not rational to presume an intent of trafficking from the mere fact of possession. Functionally, such decisions are more typical of legislative rather than of judicial functions. Politicians normally decide what issues are important enough to require legislation; that is, they fix the country's political agenda. They, too, normally have to decide whether it is defensible to interfere with the rights of the few in the interests of the many (decisions which are taken with some regard to the relative numbers and identity of the "few" and the "many"). It is they also who normally have regard to the probabilities of a statutory rule providing the right results without giving rise to legitimate complaints of an irrational impact. Yet the advent of the Charter has unquestionably put the courts in the business of deciding

---

[125][1986] 1 S.C.R. 103.

such questions — questions normally near the political end of the decision-making spectrum.

Again in *Edwards Books and Art Ltd. v. The Queen*[126] the Supreme Court had to apply s. 1 of the Charter in determining the validity of the Ontario *Retail Business Holidays Act*. A majority of 5 out of 7 found the Act to abridge religious freedom (as protected by para. 2(a) of the Charter) because of its requirements for Sunday closing. Of this majority, 4 judges found that the abridgment was justified under s. 1. In the judgment of Dickson C.J. (Chouinard and Lamer JJ. concurring) reference is made principally to a 1970 Report of the Ontario Law Reform Commission (which preceded the adoption of the Act) to support a finding that the imposition of a weekly day of rest in the retail trade is an important objective, one which *prima facie* justifies some intrusion on the freedom of religion. LaForest J. in a separate judgment agreed with this conclusion. Dickson C.J. also found the means to be rationally related to the achievement of this legitimate objective, not overly obtrusive, and proportional. LaForest J. agreed with these conclusions also although taking a somewhat narrower view of the court's role in reviewing the means employed. (Wilson J. while arguing that there was an infringement of freedom of religion, held it not to be justified under s. 1. In her view, the court should take a more stringent view of the legislation and find that the exemptions allowed in the Act for some retailers who observe Saturday as a holiday should be available to all such persons.) Again, the majority of the judges hearing the case had to make decisions about the importance of the purpose of this legislation and its suitability for that purpose, decisions akin to those which a Legislature would normally make.

Such is the role now assigned to the courts by the Charter. But it is an oversimplification to equate these decisions with political decisions taken by Legislatures. The courts in exercising their powers under s. 1 are not free to impose their views on the whole range of state activity as to what objectives are important and what means are suitable for their achievement. They only exercise this s. 1 power of review of *laws* — and only those which happen to be brought before them and which prescribe *limitations* on rights guaranteed in the Charter. Nor, it would appear, will a court measure too finely those objectives or means if they seem generally rational.

Examples of legislative-type decisions will appear in respect of many other sections of the Charter. It appears that s. 7, guaranteeing that "life, liberty and security of the person" shall not be denied "except in accordance with the principles of fundamental justice", may not confine courts to deciding if procedures have been correct (matters typical to judicial decision-making) but may enable them to decide if the law itself is just.

---

[126][1986] 2 S.C.R. 713.

This may be the result of the decision of the Supreme Court of Canada in *Reference re S. 94(2) of the Motor Vehicle Act, R.S.B.C. 1979, c. 288*,[127] where it was held that a provincial law imposing imprisonment as a possible punishment for an offence of absolute liability was contrary to fundamental justice. If this simply means that intent must be proven before serious penalties may be imposed, it may involve essentially a procedural issue familiar to courts, but if it means that a law is invalid as fundamentally unjust if it provides imprisonment for minor offences (the kind to which absolute liability normally attaches) then it may involve courts in determining the appropriateness of penalties. The fixing of penalties has been very typically a legislative function. It is done arbitrarily in the sense that one cannot demonstrate by evidence or reason or analogy, for example, that the appropriate maximum sentence for a given offence should be 2 years, 5 years, or 7 years.

Again, s. 8 of the Charter guarantees the "right to be secure against unreasonable search or seizure". As defined by the Supreme Court, in applying this section,[128]

> an assessment must be made as to whether in a particular situation the public's interest in being left alone by government must give way to the government's interest in intruding on the individual's privacy in order to advance its goals, notably those of law enforcement.

Such a balancing of public versus private interests involves a kind of utilitarianism typical of the legislative role. It has not been unknown to courts, however: some such process can be involved, for example, in determining qualified privilege in the law of defamation or in deciding on the scope of privilege for government documents whose production is sought in litigation. But those situations arise where the Legislature has not already prescribed a regime by statute. Section 8 allows a court to make such judgments even in the face of a prior legislative regime implying a different "assessment" of the relative interests.

The foregoing examples merely illustrate the point that under the Charter the courts will much more frequently be making decisions akin to political decisions. To a considerable extent they will have to make these decisions on the basis of general information rather than "adjudicative facts", and in the exercise of subjective judgments which are more intuitive than analytical. Under the constitution as revised, however, such questions are justiciable and must be addressed. In exercising this function courts must be cognisant of the limits on their mandate and on their perceived legitimacy as a non-elected branch of government. There is

---

[127][1985] 2 S.C.R. 486.
[128]*Hunter et al. v. Southam Inc.*, [1984] 2 S.C.R. 145 at 159–60.

some evidence of such concerns in recent Supreme Court decisions deal-ing with s. 1 of the Charter.[129]

C. ISSUES WAIVED BY PARTIES OR RAISED BY COURT

This subject raises different aspects of the same question: to what extent is the selection, for determination, of constitutional issues germane to a case before the court, dependent on the discretion of the parties? Can a party choose not to assert or fail to assert a constitutional point obviously in his favour, and thus preclude the court from considering it? Can or should a court raise and consider constitutional issues not insisted on by one or other of the parties? These are problems which do not appear to have received much consideration in Canadian constitutional litigation. This may be because heretofore, prior to the adoption of the Charter, the constitution provided few if any individual rights and dealt almost entirely with the distribution of powers that transcended the interests of particular individuals. Even this, however, would have provided some scope for parties ignoring, or a court raising *proprio motu*, constitutional issues.

In principle it seems that the courts should insist on respect for the constitution whatever the parties may prefer. What was formerly implicit has now been made explicit by s. 52 of the *Constitution Act, 1982*. ''The Constitution of Canada is the supreme law of Canada''. As Meredith C.J., of the Quebec Supreme Court, said in *Valin v. Langlois* in 1879:

> To me it seems plain that a statute, emanating from a legislature not having power to pass it, is not law; and that it is as much the duty of a judge to disregard the provisions of such a statute, as it is his duty to obey the law of the land.[130]

Nevertheless, it is probably necessary to distinguish between those con-stitutional norms which protect a public interest and those which protect a purely private interest which, if the individual makes a free and informed decision to abandon, the court should not insist on protecting. This dis-tinction has been recognized elsewhere in respect of waiver by an accused of procedural requirements enacted for his benefit. Such waiver is per-mitted as long as the accused has made a clear, voluntary, and informed

---

[129]See, *e.g.*, *Pub. Service Employee Regulations Act Reference, supra*, note 34, S.C.R. 391–92, 419–20; *Pub. Service Alliance of Can. v. The Queen et al.*, [1987] 1 S.C.R. 424 at 442.

[130](1879), 5 Q.L.R. 1 at 17, affd 3 S.C.R. 1, leave to appeal refused 5 App. Cas. 115 (P.C.). See generally *supra*, chapter 2.

decision to do so.[131] This would appear to be equally relevant to some of the constitutional requirements of the Charter, such as the right to be secure against unreasonable searches and seizures, to retain and instruct counsel,[132] to be tried within a reasonable time,[133] and to be tried by jury.[134] There appears to be no public interest to protect if the individual waives his own right to insist on these safeguards. On the other hand, in other sections there do appear to be public interests at stake, apart from the protection afforded individuals, such as the right to "a fair and public hearing by an independent and impartial tribunal," the right not to be subjected to cruel and unusual punishment, or perhaps the right not to be discriminated against by laws or official action. Here the courts should insist on the observance of the constitution notwithstanding any attempted waiver of rights.[135] It will not, of course, be easy in some cases to determine whether a public interest is at stake or not in many of the Charter provisions. Outside the Charter, however, where the constitutional norms are not primarily designed to protect individuals, it is hard to see how an individual can avoid judicial consideration of an issue relevant to his case simply by waiving it explicitly, or by ignoring it in his pleadings or defence. For example, if A sues B under a federal statute purporting to authorize recovery for unjust enrichment under a frustrated contract, in a matter having nothing to do with the federal government, and if B does not raise the obvious objection that the statute relied on is *ultra vires* of Parliament because it involves a matter of property and civil rights, should the court not consider this issue anyway? Surely it should not lend its authority to the application of a statute that obviously has no legal existence. There is, however, some authority that a party may be precluded on equitable grounds from relying on the constitutional invalidity of a transaction he has entered into.[136]

---

[131]*Korponey v. A.G. Can.*, [1982] 1 S.C.R. 41, 132 D.L.R. (3d) 354, 44 N.R. 103, 65 C.C.C. (2d) 65, 26 C.R. (3d) 343.

[132]*R. v. Barbon* (1986), 5 C.R. (3d) 89 (B.C. C.A.); *Clarkson v. The Queen*, [1986] 1 S.C.R. 383.

[133]See, *e.g., Balderstone v. R.*, 19 Man. R. (2d) 321, [1983] 1 W.W.R. 72, at 90, 143 D.L.R. (3d) 671, 2 C.C.C. (3d) 37, 3 C.R.R. 174 (Q.B.); *R. v. Heaslip et al.* (1983), 9 C.C.C. (3d) 480 (Ont. C.A.); *R. v. Deloli and Fowler* (1985), 33 Man. R. (2d) 262 (C.A.).

[134]See, *e.g., R. v. Gladue* (1982), 2 C.C.C. (3d) 175 (B.C. S.C.); *R. v. Turpin et al.* (1985), 18 C.R.R. 323 (Ont. H.C.).

[135]See also Gibson, *The Law of the Charter: General Principles* (Toronto: Carswell, 1986), at pp. 163–68.

[136]See, *e.g., Prov. Treas. Alta. v. Long* (1973), 49 D.L.R. (3d) 695 (Alta. S.C.); *Breck-enridge Speedway Ltd. v. The Queen* (1967), 61 W.W.R. 257, 64 D.L.R. (2d) 488 (Alta. C.A.), confirmed on other grounds [1970] S.C.R. 175, 70 W.W.R. 481, 9 D.L.R. (3d) 142.

This leads to the second aspect referred to above, namely the role of the court in raising *proprio motu* constitutional issues not raised by the parties. Analogy from other areas would appear to support such a judicial initiative. For example, courts must have regard to legal limits on their own jurisdiction even if the parties choose to ignore them.[137] It has been held that a court is bound to consider a statutory rule even if it was not specifically raised by the parties.[138] Similarly a person cannot contract out of or waive the provisions of a statute designed to protect the public interest,[139] nor can a statute be overridden by estoppel.[140] Courts should of course consider new legal issues at the appeal level only if the necessary evidence to apply the legal principles was introduced at the trial level,[141] and this would appear to be a necessary limitation even where constitutional norms are involved.[142] Also, if a constitutional issue is raised by the court which has not been raised by any party, it would appear that in the provincial courts at least the provincial statutes requiring that notice be given of constitutional issues before the court can deal with such issues would prevent the court doing so until the appropriate Attorney General had been notified.[143] The wording of the Rules of the Supreme Court of Canada confines the notice requirement to the situation where "a party to an appeal intends to raise a question as to . . . constitutional validity or the constitutional applicability of a statute of . . . Parliament or of a legislature . . ."[144] It is suggested, however, that in any court if a new constitutional issue appeared which the court felt was relevant, it should so indicate to all parties and if necessary adjourn the case in order for them all to consider and prepare to argue it. If the hearing has already

---

[137]*Re Fraser* (1912), 26 O.L.R. 508, 8 D.L.R. 955 (C.A.); *R. v. Crovi*, 20 Alta. L.R. 651, [1924] 3 W.W.R. 534, [1924] D.L.R. 1072, 43 C.C.C. 32 (C.A.); *Kowal v. New York Central Ry. Co.*, [1934] S.C.R. 214, [1934] 4 D.L.R. 440.

[138]*E.g., Banque Canadienne Nationale v. Tencha*, [1928] S.C.R. 26, [1927] 4 D.L.R. 665; *Johnston v. Anderson* (1973), 5 Nfld. & P.E.I.R. 198 (S.C.); *Collins v. Burge* (1977), 11 Nfld. & P.E.I.R. 520 (C.A.).

[139]*E.g., Equitable Life Assur. Soc. v. Reed*, [1914] A.C. 587, 111 L.T. 50 (P.C.); *Edward Ramia, Ltd. v. African Woods, Ltd.*, [1960] 1 All E.R. 627 (P.C.).

[140]*E.g., Maritime Elec. Co. v. Gen. Dairies Ltd.*, [1937] 1 D.L.R. 609 (P.C.); *Woon v. M.N.R.*, [1951] Ex. C.R. 18, [1950] C.T.C. 263; *St. Ann's Island Shooting and Fishing Club Ltd. v. The King*, [1950] S.C.R. 211; *R. v. Baig* (1979), 23 O.R. (2d) 730 (Dist. Ct.).

[141]*C.N.R. v. St. John Motor Lines Ltd.*, [1930] S.C.R. 482, [1930] 3 D.L.R. 732, 37 C.R.C. 29.

[142]*Northern Telecom Ltd. v. Communications Workers of Canada*, [1980] 1 S.C.R. 115, 98 D.L.R. (3d) 1, 28 N.R. 107.

[143]*R. v. Yorgason*, [1980] 6 W.W.R. 623 (Alta. Q.B.).

[144]*Supra*, at pp. 77–79.

been completed, argument on the new issue can be ordered.[145] This probably would be required only rarely.

Apart from these procedural considerations, the case seems compelling that a court, where satisfied that a constitutional issue not raised by the parties is relevant to the question before it, which could if considered affect the outcome, should raise that issue itself. This is subject to the right of waiver referred to above. It also is, of course, confined to the cases that are otherwise properly brought before the court and does not imply somehow that courts should commence proceedings of their own motion to ensure judicial review of some issue of which they happen to be aware. Subject to these qualifications, this appears to be required by the principle of the supremacy of the constitution which should not be subject to private selection as to which parts the courts are to respect in the course of exercising judicial authority.

D. CONCLUSION

The selection of constitutional issues for determination appears to involve a considerable element of discretion for the courts. While some issues will be central to the case and therefore inevitable, others may be unnecessary to decide in order to dispose of this particular case, may appear to be unsuitable for judicial, as opposed to political, determination, or may not be raised or pursued by the parties. We have little by way of doctrinal limitations on the courts: it is suggested here instead that the judicial limits on adjudication of such issues are self-imposed and should be applied on functional grounds. Where the issue is imprecise enough that it cannot be answered without enlarging unduly the possibility of unforeseen consequences, or if it is something that another branch of government or the voters are better able to decide because the judgments required involve arbitrary preferences rather than the application of pre-determined standards, then the courts should desist.

The adoption of the *Canadian Charter of Rights and Freedoms* has introduced new problems in the balancing of activism and restraint. On the one hand, the expansion of constitutional guarantees implies wider-ranging judicial review, and the use of rather subjective terminology in parts of the Charter seems to invite more value judgments bordering on the political. Yet for this very reason the courts may be well advised to refrain from premature generalisations about the meaning of these phrases, and instead insist on having very specific facts of a very real and pressing problem before attempting to pronounce on the meaning of such guarantees.

---

[145]As was done, for example, in respect of the *Canadian Bill of Rights* issue in *Singh et al. v. Min. of Employment and Immigration*, [1985] 1 S.C.R. 177.

Chapter 8

The Elements of a Constitutional Decision

A. THE NATURE OF CONSTITUTIONAL ADJUDICATION

With the adoption of the *Canadian Charter of Rights and Freedoms* we entered a new era of judicial review which will undoubtedly draw much from the past but also require much thoughtful innovation. In the past the courts have, in constitutional adjudication, been mostly engaged in interpretation of the distribution of powers and the characterization of laws in relation to that distribution. With the Charter, they must consider not only the characterization of laws but also of administrative practices, and they must judge, not between two levels of government, but between governmental action on the one hand and individual rights on the other.

1. Enforcement of the Distribution of Powers

It may first be useful to consider the nature of constitutional adjudication as it has developed within the context of the distribution of powers. Here the court, in determining whether an impugned statute is valid, must try to "match it up" with some head of jurisdiction in the B.N.A. Act 1867 (*Constitution Act, 1867*). This is essentially a task of characterization of laws for constitutional purposes. It includes an interpretation of those laws—that is, what they mean—but it does not end with that process. It also involves ascribing to them a quality, for constitutional purposes, that will determine if they have been enacted by the Legislature having authority to do so.

Section 91 of the *Constitution Act, 1867* declares that "the exclusive Legislative Authority of the Parliament of Canada extends to all Matters coming within the Classes of Subjects next hereinafter enumerated". Each subject enumerated in ss. 91 and 92 anticipates a legal regime related to the persons,[1] things,[2] or activities[3] referred to therein.[4] When provincial legislation is challenged, for example, it is necessary to ascertain whether the statute creates a legal regime related to certain of the phenomena in the provincial list of subjects. Only if such a relationship can be found will it be valid. An impugned federal statute will similarly be valid if related to a subject listed in s. 91. But, in addition, a federal statute, even if unrelated to any enumerated head of s. 91, so long as it is also unrelated to an enumerated head of s. 92, will be valid as an exercise of Parliament's power "to make Laws for the Peace, Order, and good Government of Canada" as conferred in the opening words of s. 91.

This states in its simplest terms a process which is full of complexity and unpredictability. It is immediately obvious that before one can "match up" an impugned statute with a subject listed in the *Constitution Act*, one must come to some conclusion with respect to what the scope of the "class of subject" is as enumerated in the constitution, and what the nature or content of the impugned statute is from a constitutional point of view.

Much has been written elsewhere in an effort to explain this decisional process of constitutional characterization of statutes. Efforts have been made to reduce it to a set of formulae for analysis of both the impugned statute and the constitution.[5] Some have suggested that construction of the impugned statute is the most important aspect of constitutional adjudication,[6] while others have stressed the importance of "the

---

[1] *E.g.* "Indians" in s. 91(24) or "Aliens" in s. 91(25).

[2] *E.g.* "Sea Coast and Inland Fisheries" in s. 91(12), or "Local Works" in s. 92(10).

[3] *E.g.* "The Regulation of Trade and Commerce" in s. 91(2) or "The Solemnization of Marriage in the Province" in s. 92(12).

[4] It might be argued that some subjects such as "Criminal Law", s. 91(27), or "Incorporation of Companies with Provincial Objects", s. 92(11), do not refer to any persons, things, or activities external to the legal phenomena therein contained. It is submitted that there is in fact an implied reference to those external physical phenomena which the framers of the original B.N.A. Act commonly understood to be associated with the legal phenomena specifically mentioned. Thus "Criminal Law" was intended to refer to forms of activity commonly considered to be dangerous to the public. See Rand J. in the Margarine Reference, *Reference re s. 5(a) of the Dairy Industry Act*, [1949] S.C.R. 1 at 50, [1949] 1 D.L.R. 433 at 473–74. That the reference to external phenomena is implied and not expressed makes interpretation more difficult, but not qualitatively different.

[5] Mundell, "Tests for Validity of Legislation under the British North America Act" (1954), 32 *Can. Bar Rev.* 813; Mundell "Tests for Validity of Legislation under the British North America Act: A Reply to Professor Laskin" (1955), 33 *Can. Bar Rev.* 915.

[6] See *e.g.* LaBrie, "Canadian Constitutional Interpretation and Legislative Review" (1950), 8 *U. Tor. L.J.* 298 at 312.

elaboration of the content of the heads of legislative power conferred by the British North America Act".[7] It is not within the scope of this work to attempt to resolve the conflicts among the authors or to seek a simple explanation for the process in question. Indeed, the decisions largely defy explanation. The better approach is to identify the factors which most probably will have some influence on the decision, without seeking to evaluate too precisely the relative weight likely to be accorded to each.

In determining the nature of the impugned statute for purposes of constitutional characterization, it now seems clear that a court may have regard to both its purpose and its effect. Previous editions of this book have questioned the relevance of "purpose", contending that for the maintenance of the distributions of powers it was only necessary to see whether the major effects of a statute went beyond those permitted to the enacting Legislature. It was argued there that purpose was not critical: a benign purpose could not save a law whose effects encroached on the jurisdiction of another level of government, nor would a bad intent invalidate a law that was, in its effects, properly confined to the area permitted to its enactor.

There had been indications in some cases, however, that purpose might be relevant to validity,[8] and more recently the Supreme Court has expressly held it to be one of the determinative criteria. In *R. v. Big M Drug Mart Ltd.*[9] the court was considering the validity of the federal *Lord's Day Act*[10] which was under attack as infringing freedom of conscience and religion as guaranteed in para. 2(a) of the Charter. It was contended by those who supported the Act that, *inter alia*, its effect was secular even if its purpose was originally to protect the Sabbath of one form of religion; or that even if its original purpose was religious in nature that purpose had changed into the secular objective of ensuring a day of rest. Although the case involved a Charter issue, the majority's statement appears to be equally applicable to distribution of power questions. It was held by Dickson J., writing for the majority, that:[11]

> In my view, both purpose and effect are relevant in determining constitutionality; either an unconstitutional purpose or an unconstitutional effect

---

[7]Laskin, "Tests for the Validity of Legislation: What's the Matter?" (1955), 11 *U. Tor. L.J.* 114 at 125.

[8]See, *e.g.*, *A.G. Alta. v. A.G. Can. et al.*, [1939] A.C. 117 at 130–31, [1938] 3 W.W.R. 337; *Reference re Anti-Inflation Act*, [1976] 2 S.C.R. 373 at 389, 68 D.L.R. (3d) 452 at 468; *Reference re Residential Tennancies Act*, [1981] 1 S.C.R. 714 at 721, 123 D.L.R. (3d) 554 at 561; *Churchill Falls (Labrador) Corp. Ltd. et al. v. A.G. Nfld.*, [1984] 1 S.C.R. 297.

[9][1985] 1 S.C.R. 295.

[10]R.S.C. 1970, c. L-13.

[11]*Supra*, note 9, at p. 331.

can invalidate legislation. All legislation is animated by an object the legislature intends to achieve. This object is realized through the impact produced by the operation and application of the legislation. Purpose and effect respectively, in the sense of the legislation's object and its ultimate impact, are clearly linked, if not indivisible. Intended and actual effects have often been looked to for guidance in assessing the legislation's object and thus, its validity.

And, further on, it was said that:[12]

If the legislation fails the purpose test, there is no need to consider further its effects, since it has already been demonstrated to be invalid. Thus, if a law with a valid purpose interferes by its impact, with rights or freedoms, a litigant could still argue the effects of the legislation as a means to defeat its applicability and possibly its validity. In short, the effects test will only be necessary to defeat legislation with a valid purpose; effects can never be relied upon to save legislation with an invalid purpose.

The majority also rejected the argument that the purpose of a law could change with the passage of time and the change of circumstances.[13]

Purpose is a function of the intent of those who drafted and enacted the legislation at the time, and not of any shifting variable.

The court then found that the purpose of the *Lord Day's Act* is and always has been—as held in numerous previous cases—"the compulsion of sabbatical observance". Its purpose being contrary to freedom of conscience and religion, the Act was invalid and the court did not need to consider its effects. Section 1 of the Charter could not be invoked to save it, because to do so it would be necessary to ascribe to the law a secular purpose (the provision of a day of rest) which could justify a reasonable limitation on the freedom of religious observance of non-Christians. Even though its effect might now be predominantly secular, a law tainted with such original sin, that is the original purpose of protecting the Christian Sabbath, could never be justified as a reasonable limitation on freedom of religion.

That this majority judgment is equally applicable to distribution of powers cases is underlined by the dissenting judgment of Wilson J.[14] She held that purpose might be a proper first condition of validity in distribution of power cases, but not in Charter cases. The Charter, she said,

---

[12]*Ibid.*, at p. 334.
[13]*Ibid.*, at p. 335.
[14]*Ibid*, at p. 356–62.

is "effects-oriented". Citing U.S. authority[15] for the proposition that absence of discriminating intent does not validate employment criteria which have a discriminatory effect, she held effect to be the primary test of infringement with Charter guarantees. Only if a *prima facie* infringement is found, and s. 1 is invoked to support the law in question, should a court consider purpose in the context of that section.

The essential point of the majority judgment in the *Big M* case would appear to be that legislation must, to be valid, meet the two tests of purpose and effect. It is not possible to say that a benign effect will save a law which is overreaching in purpose, or *vice versa*. This conclusion is at least consistent with the view of Wilson J. that, in discrimination cases, a discriminatory effect will invalidate a practice or law whose purpose is non-discriminatory. It is also consistent with what the court held shortly after in a case involving employment practices of this nature.[16]

The net result of the *Big M* decision appears to be to enlarge, or at least clarify, the vulnerability of statutes to constitutional attack. We now know that a bad purpose may destroy a good law. We also know that such purpose will always taint the law, no matter how much its effects may change over time to conform to the constitutional distribution of powers. It underlines the importance of establishing purpose and presents a challenge to judges and lawyers as to how this may be done on the basis of acceptable evidence. If, as the Supreme Court says, "purpose is a function of the intent" of those who adopted the legislation, then we are all faced with trying to divine the intent of a multi-membered law-making body. To a large extent the courts will have to rely on what that body said collectively; that is, on the words of the statute. Further, those words may disclose nothing more than what impact the statute will have; that is, its effects. It will also be necessary to recognize that a statute may have several purposes and several effects. It is difficult to imagine, by the *Big M* formulation, that a statute could have even a minor purpose that was beyond the enactor's jurisdiction and still be valid. But it is quite conceivable that a statute with a constitutionally legitimate purpose might have some secondary effects which encroach on another jurisdiction and yet be valid. The importance of such effects have to be weighed to see if they are sufficiently central to the scheme of the Act to render it *ultra vires*.

This leads to the other basic issues which must be considered in distribution of powers adjudication, that is whether the enacting Legislature ought to be permitted to adopt the purpose and achieve the effect

---

[15]*Griggs v. Duke Power Co.*, 401 U.S. 424 at 432 (1970).

[16]*Ont. Human Rights Commn. et al. v. Simpsons-Sears Ltd. et al.*, [1985] 2 S.C.R. 536; see also the *Edwards Books* case, *infra*, note 20, and accompanying text, where the majority expressly applied both tests and upheld the law.

which the court attributes to its statute. In making this decision the court must reach some conclusion as to the scope of one or more of the heads of ss. 91 or 92 of the *Constitution Act, 1867*. It will also have to make value judgments with respect to the statute in question. The statute may well have several "effects". Some of these might clearly fall within the provincial sphere, others within the federal sphere. For example, the federal *Criminal Code*[17] protects magistrates and peace officers from civil liability when carrying out their duties with respect to administration of the criminal law. This has the effect of aiding the enforcement of criminal law, but it also has the effect of taking away a civil right of a person imprisoned through some excess of jurisdiction. It is impossible to analyze fully the process by which a court would uphold the validity of such a provision. It can be argued that the court simply concludes that "criminal law" ought to include the protection of magistrates and peace officers. Or it can be said that the court considers the salient effect of the law to be the furtherance of criminal justice. Sometimes the courts express their conclusions in one form, sometimes in the other, but the results probably represent an interaction of the two concepts.

In examining the elements of a constitutional decision concerning the distribution of powers, then, it will be necessary to keep in mind the questions which the court must address. They are: (1) What is the purpose of the law in question? (2) What are its effects? and (3) Is the purpose and are the significant effects among those permitted to the enacting Legislature by the *Constitution Acts*?

2. Enforcement of the Charter

Basically the judicial task in enforcing the norms of the Charter should be very similar to that just described. As part of the Constitution the Charter is supreme; any law inconsistent with its guarantees may be held invalid, and any administrative act abridging the guarantees and freedoms it protects may be judicially constrained or remedied unless somehow justified under s. 1.

As noted in the discussion above of the *Big M* case, the dual tests of purpose and effect apply to Charter cases as well. Indeed, the majority seems to imply in that case that, if anything, purpose is a more important consideration in challenges based on the Charter.[18]

> Moreover, consideration of the object of legislation is vital if rights are to be fully protected. The assessment by the courts of legislative purpose

---

[17]R.S.C. 1970, c. C-34, ss. 33(2), 717.
[18]*Supra*, note 9, at pp. 331–32.

focuses scrutiny upon the aims and objectives of the legislature and ensures they are consonant with the guarantees enshrined in the *Charter*. The declaration that certain objects lie outside the legislature's power checks governmental action at the first stage of unconstitutional conduct. Further, it will provide more ready and more vigorous protection of constitutional rights by obviating the individual litigant's need to prove effects violative of *Charter* rights. It will also allow courts to dispose of cases where the object is clearly improper, without inquiring into the legislation's actual impact.

It was emphasized again later that a finding of an invalid purpose obviates the need for any examination (thought to be potentially more difficult) of the law's effects. It is even implied that a law with an invalid purpose cannot have legitimate effects.[19]

> If the acknowledged purpose of the *Lord's Day Act*, namely, the compulsion of sabbatical observance, offends freedom of religion, it is then unnecessary to consider the actual impact of Sunday closing upon religious freedom. Even if such effects were found inoffensive, as the Attorney General of Alberta urges, this could not save legislation whose purpose has been found to violate the *Charter's* guarantees. In any event, I would find it difficult to conceive of legislation with an unconstitutional purpose, where the effects would not also be unconstitutional.

The Supreme Court has confirmed its general approach in the *Big M* case in a later case also involving a Sunday closing law. In *Edwards Books & Art Ltd. v. The Queen*[20] the court was considering a challenge to the *Retail Business Holidays Act*[21] on both distribution of powers and Charter (freedom of religion) grounds. The majority reiterated the dual test of purpose and effect as being relevant to both grounds of attack. It found the provincial Act to have a secular purpose—the provision of a uniform holiday for retail workers—which was within provincial jurisdiction under s. 92 of the *Constitution Act, 1867*: thus the Act was not intended as an infringement of religious freedom.[22] The court therefore proceeded to consider whether its effects were inconsistent with the Charter. The majority concluded that those effects did abridge religious freedom but were justified under s. 1 of the Charter. The "limitation" of that freedom, as prescribed by the law, was valid as being within provincial jurisdiction, and was not adopted for the purpose of denying religious

---

[19]*Ibid.*, at p. 333.
[20][1986] 2 S.C.R. 713.
[21]R.S.O. 1980, c. 453.
[22]*Supra*, note 20, at p. 752.

freedom. Further it was supportable by the general tests applicable to s. 1 limitations as defined in the *Oakes* case.[23]

It is important to note precisely the role played by purpose and effect in Charter cases in the analysis of legislative or administrative activities. First, "purpose" is relevant to determining whether the law or activity in question is within the powers assigned to the relevant government by the constitution quite apart from the Charter. If it fails this test, there is no question of it being upheld *vis-à-vis* the guarantees in the Charter, nor could any such law if invalid on distribution of power grounds provide "limits prescribed by law" within s. 1. Second, purpose must be considered in connection with an initial determination as to whether *prima facie* a Charter right is infringed. The *Big M* decision clearly means that a law adopted for the very purpose of infringing a Charter right must be taken to infringe it, even if its effects are otherwise. Third, once a *prima facie* infringement is established and s. 1 is invoked as a justification, the purpose of the limit "prescribed by law" will be examined to see if it is directly intended to deny or infringe the right or freedom in question. It flows from the *Big M* decision that a limit prescribed for such a purpose cannot be justified.[24]

The effect of statutes impugned under the Charter plays a similar but not identical role. It will be equally relevant as a possible means of defeating a statute on distribution of power grounds, or of establishing *prima facie* infringement of a Charter right even if the purpose of the law is valid.[25] If at that point s. 1 is invoked to justify a law whose effects infringe Charter rights, the effects of the law will be of limited importance. It appears to flow from the *Big M* case that the very purpose of s. 1 is to validate laws which have legitimate, non-infringing purposes, but which have effects that infringe Charter rights. Therefore a finding that the law has such an effect does not (unlike a finding of an infringing purpose) affect the possibility of it being sustained under s. 1. However, it appears that in applying the tests prescribed by the Supreme Court in the *Oakes* case for determining if a "limit" to rights is justified under s. 1, the

---

[23] [1986] 1 S.C.R. 103.

[24] This appears to be consistent with the court's *obiter dicta* in *A.G. Qué v. Que. Assn. of Protestant School Bds. et al.*, [1984] 2 S.C.R. 66 at 85–88 where it was said that a law adopted with the purpose of making exceptions to the minority language education régime prescribed by s. 23 of the Charter would not be justified under s. 1. The court went on to say that neither would s. 1 sustain a law imposing a state religion.

[25] See, *e.g.*, *Protestant School Bd.* case *ibid.*, at pp. 87–88. *Cf. Ont. Human Rights Commn.* case, *supra*, note 16, where an employment policy neutral in purpose was held to be discriminatory in effect and thus susceptible to control under a provincial anti-discrimination law. The same principle would appear to be applicable to laws with valid purposes but with effects which infringe Charter rights.

nature of the effects may be quite relevant. As described in that case, a limitation on Charter rights to be justified must have a sufficiently important objective and employ appropriate means. As to the latter, the court said that the means, to meet approval (a) must be rationally connected to the objective; (b) should impair as little as possible the rights in question; and (c) in their effects be proportional to the importance of the objective being served.[26] It is clear, then, that the effect of a law will be quite relevant to applying tests (b) and (c). Here the court cannot rest simply with finding the practical effects of a law, but must also weigh those effects for severity and consider if there are possible alternatives that might have been less intrusive. Throughout these considerations may run a question as to whether the effects are such as to be acceptable in a "free and democratic society" and this may involve comparisons with the effects of laws in other countries.

The foregoing considerations relate to the characterization of a statute, or sometimes of an administrative practice, which is alleged to contravene the Charter. But just as in the application of the distribution of powers limitations, it is also necessary in applying the Charter to determine the proper scope of its guarantees. This aspect of Charter litigation has been very prominent in its early years, because of the generality of many of the Charter's terms and the lack of judicial precedents. In general it may be said that the meaning of the Charter will be sought in ways employed in the interpretation of any document. But in constitutional litigation there has been a tendency to look farther afield to find constitutional purpose, and this has been given special emphasis in Charter interpretation. For example, in the *Protestant School Board* case the Supreme Court concluded from the history of the matter that the purpose of s. 23 of the Charter was to invalidate precisely the kind of minority language education régime which existed in Québec at the time of its adoption. Hence it found that such a régime could not be sustained under s. 1.[27] This was referred to as a "teleological" interpretation of s. 23. In *Hunter et al. v. Southam Inc.* the court stated that "the proper approach to the interpretation of the *Charter of Rights and Freedoms* is a purposive one . . . ''[28] and it proceeded to interpret s. 8 on the basis of history and the common law to see its purpose. This idea was elaborated in the *Big M* case, where Dickson J. writing for the majority referred to the purposive approach approved in the *Hunter* case and said:[29]

The meaning of a right or freedom guaranteed by the *Charter* was to be

---

[26]*Supra*, note 23, at pp. 138–39.
[27]*Supra*, note 24, at pp. 79–85.
[28][1984] 2 S.C.R. 145 at 157.
[29]*Supra*, note 9, at p. 344.

ascertained by an analysis of the purpose of such a guarantee; it was to be understood, in other words, in the light of the interests it was meant to protect.

In my view this analysis is to be undertaken, and the purpose of the right or freedom in question is to be sought by reference to the character and the larger objects of the *Charter* itself, to the language chosen to articulate the specific right or freedom, to the historical origins of the concepts enshrined, and where applicable, to the meaning and purpose of the other specific rights and freedoms with which it is associated within the text of the *Charter*. The interpretation should be, as the judgment in *Southam* emphasizes, a generous rather than a legalistic one, aimed at fulfilling the purpose of the guarantee and securing for individuals the full benefit of the *Charter's* protection. At the same time it is important not to overshoot the actual purpose of the right or freedom in question, but to recall that the *Charter* was not enacted in a vacuum, and must therefore, as this Court's decision in *Law Society of Upper Canada v. Skapinker*, [1984] 1 S.C.R. 357, illustrates, be placed in its proper linguistic, philosophic and historical contexts.

That is, purpose is to be ascertained from the text of the Charter provisions together with its history and the general and particular objects of the Charter. This approach was followed at least nominally in *Reference re S. 94(2) of the Motor Vehicle Act, R.S.B.C. 1979, c. 288*, although the majority judgment seems to rely more on assumptions, rather than on the historical background of the provision, in reaching a conclusion as to the purpose of s. 7.[30] Indeed it refers to[31]

a fact which is nearly impossible of proof, *i.e.*, the intention of the legislative bodies which adopted the *Charter*.

It is difficult to reconcile this with the assurance with which the court in the *Protestant School Board* case was able to conclude that the purpose of the "framers" of s. 23 was to invalidate the "Quebec clause" in the law of that province dealing with the language of education.[32]

The problems of interpretation of particular Charter provisions will vary with each section. Some present inherent difficulties because of qualifying words such as "fundamental", "reasonable", "cruel and unusual", etc. Section 15 with its defined and undefined prohibited grounds of discrimination, and its abstract concepts such as "equal" and "discrimination" will be particularly difficult. No doubt the "purposive" approach will be much in demand in its interpretation.

---

[30][1985] 2 S.C.R. 486 at 499–500.
[31]*Ibid.*, at pp. 508–09.
[32]*Supra*, note 24, at pp. 82–85.

It may be seen then that in the enforcement of the Charter, as in distribution of powers issues, the main element for determination will be the purpose and effect of impugned laws and actions, and the proper scope of Charter provisions. Purpose will have a special emphasis here both in respect of the characterization of laws in relation to s. 1, and for the interpretation of the Charter itself.

B. NON-FACTUAL ELEMENTS

The issues that normally must be addressed in constitutional cases have been discussed in the preceding section. The main elements that go into the determination of these issues will now be addressed. Some of these elements are of a factual nature and others are non-factual. The latter will be considered first. While these may be categorized in various ways, they will (in addition to the legal presumption of validity) be gathered under the rubrics of text, doctrine, and policy. The textual approach in this analysis will include the context of the constitutional or statutory provision in question; "doctrine" describes judicial precedents which have previously interpreted the text of the constitutional or statutory provision in question in whole or in part; and "policy" covers the predominantly subjective elements which involve courts in deciding what the constitution *should* mean. These roughly correspond to the elements of Charter interpretation identified by the Supreme Court in the *Big M* case as quoted earlier.[33]

In the language often employed in discussions of judicial review in the United States,[34] interpretation based on text and doctrine is essentially "interpretive" in nature; that based on policy is essentially "non-interpretive".

1. Legal Presumption of Validity

It has long been said by the courts that they will presume an impugned law to be valid where there is an ambiguity in its scope that would otherwise allow the law to be characterized either as valid or invalid

---

[33]*Supra*, note 29, and accompanying text.

[34]See, *e.g.*, Perry, *The Constitution, The Courts, and Human Rights: An Inquiry into the Legitimacy of Constitutional Policymaking by the Judiciary* (New Haven: Yale University Press, 1982), c. 1.

depending on the meaning ascribed to it.[35] The presumption is said to apply to lead the court to conclude both that the enacting Legislature intended to stay within its assigned powers and to stay within its assigned geographical territory, unless a contrary interpretation is inevitable. This appears to be essentially a rule of statutory interpretation in determining the intended meaning of the statute.

Such a presumption permits a seemly judicial deference to the decision of another branch of government and its own implicit interpretation of the constitution. It provides a useful starting point for judicial review so that the court is not seen gratuitously to interfere with legislative judgments.[36] It is not clear, however, what practical impact the presumption has had on judicial results. Probably it has created a certain, often inarticulate, judicial inertia in favour of upholding laws where there are no compelling reasons to strike them down.

This presumption should be related to two other concepts. One is that of "reading down" a statute so as to make it applicable only where it can validly apply. This is an application of the same principle of interpretation of the law in question but is different in emphasis in that one usually speaks of "reading down" a statute only after accepting that in its essential features it is a valid law. This will be discussed briefly later.[37]

The other related concept is that of the factual presumption of validity. Whereas the legal presumption assumes a legal meaning of a contested statute which would permit its validity, the factual presumption assumes a factual context that would allow the statute or its particular application to the situation at hand to be characterized as constitutionally valid in the absence of compelling evidence to the contrary. This too will be discussed later.[38]

The legal presumption of validity, though developed in the context of distribution of powers cases, might be thought to have general appli-

---

[35]*Severn v. The Queen* (1878), 2 S.C.R. 70; *Hewson v. Ont. Power Co.* (1905), 36 S.C.R. 596; *A.G. Ont. v. Reciprocal Insurers*, [1924] A.C. 328, [1924] 2 W.W.R. 397, [1924] 1 D.L.R. 789, 41 C.C.C. 336, (P.C.); *Reference re Farm Products Marketing Act*, [1957] S.C.R. 198 at 255, 7 D.L.R. (2d) 257 at 311; *Lieberman v. The Queen*, [1963] S.C.R. 643, 41 D.L.R. (2d) 125, [1964] 1 C.C.C. 82, 41 C.R. 325; *McNeil v. N.S. Bd. of Censors*, [1978] 2 S.C.R. 662 at 687–88, 25 N.S.R. (2d) 128, 84 D.L.R. (3d) 1 at 20, 19 N.R. 570, 44 C.C.C. (2d) 316; *C.B.C. v. Cordeau*, [1979] 2 S.C.R. 618, 101 D.L.R. (3d) 24, 28 N.R. 541 (*sub nom. C.B.C. v. Quebec Police Comm.*), 48 C.C.C. (2d) 289, 14 C.P.C. 60; *R. v. Domstad* (1982), 134 D.L.R. (3d) 66 (Alta. C.A.).

[36]Hogg, *Constitutional Law of Canada*, 2nd ed. (Toronto: Carswell, 1985) at pp. 99–100 asserts this justification for the presumption.

[37]See below at pp. 300–01.

[38]See below at pp. 292, 293.

cation to Charter cases as well. As part of the Constitution, the Charter is by s-s. 52(1) of the *Constitution Act, 1982* "the supreme law of Canada" as much as are ss. 91 and 92 of the *Constitution Act, 1867*. As in distribution of powers cases, anyone wishing to establish a conflict between a law and the Charter has the initial burden to demonstrate the conflict. This has also been held to be true in respect of the burden of adducing evidence in cases where a party seeks a remedy under s. 24 of the Charter,[39] and it would appear equally true with respect to presenting legal argument.

One chief difference in Charter cases, insofar as the presumption of validity is concerned, arises if the court once finds that a Charter right is infringed. At that point, if the party responsible for defending that infringement invokes s. 1 of the Charter, the legal presumption of validity no longer applies to the law which he asserts to be a justifiable limitation on the Charter right. The onus is clearly on him to prove that that law is "reasonable" and "demonstrably justified"[40] and this excludes any further presumption of validity.

Another difference in Charter cases, whose significance is yet hard to assess, has been expressed by Beetz J. writing for the Supreme Court in *A.G. Man. v. Metro. Stores (MTS) Ltd. et al.*[41] He stated that in Charter cases

> the innovative and evolutive character of the *Canadian Charter of Rights and Freedoms* conflicts with the idea that a legislative provision can be presumed to be consistent with the *Charter*.

Further, he said this was the case whether the legislation under attack was adopted before or after the adoption of the Charter. His rationale would appear to be that, since the meaning of the Charter will be constantly changing (apparently through judicial interpretation) one cannot presume that the enacting Legislature intended to comply with the Charter.

It will be seen that such an approach leaves little room for judicial deference to other branches of governments by way of giving due weight to interpretations put on the Charter by legislatures or administrators in adopting or applying a law.

It may be noted that these comments appear to be *obiter dicta* in that the court allowed the appeal on grounds related to the proper role

---

[39]*R. v. Roach* (1985), 23 C.C.C. (3d) 262 (Alta. C.A.).
[40]*Re Fed. Republic of Germany and Rauca* (1983), 4 C.C.C. (3d) 385 at 400–01 (Ont. C.A.); *Re Ont. Film and Video Appreciation Soc. and Ont. Bd. of Censors* (1983), 147 D.L.R. (3d) at 64–65 (Ont. Div. Ct.), decided on other grounds 5 D.L.R. (4th) 766 (Ont. C.A.); *R. v. Oakes*, [1986] 1 S.C.R. 103 at 136–37.
[41][1987] 1 S.C.R. 110 at 122.

of the Manitoba Court of Appeal in reversing an exercise of judicial discretion by the trial judge. It may also be noted that the issue before the Supreme Court was the grant of an interlocutory, not a final, order: the appellant was arguing against the stay of a constitutionally-impugned order of the Manitoba Labour Relations Board prior to final determination of its validity on the ground that such validity should be presumed at this stage. Beetz J. in rejecting this contention said, however, that even when one reaches the merits (presumably at the trial stage) there was no room for the presumption of validity.

While the full implications of such an approach cannot yet be seen, the court did not exclude the possibility of a rebuttable presumption which would have the effect of placing the initial burden of proof of invalidity on he who attacks a law or administrative action, and it left open the possibility of a rule of construction by which a court should attempt to give a law a valid meaning before striking it down. These are some of the applications, referred to in this work, of the concept of presumption of constitutionality.

There remain difficult questions as to how demanding a court should be in finding that the initial burden has been met to show a conflict with the Charter. Should the court dwell on analysis of the proper scope of the guaranteed right or freedom, thus probably rejecting many claims at this stage without the need for the other party to rely on s. 1 and meet the onus thus cast on it? Or should it readily find a *prima facie* infringement, without seeking to refine the meaning of the various guarantees in the Charter, and thus place the burden on the defenders of laws of limitation to make out their case under s. 1? It is at least arguable that, given the existence of s. 1 which in effect requires legislative bodies to prescribe by law any limits that are to be placed on rights, those rights should be construed as broadly as possible. It is under s. 1 that any "balancing" should be done of private rights against the public interest.[42] No clear pattern has emerged in the jurisprudence. It is bound to vary with the particular wording of the right or freedom in question. While the Supreme Court has said that the balancing exercise under s. 1 must be kept separate from the initial determination as to infringement,[43] some guarantees have within them words which may involve some balancing – words such as "equal", "discrimination", "unreasonable", and "unusual". With respect to such a guarantee the court has not hesitated to undertake a "balancing" without going to s. 1.[44]

---

[42]See the judgment of Dickson C.J. in the *Edwards Books* case, *supra*, note 20, at pp. 756–57, where he agrees with Douglas J. in *McGowan v. Maryland*, 366 U.S. 420 at 575–76 (1961), that balancing should be done within saving clauses like s. 1, where such exist in a constitution.

[43]*Oakes* case, *supra*, note 23, at p. 134.

[44]*Hunter et al. v. Southam Inc.*, *supra*, note 28.

2. Texts of the Constitution and Impugned Laws

It is clear that the court must in each case start with an examination of the text of the constitution and of the law, if any, in question.[45] In seeking the meaning of each they can make use of the common law rules of statutory interpretation. These rules, which are uncertain in application, may not yield a final result with respect to meaning. But they may solve the easiest problems and provide a starting point for the solution of others. It must be kept in mind that the traditional rules of interpretation are related to the construction of statutes, that is, finding out what the Legislature "intended".

A few recent examples will demonstrate the use of the textual approach in interpreting constitutional provisions. Because of its novelty, the Charter has been the subject of several of these cases.

In *Law Soc. of Upper Can. v. Skapinker*[46] the Supreme Court used the heading "Mobility Rights" before s. 6 of the Charter to assist it in determining whether that section protected the right to work generally or only in respect of those who move from one province to another. In *Reference re Language Rights in Man.*[47] the court resorted to traditional interpretations of the word "shall" as expressing an imperative, in construing s. 23 of the *Manitoba Act, 1870*, a statute of the Parliament of Canada but also part of the Constitution. In *Hunter et al. v. Southam Inc.*[48] the court declined to find that the protection in s. 8 of the Charter against "unreasonable search or seizure" was confined to protection of property or was linked to trespass, in part because the text was silent on the matter.

A more controversial use of a textual approach to interpret the Charter may be seen in *Reference re S. 94(2) of the Motor Vehicle Act.*[49] There Lamer J. writing for the majority observed that ss. 7 to 14 could all have been combined into one section, with ss. 8 to 14 being merely examples of a general principle stated in s. 7. He said that "principles of fundamental justice" as referred to in s. 7 must be given a broad interpretation

---

[45]This would include an examination of the law in its legal context. That is, other statutes and judicial decisions related to it can be examined to assist in determining its meaning. See *Reference re Alberta Statutes*, [1938] S.C.R. 100, [1938] 2 D.L.R. 81; affd [1939] A.C. 117 (*sub nom. A.G. Alta. v. A.G. Can.*), [1938] 3 W.W.R. 337, [1938] 4 D.L.R. 433; *Proprietary Articles Trade Assn. v. A.G. Can.*, [1931] A.C. 310, [1931] All E.R. Rep. 277, [1931] 1 W.W.R. 552, [1931] 2 D.L.R. 1, 55 C.C.C. 241 (P.C.); *Canadian Federation of Agriculture v. A.G. Que.*, [1951] A.C. 179, [1950] 4 D.L.R. 689 (P.C.); *A.G. Can. v. C.N. Transportation, Ltd. et al.*, [1983] 2 S.C.R. 206 at 225–26; *Reference re Language Rights in Man.*, [1985] 1 S.C.R. 721 at 736–39.

[46][1984] 1 S.C.R. 357.

[47][1985] 1 S.C.R. 721 at 737.

[48][1984] 2 S.C.R. 145 at 158.

[49][1985] 2 S.C.R. 486 at 501–503.

as otherwise that section would have the effect of narrowing some of the provisions of ss. 8 to 14 presumed to be examples of the "principle of fundamental justice". This illustrates that a textual approach, seemingly objective and neutral, also involves selectivity by a court as to the factors to which it will give weight. For example, it would have been at least equally plausible to have assumed here that the eight sections in question were made separate because they were intended by the framers to have distinct meanings. It would have been easy to combine them if ss. 8 to 14 were but examples of s. 7. In fact, an earlier draft of the Charter did have them combined and this was later changed, presumably for a good reason.[50] Even the court itself in the *Skapinker* case had referred to ss. 7 to 14 as "eight disparate sections."[51]

Textual analysis may also involve the use of factual materials such as governmental statements and the factual context in which the text was adopted, but these will be dealt with below.

3. Doctrine

More important among the non-factual sources is the mass of precedent bearing on any constitutional decision. Precedent will be most influential in determining the scope of the constitutional provision in issue. This will involve some express or implied conclusion as to the proper scope of a head of ss. 91 or 92, or of a provision of the Charter. To the extent that recourse is had to precedent for this purpose the more likely it is that the rationale for judgment will be conceptual rather than functional. The reports are of course full of pronouncements on the scope of the various heads of jurisdiction in ss. 91 and 92. We have been told, for example, that "Regulation of Trade and Commerce" includes regulation of interprovincial and international commerce,[52] but not intraprovincial commerce.[53] "Criminal Law" includes the prohibition of acts combined with penal sanctions,[54] so long as the prohibition is primarily

---

[50]The text of an earlier federal proposal combining these sections was published on July 4, 1980 and may be found in McLeod, Takach, Morton, Segal, *The Canadian Charter of Rights—The Prosecution and Defence of Criminal and Other Statutory Offences* (Toronto: Carswell, 1983), Appendix C at A-128 to A-152.

[51]*Supra*, note 46 at p. 377.

[52]*Citizens' Ins. Co. v. Parsons; Queen Ins. Co. v. Parsons* (1881), 7 App. Cas. 96, 45 L.T. 721 (P.C.).

[53]*Re Board of Commerce*, [1922] 1 A.C. 191, [1922] 1 W.W.R. 20, 60 D.L.R. 513 (P.C.).

[54]*P.A.T.A. v. A.G. Can.*, *supra*, note 45.

intended to protect the public as such and is not a guise for regulating local commerce.[55]

Canadian constitutional jurisprudence on the distribution of powers abounds with such propositions. They do not necessarily yield any obvious result in a given case, however, as it is not immediately apparent how they relate to a particular statute the validity of which is in question. Is the most important feature of a statute its effect on interprovincial trade, or its effect on property and civil rights in the province? Precedent does not often give the answer to such a question, though it may.[56] The answer is more likely to come from judicial intuition or a judicial policy decision, possibly, but not probably, aided by a resort to factual material as to effect. Precedent re-emerges as a potent force after the court has singled out the important and the unimportant features of the challenged legislation. The courts are likely then to resort to the well-recognized, judicially created, principles for the determination of constitutional validity. If the major effect of a federal statute pertains to "Criminal Law", and a minor effect pertains to matters which for other purposes would fall within "Property and Civil Rights", the court will uphold the legislation possibly invoking the so-called "trenching" doctrine. If the major effect of a provincial law is the regulation of taverns or highway traffic, and federal legislation also exists regulating these matters, the court may apply the "double-aspect" doctrine and uphold both, or if it finds a "conflict" may strike down the provincial law on the basis of the "paramountcy" doctrine. If federal legislation is found to pertain to an emergency or crisis, even though not referable to one of the enumerated heads of s. 91, it may be upheld even though it may interfere with matters otherwise within the provincial sphere. These rules or doctrines are all judicial glosses on the actual terms of the *Constitution Act*.[57] They may well have hindered as much as helped in the intelligent analysis of challenged legislation.[58] So strongly has precedent operated in this area, however,

---

[55]*Canadian Federation of Agriculture v. A.G. Que., supra*, note 45.

[56]The courts have shown an unnecessarily strong tendency at times to apply, or misapply, precedent in characterizing statutes. For example, all statutory efforts of Parliament to license insurance companies have been characterized as invasions of the provincial domain over property and civil rights. Precedent was the major justification given for this finding in a series of cases. See Smith, *The Commerce Power in Canada and the United States* (Toronto: Butterworths, 1963), at 77–91.

[57]They have been amply expounded and analyzed elsewhere. See, *e.g., A.G. Can. v. A.G. B.C.*, [1930] A.C. 111, [1929] 3 W.W.R. 449, [1930] 1 D.L.R. 194; LaBrie, *supra*, note 6; Mundell, *supra*, note 5; *Laskin's Canadian Constitutional Law*, 5th ed., Finkelstein ed. (Toronto: Carswell, 1986), at pp. 242–291. Perhaps the simplest and most lucid analysis is that of Professor Lederman, "Classification of Laws and the British North America Act", in Corry, Cronkite and Whitmore, *Legal Essays in Honour of Arthur Moxon* (Toronto: U. of T. Press, 1953), 183, at pp. 201–06.

[58]See, *e.g.*, Laskin, " 'Peace, Order and Good Government' Re-examined" (1947), 25 *Can. Bar Rev.* 1054.

that a court would find it difficult to ignore these rules in reaching a final conclusion as to constitutional validity.

Precedent will be far less influential in the process of determining the effect of the impugned law or action. The effect of a particular law is likely to be unique, unless it is basically similar to other legislation not only in form but also in the context within which it is expected to operate. Each new law, each new form of administrative action, should raise a new question as to its effect. The rules of statutory interpretation or judicial experience with similar laws or Acts may yield a satisfactory answer in some cases. A resort to factual material should be permitted elsewhere. Precedent should not shut out further factual illumination.

In enforcing the distribution of powers, however, the courts have sometimes allowed precedent to preclude further inquiry as to statutory effect. With respect to one head of jurisdiction, at least, that of provincial power over "Direct Taxation within the Province", the courts have looked more to precedent than to practice in determining the effect of taxation measures. The Privy Council early adopted John Stuart Mill's definition of direct and indirect taxes: "A direct tax is one which is demanded from the very persons who it is intended or desired should pay it. Indirect taxes are those which are demanded from one person in the expectation and intention that he shall indemnify himself at the expense of another; such are the excise or customs."[59] Having accepted this as the basis of distinguishing a direct tax from an indirect tax, the courts have been unwilling to ascertain as a matter of fact whether the tax in question is or is not imposed in such a way as to permit a passing-on. They have declined to be guided by the opinions of economists on the actual effect of the tax.[60] Instead they have tended automatically to treat certain kinds of taxes as direct, other kinds as indirect. It appears to have been accepted as a matter of law that a tax on land is always a direct tax.[61] A tax on commodities is always an indirect tax, even if the possibilities of passing it on are slight.[62] Conversely, a consumption tax is a direct tax even though in a

---

[59]As approved in *Bank of Toronto v. Lambe* (1887), 12 App. Cas. 575 at 583 (P.C.).

[60]*Ibid.*, at pp. 581–82: *Cairns Const. Ltd. v. Sask.* (1958), 27 W.W.R. 297, 16 D.L.R. (2d) 465 (Sask. C.A.), appeal dismissed [1960] S.C.R. 619, 24 D.L.R. (2d) 1, 35 W.W.R. 241, without reference to this point.

[61]*A.G. B.C. v. Esquimalt & Nanaimo Ry. Co.*, [1950] A.C. 87, [1949] 2 W.W.R. 1233, [1950] 1 D.L.R. 305, 64 C.R.T.C. 165 (P.C.); *C.P.R. v. A.G. Sask.*, [1952] 2 S.C.R. 231, [1952] 4 D.L.R. 11.

[62]*A.G. B.C. v. McDonald Murphy Lumber Co.*, [1930] A.C. 357, [1930] 1 W.W.R. 830, [1930] 2 D.L.R. 721 (P.C.); *Lower Mainland Dairy Products Sales Adjustment Committee v. Crystal Dairy Ltd.*, [1933] A.C. 168, [1932] 3 W.W.R. 639, [1933] 1 D.L.R. 82 (P.C.); *Canadian Industrial Gas & Oil Ltd. v. Sask.*, [1978] 2 S.C.R. 545 at 564–66, [1977] 6 W.W.R. 607, 80 D.L.R. (3d) 449 at 461–63, 18 N.R. 107. But

large area of commercial activity it is capable of being passed on.[63]

As Professor K.C. Davis has pointed out,[64] there is a certain judicial tendency to convert difficult questions of fact into presumptions of law. For example, because it would be difficult to ascertain whether each child coming before the courts had the mental capacity to commit a crime, it came to be presumed conclusively that a child under seven could not form the intent and that one over fourteen could. This recognized tendency probably provides an explanation for the courts substituting the presumed effect for the actual effect of taxing statutes. In defence of the courts it might also be argued that a statute should be upheld if it operates "approximately" within the powers of the enacting Legislature and that peculiar circumstances in which it would transgress constitutional limitations ought not to invalidate the whole statute.[65] On the other hand, there is a strong argument for finding the statute to be "inapplicable" in such circumstances. This would equally save the statute without giving it an effect inconsistent with the constitution. It is suggested that the courts should re-examine their legal presumptions as to the effect of various forms of taxes. Equally they should be very cautious about substituting presumptions of law for findings of fact in other areas of constitutional adjudication.

At the outset of interpretation of the Charter, there were of course no binding precedents. Because of the similarity of some of its language, earlier interpretations of the *Canadian Bill of Rights* were looked to but given only limited importance. The Supreme Court has expressly rejected such interpretations as binding authority in the interpretation of the Charter on the basis that the Bill was merely a statute which was only declaratory of existing rights, not a constitutional guarantee of specified rights whether pre-existing or not.[66]

4. Policy

It has long been the reality of constitutional adjudication, and has more recently been openly recognized, that courts must often form an

---

see dissenting judgment of Dickson J. at pp. 584–86 S.C.R., pp. 476–77 D.L.R., where he makes a strong case for looking at the facts rather than automatically assuming that such a tax is indirect.

[63]*Cairns Const.* case, *supra*, note 60.

[64]Davis, 3 *Administrative Law Treatise*, 2nd ed. (1980), at 192–94.

[65]For an explanation of this principle in Australian constitutional law see Lane, *The Australian Federal System*, 2nd ed. (1979), at 1156; for an aspect of its application in U.S. law see Tribe, *American Constitutional Law* (1978), at pp. 997–99.

[66]*R. v. Big M Drug Mart Ltd., supra*, note 9, at pp. 341–44; *R. v. Oakes, supra*, note 23, at pp. 122–25. See also *R. v. Therens*, [1985] 1 S.C.R. 613 at 638–39; *Singh et al. v. Min. of Employment and Immigration*, [1985] 1 S.C.R. 177 at 208–09.

opinion as to what they think the constitution *ought* to mean. This should not be the first consideration, but it will often be necessary where the text, as interpreted in the light of its history and context, is still ambiguous or silent and there are no meaningful precedents for guidance. Such decisions involve resort to some *desiratum* which the court perceives to be implicit in the constitution, and thus they may be seen as based on the non-factual element of constitutional policy.

The subjective element in such decisions can scarcely be denied. In assessing the relative importance of various effects of a law, for example, the Privy Council has held that the salient effect of one provincial law, which reduced the principal on farm mortgages in years of crop failure, was the regulation of "interest".[67] A few years later, the Supreme Court of Canada concluded that the most significant effect of another provincial law, which authorized a reduction of both principal and interest on unconscionable contracts, was the regulation of "property and civil rights".[68] The Supreme Court was able in *Carnation Co. v. Quebec Agricultural Marketing Bd.*[69] in 1968 to find that a provincial marketing scheme by which a processor had to acquire local milk for processing and export was not directed at interprovincial trade, whereas it found in *A.G. Man. v. Manitoba Egg and Poultry Assn.*[70] in 1971 and in *Burns Foods Ltd. v. A.G. Man.*[71] in 1975 that a provincial scheme for marketing in the province farm products imported from other provinces was directed at the regulation of interprovincial trade. Logic and precedent alone would not produce such seemingly inconsistent results. Another example of an apparent policy-oriented approach may be seen in the judicial tendency to find distinct effects for provincial and federal statutes which, *prima facie*, appear to be duplicative or nearly identical.[72] This must reflect some inarticulate policy decision in favour of concurrent powers and thus the ability of provinces to impose local variations unless Parliament shows an unmistakable intent to have uniformity.

Again in determining the proper scope of the various heads of jurisdiction the policy element will frequently appear. It was a policy decision which denied to "Regulation of Trade and Commerce" the control of intraprovincial commerce, which withdrew from "Peace, Order

---

[67]*A.G. Sask. v. A.G. Can.*, [1949] A.C. 110, [1949] 1 W.W.R. 742, [1949] 2 D.L.R. 145.

[68]*A.G. Ont. v. Barfried Enterprises Ltd.*, [1963] S.C.R. 570, 42 D.L.R. (2d) 137.

[69][1968] S.C.R. 238.

[70][1971] S.C.R. 689, [1971] 4 W.W.R. 705, 19 D.L.R. (3d) 169.

[71][1975] 1 S.C.R. 494, [1974] 2 W.W.R. 537, 40 D.L.R. (3d) 731, 1 N.R. 147.

[72]For a discussion of these cases see Lederman, "The Concurrent Operation of Federal and Provincial Laws in Canada" (1963), 9 *McGill L.J.* 185; Hogg, *Constitutional Law of Canada*, 2nd ed. (Toronto: Carswell, 1985), c. 16.

and good Government'' the capacity to ''trench'' on provincial heads, and which sought means to find some limits for ''Criminal Law''. Similarly, policy considerations gave to ''Property and Civil Rights'' a meaning broad enough to cover most commercial activity not otherwise specifically described in the B.N.A. Act. Whether these were wise or unwise decisions it is unnecessary to say, but policy decisions they surely were.

Experience to date with the Charter indicates that policy considerations will have even greater importance in its interpretation. This should surprise no one. The Charter, unlike the *Constitution Act, 1867*, was born in an era of legal realism. The legal profession, the bench, and the public have all assumed a degree of judicial creativity in its interpretation never widely recognized in relation to the distribution of powers. Along with these expectations, the courts are faced with a text which is general in its terms and not yet encrusted with decades of judicial precedents. Many courts, at all levels, have to one degree or another, expressly or implicitly, brought policy considerations to bear in their decisions. Clear signals have been issued by the Supreme Court in support of this approach. The advent of the Charter has in fact caused the court to make some general pronouncements on the need for policy considerations in constitutional adjudication and it has not confined this to Charter cases. The clear adoption by the court of ''purpose'' (of statutes and of constitutional provisions) as a necessary factor for consideration has been discussed earlier in this chapter. Any emphasis on ''purpose'' is almost certain to involve the decision of policy questions. Apart from this the court very early in its interpretation of the Charter said that:[73]

> The fine and constant adjustment process of these constitutional provisions is left by a tradition of necessity to the judicial branch. Flexibility must be balanced with certainty. The future must, to the extent foreseeably possible, be accommodated in the present. The *Charter* is designed and adopted to guide and serve the Canadian community for a long time. Narrow and technical interpretation, if not modulated by a sense of the unknowns of the future, can stunt the growth of the law and hence the community it serves. All this has long been with us in the process of developing the institutions of government under the *B.N.A. Act, 1867.* . . .

Not only was this a clear indication (if implicit) that policy was to play an important role in interpreting the Charter, but it was also a recognition that similar factors had long been a part of constitutional adjudication.

This theme was expressed again shortly after, and again it was not confined to Charter interpretation.[74]

---

[73]*Skapinker* case, *supra*, note 46, at p. 366.
[74]*Hunter et al. v. Southam, Inc., supra*, note 28, at p. 155.

It is clear that the meaning of "unreasonable" cannot be determined by recourse to a dictionary, nor for that matter, by reference to the rules of statutory construction. The task of expounding a constitution is crucially different from that of construing a statute. A statute defines present rights and obligations. It is easily enacted and as easily repealed. A constitution, by contrast, is drafted with an eye to the future. Its function is to provide a continuing framework for the legitimate exercise of governmental power and, when joined by a *Bill* or a *Charter of Rights*, for the unremitting protection of individual rights and liberties. Once enacted, its provisions cannot easily be repealed or amended. It must, therefore, be capable of growth and development over time to meet new social, political and historical realities often unimagined by its framers. The judiciary is the guardian of the constitution and must, in interpreting its provisions, bear these considerations in mind. Professor Paul Freund expressed this idea aptly when he admonished the American courts "not to read the provisions of the Constitution like a last will and testament lest it become one."

While it may always be debatable which decisions have turned on policy considerations, one can readily see examples of policy-oriented results. To mention only two Charter cases, in both *Hunter et al. v. Southam Inc.*[75] and *Reference re S. 94(2) of the Motor Vehicle Act*[76] the court appears to have been deciding, in the fact of a text which it considered to be ambiguous, what the Constitution *should* mean. It largely relied on common law concepts as a source of such policy.

It is, of course, this precise area of judicial review which raises most directly the question of its legitimacy. This is no reason to reject the element of policy from the judicial function. But it is surely grounds for a cautious exercise of policy-making. Where interpretive approaches can be taken to give meaning to the constitution they are to be preferred so long as they do not lead to absurdities. Where they are not helpful, or lead to results inconsistent with the general objectives of the constitution, then policy considerations will become more acceptable. The identification and use of policy is something which should be done openly and with full explanation. The issues should first be fully canvassed with counsel who should themselves be alert to the possibility of such factors and take the initiative in laying them before the courts.

While policy will generally depend on judicial creativity, not all policy-making will be based on such non-factual elements. History and surrounding circumstances may also contribute to the determination of constitutional policy. As factual elements these will be considered below.

---

[75]*Supra*, note 28.
[76]*Supra*, note 30.

C. FACTUAL ELEMENTS

The foregoing elements have all involved factors which may contribute to a constitutional decision but in respect of which it is not necessary to receive evidence or take judicial notice of facts. We will now consider the role, and introduction, of facts in constitutional adjudication. In doing so it is necessary to keep in mind the various elements of a constitutional decision,[77] particularly the emphasis put on "purpose" both in the characterization of statutes and the interpretation of the Constitution, and the role of "effect" of statutes with respect to their characterization.

1. The Relevant Facts

(a) For Interpretation of the Constitution

To the extent that the issue is the interpretation of the 1867 constitution, facts may be of limited assistance. The courts in the past generally treated the B.N.A. Act, 1867 as a statute and in construing it did not look beyond those matters permitted by the ordinary rules of statutory interpretation.[78] Though facts have been examined in a few cases, this has usually been for the purpose of ascertaining the meaning of words in a dictionary sense and not for the purpose of determining the broad objectives or purpose of the fundamental Act.[79] Where the Supreme Court has resorted to factual history such as the Confederation Debates to determine

---

[77]Discussed, *supra*, at pp. 241–51.

[78]MacDonald "Judicial Interpretation of the Canadian Constitution" (1936), 1 *U. Tor. L.J.* 260; MacDonald, "Constitutional Interpretation and Extrinsic Evidence" (1939), 17 *Can. Bar Rev.* 77.

[79]For example, in *Edwards v. A.G. Can.*, [1930] A.C. 124, [1929] 3 W.W.R. 479, [1930] 1 D.L.R. 98 (P.C.), where Lord Sankey gave his famous description of the constitution as a "living tree", the resulting decision was based on factors examined in accordance with the conventional rules of statutory interpretation. In the *Eskimo Reference*, [1939] S.C.R. 104, [1939] 2 D.L.R. 417, considerable evidence was examined to ascertain the common understanding of the word "Indians" in 1867. Again this is within the conventional rules of statutory interpretation which permit a reference to historical context to clarify the meaning of particular words. This is clearly distinguishable from an examination of history for direct evidence of the purpose of an enactment such as the Constitution.

the meaning of the constitution[80] the results have not been reassuring.[81] The evidence of discussions and events leading up to the adoption of the original B.N.A. Act is sparse, general in nature, and at best difficult for lawyers and judges to use.[82] Also, evidence as to the situation prevailing at the time of Confederation or the intention of the framers in relation to that situation should now be considered with some hesitation. Conditions have so drastically changed since 1867 that the particular context in which the Act was passed may have little bearing on the context in which it is now expected to operate. The more crucial question now is: What would the framers have intended had conditions been in 1867 as they are today?[83] Even if the courts could now be induced to make use of external evidence as to the conditions of that time, such evidence would be of limited value in answering this hypothetical question. This is not to say, of course, that the courts should in interpreting the original B.N.A. Act take a narrow approach of a kind more suitable for interpretation of ordinary statutes. The *Constitution Act, 1867*, as it is now called, is an organic document that does require for its dynamic interpretation a generous consideration of the broad policies that underlay it at its inception so that these may be re-interpreted in the light of a changing society.[84] What is being argued here is simply that efforts to distill the long term objectives of that Act from the factual circumstances surrounding its adoption are likely to be unproductive and possibly misleading.

It may be otherwise with the interpretation of recent constitutional amendments including the Charter. Here the *travaux préparatoires* are numerous and well documented, including proceedings of federal-provincial meetings, parliamentary committees and parliamentary debates, and published official documents explaining the new provisions. The Supreme Court has not hesitated to look at extrinsic evidence for the interpretation

---

[80]*Blaikie v. A.G. Que.*, [1978] C.S. 37, 85 D.L.R. (3d) 252; affd. [1978] C.A. 351, 95 D.L.R. (3d) 42 (Que. C.A.); affd [1979] 2 S.C.R. 1016, 101 D.L.R. (3d) 394, 30 N.R. 225, 49 C.C.C. (2d) 359, rehearing [1981] 1 S.C.R. 312, 123 D.L.R. (3d) 15, 36 N.R. 120, 60 C.C.C. (2d) 524; *Re Authority of Parliament in Relation to the Upper House*, [1980] 1 S.C.R. 54, 102 D.L.R. (3d) 1, 30 N.R. 271 (*sub nom. Re British North America Act and the Federal Senate*); *Reference re Language Rights in Man.*, [1985] 1 S.C.R. 721 at 739.

[81]Kyer, "Has History a Role to Play in Constitutional Adjudication: Some Preliminary Considerations" (1981), 15 *Law Soc. of U.C. Gazette* 135; Hogg, "Comment" (1980), 58 *Can. Bar Rev.* 631.

[82]Kyer, *ibid.* at pp. 140–49; Cairns, "The Judicial Committee and its Critics" (1971), 4 *Can. J.P.S.* 301 at 337.

[83]*Labour Relations Board for Sask. v. John East Iron Works*, [1949] A.C. 134, [1948] 2 W.W.R. 1055 at 1065, [1948] 4 D.L.R. 673 at 682 (P.C.). See also *Reference re Residential Tenancies Act*, [1981] 1 S.C.R. 714, 123 D.L.R. (3d) 554, 37 N.R. 158.

[84]See, *supra*, notes 73 and 74, and accompanying text.

of the *Statute of Westminster* where the *travaux préparatoires* were also fairly numerous and readily available. In *Re Resolution to Amend the Constitution*[85] the majority which held the unilateral federal patriation initiative to be legal, made reference to the proceedings of Imperial Conferences of 1926 and 1930 and a Dominion-Provincial Conference of 1931 in interpreting the intended meaning of the subsequent *Statute of Westminster, 1931*. In this same reference a new and potentially extensive use for extrinsic evidence in constitutional adjudication was established in connection with the "recognition" of constitutional conventions. The majority of the court which found there to be a convention requiring substantial provincial consent for constitutional amendments to be requested of the United Kingdom made reference to numerous sources to identify that convention, including debates in both the Canadian and British Parliaments, a Canadian Speech from the Throne, the results of federal-provincial conferences, the proceedings of the Dominion-Provincial Conference of 1931, and a federal White Paper.

Similarly, the Supreme Court has readily considered the history of Charter provisions,[86] as have various lower courts,[87] in the course of interpreting their meanings. As will be discussed further below, the Supreme Court has, however, warned against giving evidence of parliamentary proceedings too much weight[88] because they are inherently unreliable as proof of the intention of a legislative body as a whole. This caution is no doubt wise as far as it goes, but it may have the unfortunate effect of leading courts to ignore that which is really important; namely, the scope of the intergovernmental consensus which many of the *travaux préparatoires* leading up to the Charter can elucidate. It was not a piece of legislation like any other. It was negotiated with great difficulty and the resulting consensus was fragile indeed. It will be anomalous if courts ascribe to the Charter consequences on which its framers could never reach agreement, and which were vehemently opposed by some who accepted the final text on the understanding that it did not carry such a meaning.

---

[85][1981] 1 S.C.R. 753, 11 Man. R. (2d) 1, 34 Nfld. & P.E.I.R. 1, [1981] 6 W.W.R. 1 (*sub nom. A.G. Man. v. A.G. Can.*), 125 D.L.R. (3d) 1, 39 N.R. 1, 1 C.R.R. 59.

[86]See, *e.g.*, *Protestant School Boards* case, *supra*, note 24 at 79–88; the *Motor Vehicle Act Reference, supra*, note 30, at pp. 504–09; *Pub. Service Employee Relations Act Reference*, [1987] 1 S.C.R. 313, McIntyre J. at pp. 412–14.

[87]See, *e.g., R. v. Konechny* (1983), 6 D.L.R. (3d) 350 at 357–60 (B.C.C.A.); *Reference re Education Act of Ont. and Minority Language Education Rights* (1984), 10 D.L.R. (4th) 491 at 507 (Ont. C.A.); *Reference re An Act to Amend the Education Act* (1986), 25 D.L.R. (4th) 1 at 60–63 (Ont. C.A.), affd S.C.C. June 25, 1987.

[88]*Motor Vehicle Act Reference, supra*, note 30, at pp. 507–09.

(b) For Characterisation of Laws and Actions

Facts have an even more important role in the constitutional assessment of impugned laws or administrative actions. Facts can help to establish the purpose or effect of the law or action, and the relative significance of its various effects if it has more than one. "Purpose" and "effect" are used here in their broadest sense. Their study should embrace a study of the context in which the statute is passed and is likely to operate. Such a study will aid the court in finding whether in fact, and not merely in form, the statute is within the scope of its legislative author. It may also clarify for the court the policy issue which it must face. Suppose, for example, that in a period of beef surpluses Parliament enacted legislation establishing a comprehensive quota system for sale of beef cattle. Suppose that the system could have the effect of preventing sales made solely within a province, between a local producer and a local consumer. Appropriate evidence here might show that previous surpluses had endangered interprovincial and international markets and caused a serious national problem. It might also show the curative effect which the impugned federal statute would have. Such evidence would enable the court to see that the purpose and effect of the legislation would be, not interference with local contracts, suggesting "Property and Civil Rights", but rather the protection of an important area of interprovincial and international commerce, suggesting "Regulation of Trade and Commerce" and perhaps "Peace, Order, and good Government". This evidence would also point to the policy issue. That is, is it more important to permit the national protection of this commercial activity, or to preserve intact local control over local contracts?

The relevance of these kinds of facts has been recognized in a number of situations. With respect to the constitutional relevance of a statute's factual context, the "emergency" power cases afford a ready example. To justify federal legislation which is not referable to one of the enumerated heads of s. 91, it is necessary to invoke the general power with respect to "Peace, Order, and good Government". But for such legislation to be valid, where it interferes with matters within an enumerated head of provincial jurisdiction in s. 92, it must deal with an emergency or, possibly (although recent jurisprudence casts doubt on this) a matter which is inherently of concern to the country as a whole. The courts have implicitly recognized that this raises an essentially factual issue. In most cases they have shown a great respect for the opinion of Parliament or the Government with respect to the existence of such a state of affairs, but they have always reserved the right to find the contrary on proper evidence. And on occasion they have rejected the Government's judgment that a state of affairs existed sufficient to justify the exercise of this power.[89] On other occasions they have received evidence to show that a new technological development is inherently of national concern,[90] that lack of action by the provinces has created a need for federal action to protect the national interest,[91] or that some indicators existed of an economic emergency caused by inflation,[92] thus further satisfying themselves of the correctness of Parliament's decision.

Similarly, to justify the exercise of Parliament's power over "Criminal Law" it now appears necessary to show that some danger, to the public as such, is thereby prohibited. Normally the courts will be prepared to accept Parliament's assessment of the facts.[93] But where facts are introduced which clearly demonstrate that the effect of the legislation is not to prevent some public danger or evil, an alleged criminal law enactment may be set aside as colourable.[94]

Evidence of their true effect has been used to test taxing statutes to see if their real impact goes beyond the Legislature's jurisdiction. For example, in the Alberta Bank Tax Reference[95] of 1938, the provincial statute in question imposed an annual tax on banks operating within the province at a rate specified therein, based on both the paid-up capital and the reserve fund of the banks. The question arose as to whether this was a genuine exercise of the provincial power of "Direct Taxation within the Province" or whether it was really a means of regulating "Banking", a federal matter. Both the Supreme Court of Canada and the Privy Council held it to be banking legislation. They were satisfied that the effect of such legislation, given the rates of taxation as specified, would be the destruction of banking. The accuracy of this conclusion need not now detain us, but the principal was clearly established that the practical effect

---

[89]For a more extensive discussion of this subject and the relevant cases, see *supra*, at pp. 226–28.

[90]See, *e.g., Re Regulation and Control of Radio Communication in Canada*, [1931] S.C.R. 541, [1931] 4 D.L.R. 865, affd [1932] A.C. 304, [1932] 1 W.W.R. 563, [1932] 2 D.L.R. 81, 39 C.R.C. 49 (P.C.), where an article by a radio engineer descriptive of radio communication was put before the court; and see *Johannesson v. West St. Paul*, [1952] 1 S.C.R. 292, [1951] 4 D.L.R. 609, 69 C.R.T.C. 105, where the court took account of an affidavit which indicated the national aspect of aeronautics.

[91]*Munro v. National Capital Comm.*, [1966] S.C.R. 663, 57 D.L.R. (2d) 753, affg. [1965] 2 Ex. C.R. 579.

[92]*Reference re Anti-Inflation Act*, [1976] 2 S.C.R. 373, 68 D.L.R. (3d) 452, 9 N.R. 541.

[93]For a full discussion and the relevant cases see, *supra*, at pp. 228–30.

[94]*Canadian Federation of Agriculture v. A.G. Que.*, [1951] A.C. 179, [1950] 4 D.L.R. 689 (P.C.).

[95]*A.G. Alta. v. A.G. Can.*, [1939] A.C. 117, [1938] 3 W.W.R. 337, [1938] 4 D.L.R. 433.

of an enactment is a proper consideration in constitutional adjudication. This was demonstrated by the fact that in a much earlier decision, the Privy Council had upheld provincial taxation of banks where the tax would not have this destructive effect.[96]

In *Texada Mines Ltd. v. A.G. B.C.*[97] another provincial tax was held *ultra vires* because of its prohibitive effect. Here the Legislature of British Columbia had imposed an annual tax of up to ten per cent of the value of minerals in producing areas. A contemporaneous statute provided a large bounty for iron made from ore smelted within the province. As there was at the time no smelter in the province, this was obviously designed to encourage development of a domestic iron and steel industry. The appellant company, an iron ore producer, challenged the legislation on the grounds that it created an export tax. The company introduced evidence to show that mining costs were so high that the addition of the tax would cause iron mines to operate at a substantial loss. Only where the bounty was received would iron mining be economic. As in the Alberta Bank Tax case, the Supreme Court was satisfied by this evidence that the effect of the tax would be virtually to prohibit mining for export: thus the court concluded that the nature of the measure was not the raising of revenue but the regulation of interprovincial trade.

Demonstration of the possible utility of evidence of the effect of statutes touching the regulation of trade and commerce may be found in *A.G. Man. v. Manitoba Egg & Poultry Assn.*[98] and in *Central Canada Potash Co. v. Saskatchewan.*[99] In the former case, the Manitoba Egg Marketing Reference, the court was hearing an appeal on a question referred to the Manitoba Court of Appeal on the validity of a hypothetical scheme for marketing all eggs sold in the province. Laskin J. (Hall J. concurring) lamented the absence of evidence before the court as to the nature of egg production and marketing in Manitoba. He noted that evidence indicating how significant out-of-province supplies of eggs, or markets for Manitoba eggs, might be would have been of help to the court in characterizing this scheme as essentially directed to intraprovincial trade, and thus valid, or to interprovincial trade, and thus invalid.

In the second case, *Central Canada Potash*, at issue were provincial regulations, later confirmed by statute, providing for the prorationing among potash producers in the province of allowable production, and the fixing of the price for which potash was to be sold in the province at the point of production. This scheme was attacked as an attempt to regulate

---

[96]*Bank of Toronto v. Lambe* (1887), 12 App. Cas. 575 (P.C.).

[97][1960] S.C.R. 713, 32 W.W.R. 37, 24 D.L.R. (2d) 81.

[98][1971] S.C.R. 689, [1971] 4 W.W.R. 705, 19 D.L.R. (3d) 169.

[99][1979] 1 S.C.R. 42, [1978] 6 W.W.R. 400, 88 D.L.R. (3d) 609, 23 N.R. 481, 6 C.C.L.T. 265.

interprovincial, and more particularly, international, trade and commerce. It was defended on the basis that it was in relation to local production and sale and in relation to the conservation of resources. Since on their face the regulations appeared to deal with the above mentioned matters of provincial jurisdiction, extensive evidence was submitted at trial to demonstrate their true nature and effect.[100] This evidence showed the nature of the world potash market and the important position which Saskatchewan production played in the North American and world market. It showed that virtually all Saskatchewan potash was exported from the province, and most of it from Canada, with 64% going to the United States. It indicated that, notwithstanding the justification argued for the regulations based on ''conservation'', Saskatchewan had enough reserves to supply the *world* for at least 1500 years. There was also considerable evidence about the events leading up to the adoption of the regulations, including meetings between representatives of Saskatchewan and New Mexico, the principal potash producing state, or meetings of the Governor of New Mexico with members of the provincial Cabinet, and of statements made by, *inter alia*, the premier explaining the purpose of the regulations. All of this satisfied the trial judge that the real ''aims'' and ''purposes'' of the regulations were to limit and control interprovincial and international export of potash and make it subject to provincially imposed conditions. Thus they were found *ultra vires*. (While the conclusion was stated in terms of ''aims and purposes'' it is obvious that these were determined from the real effects which the regulations would have within the factual context presented to the court.)

On appeal the Saskatchewan Court of Appeal regarded much of this evidence as inadmissible but proceeded to make findings of fact which were essentially the same and the Supreme Court later proceeded on the same findings of fact.[101] While the Court of Appeal came to the opposite conclusion to that of the trial judge on validity, the Supreme Court restored the finding of invalidity. Noting that ''the only market for which the scheme had any significance was the export market''[102] it characterized the regulations as an attempted regulation of interprovincial and international trade. The evidence was obviously important. ''This Court cannot ignore the circumstances under which the Potash Conservation Regulations came into being, nor the market to which they were applied and in which they had their substantial operation.''[103]

Apart from the question of the effect of a law if applied in accordance with its terms the fact that a statute is wrongfully administered may also

---

[100][1975] 5 W.W.R. 193, 57 D.L.R. (3d) 7 (Sask. Q.B.).

[101]*Supra*, note 99 at pp. 69–72 S.C.R., pp. 627–29 D.L.R.

[102]*Supra*, at p. 72 S.C.R., p. 629 D.L.R.

[103]*Supra*, at p. 75 S.C.R., p. 631 D.L.R.

be used to demonstrate its illegal effect. In *A.G. B.C. v. McDonald Murphy Lumber Ltd.* there was a question as to the validity of a statute similar to that in the *Texada Mines* case. Here a tax was imposed by statute on all timber cut in the province, but a rebate of all but a trifle was provided where the timber was used or manufactured in the province. The opinion of the Privy Council that this was an export tax was reinforced by the fact that the Government had not bothered to collect the small tax remaining payable on timber used locally.[104]

In spite of judicial warnings elsewhere[105] that the validity of a statute should be judged from its terms and not from the way it is administered, evidence of administration may indicate an unlawful effect. The responsibility of the courts is to keep each level of government within its proper bounds. A government which, or an official who, achieves a prohibited goal through discriminatory administration of legislation threatens the federal structure or constitutionally guaranteed rights and freedoms as much as the Legislature which enacts patently invalid legislation. Assume that instead of expressly providing for a rebate of the timber tax, the British Columbia Legislature had imposed a uniform tax on all timber produced. Suppose further that the Government collected the tax only from those who exported, but failed to collect it from the others. The court should be free to step in here to prevent what, in its practical effect, is as great an interference with free interprovincial trade as was the statute in the *McDonald Murphy* case. In such a case the court should not declare the statute to be *ultra vires*, however. It should only find that it is invalidly applied to those from whom the tax is collected, if such persons can demonstrate that the effect of government policy is to make it an export tax as applied to them.

Related to the problem of invalid effect through wrongful administration is that of invalid effect in application to particular individuals. A general statute may be valid in normal application but have an invalid effect as applied to a particular individual. Here again evidence of the effect as related to the circumstances of this individual is relevant in the judicial supervision of the federal structure. For example, in determining which government can regulate an "undertaking", it is necessary to decide whether it is local or interprovincial in nature. Here it is relevant to consider evidence as to how the undertaking is organized[106] and as to

---

[104][1930] A.C. 357 at 363, [1930] 1 W.W.R. 830, [1930] 2 D.L.R. 721 (P.C.).

[105]See Culliton J.A. in *Cairns Const. Ltd. v. Sask.* (1958), 27 W.W.R. 297 at 329, 16 D.L.R. (2d) 465 at 492 (Sask. C.A.).

[106]*A.G. Ont. v. Winner*, [1954] A.C. 541 at 581–83, 13 W.W.R. 657, 71 C.R.T.C. 225 (P.C.); *Northern Telecom Ltd. v. Communications Workers of Canada*, [1980] 1 S.C.R. 115, 98 D.L.R. (3d) 1, 28 N.R. 107.

the amount of out-of-province business carried on in relation to the amount of intraprovincial business.[107] Similarly, where evidence shows that a business is national in scope, federal legislation regulating it may not relate to purely intraprovincial trade.[108] These issues are related to the problem of "reading down" statutes which are generally valid, to avoid their application to situations where their effect would render them invalid. This will be discussed further below.[109]

It can thus be demonstrated that effect of an impugned statute is one of the most important factors in any determination as to its validity. A finding as to effect in relation to total context will enable the court to see how far the Legislature has gone, and clarify for it the policy issue of how far the Legislature should be permitted to go. The relevant facts in establishing effect are those showing the circumstances in which the Act was passed and the practical consequences of the enactment in relation to those circumstances. This analysis has been elaborated at some length because there has been a vast confusion in the case law and the literature with respect to questions of relevance, admissibility, and the objectives of proof.

Much of the confusion stemmed from an attempt to apply rules of statutory interpretation to constitutional adjudication. These rules were originally designed solely for the purpose of understanding the "meaning" of statutes in a non-federal state. In the main they proceed on the assumption that meaning can be derived from within the statute. Thus they emphasize the importance of the "literal" or "plain" meaning of the statute. If the meaning of a particular section is not apparent the statute may be examined as a whole, if necessary in conjunction with other statutes *in pari materia*. Indicia as to word usage at the time of enactment may also be considered. In case of ambiguity, the absurd result is to be avoided in favour of the less absurd (but absurdity is to be tested in relation to other parts of the same statute or other statutes *in pari materia*). Only the "mischief" rule contemplates a significant examination of external facts — those preceding the enactment of the legislation. By this rule a court may, when the meaning of a statute is not otherwise apparent, look to the preceding state of facts to find the "mischief" which the legislation was intended to cure. In spite of this rule the courts have

---

[107]*R. v. Toronto Magistrates; Ex parte Tank Tpt. Ltd.*, [1960] O.R. 497, 25 D.L.R. (2d) 161 (H.C.); affd on appeal without written reasons [1963] 1 O.R. 272n, 36 D.L.R. (2d) 636n (C.A.); *R. v. Cooksville Magistrate's Court; Ex parte Liquid Cargo Lines Ltd.*, [1965] 1 O.R. 84, 46 D.L.R. 700 (H.C.).

[108]*Reader's Digest Assn. (Canada) Ltd. v. A.G. Can.*, [1966] Que. Q.B. 725, 59 D.L.R. (2d) 54, [1965] C.T.C. 543, 66 D.T.C. 5073.

[109]See, *infra*, at pp. 300, 301.

only rarely[110] ventured to look at the factual background of legislation to ascertain its meaning.[111]

It is important to distinguish the process of "construction" of statutes, that is, statutory interpretation, from that of "characterization" of impugned laws or actions, which involves attributing to them a constitutional value. Supreme Court Justices have made frequent reference to this distinction in recent years, usually in contemplation of applying more liberal rules of evidence for purposes of characterization than for construction.[112] Construction involves essentially a pursuit of "meaning", a concern only for what the Legislature intended to convey by the words it used. The consequences of the legislation are theoretically irrelevant so long as they are those which the Legislature intended. The word "intention" is of course used here figuratively because of the difficulty of ascribing an intention in the human sense to an elected assembly. This has led to a preoccupation with the words of the statute because they are the expression of this imaginary "intention" and it has inhibited the examination of the statute's essence.

The process of constitutional adjudication is different. Here the essential question is not the meaning, but, as is now confirmed by the Supreme Court, the purpose and effect, of the statute. It must pass both tests. In the majority of cases the two may be identical. But even if the purpose is acceptable the court must see what the statute really does. Does a provincial statute revising loan contracts have the principal effect of altering "interest"? Does a federal statute introducing unemployment insurance principally disrupt contractual relations between employer and employee? These are the important questions to ask if the court is to maintain the division of powers or to protect guaranteed rights and freedoms as contemplated by the constitution. This process must by its nature be much more dynamic than the interpretation of statutes. Statutes are capable of greater specificity because of the greater ease with which they may be amended as a result of changed circumstances. Con-

---

[110]See, *e.g., Eastman Photographic Materials v. Comptroller-General of Patents*, [1898] A.C. 571, 79 L.T. 195 (H.L.).

[111]For discussions of the rules of statutory interpretation see 44 Halsbury *Laws of England*, 4th ed. (London: Butterworths, 1983), at 522–555; *Maxwell, on the Interpretation of Statutes* 12th ed. (London: Sweet & Maxwell, 1969), at 28–75; Driedger, *The Construction of Statutes*, 2nd ed. (Toronto: Butterworths, 1983).

[112]See, *e.g.,* Laskin J. in *A.G. Man. v. Manitoba Egg & Poultry Assn.*, [1971] S.C.R. 689 at 704–06, [1971] 4 W.W.R. 705, 19 D.L.R. (3d) 169 at 181–82; *Reference re Anti-Inflation Act*, [1976] 2 S.C.R. 373 at 387, 68 D.L.R. (3d) 452 at 467, 9 N.R. 541 *per* Laskin C.J.; at pp. 470–71 S.C.R., p. 534 D.L.R. *per* Beetz J.; *Reference re Residential Tenancies Act*, [1981] 1 S.C.R. 714 at 722–24, 123 D.L.R. (3d) 554 at 562–63, 37 N.R. 158 *per* Dickson J; *Churchill Falls Reference, supra*, note 8, at p. 318; *Skapinker* case, *supra*, note 46, at pp. 365–66.

stitutions must stand a greater test of time and therefore must be more general in wording. Courts must recognize the difficulties of amendment and therefore be prepared to develop and adopt the general text to a variety of changing circumstances. To do this they must not confine themselves to the bare language of the constitution or the impugned law but should be prepared where necessary to look at the surrounding factual context in which the constitution and the law must operate to see if the essential values of the constitution are being respected. As Dickson J. said for the Supreme Court in *Reference re Residential Tenancies Act*,[113] the characterization or, as he called it, "classification" process "joins logic with social fact, value decisions and the authority of precedents".

In the Charter era, the difference between constitutional adjudication and statutory interpretation has become even more marked.

First, the Supreme Court in the *Big M* case has clarified and emphasized the role of "purpose" as a distinct criterion for determination of a statute's validity. Consequently, to the extent that purpose is not abundantly apparent from the words of the statute and must be proven otherwise, it makes relevant a variety of facts.

Second, in cases involving the Charter, where a *prima facie* infringement of a guaranteed right or freedom is established and s. 1 is invoked, several issues are automatically raised to which facts may be relevant. These issues are now clearly defined by the Supreme Court decision in *R. v. Oakes*.[114] Briefly put, they involve questions as to both the objective of the legislation and the proportionality of the means adopted. As to objective, evidence may be relevant to show the relative importance of the purpose of the limits prescribed by law. This may necessitate a demonstration by facts of the seriousness of the problem which the Legislature sought to overcome. As to proportionality of means, evidence may be relevant as to the effect or anticipated effect of the law and as to the possibility of alternative means which would be less intrusive.[115] The court in *Oakes* did not address specifically the appropriate test of what is suitable in a "free and democratic society". It did refer, however, to both the gravity of the domestic problem of drug trafficking, and the measures taken by other nations and through international agreements to control this problem. Evidence on such matters (keeping in mind that foreign law must be proven as a fact) is no doubt desirable even if not in all cases available.

Third, s. 15 of the Charter may generate a number of fact-issues on which evidence will be needed. Much will depend on whether the courts

---

[113]*Supra*, note 112 at pp. 720–21 S.C.R., pp. 560–61 D.L.R.

[114]*Supra*, note 23 at pp. 138–41.

[115]For a good example of the extensive use of evidence in respect of such issues see *R. v. Seo* (1986), 27 D.L.R. (4th) 496 (Ont. C.A.).

finally adopt tests to qualify the guarantees of equality in s. 15, applying such tests in order to decide if legislative or administrative distinctions are really discriminatory before considering possible justifications under s. 1. To date, some courts have articulated such tests as whether the distinction is "reasonable or fair" (*i.e.*, "not unduly prejudicial" to those affected by it)[116] or whether persons similarly situated are being treated similarly.[117] If such tests are applied to the initial application of s. 15 in finding whether or not there has been "discrimination", it is easy to foresee many factual issues being canvassed. On the other hand, the *Oakes* case appears to imply that no tests such as proportionality should be applied except at the s. 1 stage and this may preclude some consideration of the reasonability of a distinction at the initial stage of determining whether there has been discrimination.[118] This would in turn narrow the range of fact-finding in s. 15 cases.

Whether a court is dealing with distribution of powers or Charter issues, it is necessary to distinguish between the rules of evidence in ordinary litigation and the rules of evidence in constitutional litigation. Ordinary litigation involves facts pertaining to the immediate parties, sometimes called "adjudicative facts". These must be strictly proven. The court would be remiss here in going outside the record to consider facts not properly introduced as evidence. In constitutional cases there may also be "adjudicative facts" to the extent that issues involve the status and circumstances of parties before the court. But when the court turns to the question of the validity of the statute or administrative act challenged in the proceedings, it is performing a legislative function. That is, it is about to make a determination as to validity which may affect not only the parties before the court but the public at large. Moreover, the decision will proceed not merely from given findings of pre-existing fact and law, but may also involve questions of policy. To aid in deciding such questions the courts may have to resort to "constitutional facts", facts of a general nature concerning the economic and social context of legislation or official acts, since such facts are logically relevant to this process. To the extent that the courts are prepared to acknowledge this legislative aspect of their function, they should be more flexible in applying the rules of proof.[119]

---

[116] See, *e.g.*, *Andrews v. Law Soc. of B.C. et al.* [1984] 4 W.W.R. 242 at 252–54 (B.C.C.A.), leave to appeal to S.C.C. granted Nov. 27, 1986.

[117] See, *e.g.*, *R. v. R.L.* (1986), 26 C.C.C. (3d) 417 at 424–25 (Ont. C.A.); *Smith, Kline & French Laboratories Ltd. et al. v. A.G. Can.* (1986), 34 D.L.R. (4th) 586 (Fed. C.A.), leave to appeal to S.C.C. refused April 9, 1987.

[118] This would appear to flow from the *Smith, Kline* decision at 34 D.L.R. (4th) 586 at 591–93.

[119] See also Hogg, "Proof of Facts in Constitutional Cases" (1976), 26 *U. Tor. L.J.*

2. Forms of Evidence

Having thus identified many of the kinds of facts which are relevant in constitutional adjudication, and the general considerations which ought to guide the courts in determining relevancy, we can examine the rules respecting admissibility of particular forms of evidence. In doing so it is important to keep in mind that not only have the Supreme Court Justices in recent years confirmed the relevancy of extrinsic evidence of effect,[120] but they have also cautioned against any "general principle of admissibility or inadmissibility"[121] of such evidence or against "any inflexible rule governing the admissibility of extrinsic materials in constitutional references. The effect of such a rule might well be to exclude logically relevant and highly probative evidence".[122] This suggests that admissibility may be a problem for relevant evidence only where its weight is so insubstantial that it should not be put before the court.[123]

Following is a discussion of the principal forms of evidence which are used in constitutional cases. The first two (statements by legislators, official reports) are, of course, particular examples of the other three, and might be put in evidence through them; that is, by direct evidence, admissions, or judicial notice (although most commonly by judicial notice). They deserve separate treatment, however, because of the special issues which they raise and the degree of attention they have received in the courts.

(a) Legislative Proceedings and Government Statements

(i) Use for Statutory Interpretation

Traditionally in cases involving only statutory interpretation such evidence has been held to be inadmissible.[124] Those who support its use

---

386; Buglass, "The Use of Extrinsic Evidence and the Anti-Inflation Act Reference" (1977), 9 *Ottawa L. Rev.* 183; Lane, *The Australian Federal System*, 2nd ed. (1979), at 1083 *ff.*

[120]*Reference re Anti-Inflation Act, supra,* note 112 at pp. 387–89 S.C.R., pp. 467–68 D.L.R.: *Reference re Residential Tenancies Act, supra,* note 112 at p. 721 S.C.R., p. 561 D.L.R.; *Churchill Falls* case, *supra,* note 8.

[121]*Reference re Anti-Inflation Act, supra,* note 112 at p. 389 S.C.R., pp. 467–68 D.L.R.

[122]*Reference re Residential Tenancies Act, supra,* note 112 at p. 722 S.C.R., p. 562 D.L.R.

[123]See also Lyon, *Comment* (1982), 16 *U.B.C. L. Rev.* 131.

[124]*E.g., R. v. West Riding of Yorkshire County Council,* [1906] 2 K.B. 676 at 700, 716

argue that the purpose of statutory interpretation is to find the intention of the Legislature, and the statements by members of the Legislature in relation to the statute are logically relevant to this inquiry. While there is a danger that they may not reflect the intention of the majority, or may be misleading or self-serving, it is contended that this creates a problem of weight rather than of admissibility.[125] Dr. Driedger suggested that the speech of a minister in proposing legislation in Parliament might at least be relevant to the question of the "mischief" that the statute is designed to remedy.[126] Opponents of such evidence contend, however, that statements of members may have little or no logical connection with the actual meaning of the statute. They have seen a danger in introducing such evidence because it may divert attention from what the statute actually says. Distinctions have been drawn between Canadian and United States legislative practice. It is said that, in the latter, committee proceedings are less dominated by political partisanship and that committee reports are more cohesive and informative. Thus there is more justification for the admission of such evidence in the courts of the United States.[127]

This rule of exclusion in cases of statutory interpretation has been unnecessarily restrictive, as the statements of legislators would seem to have relevance in explaining the meaning of obscure legislation particularly on the matter of the problem that was being addressed. The dangers of admitting such evidence are exaggerated. It would be a rare case where suitable evidence bearing on a particular point of interpretation could even be produced. When produced, its weight would be assessed by the court. In most cases it would probably be given very little weight. But there are situations where it might prove useful.[128]

Indeed a decision of the Supreme Court would suggest that it is now prepared in a proper case to refer to debates in Parliament as an aid to

---

(C.A.), revd. [1907] A.C. 29 (H.L.) on other grounds; *Hollinshead v. Hazleton*, [1916] 1 A.C. 428 at 438, [1914–15] All E.R. Rep. 117 (H.L.); *Gosselin v. the King* (1903), 33 S.C.R. 255, 7 C.C.C. 139; *Hadmor Productions Ltd. v. Hamilton*, [1983] A.C. 191, [1982] 2 W.L.R. 323 (H.L.).

[125]See, *e.g.*, Kilgour, "The Rule Against the Use of Legislative History: 'Canon of Construction of Counsel of Caution'?" (1952), 30 *Can. Bar Rev.* 769.

[126]Driedger, *supra*, note 111 at pp. 156–58.

[127]See, *e.g.*, Corry, "The Use of Legislative History in the Interpretation of Statutes" (1954), 32 *Can. Bar Rev.* 624.

[128]See, *e.g.*, *Canadian Wheat Bd. v. Nolan*, [1951] S.C.R. 81, [1951] 1 D.L.R. 466, revd (*sub nom. A.G. Can. v. Hallett & Carey Ltd.*), [1952] A.C. 427, 6 W.W.R. 23, [1952] 3 D.L.R. 433 (P.C.); relevant parliamentary debates were ignored: see criticism in Kilgour, *supra*, note 125.

statutory interpretation. In *R. v. Vasil*[129] the court was considering the meaning of the words "unlawful object" in para. 212(*c*) of the *Criminal Code* dealing with constructive murder. The phrase seemed ambiguous on the point of whether it required an act involving *mens rea* to constitute the offence where death ensued. This provision had been largely copied from the English Draft Criminal Code of 1879 and the court was invited to consider the Report of the Royal Commission which prepared the English Code and the statements of the Canadian Minister of Justice in Parliament when the Criminal Code provisions were debated in Ottawa. (The Minister had made frequent reference to the English Royal Commission Report.) Lamer J., on behalf of a majority of the court, considered these statements, perceived from them that it was the intention of Parliament to adopt "not only the British Commissioners' proposed sections but also their reasons", and thus ascribed to the section the meaning most consistent with the recommendations of the British Royal Commission of 1879. This was seemingly done with only a passing observation that "Reference to Hansard is not usually advisable", and with the approval of all judges sitting on the case.[130] In the circumstances this seems to be a good use of debates since the evidence was clear, and was relevant in showing the reason for the choice of language employed in relation to contemporaneous statutory and common law. The subject matter would not suggest that the minister's statement would be partisan or self-serving.

(ii) Use for Characterization of Statutes

With respect to the characterization of laws, the admissibility of statements of legislators and of governmental pronouncements on the purpose or effect of legislation has evolved markedly. In 1938 Lord Maugham L.C. said, in *A.G. Alta. v. A.G. Can.* (Bank Tax Reference) that "the object or purpose of the Act, in so far as it does not plainly appear from its terms and its probable effect, is that of an incorporeal entity, namely, the Legislature, and generally speaking, *the speeches of individuals would have little evidential weight*."[131] This implies that such evidence would be admissible but of little value.

Later, the Supreme Court of Canada appeared to rule against the admissibility of all such evidence in constitutional cases. In *Texada Mines*

---

[129][1981] 1 S.C.R. 469, 121 D.L.R. (3d) 41, 35 N.R. 451, 58 C.C.C. (2d) 97, 20 C.R. (3d) 193. See also *Babineau v. Babineau* (1981), 32 O.R. (2d) 545 at 550, 122 D.L.R. (3d) 508 (H.C.); affd 37 O.R. (2d) 527n, 133 D.L.R. (3d) 767n (C.A.).

[130]*Supra*, at pp. 487–90 S.C.R., pp. 469–71 N.R.

[131][1939] A.C. 117 at 130–31, [1938] 3 W.W.R. 337, [1938] 4 D.L.R. 433 (P.C.)(emphasis added).

Ltd. v. A.G.B.C.[132] those attacking the tax on iron production sought to characterize it as an export tax. When the matter reached the Supreme Court, Locke J., delivering the unanimous judgment of the court, commented on the trial judgment.

> While that learned judge, in the course of his judgment, referred to certain statements purporting to have been made by the Premier of the Province and the Minister of Mines to the effect that the legislation was designed to discourage the export of iron ore so that eventually an integrated steel industry could be established in the province, he made it clear that he came to his conclusion without reference to this. That such statement had been made was not proven at the trial and had the evidence been tendered it would, no doubt, have been rejected as inadmissible.[133]

This was *obiter dicta* only, as no such evidence had been presented. Nevertheless it indicated that the court was unanimous in its view that the statements of legislators should not be admitted in proceedings involving the constitutional validity of legislation.

This view was reaffirmed in *ratio decidendi* in *A.G. Can. v. Reader's Digest Assn. (Canada) Ltd.*[134] In 1956 the federal Government introduced in Parliament certain amendments to the *Excise Tax Act* which would have imposed a tax on advertising placed in any periodical containing at least 25% editorial material identical to that contained in a non-Canadian periodical. Reader's Digest, to which the tax would have applied, sought a declaration that the amendments were *ultra vires*. It contended that the real purpose of the legislation was to discriminate against publications such as its own and in favour of purely Canadian publications. This was said to make the legislation not taxation but an interference with property and civil rights. To support its argument as to the real purpose of the legislation, Reader's Digest sought to introduce evidence as to statements with respect to the amendments made by the Minister of Finance both inside and outside Parliament. The trial judge refused to admit such evidence. When the appeal on this point reached the Supreme Court this view was upheld. All of the judges held the evidence as to the Minister's

---

[132][1960] S.C.R. 713, 32 W.W.R. 37, 24 D.L.R. (2d) 81.

[133]*Supra*, at p. 720 S.C.R., p. 87 D.L.R.

[134][1961] S.C.R. 775, 30 D.L.R. (2d) 196, [1961] C.T.C. 530, 61 D.T.C. 1273. Followed in *Saumur v. A.G. Que.*, [1963] Que. Q.B. 116 at 123, 135, 37 D.L.R. (2d) 703 at 712, 719, affd [1964] S.C.R. 252, 45 D.L.R. (2d) 627, without reference to this point. Also followed in *B.C. Power Corp. v. A.G. B.C.; Copithorne v. B.C. Power Corp. Ltd.; Royal Trust Co. v. B.C. Power* (1963), 44 W.W.R. 65 at 172, 47 D.L.R. (2d) 633 at 733–34 (B.C. S.C.); *Canex Placer Ltd. v. A.G. B.C.*, [1976] 1 W.W.R. 644, 63 D.L.R. (3d) 282 (B.C. S.C.).

statements to be inadmissible, and seven of them expressly approved Mr. Justice Locke's *dictum* in the *Texada Mines* case.

More recent cases, however, demonstrate a relaxation in the rule against the use of statements by legislators for purposes of constitutional adjudication. In the *Central Canada Potash* case, in the trial court,[135] Disbery J. while accepting the binding effect of the Supreme Court's pronouncement on this subject in the *Texada Mines* and *Reader's Digest* cases, distinguished them from the case before him which dealt with characterization of regulations, not statutes. On the rationale that such evidence is tendered to prove object or purpose of legislation, and that the evidence of a member of a Legislature is "not relevant evidence to prove the fact of what the intent of the Legislature was as a collective body",[136] he distinguished the workings of the provincial Cabinet from those of the Legislature. He did this on the basis that, because of the convention of cabinet responsibility and solidarity, all decisions are deemed to be unanimous. Cabinet speaks with one voice and therefore can be assumed to have a common intent.[137] He therefore admitted evidence to prove the intent of cabinet, including a news release and television statements by the Premier, and direct evidence from the former Attorney General who had been a member of that cabinet. On appeal the Court of Appeal, while saying that most of the extrinsic evidence admitted by the trial judge was "inadmissible and unnecessary"[138] did not specify what its view was on this particular evidence, nor did the Supreme Court on further appeal.[139] Accepting the premise that object and purpose (in the subjective sense of the intention of its authors) of a law are relevant, then there is a logic in attributing to a cabinet, where in theory there is only one opinion, a common intention to which its individual members can attest.

Subsequently, the Supreme Court has gone well beyond the *Central Canada Potash* case and has considered legislative debates or government policy statements in constitutional adjudication. In *Reference re Anti-Inflation Act*, Laskin C.J. (Judson, Spence, Dickson JJ. concurring) in espousing a flexible approach to the use of extrinsic evidence appeared to put the emphasis on relevancy as the most important consideration and suggested no absolute bar to ministerial statements.[140] He also made at

---

[135][1975] 5 W.W.R. 193, 57 D.L.R. (3d) 7 (Sask.Q.B.).

[136]*Supra*, at p. 214 W.W.R., p. 33 D.L.R.

[137]*Supra*, at pp. 215, 219 W.W.R., pp. 34, 38 D.L.R.

[138][1977] 1 W.W.R. 487 at 504, 79 D.L.R. (3d) 203 at 217 (Sask. C.A.).

[139][1979] 1 S.C.R. 42, [1978] 6 W.W.R. 400, 88 D.L.R. (3d) 609, 23 N.R. 481, 6 C.C.L.T. 265.

[140][1976] 2 S.C.R. 373 at 387–91, 68 D.L.R. (3d) 452 at 467–70, 9 N.R. 541; see also

least passing reference to a Government White Paper which was a policy statement of the Minister of Finance tabled in the House of Commons prior to the introduction of the Bill in question.[141] Ritchie J. (Martland and Pigeon JJ. concurring) gave great weight to the White Paper.[142] This White Paper had, however, been attached to the Order of the Governor-in-Council referring the validity question to the court so that the court was probably obliged in any event to consider it. Nevertheless these references to it by a majority of the court indicate that they found it to be relevant in determining that sufficient evidence existed of an economic crisis to avoid any conclusion that the Act was colourable. Beetz J. (de Grandpré J. concurring), while not using the White Paper, and while holding that Parliament had not by the language of the Act properly invoked the emergency power, reinforced this view with a reference to statements by Ministers in the House of Commons and its Committee. He observed that if the court could look at the White Paper, then "it is not improper for us to read Hansard in this case, in order not to construe and apply the provisions of the Anti-Inflation Act, but to ascertain its constitutional pivot".[143]

Dickson J., writing for the court in *Reference re Residential Tenancies Act*,[144] in the context of warning against inflexible rules which might exclude "logically relevant and highly probative" extrinsic evidence in constitutional cases, observed that where the object or purpose of an Act had to be considered speeches made in the Legislature at the time of its passage "are inadmissible as having little evidential weight". Here, however, the criterion appears to be weight, a more flexible test, and no absolute bar to such evidence is implied.

In *Re Resolution to Amend the Constitution*[145] the six judges who formed the majority in favour of finding a convention of the constitution requiring substantial provincial consent for a request to be made to Westminster made considerable reference to statements in the House of Commons both in Ottawa and in London. This was distinguishable from the use of such statements in the characterization of legislation as they were used here to help establish the existence and nature of the convention. It was agreed on all sides that one of the tests for a convention is the belief

Société Asbestos Ltée v. Société de l'Amiante, [1981] C.A. 43, 128 D.L.R. (3d) 405, 24 L.C.R. 17.

[141]*Supra*, note 140 at p. 426 S.C.R., p. 498 D.L.R.

[142]*Supra*, note 140 at pp. 438–39 S.C.R., pp. 508–09 D.L.R.

[143]*Supra*, note 112, at p. 470 S.C.R., pp. 534–35 D.L.R. This approach was followed in *Re Clearwater Well Drilling Ltd.* (1981), 46 N.S.R. (2d) 606, 124 D.L.R. (3d) 447 (S.C.), revd 52 N.S.R. (2d) 418, 135 D.L.R. (3d) 142 (C.A.).

[144][1981] 1 S.C.R. 714 at 721–22, 123 D.L.R. (3d) 554 at 561–62, 37 N.R. 158.

[145]*Supra*, note 85, at p. 753 S.C.R., p. 1 D.L.R.

in its existence by the political actors, and such statements could help, particularly where they were made against interest. (It must be conceded, of course, that no objections were raised to the use of such materials, which were liberally referred to by parties on both sides.)

That this was no aberration has been amply demonstrated since. In *Reference re Exported Natural Gas Tax*[146] the court looked at a federal government policy publication, "National Energy Program, 1980", and at budget documents tabled in Parliament to help characterize a federal statute as a matter of taxation and not regulation. In the *Churchill Falls Reference*[147] while rejecting certain "speeches and public declarations by prominent figures in the public and political life of Newfoundland" as not constituting expression of the intent of the Legislative Assembly of that province, the court nevertheless accepted a government pamphlet as evidence of the intent and purpose of the provincial statute in question for the purpose of constitutional characterization. In the *Edwards Books & Art Ltd.*[148] case the court looked at debates in the Ontario Legislature on the occasion of the adoption of the *Retail Business Holidays Act* to confirm that its purpose was secular and thus not automatically proscribed by the Charter. Use of such materials will no doubt increase since the Supreme Court clearly adopted the "purpose" test in the *Big M* case. Such evidence is obviously relevant to a search for the "purpose" of the Legislature.

(iii) Use for Interpretation of the Constitution

It has also become accepted that the meaning of provisions of the Constitution can be clarified by resort to legislative debates and similar materials purporting to indicate the intention of the framers. This is true even with respect to pre-1982 constitutional provisions. For example, in *A.G. Can. v. C.N. Transportation, Ltd. et al.*[149] Laskin C.J. mentioned the examination he had made of the Confederation Debates to seek illumination on the meaning of the criminal law power in head 91[27] of the *Constitution Act, 1867*. In *Reference re Manitoba Language Rights* resort was had by the court to the Confederation Debates to assist in interpreting s. 133 of the 1867 Act, this being a guide to the proper interpretation of the *Manitoba Act, 1870*.

Since the advent of the Charter use of such materials has proliferated in part from the need to find a meaning for new provisions for which

---

[146][1982] 1 S.C.R. 1004.

[147]*Supra*, note 8, at p. 319.

[148]*Supra*, note 20, at pp. 745, 749. For another example of the use of legislative debates, see *R. v. Seo* (1986), 27 D.L.R. (4th) 496 at 506 (Ont. C.A.).

[149][1983] 2 S.C.R. 206 at 225–26.

there is no authoritative interpretation, and in part from the opportunity provided by the volume and freshness of available material. This issue was addressed directly by the Supreme Court in the *B.C. Motor Vehicle Act Reference*[150] in relation to the use of proceedings of the Special Joint Committee of the Senate and House of Commons on the Constitution which studied the proposed Charter intensively and reported to Parliament after making several amendments to the government's original proposal. Certain evidence of the Minister of Justice and federal officials had been relied on by counsel supporting the provincial statute, to demonstrate that the intention of the framers was to limit the guarantees in s. 7 to procedural matters only. Lamer J. writing for the majority held such evidence to be admissible but was entitled to only "minimal weight" as evidence of the intention of those who adopted the Charter. He also referred to the statement of Dickson C.J. in *Reference re Residential Tenancies Act*, quoted above, that speeches made in the Legislature "are inadmissible as having little evidential weight", in the determination of legislative purpose. He thus appeared to be distinguishing speeches in Parliament or legislature from evidence before a parliamentary or legislative committee, with the former being inadmissible and the latter being admissible. The comment on speeches was probably *obiter* and appears not to have been the last word on this subject.[151]

There is need for further consideration of the use of the *travaux préparatoires* leading up to the adoption of the Charter and the other amendments in 1982. It is true, of course, that the opinions of individual ministers or officials can not be taken out of context as proof of the intent of those various governments and the Parliament of Canada which collectively expressed the consensus of the Canadian people on the contents of the Charter. But a more extensive examination of the committee proceedings, and of other available materials on positions of various governments and parliamentarians, may indeed be very useful in gaining an understanding of that consensus, which is after all the only source of legitimacy for judicial review under the Charter. Those materials might well include speeches in Parliament, if such speeches for example explained the concerns which led to a compromise or the choice of certain language in the Charter. All of these matters should be admissible, but viewed very carefully as to the weight which should be accorded to them having regard to the particular circumstances.

The value of such an approach can be seen in *Reference re Education Act*[152] where the Ontario Court of Appeal had to interpret s. 29 of the

---

[150]*Supra*, note 49 at pp. 504–07.
[151]*Cf. Pub. Service Alliance et al. v. The Queen et al.*, [1987] 1 S.C.R. 424, Dickson C.J., at pp. 444–45.
[152]*Supra*, note 87, at pp. 60–63. On appeal the Supreme Court used a textual approach instead.

Charter. This section preserves, from being affected by the Charter, "any rights or privileges guaranteed *by or under* the Constitution" with respect to separate schools. The question was whether this would save from conflict with the Charter certain rights or privileges granted by law but not by the Constitution. The court looked at the legislative history of this section and noted: that it was not in the original proposed Charter submitted to the Parliamentary Committee; that there had been a submission on this subject and in response a proposed opposition amendment which would have been rather narrow in its effect; that there had been an amendment to that amendment introduced by government members in the form which s. 29 now takes; and in particular, that in explaining this latter amendment a government member made clear that it was designed, *inter alia*, to protect rights granted by provincial law and not by the Constitution, hence the use of the words "or under". This amendment was accepted. Thus the section was held to protect such provincial laws made under the Constitution in exercise of provincial jurisdiction over education.[153]

(b) Royal Commission or Similar Reports

It is not uncommon in Anglo-Canadian governmental practice for a serious problem to be considered initially by a Royal Commission, a Law Reform Commission, a Task Force or some other specialized body. The resulting report sets out its findings of fact and recommendations for solution. The latter may be brought to varying degrees of fruition by subsequent legislation. The question arises as to what extent such reports may be admissible in evidence to aid in analyzing the subsequent legislation.

Where the issue is solely one of statutory interpretation the conventional view has been that a Royal Commission report is not admissible proof of "intention" *per se*. In *Assam Rys. & Trading Co. Ltd. v. Commrs. of Inland Revenue*[154] the company contended that a Royal Commission report which preceded the taxation statute in question would show that the interpretation most favourable to them was intended. Writing the judgment for the House of Lords, Lord Wright said that the commissioners' report was not proper evidence of Parliament's intention "because it does not follow that their recommendations were accepted".[155] But where a court by the use of the mischief rule becomes involved in an examination of the problem which Parliament obviously hoped to overcome, a commission report may be examined. Lord Wright

---

[153]See also a similar use of Committee proceedings in *Deutsch v. Law Soc. of Upper Can. Legal Aid Fund et al.* (1985), 48 C.R. (3d) 166 (Ont. Div. Ct.).

[154][1935] A.C. 445, [1934] All E.R. Rep. 646 (H.L.).

[155]*Ibid.*, at p. 458 A.C.

was careful to distinguish the *Assam* case from the type of situation which
had arisen in *Eastman Photographic Materials v. Comptroller-General
of Patents.*[156] In the *Eastman* case the House of Lords had to decide what
an "invented word" was within the meaning of the Patent Acts. By
looking at a Royal Commission report the judges ascertained the basic
problem and the purpose of the legislation in relation thereto. Hence they
concluded that the trade name in dispute before the House adequately
qualified as an "invented word". The distinction between the two cases
would appear to be that in *Assam* the report was rejected as subjective
evidence of the state of mind of Parliament, whereas in *Eastman* it was
accepted as objective evidence of the state of affairs with respect to which
the legislation was enacted. The recommendations of the report in the
Assam case would have no necessary relationship to Parliament's intention
because Parliament might or might not have intended to adopt them in
its legislation. But the facts as found in the report in the *Eastman* case
would have some logical relevance to ensuing legislation on the subject
whether the recommendations of the report were adopted or rejected.[157]

The *Eastman* case pointed the way to the use of Royal Commission
and similar reports in constitutional litigation. Just as in statutory interpretation it is relevant to know the circumstances in which a law was
passed to ascertain the mischief remedied, so in constitutional litigation
it is relevant to know those circumstances in order to assess the effects
of the law. A prior report which studies that situation and makes recommendations on it is surely relevant to determining the effects of the
ensuing law. Its weight may of course vary depending on the nature of
the Commission and the closeness of the ensuing legislation in time and
connection.

For many years Canadian courts and the Judicial Committee of the
Privy Council were ambivalent on the use of such materials. For the most
part they were prepared to consider them if put before them without
objections from either side,[158] where they were submitted by agreement,[159]
where they were put before the court in an order of reference,[160] and even

---

[156][1898] A.C. 571, 79 L.T. 195 (H.L.).

[157]See also Lord Denning M.R., in *Letang v. Cooper*, [1965] 1 Q.B. 232 at 240–41,
[1964] 2 All E.R. Rep. 929 (C.A.); *Laidlaw v. Metropolitan Toronto*, [1978] 2 S.C.R.
736 at 743, 87 D.L.R. (3d) 161 at 165, 20 N.R. 515, 15 L.C.R. 24.

[158]*Ladore v. Bennett*, [1939] A.C. 468, [1939] 3 All E.R. 98, [1939] 2 W.W.R. 566,
[1939] 3 D.L.R. 1, 21 C.B.R. 1 (P.C.)

[159]*Walter v. A.G. Alberta* (1966), 58 W.W.R. 385, 60 D.L.R. (2d) 253 (Alta. C.A.).
The Supreme Court on appeal appears not to have considered the reports [1969] S.C.R.
383, 66 W.W.R. 513, 3 D.L.R.(3d) 1. See also *Re Agricultural Products Marketing
Act*, [1978] 2 S.C.R. 1198, 84 D.L.R. (3d) 257, 19 N.R. 361.

[160]*A.G. B.C. v. A.G. Canada*, [1937] A.C. 368, 156 L.T. 308 (P.C.).

where they were submitted over the objection of the opposing party.[161] In all of these cases the reports were, when used by the judges, obviously considered to be relevant to the issues before them. In one case where Cartwright J. (Locke J. concurring) in dicta in the Supreme Court said that a Royal Commission report would not be admissible to determine constitutionality, he appeared to be recognizing the relevance of such reports but found them unacceptable on the "technical rules as to admissibility".[162]

Happily the uncertainty in this area was largely disposed of by the judgment of Dickson J. for the Supreme Court in *Reference re Residential Tenancies Act*. The Ontario Government had referred to the Ontario Court of Appeal questions concerning the validity of this legislation enacted in 1979. Prior to the hearing in the Court of Appeal the Government filed reports of the provincial Law Reform Commission of 1968, 1972, and 1976 concerning problems and possible reforms in this area, together with a Government Green Paper of 1978 containing various policy options. The Court of Appeal did not rule on the admissibility of this material but when the case reached the Supreme Court Dickson J. thought it was appropriate to decide that question. He made various general comments, referred to earlier, as to the need to avoid inflexible rules on admissibility of extrinsic evidence for purposes of characterization and laid down the general proposition that "Material relevant to the issues before the court, and not inherently unreliable or offending against public policy should be admissible".[163] With respect to the admissibility of such reports he held that

> Generally speaking, for the purpose of constitutional characterization of an act we should not deny ourselves such assistance as Royal Commission reports or Law Reform Commission reports underlying and forming the basis of the legislation under study, may afford. The weight to be given such reports is, of course, an entirely different matter. They may

---

[161]*Home Oil Distributors v. A.G. B.C.*, 53 B.C.R. 355, [1939] 1 W.W.R. 49 at 51, [1939] 1 D.L.R. 573 at 574 (C.A.). In the Supreme Court of Canada on appeal, Kerwin J. (Rinfret J. concurring) dealt with this issue, holding the Royal Commission report to be admissible. Davis J. held it inadmissible without consent of all parties and the other three judges ignored the report: [1940] S.C.R. 444, [1940] 2 D.L.R. 609; *Canadian Indemnity Co. v. A.G. B.C.*, [1975] 1 W.W.R. 481 at 554–55, 56 D.L.R. (3d) 1 at 76–77, 21 C.P.R. (2d) 1 (B.C. S.C.), apparently approved in [1976] 2 W.W.R. 499, 63 D.L.R. (3d) 468 at 470, 24 C.P.R. (2d) 10 (B.C. C.A.); the Supreme Court did not refer specifically to the issue, [1977] 2 S.C.R. 504, [1976] 5 W.W.R. 748, 73 D.L.R. (3d) 111, 1 N.R. 466, 30 C.P.R. (2d) 1.

[162]*Reader's Digest* case *supra*, note 134, at p. 789 S.C.R., pp. 308–09 D.L.R.

[163][1981] 1 S.C.R. 714 at 723, 123 D.L.R. (3d) 554 at 562–63, 37 N.R. 158. *Cf.* 1st edition of this book, p. 171.

carry great, little, or no weight, but at least they should, in my view, generally be admitted as an aid in determining the social and economic conditions under which the Act was enacted. . . . The mischief at which the act was directed, the background against which the legislation was enacted and institutional framework in which the act is to operate are all logically relevant. . . . [164]

With respect, this expresses with great clarity the rationale for the admission of such materials.

It appears to have put at rest any lingering doubts on the subject, not only with respect to references but in other cases as well. The Charter has in fact created new uses for such materials, particularly in relation to the application of s. 1. In the *Oakes* case[165] the Supreme Court considered the report of a Senate committee, and of a royal commission, on the subject of narcotics in determining whether s. 8 of the *Narcotic Control Act* had a sufficiently important objective to justify the limitation it imposed on Charter rights. In *R. v. Seo*[166] the Ontario Court of Appeal made use of reports on driving after drinking, and the effectiveness of roadside testing, in measuring the importance of the objective to be served by such testing. In *Edwards Books & Art Ltd.*[167] the Supreme Court examined a report of the Ontario Law Reform Commission on Sunday observance legislation as accurately reflecting the purposes of the *Retail Business Holidays Act* which followed it. Those purposes being secular, they did not preclude the invocation of s. 1 to justify certain infringements on freedom of religion. Such reports have also been considered in relation to s. 15 of the Charter.[168]

(c) Direct Evidence

Consistently with the Supreme Court's view in *Reference re Residential Tenancies Act* referred to above, that "Material relevant to the issues before the court, and not inherently unreliable or offending against public policy should be admissible" it is clear that sworn evidence as to the effect of a statute or of administrative action, if it otherwise meets

---

[164]*Supra*, at p. 723 S.C.R., p. 562 D.L.R. Folld *Schneider v. The Queen*, [1982] 6 W.W.R. 673 at 691, 139 D.L.R. (3d) 417 at 434, 39 B.C.L.R. 273, 43 N.R. 91, 68 C.C.C. (2d) 449.

[165]*Supra*, note 23, at p. 140.

[166]*Supra*, note 115, at p. 506.

[167]*Supra*, note 20, at p. 745.

[168]*Smith, Kline & French Laboratories Ltd. et al. v. A.G. Can.*, [1986] 1 F.C. 274 at 321–27 (T.D.), affd 34 D.L.R. (4th) 586 without reference to this point (Fed. C.A.).

these tests, should be admitted. This can include, for example, evidence of persons with first-hand knowledge of the situation dealt with by the statute or affected by the administrative action. It could also include opinion evidence of experts knowledgeable about, for example, the state of the economy, the costs of running minority language schools (in the determination of entitlement to such schools where "the number of children . . . is sufficient to warrant the provision to them out of public funds of minority language instruction" under s. 23 of the Charter), the trading patterns in a commodity, or the nature of a substance outlawed by Parliament as dangerous (and thus a fit subject for the "Criminal Law").

An example of the use of such evidence may be seen in *Johannesson v. West St. Paul*[169] where an affidavit of one of the parties, setting out certain facts about aerial navigation and commercial flying, was considered by the Supreme Court. This assisted it in finding that the federal *Aeronautics Act* regulated a matter going beyond purely provincial concern and was *intra vires*. Another dramatic example of the use of such evidence was in the trial of the *Central Canada Potash* case[170] where various participants in events surrounding the adoption of the regulations were called as witnesses. These included the former Governor of New Mexico and the former Attorney General of Saskatchewan. Other witnesses testified concerning the nature of the potash industry and its markets. As noted above, the higher courts on appeal did not specify which aspects of this evidence were, in their view, admissible or inadmissible, but no suggestion was made that the use of direct evidence *per se* was unacceptable. Similarly, in *Canadian Indemnity Co. v. A.G. B.C.* where a provincial statute creating a provincial public monopoly in automobile insurance was attacked, *inter alia*, as a regulation of trade and commerce, direct evidence was admitted at trial with respect to the nature of the insurance business and of the problems created by automobile accidents.[171]

In Charter cases direct evidence of effect of statutes has become quite common. For example, in the *Protestant School Board*[172] case involving the "Quebec clause" of Bill 101, the Supreme Court heard a variety of expert witnesses in relation to s. 1 issues. In *Re Lavigne and Ont. Pub. Service Employees Union et al.*[173] the High Court of Ontario admitted

---

[169][1952] 1 S.C.R. 292, [1951] 4 D.L.R. 609, 69 C.R.T.C. 105. See also *Texada Mines Ltd. v. A.G. B.C.*, [1960] S.C.R. 713, 32 W.W.R. 37, 24 D.L.R. (2d) 81.

[170][1975] 5 W.W.R. 193, 57 D.L.R. (3d) 7.

[171][1975] 1 W.W.R. 481, 56 D.L.R. (3d) 7, 21 C.P.R. (2d) 1 (B.C. S.C.). It is not clear to what extent this admissibility ruling was accepted by the higher courts.

[172]*Que. Assn. of Protestant School Bds. et al. v. A.G. Que. et al. (No. 2)* (1982), 140 D.L.R. (3d) 33 at 67–68, affd 1 D.L.R. (4th) 573 (Que. C.A.), affd [1984] 2 S.C.R. 66.

[173](1986), 55 O.R. (2d) 449 at 513.

numerous affidavits which were submitted to assist in determining the governmental objective of legislation, for s. 1 purposes.

(d) Admissions

It is open to the parties to admit any relevant facts even though these might not be otherwise capable of proof. Facts may readily be admitted through the pleadings, where the matter commences as an ordinary action,[174] or by an agreed statement of facts.[175] In the appellate courts they may be introduced through the appeal book or "case" containing the evidence, the contents of which are subject to agreement by the parties. Perhaps more commonly, as the scope for intrinsic evidence has expanded with the Charter, facts are admitted more informally simply through a failure to take objection. For example, material such as foreign law of which a court should not, strictly speaking, take judicial notice, is readily used without objection from opposing counsel. Courts should, of course, take care not to accept "admissions" of constitutional facts where these may be to the advantage of both parties and inconsistent with reality and the public interest.

(e) Judicial Notice

As noted earlier, judicial notice can be one means of introducing certain of the materials already referred to. By the ordinary rules of evidence, a court can take judicial notice only of "notorious" facts or facts of public, general knowledge, although in doing this the court can resort to sources in books, and similar sources whose accuracy cannot reasonably be questioned.[176] While there appears to be a large area of discretion as to what facts the courts will judicially notice, in ordinary litigation they have frequently limited themselves to matters of which virtually everyone would be aware.

Even in more traditional distribution of powers cases, however, the courts have not confined themselves to a narrow concept of judicial notice when constitutional issues were involved. In the Alberta Bank Taxation

---

[174]See, *e.g.*, *Walter* case, *supra*, note 159.

[175]*E.g.*, *Duplain v. Cameron*, [1961] S.C.R. 693, 36 W.W.R. 490, 30 D.L.R. (3d) 348.

[176]See generally Sopinka and Lederman, *The Law of Evidence in Civil Cases* (Toronto: Butterworths, 1974), at 357–65; Schiff, 2 *Evidence in the Litigation Process* 2nd ed. (Toronto: Carswell, 1983), at pp. 643–724.

Reference both the Supreme Court and the Privy Council[177] took judicial notice of the fact that the Alberta tax if similarly applied by every province would prohibit the carrying on of banking in Canada. This led each court to conclude that the tax was invalid. The only direct evidence which had been introduced merely indicated the amount of the increase in bank taxation in Alberta. Such evidence did not *per se* disclose that this rate of tax would be prohibitive of banking in Alberta or in Canada as a whole. The "facts" of which these highest tribunals took notice were scarcely "notorious" facts within the normal scope of judicial notice. The court exercised its discretion creatively in this instance to enable it to assess the effect of the statute.

The Exchequer Court of Canada in *National Capital Comm. v. Munro*[178] took judicial notice of a wide range of facts, though the Supreme Court of Canada on appeal found it unnecessary in upholding the decision to rely on these facts or to comment on their use. In deciding that the creation of a "green belt" around Ottawa was a legitimate exercise of Parliament's power with respect to the "Peace, Order, and good Government" of Canada, Mr. Justice Gibson of the Exchequer Court took note of the pattern of development of other national capitals. He referred to such material as a memorandum on the development of Washington, D.C., issued by the late President Kennedy, to support his conclusion that the proper planning of national capitals is a matter inherently of national concern.

Another example of judicial notice in a constitutional case may be found in *Montcalm Const. Inc. v. Minimum Wage Comm.* Here there was a question as to whether a contractor, because it was engaged in construction of a federally owned and regulated airport, was within federal jurisdiction in matters of minimum wages. The Supreme Court apparently thought that an important factor would be whether the contractor's work was limited to this or similar federal projects or whether it carried on general construction work for various parties. The court took judicial notice of "the conditions of work generally prevailing in the construction industry"[179] and presumed that these applied to the contractor here. In a quasi-constitutional case, *Curr v. The Queen*, the Supreme Court was considering an argument that *Criminal Code* provisions requiring breath

---

[177]*Reference re Alberta Statutes*, [1938] S.C.R. 100 at 128, [1938] 2 D.L.R. 81 at 103, affd (*sub nom. A.G. Alta. v. A.G. Can.*), [1939] A.C. 117 at 131–32, [1938] 3 W.W.R. 337, [1938] 4 D.L.R. 433. For another example of a court taking notice of "ordinary economic considerations" see *Min. of Finance of N.B. et al. v. Simpson-Sears Ltd.*, [1982] 1 S.C.R. 144 at 161.

[178][1965] 2 Ex. C.R. 579, affd [1966] S.C.R. 663, 57 D.L.R. (2d) 753.

[179][1979] 1 S.C.R. 754 at 775, 93 D.L.R. (3d) 641 at 658, 25 N.R. 1, 79 CLLC 14, 190.

tests on persons suspected of drunken driving, making it an offence to refuse such tests and allowing evidence of refusal to be introduced in trials for impaired or drunken driving, violated due process and the protections of the *Canadian Bill of Rights*. Laskin J. in the judgment in which a majority concurred, observed that

> I am, moreover, of the opinion that it is within the scope of judicial notice to recognize that Parliament has acted in a matter that is of great social concern, that is the human and economic cost of highway accidents arising from drunk driving, in enacting s. 223. . . . [180]

This consideration was apparently thought to be relevant to the question of whether normal procedural safeguards might be modified in such circumstances and still not violate the "due process" required by the Bill of Rights.

The use of history, legislative debates and conference proceedings in connection with the references *Re Authority of Parliament in Relation to the Upper House* and *Re Resolution to Amend the Constitution* has been discussed earlier. [181]

The adoption of the *Canadian Charter of Rights and Freedoms* has brought with it a need, and an opportunity, for more extensive use of judicial notice. Section 1, for example, requires for its application facts of a general nature concerning the importance of legislative objectives, [182] the rationality of means adopted by the Legislature, and the norms of a free and democratic society. [183] Section 15, for example, will require insight into the true effect of legislation and the reasonability of different treatment of individuals. [184] Interpretation of the Charter itself may require

---

[180][1972] S.C.R. 889 at 902–03, 26 D.L.R. (3d) 603 at 616, 7 C.C.C. (2d) 181, 18 C.R.N.S. 281.

[181]See, *supra*, at pp. 264, 265. See also *Jones v. A.G. N.B.*, [1975] 2 S.C.R. 182, 7 N.B.R. (2d) 526, 45 D.L.R. (3d) 583 (*sub nom. Jones v. A.G. Can.*), 1 N.R. 582 (*sub nom. Reference re Official Languages Act*), 16 C.C.C. (2d) 297.

[182]See, *e.g.*, *R. v. Oakes, supra*, note 23, at pp. 140–41; *Re Red Hot Video Ltd. and City of Vancouver* (1983), 5 D.L.R. (4th) 61 at 66 (B.C.S.C.); *R. v. Keegstra* (1984), 19 C.C.C. (3d) 254 (Alta. Q.B.); *Reference re S. 94(2) of the Motor Vehicle Act, supra*, note 30, at p. 521.

[183]See, *e.g.*, *Re Fed. Republic of Germany and Rauca* (1982), 141 D.L.R. (3d) 412 at 425 (Ont. H.C.), affd 41 O.R. 225 (C.A.); *Reference re Procedures and Mental Health Act* (1984), 5 D.L.R. (4th) 577 at 589–90 (P.E.I. S.C. *in banco*); *Re Southam Inc. and the Queen (No. 1)* (1983), 41 O.R. (3d) 113 at 131–34 (Ont. C.A.).

[184]For some other Charter decisions using judicial notice, see, *e.g.*, *A.G. N.S. and Lynch et al. v. Phillips* (1986), 27 D.L.R. (4th) 156 (N.S.S.C.), C.A. decision affg of Nov. 27, 1986 not reported; *Jones v. The Queen*, [1986] 2 S.C.R. 284 at 299–301; *Edwards Books* case, *supra*, note 20, at pp. 802–806; *Collins v. The Queen*, [1987] 1 S.C.R.

resort to its history through the use of judicial notice.[185] It must be noted that courts have not always articulated clearly that they are resorting to judicial notice, even when that seems to be what they have done.

It appears that while parties normally bring to the attention of the court those well-known facts of which they wish it to take judicial notice, it should be open to the court to take notice of such facts on its own initiative.[186]

There is, however, a need to ensure that fair procedure will be followed if a court is to take judicial notice either at the initiative of one of the parties or on its own initiative. While there has been some debate in the past as to whether, in ordinary litigation, it should be possible for a party to attempt to refute facts judicially noticed, the logic that might argue against the opportunity for refutation was not compelling and should not be extended to the area of constitutional facts. That is, in the case of adjudicative facts judicial notice has been generally restricted to notorious and indisputable facts. But the argument that is being made here is that for "contitutional facts" judicial notice should embrace economic and social facts that may not be so notorious. And in any event it should always be open to a party of opposing interest to argue that a particular fact does not come within the scope of proper judicial notice.

This broader approach to judicial notice, combined with some procedural safeguards, was taken by the Law Reform Commission of Canada in its *Report on Evidence* of 1975. In its proposed Code the Commission specifically recommended more generous rules for judicial notice in constitutional cases. Whereas in other cases judicial notice could be taken of facts "generally known" and in certain cases "of facts capable of accurate and ready determination by resort to sources whose accuracy respecting such facts cannot reasonably be questioned", they simply proposed that "judicial notice may be taken of any fact in determining the law or the constitutional validity of a statute". Their Code also had a requirement for notice to be given to the other party by a party seeking to have certain kinds of facts noticed, or by a judge where he proposed to take such notice. These requirements would have been of limited application and would not have covered the special provision dealing with judicial notice in constitutional cases.[187]

After lengthy consideration by a special federal-provincial task force of this and other proposals the Uniform Law Conference of Canada

---

265. Lamer J. at pp. 270; *Pub. Service Employee Relations Act Reference, supra*, note 86. Dickson C.J., at p. 374–75.

[185]Discussed, *supra*, at nn. 281–83.

[186]See LaForest J. in the *Edwards Books* case, *supra*, note 20, at pp. 802–03.

[187]Law Reform Commission of Canada, *Report on Evidence* (1975), at 44–46, 103–06. See also its Evidence Project, *Study Paper No. 6*, "Judicial Notice" (1973).

proposed a Uniform Evidence Act for possible adoption by all jurisdictions, federal and provincial. Its provisions on judicial notice are simpler than those of the Law Reform Commission.[188] It essentially codifies the common law as to what facts can be noticed, those that are generally known and accepted as well as those which are capable of ready determination from sources whose accuracy cannot reasonably be questioned. But then there follows a general requirement:

> Before taking judicial notice of any matter, the court shall afford the parties an opportunity to be heard on the question whether judicial notice should be taken.

This approach does not directly encourage a wider use of judicial notice although it may be that, with the requirement of the parties having an opportunity to be heard, a court operating under such an Evidence Act would feel able to venture further afield in taking judicial notice.

The case then to be made for a more generous use of judicial notice in constitutional cases is that such cases normally transcend the interests of the immediate parties before the court and frequently involve questions of economic or social fact which either cannot readily be proven by conventional techniques of direct evidence or are sufficiently obvious that they should not have to be proven. They are "obvious" in the sense, not that everyone can be assumed to know them but that they can be ascertained from reliable sources which would nevertheless not likely pass the conventional admissibility tests for direct evidence. Because of the nature and importance of constitutional facts, it is suggested that judicial notice might be taken of facts which, even if not utterly undisputable, might be regarded as presumptively correct unless the other party, through an assured fair process, takes the opportunity to demonstrate that those facts are incorrect, partial, or misused. If such a procedure is not implemented legislatively the courts might, in the exercise of their discretion concerning the use of judicial notice, combine a requirement of notice and a right of reply with a more extended use of this technique of fact-gathering in constitutional cases.

3. The Factual Presumption of Validity

This presumption underlies the whole process of fact consideration in constitutional cases. It is really a rule to govern situations where there is no evidence presented to the court by the parties on issues germane to constitutionality. It is distinguishable from the legal presumption of validity

---

[188]Uniform Law Conference of Canada, *Uniform Evidence Act* (1981), ss. 18–21.

discussed above.[189] The legal presumption has to do with meaning of the law: it permits the court to give a favourable interpretation to a law where there is ambiguity as to whether it is intended to apply in a way which would be invalid. The factual presumption has to do with effect of the law: it allows the court to assume, if it has no evidence to the contrary, that the relevant facts are such as to allow the effect of the law to be within the permitted scope of the Legislature.

This factual presumption has been referred to several times in recent years. For example, in the absence of evidence to the contrary it was presumed that the principal effect of a provincial wildlife law was conservation of the resources and not the regulation of Indians,[190] that the nature of a contractor's business was such that a provincial minimum wage law could validly apply to him,[191] or that an employer's undertaking was such as to bring it within federal jurisdiction and thus subject to a certification order of the Canada Labour Relations Board.[192]

Such cases have dealt with distribution of powers problems, and it is not yet entirely clear how the factual presumption of validity should apply in Charter cases. It may be possible to argue that the factual presumption is applicable in an initial determination of whether a law or administrative action is in fact violating a Charter right or freedom, but that it ceases to be applicable when a party relies on the defence that the right or freedom has been limited by a law justifiable under s. 1. As noted previously, s. 1 puts the onus on the party invoking it. While facts might be relevant in showing that a law is justified, those facts cannot be presumed.

A concern should also be noted that the parties in constitutional litigation should not be able to force a result clearly inconsistent with the constitution merely through the failure to call evidence. This could be a result of incompetence or collusion, just as in the case of self-serving admissions.[193] For this reason it should always be open to a court to decline to apply the factual presumption of validity if there is a suspicion of collusion or where the presumption of the necessary facts would clearly appear to be inconsistent with facts of which the court is able to take judicial notice on its own initiative.

---

[189]See, *supra*, at pp. 251–54.

[190]*Kruger v. The Queen*, [1978] 1 S.C.R. 104, [1977] 4 W.W.R. 300, 75 D.L.R. (3d) 434, 14 N.R. 495, 34 C.C.C. (2d) 377.

[191]*Montcalm Const. Inc. v. Minimum Wage Comm.*, *supra*, note 179.

[192]*Northern Telecom Ltd. v. Communications Workers of Canada*, [1980] 1 S.C.R. 115, 98 D.L.R. (3d) 1, 28 N.R. 107. See also Magnet, "The Presumption of Constitutionality" (1980), 18 *Osgoode Hall L.J.* 87.

[193]Discussed, *supra*, at p. 288.

4. The Use of Factual Material in Constitutional References

It remains to note the special problem of fact-introduction associated with constitutional references. Here there are no pleadings and no trial. There is no contest in the usual sense, though the courts usually assure argument on all sides of the issue by appointing counsel to speak for unrepresented interests.

At one time little attention was paid to the use of evidence in references and indeed it was suggested that, since the result of a reference is an opinion and not a judgment it ought to be based solely on the material submitted to the court in the reference order.[194] There were certainly many examples of opinions being given with a minimum of factual background with results that were abstract and hypothetical.[195]

The modern view is, however, that evidence is equally important in reference cases so that the court may have a specific factual context in which to assess the effect of impugned laws. This approach, though previously urged at times by commentators,[196] received its first major judicial articulation by Laskin J. in *A.G. Man. v. Manitoba Egg and Poultry Assn.*[197] in 1971. The reference was patently hypothetical, representing one of the less felicitous uses of this device. It had its origins in the "chicken and egg war",[198] when Quebec erected barriers to the entry of eggs from out of province through a compulsory marketing scheme for all eggs marketed in the province. Manitoba was particularly offended by this scheme, in part because the distances involved to the Quebec market made the avoidance of Quebec controls, affecting the entry of out of province eggs, difficult for Manitoba producers. Anxious to have further judicial review of the scheme, Manitoba first sought to bring this Quebec law before the Supreme Court directly, arguing that the court had an original jurisdiction.

Failing in this,[199] the Manitoba Government then drafted regulations for a hypothetical egg marketing scheme in Manitoba, of the same nature as the Quebec scheme, and referred to its Court of Appeal the question

---

[194]Rinfret C.J. in *Reference re Wartime Leasehold Regulations*, [1950] S.C.R. 124, [1950] 2 D.L.R. 1.

[195]*E.g., Reference re Farm Products Marketing Act*, [1957] S.C.R. 198, 7 D.L.R. (2d) 257.

[196]*E.g.,* Davison, "The Constitutionality and Utility of Advisory Opinions" (1938), 2 *U. Tor. L.J.* 254; MacDonald, "The Privy Council and the Canadian Constitution" (1951), 29 *Can. Bar Rev.* 1021; 1st edition of this work, chapter 6.

[197][1971] S.C.R. 689, [1971] 4 W.W.R. 705, 19 D.L.R. 169.

[198]Described, *e.g.,* in Safarian, *Canadian Federalism and Economic Integration* (1974), at 51–53.

[199]*Govt. of Manitoba v. Govt. of Québec*, leave to appeal to S.C.C. refused October 19, 1970, [1970] S.C.R. x.

of whether such a scheme would be valid. As far as can be ascertained, there was never any intention to bring such a scheme into effect in Manitoba and therefore the question was hypothetical and lacking any factual context. The only material put to the Manitoba Court of Appeal, and before the Supreme Court on appeal, was the order of reference with the hypothetical regulations attached. Laskin J. (Hall J. concurring), while agreeing with the majority in the result, specifically commented on this lack of factual material.[200]

> The utility of the Reference as a vehicle for determining whether actual or proposed legislation is competent under the allocations of power made by the *British North America Act* is seriously affected in the present case because there is no factual underpinning for the issues that are raised by the Order of Reference. Marketing data to illuminate those issues might have been set out in the Order itself (as was done, for example, in the *Margarine* Reference), or in an agreed statement of facts, or, indeed, might have been offered to the court to indicate the circumstances which prompted the questions addressed to it.
>
> As it is, I know nothing of the nature of the market for eggs in Manitoba or outside of it, nothing of the production of eggs in that province, nothing of the uses to which the production is put, nothing of the number of producers in Manitoba, nothing of any problems that may have been created in relation to quality, price or otherwise by the entry of out-of-province eggs. I know only, and then in the broad terms set out in the first two recitals in the Order of Reference (and of which matters I could, in any event, have taken judicial notice) that (to quote them) "many Provinces of Canada, including the Province of Manitoba, have enacted legislation pertaining to the regulation and control of marketing of agricultural products" and "certain of the marketing agencies established under the aforementioned legislation in some of the Provinces assert the right to prohibit, regulate and control the marketing within a Province of agricultural products produced outside that Province".
>
> A knowledge of the market in Manitoba, the extent to which it is supplied by Manitoba producers, and of the competition among them as it is reflected in supply, quality and price, would be of assistance in determining the application of the proposed legislative scheme.

This comment has since been quoted frequently in lower courts and has no doubt influenced in a positive way the greater use of evidence in references. In the *Reference re Anti-Inflation Act* Laskin C.J. (Judson, Spence, and Dickson JJ. concurring) elaborated further the rationale for use of extrinsic material in constitutional cases (apparently not distinguishing between references and ordinary cases) indicating that they were to be used for characterization, not construction, of statutes and that their

---

[200]*Supra*, note 197 at pp. 704–05 S.C.R., p. 181 D.L.R.

relevance and weight depended on the nature of the legislative power being asserted.[201]

The definitive view of the Supreme Court was stated in *Reference re Residential Tenancies Act* where Dickson J., writing on behalf of the court, stated the general proposition that all relevant material "not inherently unreliable or offending against public policy" should be admissible for purposes of constitutional characterization. With respect to reference cases in particular he noted the difficulty for the court "when only the bare bones of the statute arrive for consideration". He specifically rejected the view of an earlier Chief Justice that references should be decided only on the material submitted in the order of reference[202] and said the court should not adopt any inflexible rule governing the admissibility of extrinsic materials in references.[203] The court then proceeded to consider such materials as Law Reform Commission reports to assist in characterizing subsequent legislation.

Following the *Residential Tenancies Act* case, a very broad range of factual material has been used in references with little or no question. There has been extensive use of history,[204] and consideration of such matters as the development of international law,[205] demographic statistics,[206] and even election results.[207]

The principle thus appears to be well established that in reference cases, as in other constitutional litigation, extrinsic material is admissible and desirable, provided it is relevant to the characterization of the law or action in question. One can expect the attitude of lawyers and judges to be much more oriented to the use of such materials in future references. It remains to note the principal ways in which such materials may be introduced in a proceeding without evidence or pleadings.

The traditional way of placing material before the court was in the

---

[201]Discussed, *supra*, at pp. 272, 273.

[202][1981] 1 S.C.R. 714, at 720–24, 123 D.L.R. (3d) 554 at 561–63, 37 N.R. 158.

[203]*Supra*, at pp. 720–24 S.C.R., pp. 561–63 D.L.R. This approach was reaffirmed by the court in *Reference re Proposed Federal Tax on Exported Natural Gas*, [1982] 1 S.C.R. 1004, [1982] 5 W.W.R. 577, 136 D.L.R. (3d) 385, 42 N.R. 361.

[204]*Reference re Nfld. Continental Shelf*, [1984] 1 S.C.R. 86, especially at 106–09; *Reference re Upper Churchill Water Rights Revision Act, supra*, note 8, at pp. 315–19, 332–33; *Reference re Ownership of the Bed of the Strait of Georgia and Related Areas*, [1984] 1 S.C.R. 388, especially at 403–09; *Reference re Education Act of Ont. and Minority Language Education Rights, supra*, note 87, at pp. 505–17; *Reference re Man. Language Rights, supra*, note 47, at pp. 731–32.

[205]*Nfld. Continental Shelf* case, *ibid.*, at pp. 120–21.

[206]*Reference re Yukon Election Residency Requirements* (1986), 27 D.L.R. (4th) 146 at 149 (Y.T. C.A.).

[207]*Ibid.*

order of reference. Here the "facts" become part of the question and may be hypothetical[208] or real.[209] Documents may be filed with the court by either party, through a factum or otherwise, and then their contents admitted in whole or in part on the basis of general rules of judicial notice and of relevance.[210] With the leave of the court, material may be put in by affidavit.[211] Material can also be put in by agreement through the "case" (appeal book) subject to judicial determination of its relevance and weight.

A problem where such material is submitted by one party for possible judicial notice is that the other party might be taken unaware or denied a practical opportunity for rebuttal. A court could properly question such a process[212] and should where warranted refuse to take judicial notice under such circumstances. A more suitable process is that followed in the *Reference re Anti-Inflation Act* where on the application of the Attorney General of Canada the Supreme Court gave directions as to what material he could file and then prescribed dates allowing opposing parties to file material in response, with a further date for all parties to file yet further material in response to anything filed before.[213]

Another technique available in the Supreme Court of Canada is the appointment of the registrar to hear evidence in advance of the argument of the reference. This device has apparently been used only once[214] and a great deal of evidence both oral and written was thereby taken for insertion in the "case" subject to the ultimate decision of the court as to its admissibility. This method has the advantage of allowing a full right of challenge and rebuttal in a more typical adversary process of fact-introduction.

With more modern views favouring the use of extrinsic facts in references, better methods may be developed to allow the courts to have all relevant facts by a process that ensures fairness to all interests represented.

---

[208]*E.g., A.G. Man. v. Manitoba Egg & Poultry Association, supra,* note 195.

[209]*E.g., Reference re Natural Gas Tax, supra,* note 203; *Reference re Education Act of Ont. and Minority Language Education Rights, supra,* note 87, at 498.

[210]*E.g., Reference re Anti-Inflation Act,* [1976] 2 S.C.R. 373, 68 D.L.R. (3d) 452, 9 N.R. 541; *Reference re Residential Tenancies Act, supra,* note 203; *Reference re Natural Gas Tax Act, supra,* note 203.

[211]*Churchill Falls* case, *supra,* note 8, at pp. 315–16.

[212]See *Reference re Waters and Water Powers,* [1929] S.C.R. 200, [1929] 2 D.L.R. 481; record of oral argument at 1–41, 1253; *Nfld. and Labrador Corp. Ltd. et al. v. A.G. Nfld.,* [1982] 2 S.C.R. 260 at 279. See also *Montreal v. Arcade Amusements Inc.,* [1985] 1 S.C.R. 368 at 381, a non-reference case.

[213]Discussed in Hogg, "Proof of Facts in Constitutional Cases" (1976), 26 *U. Tor. L.J.* 386, at 399 *ff.*

[214]*Reference re Eskimos,* [1939] S.C.R. 104, [1939] 2 D.L.R. 417.

D. PLEADINGS

Having seen what evidence may be relevant in constitutional cases and how it may be admitted, it may be useful to consider the general principles governing to pleadings in civil cases and how these may be applicable.

There is very little jurisprudence specifically on the subject of written pleadings in constitutional cases. While this may indicate a minimum of problems, it is well to remember that here, just as in other litigation, the groundwork for defining the issues and for the presentation of evidence must be laid in the framing of the pleadings.

The general requirement for a written pleading is that it set out the material facts upon which the party pleading relies. He must also plead any matter which, if not specifically pleaded, might take the other party by surprise. He may raise a point of law in his pleading but if he seeks to assert a conclusion of law he must plead the facts which would support that conclusion.[215]

The nature of the pleadings required may then generally be seen by considering the relevant issues which must be addressed as discussed earlier.[216] In distribution of powers cases, it may be necessary to make certain allegations as to both the purpose and the effect of the law under attack. With respect to effect, consideration should be given as to whether one intends to allege that the effect of the statute makes it generally invalid, or only as it applies to the particular litigant. This distinction can be quite important in the definition of the issues, the determination of the scope of examination for discovery and of the admissible evidence at trial.

Where civil litigation involves the Charter, there will be a similar need to follow the normal rules with respect to pleadings. As McIntyre J. noted, albeit in a criminal matter,

> the *Charter* was not enacted in a vacuum. It was created to form a part — a very important part — of the Canadian legal system and, accordingly, must fit into that system. It will be noted at once that s. 24(1) gives no jurisdictional or procedural guide. This absence makes it clear that the procedures presently followed must be adapted and used for the accommodation of applications for relief under s. 24(1).[217]

Thus, if the purpose or effect of a law, or of an administrative practice

---

[215]See, *e.g.*, *Federal Court Rules*, C.R.C. 1978, c. 663, Rules 408, 409, 412; Ont. *Rules of Civil Procedure*, O. Reg. 560/84, Rules 25.06, 25.07, 25.08.

[216]*Supra,* at pp. 241–51.

[217]See *Mills v. The Queen*, [1986] 1 S.C.R. 863 at 956–57.

or act, is thought to contravene the Charter, any relevant facts to support such an allegation must be pleaded. Special problems will arise under certain sections, however. It is still not clear what criteria will be adopted to apply s. 15, particularly in respect of what will constitute "discrimination" or equality under that section. But it is probable that allegations will often be necessary as to the nature of the class to which the complainant is said to belong or from which he has been distinguished by the law or action under attack, and the nature and purpose of such alleged distinctions.

With respect to s. 1, a preliminary question arises as to whether it must be pleaded. If a government or other party is defending a law or action which *prima facie* appears to infringe Charter rights, must it plead s. 1 in order for the court to take that section into account? As has been noted earlier,[218] it is clear that the onus is on the one who invokes s. 1 to prove that there is a reasonable limit prescribed by law which is justified in a free and democratic society. This would suggest that unless he pleads the necessary facts and supports them by evidence at trial, he cannot rely on the exception which s. 1 creates to the general guarantees set out in the Charter. Further, it is at least arguable that this is the kind of matter which that party should plead to avoid surprise: that is, it raises a matter which presumably has not been raised in the preceding pleadings. The cases so far do not seem very settled on this question, however.[219]

E. REMEDIES

If a court determines that a law or an administrative act is contrary to the constitution, what are the consequences? What remedy can it give? In the past, in distribution of power cases, remedies have been shaped, granted, or denied on the basis of general principles of legal invalidity of an Act or contract. In recent years there has been a growing awareness of the particular requirements of constitutional remedies, and this has been much accelerated by the adoption of the *Constitution Act, 1982.* As we have seen earlier,[220] s. 52 of that Act which renders "of no force and effect" any law inconsistent with the Constitution is really only a continuation of the rule in s. 2 of the *Colonial Laws Validity Act* whose application to Canada was terminated in 1982. It enables courts to treat

---

[218]See, *supra*, at pp. 60, 253.
[219]*Cf. Re Reich and College of Physicians and Surgeons of Alta. et al. (No. 2)* (1984), 8 D.L.R. (4th) 696 at 714–15 (Alta. Q.B.); *Hunter et al. v. Southam Inc.*, [1984] 2 S.C.R. 145 at 169–70.
[220]*Supra*, at pp. 31, 32.

unconstitutional laws as nullities. Section 24 of the 1982 Act, forming part of the Charter, while authorizing any "court of competent jurisdiction" to grant such remedy for Charter infringement "as the court considers appropriate and just in the circumstances", a phrase which appears to invite a greater breadth of remedies, is nevertheless confined to violations of rights "guaranteed" by the Charter and does not apply to conflicts with the rest of the Constitution. Thus, for example, s. 24 does not apply to infringement of aboriginal rights which are "affirmed" in s. 35 which is outside the Charter.[221]

It will not be sought here to treat comprehensively the subject of constitutional remedies. Section 24 of the Charter has been written about extensively elsewhere.[222] But a few salient aspects of the subject will be considered.

1. Findings of Invalidity of Laws

Assuming that at the end of its analysis a court finds a law or part of a law to be capable of a characterization or application that would be contrary to the constitution, must it automatically find the whole law to be invalid? Must it equally invalidate everything purportedly done under that law? Two possible means for reducing the impact of such a finding are discussed below.

(a) "Reading Down"

The affinity of this technique to the legal presumption of validity has been noted in the discussion above of that presumption.[223] "Reading down" is employed in a context where a statute appears to be generally valid but where it has some broad terms which could be applied in a way to contravene the constitution. If the language of the Act does not clearly require such an application, then courts will normally interpret the general clauses in a way which restricts their application to those matters within the jurisdiction of the enacting Legislature. This restrictive interpretation

---

[221]Lysyk, in Tarnopolsky and Beaudoin, *Canadian Charter of Rights and Freedoms Commentary* (Toronto: Carswell, 1982), at p. 477.

[222]*E.g.*, Gibson, *The Law of the Charter: General Principles* (Toronto: Carswell, 1986), c. 6; Sharpe, *Charter Litigation* (Toronto: Butterworths, 1987), chaps. 10, 11.

[223]*Supra*, at p. 252.

is used in the application of laws with respect to territorial,[224] subject matter,[225] and Charter, limitations on legislative power.

If, on the other hand, the intent of the Act to apply to matters outside the jurisdiction of its legislators is clear, there is no place for reading down and even a specific interpretation provision calling for an interpretation that will keep the statute within permissible constitutional bounds will be ineffective.[226]

In the wake of the Charter there has been increased attention to the possibility of "reading down" a statute by "reading in" certain qualifications which would make its provisions consistent with the Charter. The courts have taken a generally negative approach to such suggestions, essentially on the basis that it is not for them to usurp the function of the Legislatures.[227] It is apparently thought to be presumptuous for a court to supplement the words of the legislator with additional words which have no legislative mandate, it being assumed that if Parliament, for example, had wanted to qualify its enactment with additional conditions it would have said so.[228]

(b) Severability

Taking the process one step further, suppose that the court finds that certain provisions of a law standing alone would be valid whereas certain others would be invalid. Must it find the whole law to be invalid?

---

[224]*E.g., Hewson v. Ontario Power Co.* (1905), 36 S.C.R. 596; *A.G. Ont. v. Reciprocal Insurers*, [1924] A.C. 328, [1924] 2 W.W.R. 397, [1924] 1 D.L.R. 789, 41 C.C.C. 336 (P.C.); *Reference re s. 31 of the Municipal District Act Amendment Act 1941*, [1943] S.C.R. 295, [1943] 3 D.L.R. 145; *Société Asbestos Ltée v. Société de l'Amiante*, [1981] C.A. 43 at 57–58, 128 D.L.R. (3d) 405 at 431–32, 24 L.C.R. 17.

[225]*E.g., Reference re Minimum Wage Act of Saskatchewan*, [1948] S.C.R. 248, [1948] 3 D.L.R. 801, 91 C.C.C. 366; *McKay v. The Queen*, [1965] S.C.R. 798, 53 D.L.R. (2d) 532; *Re Agricultural Products Marketing Act*, [1978] 2 S.C.R. 1198, 84 D.L.R. (3d) 257, 19 N.R. 361; *C.B.C. v. Cordeau*, [1979] 2 S.C.R. 618, 101 D.L.R. (3d) 24, 28 N.R. 541 (*sub nom. C.B.C. v. Quebec Police Comm.*), 48 C.C.C. (2d) 289, 14 C.P.C. 60.

[226]*A.G. Alta. v. A.G. Can.* (Debt Adjustment Act), [1943] A.C. 356 at 376, [1943] 1 All E.R. 240, [1943] 1 W.W.R. 378 at 394, [1943] 2 D.L.R. 1.

[227]*R. v. Rao* (1984), 9 D.L.R. (4th) 542 (Ont. C.A.); *R. v. Coombs* (1985), 56 Nfld. & P.E.I.R. 152, 23 C.C.C. (3d) 356 (Nfld. S.C.).

[228]*Hunter et al. v. Southam, supra*, note 28, at pp. 168–69; *R. v. Oakes* (1983), 145 D.L.R. (3d) 123 at 148, affd [1986] 1 S.C.R. 103; *R. v. Burton* (1983), 1 D.L.R. (4th) 152 (Nfld. C.A.); *Re Print Three Inc. et al. and The Queen* (1985), 51 O.R. (2d) 321 (C.A.); *R. v. Varga* (1985), 15 C.R.R. 122 (Ont. C.A.); *R. v. Videoflicks Ltd. et al.* (1984), 48 O.R. (2d) 395 at 430, revd on other grounds by S.C.C. in *Edwards Books* case, *supra*, note 20.

The classic test is well expressed in a 1947 judgment of the Judicial Committee of the Privy Council in *A.G. Alta. v. A.G. Can.* (Bill of Rights Reference) where it was said that if certain sections of a law are found to be invalid

> The real question is whether what remains is so inextricably bound up with the part declared invalid that what remains cannot independently survive or, as it has sometimes been put, whether on a fair review of the whole matter it can be assumed that the legislature would have enacted what survives without enacting the part that is ultra vires at all.[229]

The courts have more commonly found against severability, usually finding that the otherwise valid portions are inextricably linked with the invalid provisions.[230] They have refused to uphold remaining sections even where the legislators specifically provided that in case of a finding of invalidity of some provisions the remaining ones should not be held invalid, "the intention of Parliament being to give independent effect to the extent of its powers to every enactment and provision in this Act contained".[231] The Judicial Committee found that despite the clear statement of legislative intent that Parliament would have passed the various provisions individually, the marketing scheme in question was so interconnected that the detailed provisions of the scheme would not stand without the board and the basic marketing arrangement which had been held *ultra vires*. This suggests that severability is as much a matter of functional considerations as it is of legislative intent and that the courts will have the last word. This is a proposition which must be viewed with some scepticism, as it should not be for the court to decide that a truncated Act is nonsensical and therefore non-existent, if the Legislature has clearly said that it wishes surviving sections which are not *per se* invalid to remain.

An example of severance may be found in the Margarine Reference where the Supreme Court of Canada was able to strike down the section of the federal *Dairy Industry Act* which prohibited the manufacture of margarine (this being a provincial matter) but upheld the remaining sections which prohibited importation (a federal matter of regulation of trade

---

[229][1947] A.C. 503 at 518, [1947] 2 W.W.R. 401, [1947] 4 D.L.R. 1 at 11.

[230]*E.g., A.G. Alta. v. A.G. Can.* (Debt Adjustment Act), [1942] S.C.R. 31, [1942] 1 D.L.R. 1; *A.G. Can. v. A.g. Ont.* (Unemployment Insurance), [1937] A.C. 355, [1937] 1 W.W.R. 312, [1937] 1 D.L.R. 684; *Canadian Bankers Assn. v. A.G. for Sask.*, [1956] S.C.R. 31, [1955] 5 D.L.R. 736, 35 C.B.R. 135.

[231]*A.G. B.C. v. A.G. Can.* (Natural Products Marketing Act, 1934), [1937] A.C. 377 at 388, [1937] 1 W.W.R. 328, [1937] 1 D.L.R. 691 at 693, 67 C.C.C. 337.

and commerce).[232] The tests of both intent and functionalism were applied in support of this conclusion.[233]

2. Effect of a Finding of Invalidity

Assuming that a court finds that a law is invalid, does this mean that such law is without any legal consequence because of the violation of a constitutional requirement? Until recently there had been some debate in Canada as to whether some constitutional norms might be regarded as directory only. That is, where there is failure to comply with a directory norm the result would not be invalidity, even though there might be means to prevent the repetition of the constitutional violation.

There may still be some scope for the concept of directory constitutional provisions. For example, internal procedural requirements for Parliament and Legislatures not directly affecting members of the general public would probably be treated as directory only, partly (as discussed in chapter 7) because of the deference the courts should show to legislative bodies concerning their internal processes, and partly because of the inconvenience that would otherwise result.[234] Similarly, a requirement for the timing of elections might be regarded as directory only,[235] even though some remedies other than a finding of invalidity might be necessary.

The Supreme Court of Canada in *Reference re Language Rights in Manitoba*[236] has strongly confirmed, however, that in general the consequence of a law being inconsistent with the constitution is total invalidity. This was pronounced in a case where the consequences were quite dramatic; namely that all laws passed by the Manitoba Legislature in English only since 1890 were held to be invalid. Although this meant on its face that nothing that had happened since 1890 that depended on such laws, nor the institutions which were created by them, had any legal validity, the court proceeded to find means for the maintenance of an orderly society.

---

[232][1949] S.C.R. 1, [1949] 1 D.L.R. 433, affd. [1951] A.C. 179 (*sub nom. Can. Fed. of Agriculture v. A.G. Que.*), [1950] 4 D.L.R. 689.

[233]See also, *e.g., Bernstein v. Thurston* (1961), 46 M.P.R. 308, 132 C.C.C. 27 (N.B. C.A.); *La Caisse Populaire Notre-Dame Ltée v. Moyen* (1967), 59 W.W.R. 129, 61 D.L.R. (2d) 118 (Sask. Q.B.); *Alaska Training Corp. v. Pacific Pilotage Authority*, [1981] 1 S.C.R. 261, 35 N.R. 271.

[234]*Namoi Shire Council v. A.G. N.S.W.* (1980), 2 N.S.W.L.R. 639; Swinton, "Challenging the Validity of an Act of Parliament: the Effect of Enrolment and Parliamentary Privilege" (1976), 14 *Osgoode Hall L.J.* 345.

[235]*Simpson v. A.G. New Zealand*, [1955] N.Z. L.R. 271 (C.A.).

[236]*Supra*, note 47.

The Supreme Court relied heavily on the principle of the rule of law, now expressly made part of our Constitution by recognition in the preamble of the Charter and always implicitly part of it. The rule of law, it held, required that acts carried out in the past under colour of authority would have to be treated as valid, on the basis of the *de facto* doctrine. This doctrine, as the court noted, had long been accepted in Canada as a basis for validating the actions of unauthorized officers who nevertheless acted under colour of authority. The court then described as follows the application of the *de facto* doctrine to the case before it.[237]

> The application of the *de facto* doctrine is, however, limited to validating acts which are taken under invalid authority: it does not validate the authority under which the acts took place. In other words, the doctrine does not give effect to unconstitutional laws. It recognizes and gives effect only to the justified expectations of those who have relied upon the acts of those administering the invalid laws and to the existence and efficacy of public and private bodies corporate, though irregularly or illegally organized. Thus, the *de facto* doctrine will save those rights, obligations and other effects which have arisen out of actions performed pursuant to invalid Acts of the Manitoba Legislature by public and private bodies corporate, courts, judges, persons exercising statutory powers and public officials. Such rights, obligations and other effects are, and will always be, enforceable and unassailable.
>
> The *de facto* doctrine will not by itself save all of the rights, obligations and other effects which have purportedly arisen under the repealed and current Acts of the Legislature of Manitoba from 1890 to the date of this judgment. Some of these rights, obligations and other effects did not arise as a consequence of reliance by the public on the acts of officials acting under colour of authority or on the assumed validity of public and private bodies corporate. Furthermore, the *de facto* authority of officials and entities acting under the invalid laws of the Manitoba Legislature will cease on the date of this judgment since all colour of authority ceases on that date. Thus, the *de facto* doctrine only provides a partial solution.

Briefly put, then, if a law is administered and is subsequently found by a court to be invalid, steps taken in accordance with the law and rights accrued pursuant to the law will continue to be recognized, on the basis of the *de facto* doctrine, after a finding of invalidity of the law itself. As the court emphasized, the law itself is invalid *ab initio* and the *de facto* doctrine cannot change that.

3. Prospective Overruling

But what of the future where a law or a system of laws is wiped out at the stroke of the judge's pen? As the Supreme Court stressed in

---

[237]*Ibid.*, at pp. 756–57.

the above passage from the *Manitoba Language Reference*, all colour of authority of those acting under an impugned statute ceases the day the court holds it invalid. In some cases this may not cause serious problems. The law may no longer be necessary or, as a single piece of legislation, may be cured of its defect and re-enacted soon in an amended form. But in the case of Manitoba, where virtually all laws had been wiped out by this decision, it was impossible to effect a quick remedy. All unilingual laws had to be re-enacted, but this time in both languages. This would require a considerable time to accomplish, and in the meantime all validity and all "colour of authority" of the old laws had disappeared. The court thus devised a solution: it ordered that all Acts which would otherwise have been in force, save for their unilingual nature, were "deemed temporarily valid and effective from the date of this judgment" to the expiration of the period necessary for translation and re-enactment of the statutes of Manitoba. The court held a subsequent hearing to fix the length of this period, giving the province over 3 years to re-enact in bilingual form its current statutes.[238] Although not so described, this amounted to prospective overruling of the statutes of Manitoba, avoiding legal chaos but ultimately ensuring the enforcement of the Constitution. While the Manitoba situation was unique, this case will serve as a potential model for other decrees where a judicial determination of invalidity of a law— or perhaps of an administrative practice—would create a legal crisis.[239]

4. Mandatory Orders to Enforce the Constitution

The *Manitoba Language Reference* decision is one novel form of judicial enforcement of a constitutional norm by requiring corrective action by government. While there was no order in the nature of an injunction or *mandamus* — indeed, there could not have been, it being only a reference — the result was certainly effectively designed to get the attention of the Manitoba Legislature and indeed its compliance: if the necessary legislative action is not taken by the end of 1988, most of Manitoba's laws will disappear. This achieves indirectly what probably no court could achieve directly — the enactment of legislation.

There are other more traditional ways for courts to compel compliance with the constitution, going beyond mere determination of invalidity of laws or administrative action. Provided that the remedy is otherwise appropriate in terms of the party against whom it is sought, and in terms

---

[238][1985] 2 S.C.R. 347.

[239]For a further analysis of the implications, see Gibson and Lercher, "Reliance on Unconstitutional Laws: The Saving Doctrines and Other Protections" (1986), 15 *Man. L.J.* 305.

of the normal conditions being present for granting that remedy, and provided such remedy is available in the court in question, the latter may issue orders such as *mandamus*, prohibition, and injunction for this purpose. Where the constitutional duty is sufficiently precise, it cannot be said that any officer of government has a duty to the Crown to disobey the constitutional imperative. Therefore the outmoded concept of "servants of the Crown" (not subject to *mandamus*) contrasted with "servants of the legislature" (subject to *mandamus*) is even less relevant than it was when adopted. The issue is the existence of a precise constitutional duty and its application in the specific situation before the court.[240]

In interlocutory proceedings, however, the courts have in the past normally been reluctant to issue orders premised on the probable invalidity of a law. This has been true both with respect to applications for prohibitory injunctions[241] and for mandatory injunctions,[242] the rationale generally being that the law was presumptively valid until proven otherwise, and further, that interim and interlocutory injunctions are designed to preserve the *status quo* until trial, not give the plaintiff everything he might win at trial.

The Supreme Court of Canada has recently had occasion to review the principles applicable to such interlocutory orders. In *A.G. Man. v. Metro. Stores (MTS) Ltd. et al.*[243] the court was dealing with the stay of an order of the Manitoba Labour Board pending a court decision as to possible conflict between the Charter and the Board order for which the stay was sought. Beetz J. writing for the court equated stays with interlocutory injunctions in constitutional cases, insofar as the relevant principles are concerned. He first virtually dismissed the presumption of validity of legislation as a rationale for refusing such injunctions, at least in Charter cases. While he appeared to accept the validity of that presumption for certain purposes in distribution of powers litigation, he dismissed its relevance to Charter cases because of the "innovative and evolutive character" of the Charter.[244] This apparently means that as the interpretation of the Charter is expected to be in a state of constant evolution, one cannot presume that legislatures intended to comply with it. This attenuation of the presumption of validity is, however, expressed in the context of a general approach that the merits of the case normally cannot be adequately addressed on interlocutory proceedings, given the

---

[240]*Air Can. v. A.G. B.C.*, [1986] 2 S.C.R. 539; *Lévesque v. A.G. Can. et al.* (1985), 25 D.L.R. (4th) 184 (F.C. T.D.).

[241]*Morgentaler v. Ackroyd* (1983), 42 O.R. (2d) 659 at 668 (H.C.).

[242]*Gould v. A.G. Can.*, [1984] 1 F.C. 1133 (C.A.), affd [1984] 2 S.C.R. 124; *Marchand v. Simcoe County Bd. of Educ. et al.* (1984), 10 C.R.R. 169 (Ont. H.C.).

[243][1987]1 S.C.R. 110.

[244]*Ibid.*, at pp. 121–25.

limited time and evidentiary basis available to the motions judge. Thus, the court put greater emphasis on the balance of convenience as the chief determinant as to whether an injunction or stay should issue. It emphasized that we must place in the balance in favour of the respondent official or agency, against whom an injunction is sought to prevent the administration or use of a constitutionally impugned law or practice, the interests of the public. The court seemed prepared to assume that legislation is enacted in the public interest, and therefore the public interest is threatened if its use is enjoined.[245] It does distinguish between an injunction which would involve a total "suspension" of a law or practice, and one which would only involve an "exemption" for the particular party seeking the injunction. While recognizing that the public interest will normally be more seriously threatened by a "suspension", it notes that even "exemptions" will probably have precedential effects almost as harmful to the public interest.

Thus the criteria for the exercise of discretion in granting interlocutory relief in constitutional cases would now appear to be related principally to the balance of convenience with little or no emphasis on the merits of the case (the merits often involving the issue of presumption of constitutionality).

5. Restoration of *Status Quo Ante*

To what extent can the courts seek to restore parties to a position they might have enjoyed had the invalid law not been passed?

As was noted in the *Manitoba Language Reference*[246] there are various doctrines of the law which militate against that restoration. The doctrine of *res judicata* means that cases decided by the courts, even on the basis of an invalid law, cannot be reopened if the appeal period has passed. The Supreme Court also referred to the rule against recovery of money paid under a mistake of law, although, as will be noted below, this is a rule now full of exceptions.

Two possible means of restoration or compensation will be considered.

(a) Damages

There appears to be a well established common law doctrine that where an official has acted in good faith under the colour of authority of

---

[245]*Ibid.*, at p. 138.
[246]*Supra*, note 47, at p. 757.

a statute later found to be invalid, he should not be liable in damages.[247] Further, it is permissible for a Legislature to protect him from liability in such circumstances.[248]

But what of the official who undertakes administrative actions which are not specifically required of him by any statute or regulation and which amount to an unconstitutional way of performing his duties? And what of the position of his employer? Should either or both be liable?

These questions have become much more pressing with the Charter which by implication imposes new standards of care on public officials. The answer may be more obvious under the *Civil Code* of Quebec in which art. 1053 recognizes a general duty not to injure others. In the common law, with its system of nominate torts, it is more difficult to find a basis for liability in the case of violation of the Charter, if the offending act does not also amount to a recognized tort such as assault or trespass. It now seems clear that violation of the standards prescribed by a statute does not automatically give rise to an actionable tort where injury ensues.[249] It can be argued that the same is true where the standards are imposed by the Charter and not observed by officials, with a resulting denial of Charter rights.

It has been suggested that Canadian courts should take inspiration from the U.S. law and practice, where by both statute and decisional law plaintiffs have been able to sue officials and their employing agencies where constitutional rights have been infringed.[250] There have been a few cases in which damages[251] or costs[252] have been awarded, apparently on the sole basis of Charter violation. It has been held, however, that such claims for damages for Charter violation, if they exist, must be by the procedure normally applicable to damage claims.[253]

There are thus some precedents, and, it would seem, some principles, which would sustain actions in damages for breach of the Charter. Although

---

[247]*Central Can. Potash Co. v. Sask.*, [1979] 1 S.C.R. 42 at 90; *Vespoli et al. v. The Queen et al.* (1984), 12 C.R.R. 185 at 188–89 (Fed. C.A.); *Crown Trust Co. et al. v. The Queen in Right of Ont. et al.* (1986), 14 O.A.C. 137 at 144 (Div. Ct.).

[248]*Crown Trust* case, *ibid.*; *Kohn v. Globerman et al.* (1986), 27 D.L.R. (4th) 583 at 599 (Man. C.A.); leave to appeal to S.C.C. refused 44 Man. R. (2d) 160n.

[249]*R. v. Sask. Wheat Pool*, [1983] 1 S.C.R. 205.

[250]Manning, "Constitutional and Statutory Created Torts and Liability for Breaches Thereof" (1983), *L.S.U.C. Special Lectures* 221; Pilkington, "Damages as a Remedy for the Infringement of the Canadian Charter of Rights and Freedoms" (1984), 62 *Can. Bar Rev.* 517.

[251]*Crossman v. The Queen* (1984), 9 D.L.R. (4th) 588 (Fed.T.D.); *Lord v. Allison et al.* (1986), 3 B.C.L.R. (2d) 300 (S.C.); see also *obiter dicta* in the *Vespoli* case, *supra*, note 247, at p. 189.

[252]*R. v. Volpi* (1985), 19 C.R.R. 46 (Ont. H.C.).

[253]*Lussier v. Collin* (1984), 20 C.R.R. 29 (Fed. C.A.).

in the *Sask. Wheat Pool* case[254] the Supreme Court confirmed that there is no automatic right to sue in tort for breach of statute, this was a situation where the Act was at best silent on the matter, and even implied in providing specifically for penalties for breach that no other sanctions were contemplated. But s-s. 24(1) of the Charter virtually proclaims the intention that a court which finds a Charter violation may order any remedy available in that court against the kind of defendants or respondents before it. It implies that the breach of the Charter is a civilly wrongful act, and arguably any remedy available in that court for wrongful acts should be available to the person who has suffered the wrong. There may well be limitations as to the persons or bodies against whom such remedies are available. Since the Charter creates the liability, it must be defined in terms of the Charter. Thus, since s. 32 of the Charter makes it applicable to Parliament, Legislatures, and governments, arguably only those bodies incur liability for its breach. While public officers may be restrained in various ways from exercising governmental powers in a way that would contravene the Charter, there is a serious question as to whether they can be held personally liable, in an action by another private party, for Charter breaches. This may not be an important problem in many cases where their employer, if a governmental organ, is amenable to suit. Even when vicarious liability is not available, the state may arguably be held liable.[255] Also, if general rules of law apart from s-s. 24(1) would support an action against a private defendant for damages for invasion of recognized private rights through excess of authority (authority here having been limited by the Charter) then such officer can probably be sued in his personal capacity.[256] It is probable, however, that many rights protected by the Charter — *e.g.*, privacy under s. 8 — do not give rise to a private cause of action for their breach, at least in common law.

(b) Recovery of Money Paid Under Invalid Law

Such moneys are essentially paid under a mistake of law—a mistake as to the validity of the Act requiring their payment. The traditional general principle of law is that money paid under a mistake of law cannot be recovered,[257] but it is a principle to which there are numerous excep-

---

[254]*Supra*, note 249.

[255]See *Maharaj v. A.G. Trinidad and Tobago (No. 2)*, [1979] A.C. 385 (P.C.); *Germain v. The Queen* (1984), 10 C.R.R. 232 at 244–45 (Alta. Q.B.).

[256]But see Gibson, *supra*, note 222 at pp. 110–19, where he argues that even purely private activity is governed by the Charter.

[257]See, *e.g.*, *Hydro Elec. Commn. of Twp. of Nepean v. Ont. Hydro*, [1982] 1 S.C.R. 347.

tions. One of the important exceptions is that when such money has been paid under duress it is recoverable.[258] In the constitutional context the Supreme Court has assumed that there is a common law right to recover from a government taxes paid under duress, and that neither the Legislature[259] nor the executive government[260] can constitutionally impair that recovery. Presumably the same principles of recovery would apply where a private individual has paid to another private individual sums as required by a statute which is subsequently found to be invalid. A more difficult issue arises where a subordinate public agency or private individual has expended sums for the benefit of numerous third parties, as required by a statute which later proves to be invalid. Recovery from those benefitted may be impractical. Can it or he look to the government whose legislative branch enacted the law, for recovery of the money paid under a mistake of law?[261]

6. Section 24 Remedies Under the *Charter*

This subject has been dealt with extensively in relation to the subjects of "court of competent jurisdiction",[262] standing,[263] and damages.[264] It is a subject which has been treated at length elsewhere by others in a way which is not possible in this work.[265] It will suffice to summarize, with respect to s. 24, what has been said here previously, namely: that s. 24 should be regarded as broadening, not narrowing, available remedies and standing to seek such remedies; that it does not create new jurisdiction for any court in respect of subject-matter, remedies, or parties, but it may enable a court to vindicate new rights guaranteed by the Charter through the exercise of accustomed jurisdiction; that it probably only allows remedies against government or officials acting in a public capacity, but not against private individuals as such; and that s-s. 24(2) does modify the law with respect to admissibility of evidence but that the judicial discretion exercisable thereunder should normally only be exercised at trial.

---

[258]See, *e.g.*, *Eadie v. Brantford*, [1967] S.C.R. 573.
[259]*Amax Potash Ltd. et al. v. Sask.*, [1977] 2 S.C.R. 576.
[260]*Air Can. v. A.G. B.C.*, *supra*, note 240.
[261]See *Regional Municipality of Peel v. The Queen* (1987), 7 F.T.R. 213 (F.C. T.D.).
[262]*Supra*, at pp. 70–73.
[263]*Supra*, at pp. 185–87.
[264]*Supra*, at pp. 307–09.
[265]See, *e.g.*, works cited, *supra*, notes 222, 250.

Chapter 9

Constitutional References

A. HISTORY

One of the most distinctive features of Canadian judicial review is its frequent resort to the constitutional reference. This frequency can be demonstrated by a survey of the leading cases: those reaching the Privy Council up to 1949, the Supreme Court of Canada thereafter, decided from 1867 to 1986. Of 352 cases involving constitutional issues, 91 had their origins in a constitutional reference while 261 involved concrete cases. Nor does the fact that over a quarter of the leading decisions were given in such proceedings reveal the full significance of constitutional references. In terms of impact on the political, social, and economic affairs of the country the decisions in these cases have had an effect far beyond their numerical proportion. It is therefore essential in any study of judicial review of legislation in Canada to give some particular attention to this device.

The statutory reference system can claim ancestry in English common law. There were some examples of both the Crown[1] and certain courts[2] referring difficult questions to the judges for an opinion. More closely related was the precedent set by the *Judicial Committee Act* of 1833, s. 4 of which conferred on the Crown the power to refer to that body "any such other matters whatsoever as His Majesty shall think fit".[3]

It was the provision in the *Judicial Committee Act* which apparently inspired the introduction of this system into Canada in 1875.[4] In that year

---

[1]See, *e.g.*, Inderwick, *The King's Peace* (1895), at 174–75; Plucknett, *A Concise History of the Common Law*, 5th ed. (1956), at 162.

[2]Plucknett, *supra*, at pp. 162, 213, 347. For examples of this procedure see *Re London and Westminster Bank* (1834), 2 Cl. & F. 191, 6 E.R. 1127; *M'Naghten's Case* (1843), 10 Cl. & F. 200, 8 E.R. 718; *Hollins v. Fowler* (1875), L.R. 7 H.L. 757, [1874–80] All E.R. Rep. 118.

[3]3 & 4 Wm. IV, c. 41 (U.K.). Used in *Re Cape Breton* (1846), 5 Moo. P.C.C. 259, 13 E.R. 489; *Re Parliamentary Privilege Act, 1770*, [1958] A.C. 331, [1958] 2 All E.R. 329 (P.C.). See also Tarring, *The Law Relating to the Colonies* (1913), at 162–63 for other cases pertaining to colonial laws and powers.

[4]Acknowledged in *A.G. Ont. v. A.G. Can.*, [1912] A.C. 571 at 585, 3 D.L.R. 509 (P.C.).

311

the Supreme Court of Canada was created, and its founding statute conferred on it this power and duty. The *Supreme and Exchequer Court Act* provided as follows:

> 52. It shall be lawful for the Governor in Council to refer to the Supreme Court for hearing or consideration, any matters whatsoever as he may think fit; and the Court shall thereupon hear and consider the same and certify their opinion thereon to the Governor in Council: Provided that any Judge or Judges of the said Court who may differ from the opinion of the majority may in like manner certify his or their opinion or opinions to the Governor in Council.[5]

Section 53 also permitted the Senate or House of Commons to refer bills before it to the court for a report. These reference provisions proved to be inadequate and were not used extensively in the next 15 years. Normally there was no argument presented to the court in reference cases. The court took the view that it should not give reasons for its answers, but should only state its conclusion as to the validity or invalidity of legislation. The result was particularly unsatisfactory in the *McCarthy Act Reference*[6] in 1885 where a federal statute regulating the liquor traffic was found by the Supreme Court to be *ultra vires*. That court and the Judicial Committee on appeal both declined to give reasons for their conclusions. As a result it was extremely difficult for Parliament or the Government to ascertain the probable limits of federal power insofar as future legislation might be contemplated.

Edward Blake, a member of the opposition but a former Attorney General, pointed out these and other defects in a speech to the House of Commons in 1890.

> Our present powers, Sir, are wholly inadequate for the effectual execution of the project in hand. There is no certainty — there is in ordinary cases rather an improbability — of our being able to reach the Judicial Committee; and as to all the three possible appeals or references, the Judicial Committee of the Privy Council, the Supreme Court, and the Imperial law officers, the machinery is extremely defective. There is no provision for the representation of the different interests; there is no provision for the ascertainment of facts; there is no provision for the reasoned opinion of the tribunal.[7]

Noting that in the *McCarthy Act Reference* and one other case special

---

[5]S.C. 1875, c. 11, s. 52.
[6]Decision reported *Sess. Papers* No. 85a, 1885 (Can.), at 12–13; argument reported at 42–244. For a discussion of this case see Smith, *The Commerce Power in Canada and the United States* (Toronto: Butterworths, 1963), at 49–57.
[7]2 H.C. Deb., 6th Parl., 4th Sess., 1890, at 4089–90.

provision had been made for the appearance of counsel to represent the various interests, he considered that the results were still unsatisfactory because of the absence of a reasoned opinion. Consequently, Blake, by a resolution, sought an amendment to correct these defects, but only for limited purposes. He proposed an improved reference system to be used only with respect to questions of law and fact pertaining to the federal Government's use of the power to disallow provincial legislation and its appellate power in educational matters. The Government accepted Blake's resolution, and Sir John A. Macdonald assured him that a suitable amendment would be introduced at the next session.

As a result the *Supreme and Exchequer Courts Act* was amended in 1891, the reference section quoted above being replaced by more elaborate provisions. In spite of Blake's preference for a broadened reference system applicable only to matters of disallowance and education, the new section extended as well to questions of law or fact touching the constitutionality of any provincial or federal legislation, and to "any other matter with reference to which he [the Governor in Council] sees fit to exercise this power". The court was obliged to certify its opinion "with the reasons therefor, which shall be given in a like manner as in the case of a judgment upon an appeal to the said court". Where provincial legislation was involved the appropriate Attorney General was to be notified and permitted to be heard. The court could direct that other interested persons could be heard, and it could appoint counsel to represent interests otherwise unrepresented. The opinion of the court, though "advisory only", was to be treated for purposes of appeal to the Judicial Committee "as a final judgment of the said court between parties". The court was also empowered to make such rules as might "seem best for the investigation of questions of fact involved in any reference thereunder".[8] Thus Blake's criticisms of the former provisions were largely met. There was to be representation of different interests, a clear right of appeal to the Judicial Committee, and, most importantly, a reasoned decision. The court was enabled to make appropriate rules for fact-finding in reference cases.[9] In this way the reference system was immeasurably strengthened, a vast improvement on the procedure after which it was

---

[8]*An Act to amend Chapter one hundred and thirty-five of the Revised Statutes intituled, "An Act respecting the Supreme and Exchequer Courts"*, S.C. 1891, c. 25, s. 4.

[9]The only rule made by the court in this respect allows it to review or require further evidence but this is limited to use in references by the Governor in Council asking what disposition the court would have made of a case already decided by a court of appeal (*i.e.*, where no appeal has been taken to the Supreme Court or for which leave to appeal was not given). The present Rule 31, SOR/83–74, is broader than its predecessor which limited the receiving of such evidence to criminal cases. The only other kind of measure the court has taken with respect to reference cases was to order the registrar to receive further evidence under s. 67 of the (present) Act. See, *supra*, at p. 297.

originally patterned. Apart from some clarifications introduced in 1906[10] these provisions remain substantially unchanged in the present *Supreme Court Act*,[11] the reference to Judicial Committee appeals having been deleted in 1956.

The federal reference system, though it had achieved a technical acceptability by 1891, had yet to establish its constitutional legitimacy. Some of the provinces objected to federal references on two grounds. First, it was contended that any reference of provincial legislation to a federal court was an invasion of the provincial field of jurisdiction to which the legislation pertained. Further, it was contended that this was not a proper judicial function, and that Parliament in the exercise of its power under s. 101 of the B.N.A. Act to create a "General Court of Appeal for Canada" could not confer on the "court" a non-judicial function. These objections were finally put to rest in *A.G. Ont. v. A.G. Can.*[12] The Privy Council upheld the federal reference system as incidental to the establishment of a Court of Appeal. It regarded the answering of such questions as a non-judicial function, but nevertheless a duty properly imposed on the court by statute.[13]

The provinces had other objections to the federal reference system as well. The period from Confederation up to 1896 had been marked by a vigorous assertion of federal jurisdiction. One manifestation of this was the frequent disallowance of provincial legislation by the federal Government. Another was the creation of the Supreme Court of Canada, including the conferral of power on the federal cabinet to refer questions of legislative validity to that tribunal. The provinces apparently regarded this reference system as a sinister device intended primarily to enable the federal authorities to attack provincial legislation in a federally created court before which the province had no automatic right to appear. Provincial statesmen reacted with demands for increased provincial autonomy or equality of rights. Their views found expression in the interprovincial conference of 1887 in Quebec where five of the seven provinces were represented. The conference passed a series of resolutions calling for constitutional changes. The second resolution, noting that it was just as important that Parliament not assume to exercise provincial powers as that the provinces not assume to exercise federal powers, urged

. . . that to prevent any such assumption, there should be equal facilities

---

[10]*An Act to amend the "Supreme and Exchequer Courts Act"*, S.C. 1906, c. 50, s. 2.
[11]R.S.C. 1970, c. S-19, ss. 55 and 103(1)(*f*).
[12]*Supra*, note 4.
[13]For a full discussion of these issues, see, *supra*, at pp. 137–40. If the accord signed by the First Ministers on June 3, 1987, is implemented by constitutional amendments, a new section 101E of the *Constitution Act, 1867*, will specifically preserve the power of Parliament to provide for references to the Supreme Court.

to the Federal and Provincial Governments for promptly obtaining a judicial determination respecting the validity of Statutes of both the Federal Parliament and Provincial Legislatures; that Constitutional provision should be made for obtaining such determination before, as well as after, a Statute has been acted upon; and that any decision should be subject to Appeal as in other cases, in order that the adjudication may be final.[14]

Their faith in a reference system to which either level of Government would have equal access was attested to by the third resolution. This proposed that private litigants should be able to challenge the validity of legislation, federal or provincial, only within two years after enactment. Thereafter it should be challengeable only at the instance of the federal or provincial Government.[15] This presumably contemplated the use of a reference in any dispute as to validity after the initial two–year period.

While no such constitutional changes were ever effected, the resolutions of 1887 appear to have brought about the introduction, through provincial legislation, of provincial reference systems. It is surely no coincidence that three of the five provinces represented at the interprovincial conference introduced virtually identical legislation on this subject in 1890.[16] Over the course of the next 63 years the other provinces[17] followed the lead taken by these autonomy-conscious statesmen at the end of the nineteenth century.

The scope of the provincial reference power was from the beginning stated quite broadly. Typical of the 1890 statutes was Manitoba's which provided that:

> 1. The Lieutenant-Governor-in-Council may refer to the Court of Queen's Bench or a Judge thereof, for hearing or consideration any matter which he thinks fit to refer, and the court shall thereupon hear or consider the same.

---

[14]*Official Proceedings of the Inter-Provincial Conference, Quebec, 1887* (1887), at 28.
[15]*Ibid.*
[16]*An Act for Expediting the Decision of Constitutional and other Provincial Questions*, S.M. 1890, c. 16; *An Act for expediting the decision of Constitutional and other Provincial Questions*, S.N.S. 1890, c. 9; *An Act for expediting the decision of Constitutional and other provincial Questions*, S.O. 1890, c. 13.
[17]*An Act for expediting the decision of Constitutional and other Provincial Questions*, S.B.C. 1891, c. 5; *An Act to authorize the reference, by the Lieutenant-Governor in Council, of certain questions to the Court of Queen's Bench*, S.Q. 1898, c. 11; *An Ordinance for expediting the decision of Constitutional and other Legal Questions*, Ord. N.W.T. 1901, c. 11 (carried forward into the laws of Alberta and Saskatchewan when they were created out of the Northwest Territories); *An Act to provide for references by the Governor-in-Council to the Appeal Division of the Supreme Court*, S.N.B. 1928, c. 47; *An Act to Amend the Judicature Act*, S.P.E.I. 1941, c. 16, s. 10; *The Judicature (Amendment) Act*, 1953, S.N. 1953, No. 3.

This was obviously copied from the *Judicial Committee Act* of 1833 and the *Supreme and Exchequer Court Act* of 1875. It stated the power in the broadest terms possible, allowing the provincial cabinet to refer all matters which it "thinks fit". This could include questions of the validity of federal as well as provincial laws. It would permit the referral of bills not yet enacted.[18] Issues of fact as well as of law could apparently be raised.

Identical or similar terminology has been adopted by nine of the ten provinces and continued in current statutes.[19] Only New Brunswick expressed the reference power differently. When it introduced references in 1928 it followed the pattern of the *Supreme Court Act* as revised in 1891 and 1906. The net effect of its legislation[20] would appear to be the same, however. One minor variation among the existing provincial statutes is the court to which such questions are to be referred. All provinces now provide for a reference directly to the highest provincial appellate court. But, in addition, Manitoba and Ontario permit a reference to the superior trial court or judge thereof, though this alternative is rarely used.

The original provincial reference statutes of 1890 in other respects were an improvement over, not an imitation of, the existing federal legislation. They sought to cure most of the defects which, in the same year, Edward Blake had ascribed to the reference provision in the *Supreme Court Act*. It will be remembered that these defects included the lack of opportunity for the various interests to be represented and heard, the lack of expressed reasons for the conclusions reached by the court, and the uncertainty with respect to the right of appeal from such decisions. The provincial statutes required the giving of reasons. They allowed the court to permit various interests to be heard, and to appoint counsel at public expense to represent unrepresented interests. The opinion of the court was to be "deemed a judgment . . . and an appeal shall lie therefrom as in the case of a judgment in an action". In these provisions the early provincial statutes anticipated the changes made in the *Supreme Court Act* in 1891. These provisions still appear in almost identical terms in the current reference statutes of all provinces. Small exceptions may be

---

[18]*Reference re Labour Relations Act*, s. 46A (1962), 40 W.W.R. 354, 36 D.L.R. (2d) 560 (Man. C.A.).

[19]*Judicature Act*, R.S.A. 1980, c. J-1, s. 27; *Constitutional Question Act*, R.S.B.C. 1979, c. 63, s. 1; *The Constitutional Questions Act*, C.C.S.M., c. C180, s. 1; *Judicature Act, 1986*, S.N. 1986, c. 42, s. 13; *Constitutional Questions Act*, R.S.N.S. 1967, c. 51, s. 2; *Courts of Justice Act, 1984*, S.O. 1984, c. 11, s. 19; *Judicature Act*, R.S.P.E.I. 1974, c. J-3, s. 38; *Court of Appeal Reference Act*, R.S.Q. 1977, c. R-23, s. 1; *Constitutional Questions Act*, R.S.S. 1978, c. C-29, s. 2.

[20]*Judicature Act*, R.S.N.B. 1973, c. J-2, s. 23, am. 1978, c. 32, s. 18; 1980, c. 28, s. 6; 1982, c. 3, s. 39(1).

seen in Quebec where an opinion given in a reference is not subject to appeal,[21] and in British Columbia, New Brunswick, and Quebec where no provision is made for appointment of counsel at public expense to appear for interests not otherwise represented.

As a result of this legislation the provinces achieved essentially all they had sought in the resolution at the 1887 interprovincial conference. They had provided for themselves "equal facilities . . . for promptly obtaining a judicial determination respecting the validity of Statutes of both the Federal Parliament and Provincial Legislatures". They could not refer a matter directly to the Supreme Court of Canada but they could obtain a respected opinion from the highest provincial court. While the purported right of appeal from a reference decision of a provincial court to the Supreme Court of Canada was initially held invalid by the latter,[22] an amendment[23] to the *Supreme Court Act* in 1922 specifically permitted such appeals to that body. Meanwhile the Privy Council had willingly entertained appeals brought directly from provincial courts in reference cases.[24] Though appeals to the Supreme Court were governed by the restrictions of the *Supreme Court Act*, the provinces themselves seemingly had jurisdiction to create a right of appeal from their courts to the Privy Council. Moreover the Privy Council could always exercise the prerogative right of granting leave to appeal where the right was not conferred by law.[25] Thus, by referring a question to its local court, a provincial Government could expect an answer ultimately from the Privy Council or, more recently, from the Supreme Court of Canada.

From this brief historical review of the reference system two facts emerge which place it in an interesting perspective. First, it may be seen that at both the federal and the provincial level this device was looked upon as an integral part of the functioning of the constitution. After several years of experience with the reference power under the *Supreme Court Act*, unsatisfactory as it had been, both Government and Opposition in the House of Commons were agreed that it should be retained. The debates

---

[21]Special legislation has been passed when an appeal was desired; see, *e.g., An Act respecting a reference to the Court of Appeal*, S.Q. 1980, c. 24; S.Q. 1981, c. 17. Such a provincial law is required to meet the conditions prescribed by s. 37 of the *Supreme Court Act* that, for the Supreme Court to hear such appeals, they must be authorized under provincial law by the reference opinion being thereby deemed a judgment and made subject to appeal.

[22]*Union Colliery Co. v. A.G. B.C.* (1897), 27 S.C.R. 637. For a full discussion see, *supra*, at pp. 139, 140.

[23]*An Act to amend the Supreme Court Act*, S.C. 1922, s. 48, s. 1.

[24]See, *e.g., A.G. Ont. v. A.G. Can.*, [1894] A.C. 189, 11 Can. Rep. 13 (P.C.); *A.G. Ont. v. Hamilton Street Ry.*, [1903] A.C. 524, 2 O.W.R. 672, 7 C.C.C. 326 (P.C.); *A.G. Can. v. A.G. Que.*, [1921] 1 A.C. 413, 56 D.L.R. 358 (P.C.).

[25]See, *supra*, at pp. 11, 12, 22–27.

in 1890 and 1891 primarily reveal a concern that the system should be made to operate properly. There was a general assumption that this was an important device for ensuring that neither Parliament nor the Legislatures exceeded their constitutional powers. Similarly, the resolutions at the 1887 interprovincial conference show that the provinces placed great emphasis on this device, their concern being that they should be equally entitled to resort to it. They also apparently felt that the role of private litigants in judicial review of legislation should be drastically limited.

Second, it is clear that both Parliament and the Legislatures intended that the procedure in reference cases should be as similar as possible to the procedure employed in ordinary litigation. Issues were to be fully argued by opposing counsel, and reasons were to be given by the court for its decision. The debates in Parliament and the revised section of the *Supreme Court Act* also reveal a hopeful expectation that the Supreme Court would contrive methods to acquire more effectively the factual background upon which the opinions would be given. This particular hope has now been largely fulfilled, not by positive action by the court but through the ready admission of facts presented by participants in references.[26] The overall objective of "judicializing" the reference procedure has thus been achieved. The approach taken by both bench and bar in references is scarcely distinguishable from an ordinary appeal. This is obviously what the nineteenth-century legislators sought to ensure.

B. AN ASSESSMENT

1. Advantages

To the extent that problems of standing can still prevent judicial review on constitutional grounds, references provide a means whereby constitutional issues may be placed before the courts.

We have seen in chapter 6 that rules of standing in constitutional cases have largely depended in the past on the requirements of particular remedies and that as a result certain remedies may be available for judicial review only to persons with an "interest" distinct from that of the general public. At best the applicant for a declaration, injunction, *certiorari* or prohibition, who does not have such a specific interest, will be subject to the discretionary power of the court to grant or withhold standing, and in the case of *mandamus* he will not be able to proceed.[27] There may be

---

[26]See, *supra*, 294–97.

[27]See, *supra*, at pp. 148–70.

certain constitutional norms, such as the requirements for distribution of constituencies[28] or of periodic elections, in which no individual would be regarded as having a sufficient interest in such judicial review. There may be issues, such as the validity of the federal spending power when used in areas of provincial legislative jurisdiction, or the propriety of constitutional amending procedures,[29] where no individual could persuade a court to grant him standing.

It must be recognized, however, that if the recent trend continues with respect to the discretionary grant of standing in declaratory actions for judicial review, the resort to references to overcome standing problems in constitutional cases may be of marginal importance.

As well as permitting initial judicial review where it would not otherwise be available, a reference may be used to obtain the opinion of a higher court where an appeal would not lie.[30] It is improbable that this precise type of situation would arise now with respect to an appeal from the highest court of a province to the Supreme Court of Canada. Since 1949 the *Supreme Court Act* has permitted appeals where either the provincial appellate court (subject to certain limitations) or the Supreme Court gives leave. In a constitutional case leave would almost certainly be forthcoming from either court. Yet the reference will still be a good substitute for an appeal in some cases. In some provinces there may be situations where an appeal to the highest court is not available, and a reference may be used. Or the parties to the original litigation may not wish to carry a case to the Court of Appeal or the Supreme Court and the provincial or federal Attorney General may be powerless to do so.[31] There is also the possibility that the courts may refuse leave to appeal a case which the Government feels should be appealed. While the Government's power should not be used lightly in such circumstances, the court could be forced by a reference to deal with the issue on which they had refused leave to appeal.[32] Or a reference could be used instead of an

---

[28]As tested by a reference in *A.G. P.E.I. v. A.G. Can.*, [1905] A.C. 37, 13 Can. Rep. 341 (P.C.).

[29]As tested by reference in *Re Authority of Parliament in Relation to the Upper House*, [1980] 1 S.C.R. 54, 102 D.L.R. (3d) 1, 30 N.R. 271 (*sub nom. Re British North America Act and the Federal Senate*). *Re Resolution to Amend the Constitution*, [1981] 1 S.C.R. 753, 125 D.L.R. (3d) 1; see also *Re A.G. Que. and A.G. Can.*, 140 D.L.R. (3d) 385, 45 N.R. 317 (*sub nom. Quebec Constitutional Amendment Reference (No. 2)*). For standing on spending power issues *cf. Finlay v. Min of Finance*, [1986] 2 S.C.R. 607.

[30]As was done, for example, in *Reference re Saskatchewan Minimum Wage Act*, [1948] S.C.R. 248, [1948] 3 D.L.R. 801, 91 C.C.C. 366.

[31]See, *supra*, at pp. 81–83, 174.

[32]*Cf. Reference re R. v. Coffin*, [1956] S.C.R. 186, 7 D.L.R. (2d) 568; ''Comment''

appeal to raise related issues not involved in the lower court.[33]

In cases where judicial review will be ultimately possible through private litigation, a reference may nevertheless be desirable to hasten the process. To facilitate public or private planning it may be very valuable to have a judicial opinion in advance with respect to the legality of a particular course of action. For example, the Government may wish to have clarified the constitutionality of a nation-wide unemployment insurance scheme or a marketing scheme[34] before establishing elaborate machinery for its operation. A vivid example of this kind of situation may be found in *Reference re Anti-Inflation Act*.[35] In order to move swiftly to combat a high rate of inflation Parliament had passed this Act on December 15, 1975, effective October 14, 1975 directly imposing wage and price controls in the federal public and private sectors, and providing for the imposition of similar controls in the provincial sector where any province entered into an agreement to have those controls apply along with federal administration thereof. All provinces except Quebec entered into such agreements and Quebec established parallel controls. Questions were soon raised as to the validity of the federal law, and its application by agreement to the Ontario provincial domain was being challenged in an action commenced in the courts of that province. Other cases were contemplated elsewhere in Canada. Since the application of the law would disrupt a myriad of transactions throughout the country it was urgent that the constitutional position be clarified. It was referred to the Supreme Court on March 11, 1976, argued on May 31–June 4, 1976, and judgment was given on July 12, 1976, generally upholding the validity of these arrangements. Thus within seven months of the passage of the Act a definitive ruling of the highest court had been obtained as to its validity. The disruptive effect of continuing uncertainty, and the probability of much longer delays before all the issues would otherwise have reached the Supreme Court by ordinary appeal, made the reference device a valuable means of clarifying the situation.

It may be important to businessmen to know under which level of Government they are to operate, and speed of clarification of this issue

---

(1956), 34 *Can. Bar Rev.* 966; *Reference re R. v. Truscott*, [1967] S.C.R. 309, 62 D.L.R. (2d) 545, [1967] 2 C.C.C. 285, 1 C.R.N.S. 1.

[33]*E.g., Reference re S. 6 of the Family Relations Act*, [1982] 1 S.C.R. 62, 36 B.C.L.R. 1, [1982] 3 W.W.R. 1, 131 D.L.R. (3d) 257, 40 N.R. 206, 26 R.F.L. (2d) 113; *Reference re Language Rights in Man.*, [1985] 1 S.C.R. 721, referred after the Manitoba Court of Appeal decision in *Bilodeau v. A.G. Man.*; [1981] 5 W.W.R. 393, [1986] 3 W.W.R. 673 (S.C.C.). For an explanation of this reference see *House of Commons Debates*, June 12, 1984, at p. 4584.

[34]*E.g., A.G. Can. v. A.G. Ont.*, [1937] A.C. 355, [1937] 1 W.W.R. 312, [1937] 1 D.L.R. 684 (P.C.); *A.G. B.C. v. A.G. Can.*, [1937] A.C. 377, [1937] 1 W.W.R. 328, [1937] 1 D.L.R. 691, 67 C.C.C. 337 (P.C.).

[35][1976] 2 S.C.R. 373, 68 D.L.R. (3d) 452, 9 N.R. 541.

may be useful in encouraging economic development. This justification has been used, for example, in connection with references to the courts to seek judicial opinions on questions of jurisdiction and ownership over offshore resources.[36]

There will also be situations where speedy determination is more of a necessity than a convenience. Emergency conditions such as war make it imperative that the Government be assured at once of the validity of proposed action. For example, if it wishes to create a regulatory system to ensure the maintenance of vital supplies and the prevention of waste, it cannot afford the luxury of waiting for chance litigation to uphold or strike down the scheme.[37]

A reference may also provide relief where a private citizen would not find it convenient to take a constitutional case to the higher courts. A litigant may have grave doubts about the validity of a statute applied against him, but it may be less expensive for him to drop his objections than to carry the case to an appeal. Yet such a statute applied similarly to dozens or hundreds of people may collectively cause great expense or injustice. In addition, various lower courts may hold conflicting views as to the validity of the law, some upholding it and others deeming it invalid. If no affected individual is prepared to undertake the expense and trouble of appeal, the enforcement of the statute will fall into chaos and the law itself into discredit. A reference to an appellate court may provide the authoritative decision required to restore order. If the statute is held invalid, numerous citizens will be relieved from compliance with legislation which it was not practical for them to contest individually.[38]

With respect to issues which the courts usually regard as non-justiciable a reference might be used to permit judicial determination. There are obviously many non-justiciable issues where the decision ought not to be made by the judiciary, in any form of procedure, because a policy determination is required and there are no objective criteria for guidance. But there are other areas, such as the propriety of parliamentary procedure, where pre-established norms are available for application. It seems

---

[36]See, *e.g.*, statement of Prime Minister Pearson to a Federal-Provincial Conference on July 19, 1965, *Proceedings* at 29–33, concerning the B.C. offshore, followed by the Supreme Court reference (*Reference re Offshore Mineral Rights*) which resulted in a decision at [1967] S.C.R. 792, 62 W.W.R. 21, 65 D.L.R. (2d) 353. With respect to the reference to the Supreme Court of Canada concerning the Newfoundland offshore see House of Commons Debates, May 19, 1982 at 17586–88; that reference was decided in [1984] 1 S.C.R. 86.

[37]See, *e.g.*, *Reference re Regulations in Relation to Chemicals*, [1943] S.C.R. 1, [1943] 1 D.L.R. 248, 79 C.C.C. 1.

[38]For example, the situation in *Reference re Anti-Inflation Act, supra*, note 35; or *Reference re Criminal Law Amendment Act 1968–69*, [1970] S.C.R. 777, 74 W.W.R. 167, 10 D.L.R. (3d) 699, [1970] 3 C.C.C. 320, 12 C.R.N.S. 28.

probable that a court would review a federal statute on the basis that it was passed by a procedure not in accordance with the *Constitution Act*.[39] The directions of the Act in this regard are as clear as those of sections 91 and 92 which the courts constantly apply.

Finally, references provide a flexible means for each level of Government to challenge the constitutional authority of the other level of Government. The federal Government was given this power in another form through the disallowance procedure. But federal disallowance of provincial legislation on the sole grounds that it was *ultra vires* fell into disfavour and by 1935 was expressly abandoned.[40] Even where the power was exercised on this ground, it was common for the federal Government first to refer the question of validity to the Supreme Court and be guided by its advice. The reference is now the principal means for the Government of Canada to challenge the validity of provincial legislation. It may of course refer such legislation on its own initiative[41] or at the request of the province concerned.[42] Equally, the provinces may challenge the validity of federal legislation[43] or even a parliamentary resolution[44] by referring it to a provincial court, in this way ensuring that it will ultimately reach the highest tribunals. In Ontario the Attorney General may, in the alternative, seek a declaration that an Act of Parliament is invalid,[45] but presumably the reference procedure would be speedier.

The essential advantage of the reference system thus appears to be facilitation of judicial review. In some cases it makes the impossible

---

[39]See, *supra*, at pp. 222, 223.

[40]Report of Hon. E. Lapointe, Minister of Justice, reproduced in La Forest, *Disallowance and Reservation of Provincial Legislation* (1955), at 77. In subsequent cases of disallowance additional grounds were asserted.

[41]*E.g., A.G. Ont. v. A.G. Can.*, [1896] A.C. 348, 74 L.T. 533 (P.C.); *A.G. Sask. v. A.G. Can.*, [1949] A.C. 110, [1949] 2 D.L.R. 145, [1949] 1 W.W.R. 742.

[42]*E.g., Reference re Farm Products Marketing Act*, [1957] S.C.R. 198, 7 D.L.R. (2d) 257.

[43]*E.g., A.G. Ont. v. Reciprocal Insurers*, [1924] A.C. 328, [1924] 2 W.W.R. 397, [1924] 1 D.L.R. 789, 41 C.C.C. 336 (P.C.); *A.G. Ont. v. Canada Temperance Fed.*, [1946] A.C. 193, [1946] 2 W.W.R. 1, [1946] 2 D.L.R. 1, 85 C.C.C. 225, 1 C.R. 229 (P.C.); *A.G. Can. v. C.P.R.*, [1958] S.C.R. 285, 12 D.L.R. (2d) 625, 76 C.R.T.C. 241; *Jones v. A.G. N.B.* [1975] 2 S.C.R. 182, 45 D.L.R. (3d) 583 (*sub nom. Jones v. A.G. Can.*), 1 N.R. 582 (*sub nom. Reference re Official Language Act*), 16 C.C.C. (2d) 297, 7 N.B.R. (2d) 526; *Reference re Agricultural Products Marketing Act*, [1978] 2 S.C.R. 1198, 84 D.L.R. (3d) 257, 19 N.R. 361.

[44]*Re Resolution to Amend the Constitution*, [1981] 1 S.C.R. 753, 11 Man. R. (2d) 1, 34 Nfld. & P.E.I.R. 1, [1981] 6 W.W.R. 1 (*sub nom. A.G. Man. v. A.G. Can.*), 125 D.L.R. (3d) 1, 39 N.R. 1, 1 C.R.R. 59.

[45]See, *supra*, at pp. 121, 122.

possible, in others it speeds the process where time is of the essence. To those for whom enforced judicial activism poses no threat, the constitutional reference may appear as an unmixed benefit. But it is also essential to consider some of the problems which arise out of its use.

2. Disadvantages

Two principal disadvantages of references can be identified: they may foster abstract jurisprudence because they require an opinion from the court without the benefit of an adequate factual context; and they may cause the court to decide issues which are not really justiciable because Governments are seemingly unlimited in the questions they can refer. These difficulties flow from the very nature of references: that is, they do not arise out of a specific controversy between parties whose legal rights are in issue.

The first problem mentioned, the lack of an adequate factual basis, has been thought not only to hinder sound characterization of laws, but also to lead more frequently to a finding of invalidity.

The suspicion that they favour findings of invalidity cannot be clearly confirmed on a statistical basis. A survey of leading constitutional cases from 1867 through 1986, those reaching the highest tribunal available, either the Privy Council or the Supreme Court, shows that the results in the courts for each level of Government were not dramatically different as between references and ordinary litigation. Of cases involving provincial competence, in 51 references provincial authority was upheld in 24 cases and found lacking in 27 cases—a failure rate of about 53%. In ordinary litigation, in 164 cases the provinces succeeded in 102 and lost in 61, a failure rate of about 37%. For the federal authority, in 42 references there was a finding of invalidity in 13 cases, a loss rate of about 31% whereas the loss rate in ordinary litigation was 18 of 82 cases, or about 22%. So the contrasts are far from marked as between results achieved in references and ordinary litigation. The statistical results[46] are unreliable because of the relatively small numbers and the probable ex-

---

[46]The number of cases referred to here when totalled will not equal the total of constitutional cases referred to elsewhere in this chapter, as the figures here reflect the fact that some cases involve both federal and provincial laws with the result that some cases are counted twice. But the figures here do not include constitutional cases, counted elsewhere, involving interpretation issues not going to the validity of laws.

istence of other factors involved as between references and litigation[47] and as between federal and provincial results.[48]

It is interesting, however, to look at some of the most abstract and influential reference decisions in our constitutional history to understand the nature of this problem. One need only look at a few examples. In the 1916 *Reference re Insurance Act* the Supreme Court was asked for an opinion as to the validity of certain sections of the federal *Insurance Act, 1910*. This legislation required the federal registration of insurance companies before they could carry on business. It was broad enough to cover provincially incorporated companies carrying on business in Canada outside the province of incorporation. A majority of the Supreme Court confined itself to an exercise in semantics, holding that the federal power to regulate "trade and commerce" could not include "a trade". The insurance business was regarded as "a trade", hence not susceptible to federal control.[49] One of the dissenting judges, Davies J., took a more functional approach. He took judicial notice of the national significance of the insurance business, the mobility of insured persons, and the possible national repercussions of the failure of a major company. This enabled him to find that the business of insurance was clearly a matter of national trade and commerce.[50] But the Privy Council on appeal sided with the majority below, Viscount Haldane at his dogmatic best holding that

> . . . it must now be taken that the authority to legislate for the regulation of trade and commerce does not extend to the regulation by a licensing system of a particular trade in which Canadians would otherwise be free to engage in the provinces.[51]

Here was a reference involving the bare question, "Are sections 40 and 70 of the 'Insurance Act, 1910', or any or what part or parts of the said sections, *ultra vires* of the Parliament of Canada?" No factual information was included with the reference, nor apparently was any otherwise presented to the court. Without consideration of the factual context in which the legislation would operate, the majority of the Supreme Court and the Privy Council set aside the legislation on a conceptual analysis of the word "trade". The net result was to bar the Parliament of Canada from regulating businesses which were interprovincial in scope, because their

---

[47]It could be argued, for example, that statutes are referred to the courts only where there are serious doubts as to validity, whereas private litigants frequently raise insubstantial constitutional issues in the course of proceedings primarily involving other issues.

[48]It may be noted that most of the references of federal legislation were taken at a time when judicial trends generally were against federal power.

[49](1913), 48 S.C.R. 260, 5 W.W.R. 488, 15 D.L.R. 251, affd [1916] 1 A.C. 588 (*sub nom. A.G. Can. v. A.G. Alta.*), 25 Que. K.B. 187, 10 W.W.R. 505, 26 D.L.R. 288.

[50]For a discussion of the decision see Smith, *supra*, note 6 at pp. 80–84.

[51]*A.G. Can. v. A.G. Alta.*, *supra*, note 49, at p. 596 A.C.

operations could be analytically dismembered into a collection of "particular trades" carried on in particular provinces.

Three decisions from 1937 provide similar examples. The Natural Products Marketing Act Reference[52] concerned the validity of federal legislation purporting to authorize federal regulation of marketing of certain agricultural products. Marketing schemes were to be confined to commodities whose "principal market" was outside the province of growth. While it probably could have been demonstrated that the regulation of local sales was inextricably linked with the control of interprovincial and international marketing (clearly a federal matter), both the factums and the judgment ignore such factual considerations. The Judicial Committee proceeded on a series of abstract propositions, foremost of which was the prohibition against federal control of trade which is "exclusively local". In this it assumed a separability between local and non-local trade which the facts would probably have refuted.[53]

The second of these cases was the Employment Insurance Reference.[54] The federal statute in question would have established a system of compulsory insurance against unemployment, to be paid for in part by "contributions" required of both employers and employees. Federal counsel did introduce through his factum some impressive economic data showing the grave and national character of the unemployment problem.[55] But the Privy Council ignored the factual context of the legislation, confining itself to more familiar and congenial conceptualism. The only important consequences of this legislation it could see were compulsory alteration of contracts of employment through forced insurance deductions, and the operation of an insurance business. These automatically made the federal legislation a usurpation of the provincial "property and civil rights" jurisdiction. The fact that the effect on contracts and insurance was a mere incident of a scheme essentially directed to the relief of nation-wide hardship, the greater rationalization of federal-provincial financial relations, and the stabilization of the national economy, was completely ignored by the Judicial Committee.

The other reference in this trilogy pertained to federal legislative

---

[52]*A.G. B.C. v. A.G. Can.*, [1937] A.C. 377, [1937] 1 W.W.R. 328, [1937] 1 D.L.R. 691 (*sub nom. Reference re Natural Products Marketing Act, 1934*), 67 C.C.C. 337 (P.C.).

[53]See *R. v. Klassen* (1959), 29 W.W.R. 369, 20 D.L.R. (2d) 406, 31 C.R. 275 (Man. C.A.); *A.G. Man. v. Manitoba Egg and Poultry Assn.*, [1971] S.C.R. 689, [1971] 4 W.W.R. 705, 19 D.L.R. (3d) 169, judgment of Laskin J. (Hall J. concurring) at pp. 716–17 S.C.R., pp. 189–90 D.L.R.; *Cf. U.S. v. Darby*, 312 U.S. 100 (1941); *Wickard v. Filburn*, 317 U.S. 111 (1942).

[54]*A.G. Can. v. A.G. Ont.*, [1937] A.C. 355, [1937] 1 W.W.R. 312, [1937] 1 D.L.R. 684 (*sub nom. Reference re Employment and Social Insurance Act, 1935*) (P.C.)

[55]For introduction of facts in references, generally, see *supra*, at pp. 294–97.

attempts in the fields of labour relations and treaty implementation. Canada had ratified certain conventions adopted by the International Labour Organization with respect to labour standards. Subsequently Parliament enacted three statutes, the *Weekly Rest in Industrial Undertakings Act,* the *Minimum Wages Act,* and the *Limitation of Hours of Work Act.* On the basis of earlier decisions it was clear that these statutes infringed on provincial jurisdiction over property and civil rights (*i.e.,* contracts of employment) unless they could be justified under some overriding federal power. In the Labour Conventions Reference[56] the federal Government contended, *inter alia,* that once a matter had become of international concern and the subject of a treaty, it ought to be considered within federal legislative jurisdiction over the "peace, order, and good government" of Canada. The arguments and the judgment all proceeded by a series of abstract precepts, with the Privy Council once again characterizing the legislation as an unwarranted interference with "property and civil rights".

Numerous other examples could be cited to support the claim that reference decisions are frequently abstract. These particular ones were selected because of their far-reaching consequences.

The 1916 Insurance Reference was influential in a number of later cases where Parliament was denied the power to cope with nation-wide commercial problems because this was characterized as regulation of a particular trade within each province.[57]

The Natural Products Marketing Act Reference created a constitutional impasse in the regulation of agricultural marketing. It made clear that though the provinces could not regulate local trade in such a way as to interfere with interprovincial trade, neither could Parliament interfere with intraprovincial trade in the course of regulating interprovincial or international trade. As the normal flow of trade in agricultural products does not readily break down into these constitutionally distinct categories until almost the time of consumption, it is impossible to ascertain which Government can regulate production quotas, inspection, or grading of a given item of produce.[58] A literal application of the Privy Council's edicts would at best have resulted in confusion and expensive duplication of

---

[56]*A.G. Can. v. A.G. Ont.,* [1937] A.C. 326, [1937] 1 W.W.R. 299, [1937] 1 D.L.R. 673 (*sub nom. Reference re Weekly Rest in Industrial Undertakings Act*) (P.C.).

[57]*Re Board of Commerce Act,* [1922] 1 A.C. 191, [1922] 1 W.W.R. 20, 60 D.L.R. 513 (P.C.); *A.G. Ont. v. Reciprocal Insurers,* [1924] A.C. 328, [1924] 2 W.W.R. 397, [1924] 1 D.L.R. 789, 41 C.C.C. 336 (P.C.); *Toronto Electric Commrs. v. Snider,* [1925] A.C. 396, [1925] 1 W.W.R. 785, [1925] 2 D.L.R. 5 (P.C.).

[58]See Corry, "Difficulties of Divided Jurisdiction", in *Report of the Royal Commission on Dominion-Provincial Relations, 1940,* Appendix 7, *passim*; Smith, *supra,* note 6, at pp. 139–43.

effort. The situation has been partially relieved only through the inter-delegation of administrative authority.

The Employment Insurance Reference created an obstacle, partially legal and partially psychological, to future proposals for federal social security measures. The effect with respect to unemployment insurance itself was overcome by a 1940 constitutional amendment[59] expressly conferring jurisdiction on Parliament. But when in 1950 consideration was being given to a possible federal contributory old-age pension scheme the deputy minister of justice advised that Parliament would be precluded from enacting such a measure by virtue of the 1937 Privy Council decision.[60] The Government apparently accepted this view and obtained a constitutional amendment the next year.[61] However, it was not until a further 14 years and another constitutional amendment[62] that Parliament actually introduced a contributory scheme.[63] Other federal social security measures such as hospitalization insurance and medical care insurance have proceeded on the assumption that the proper role of the Government of Canada is cost-sharing. These insurance plans operate under provincial law with large subventions from the general revenues of the federal Government.

The Labour Conventions Reference, denying Parliament the power to implement treaties properly entered into by the Crown in right of Canada, has been a continuing source of difficulty in the conduct of foreign affairs.[64] It has also given rise to exaggerated provincial claims. In the negotiation of the Columbia River Treaty and its Protocol, for example, the Government of British Columbia could take the position that it would not proceed to implement the treaty unless it was revised to meet provincial demands. This posed problems in the conduct of negotiations with the United States—problems in an area for which the province had no political responsibility. Quebec has sometimes contended that, because Ottawa cannot implement treaties involving matters within provincial jurisdiction, the provincial and not the federal Government should negotiate and sign such treaties. While not accepting this position,

---

[59]*British North America Act*, 1940, 3–4 Geo. VI, c. 36 (U.K.) (now *Constitution Act, 1940*).

[60]*Minutes, Joint Committee of the Senate and the House of Commons on Old Age Security* (Wednesday, May 31, 1950), at 1161–71.

[61]B.N.A. Act, 1951, 14–15 Geo. VI, c. 32 (U.K.) (repealed by *Constitution Act, 1982*).

[62]B.N.A. Act, 1964, 12–13 Eliz. II, c. 73 (U.K.) (now *Constitution Act, 1964*).

[63]*Canada Pension Plan*, S.C. 1964–65, c. 51, now R.S.C. 1970, c. C-5.

[64]See Szablowski, "Creation and Implementation of Treaties in Canada" (1956), 34 *Can. Bar Rev.* 28 at 54–56; Lederman, "Legislative Power to Implement Treaty Obligations in Canada", in Aitchison, *The Political Process in Canada* (Toronto: University of Toronto Press, 1963), at 171.

the Government of Canada seeks provincial views on prospective treaties if they involve matters which domestically are of provincial jurisdiction.[65] The Labour Conventions Reference has thus had a pervasive effect on Canada's international posture.

This examination of a few major reference decisions of historic importance illustrates their potential for creating abstract jurisprudence. There are, however, several mitigating factors which should be recognized in assessing the merits of the reference system by this standard.

First it should be recognized that while such decisions were conceptual rather than functional, this was also true of contemporary decisions in normal litigation. There were many concrete cases where facts were probably available but not relied on.[66] In defence of the Privy Council decisions of this period, whether on references or in litigation, it has been argued that, whatever their economic validity, they were politically realistic.[67]

Second, there are situations where there is arguably no need for a factual study of legislative effect or administrative action. This arises where the issue is solely that of an interpretation of a section of the constitution, where no legislation is involved, no official action is being questioned, and where the court is prepared to make a decision based on the text and its history without resort to policy considerations. These cases will be rare, and the decisions therein may be of limited use. But occasionally they will be valuable, where the issue in question is sufficiently narrow. For example in *Edwards v. A.G. Can.*[68] the question was whether the word "persons" in s. 24 of the B.N.A. Act included women, thus making the latter eligible for appointment to the Senate. The answer turned completely on internal evidence in the Act. The effect of each possible interpretation was readily apparent. A similar decision was necessary in the *Reference re Eskimos*[69] where the court had to decide whether the word "Indians" in s. 91(24) included Eskimos, thus bringing them under federal jurisdiction. The affirmative answer given by the Supreme Court was very helpful, because the extent of federal power over Indians was already well defined. It only remained to exercise the same powers with respect to Eskimos. While facts were considered in the rendering of the opinion, they were facts pertaining to the meaning of words as employed by the Imperial Parliament in 1867. There were no other facts

---

[65]See, *e.g.*, Government of Canada, *Federalism and International Relations* (1968), at 30–33. A recent example is that of consultations with provincial governments in relation to negotiations with the United States on free trade.

[66]See, *e.g.*, *Board of Commerce Act* case, *supra*, note 57 and the *Toronto Electric Commrs.* case, *supra*, note 57.

[67]Cairns, "The Judicial Committee and its Critics" (1971), 4 *Can. J.P.S.* 301.

[68][1930] A.C. 124, [1929] 3 W.W.R. 479, [1930] 1 D.L.R. 98 (P.C.).

[69][1939] S.C.R. 104, [1939] 2 D.L.R. 417.

which could have been considered, because there was no legislative scheme purporting to regulate Eskimos. Thus it may be seen that where an opinion may usefully be rendered as to the meaning of the constitution, even in the absence of a legislative scheme and facts showing legislative effect, a reference is legitimate. Though the decision may be abstract in one sense, it will be useful because of the context in which it is given. Such a use of the reference must be viewed with great caution, however. In the Senate Reference,[70] there was no specific legislation to be considered but only a series of questions about the validity of various kinds of Senate reforms. This might have appeared on its face to be a situation where one had little need of evidence because there was no specific legislation whose effect required examination. The Supreme Court, however, construed Parliament's amendment power over the Senate to be limited to what it called "housekeeping" matters but not to include changes that would alter the "fundamental features" of the Senate. Having created this distinction, it then refrained from answering certain of the questions which, in the absence of specific legislation, did not provide enough detail for the court to decide whether they contemplated "housekeeping" or "fundamental" changes.

Third, the remedy for abstract reference decisions should not be total abandonment of this sometimes useful device, but rather a more selective use of it accompanied by adequate fact-introduction. The argument for use of facts in constitutional cases generally,[71] and references in particular,[72] has been made in chapter 8. It has been demonstrated that the Supreme Court has led the way in emphasizing the importance of facts in references and the trend appears to be for counsel to meet these judicial expectations. What we are seeing in reality is a rather unsteady movement from the conceptual jurisprudence so beloved by the Judicial Committee and its followers to a more functional jurisprudence in which facts are all important. Therefore much of this particular problem traditionally associated with the reference process may disappear, although the inherent nature of the device is a reminder that constant care must be exercised in its use. There should be a careful framing of questions so that issues may be raised as precisely as possible. Courts should refuse to answer questions which are too general or which require a factual context if none is provided. They should also avoid answering questions not clearly included in the reference order.[73] If these principles are faithfully applied in reference cases, there will be far less complaint of abstractness.

---

[70]*Re Authority of Parliament in Relation to the Upper House*, [1980] 1 S.C.R. 54, 102 D.L.R. (3d) 1, 30 N.R. 271 (*Sub nom. Re British North America Act and the Federal Senate*).

[71]*Supra*, at pp. 263, 264.

[72]*Supra*, at pp. 294–97.

[73]*Reference re Magistrate's Court Act*, [1965] S.C.R. 772, 55 D.L.R. (2d) 701.

The second major problem with references noted above is that they may call upon a court to answer questions that are not justiciable. Reference statutes at both the federal and provincial level allow Governments to refer any "matter" to the courts. This would appear on its face to include any question not only of law, but also of politics, science, or taste. It was held, however, by a majority of seven in the Supreme Court in the *Re Resolution to Amend the Constitution* that such a provincial statute

> . . . is wide enough to saddle the respective courts with the determination of questions which may not be justiciable and there is no doubt that those courts, and this Court on appeal, have a discretion to refuse to answer such questions.[74]

Given the lack of a clear separation of powers in our system it is perhaps not surprising that the court did not on that occasion deny itself the right to decide non-justiciable questions but only asserted a power to decline to do so at its discretion. It is encouraging to know that courts should not feel obliged to decide questions which functionally belong elsewhere. But at the same time it must be noted that, having asserted the right to refuse to answer, the court in this same case proceeded to answer questions posed by provincial Governments to their courts and appealed to the Supreme Court as to the existence and nature of a political convention concerning the use of legal powers.

While Legislatures have thus authorized Governments to refer non-justiciable questions to the courts, normally they do not do so nor, it is submitted, should they do so if they wish to protect the courts from undue political controversy and resulting hazards to their legitimacy. The federal Government has in fact articulated such a principle in the course of resisting pressures for references to the Supreme Court.[75]

When Governments do not exercise self-restraint in this respect, it is open to the courts to do so and to decline to decide such issues. When these safeguards are not employed, the reference system does thrust the courts into the decision of non-justiciable issues that may in the long term impair their effectiveness.

Lesser criticisms of the reference system include that of possible

---

[74][1981] 1 S.C.R. 753 at 768, 125 D.L.R. (3d) 1 at 16, 11 Man. R. (2d) 1, 34 Nfld. & P.E.I.R. 1, [1981] 6 W.W.R. 1 (*sub nom. A.G. Man. v. A.G. Can.*), 39 N.R. 1, 1 C.R.R. 59; see also *McEvoy v. A.G.N.B.*, [1983] 1 S.C.R. 704.

[75]See, *e.g.*, correspondence between Prime Minister Trudeau and the Quebec Association of Protestant School Boards, tabled in the House of Commons July 21, 1975, Sessional Papers No. 301–5/185; statement of Hon. O.E. Lang, Minister of Justice, to Special Joint Committee on the Constitution, Proceedings of August 31, 1978, at 8:14–15.

interference with private rights. Judges have occasionally hesitated to answer a referred question because, though worded generally, it may include issues on which the rights of specific individuals may turn. It is thought unfair to render such decisions where individuals who may be seriously affected are not represented before the court. As previously noted, this criticism appears specious for the same may be said of almost any decision. A case between litigants A and B may involve issues similar to those at stake between C and D. An unfavourable decision in A v. B, for example, may have grave implications for C. But it has never been suggested that C should be a party in A v. B. References are actually more flexible in this matter because the court is at liberty to permit almost anyone to participate in the argument.[76]

The real fault lies, not in the initial reference decision having possible implications for private individuals, but rather in the misplaced fidelity with which such decisions are subsequently followed. This is part of the broader complaint that reference decisions have generally been given undue precedential value. In other words, what were originally intended to be opinions only have been treated as judgments.

When the *Supreme Court Act* was amended in 1891, reference opinions were described as "advisory only". This was soon ignored and the Privy Council and Supreme Court expressly followed the decisions in earlier federal references with undiscriminating zeal.[77] Not until 1957, after the "advisory only" provision had actually been dropped from the *Supreme Court Act*, did the Supreme Court suggest the possibility that it would ignore earlier reference decisions, even those of the Judicial Committee. It then stated that it was not bound by a decision of the Judicial Committee rendered in a reference involving some of the same issues and parties now before it in a concrete case. It may be noted, however, that this was *obiter dicta*, for the Supreme Court accepted the opinion of the Privy Council.[78]

It is to be hoped nevertheless that this judicial declaration of independence will not be forgotten. Uncritical following of reference decisions brings discredit on the whole reference system. The rendering of opinions on hypothetical questions or on issues affecting private rights would create few problems if they were not subsequently treated as conclusive. An opinion on an abstract question should be regarded as of limited value, valid only in relation to the assumptions and facts on which it was ren-

---

[76]For a full discussion of this point see, *supra*, at pp. 210, 211.

[77]See Rubin, "The Nature, Use and Effect of Reference Cases in Canadian Constitutional Law" (1959), 6 *McGill L.J.* 168 at 175–79.

[78]*C.P.R. v. Town of Estevan*, [1957] S.C.R. 365, 7 D.L.R. (2d) 657, 75 C.R.T.C. 185. See also dicta in *Reference re R. v. Coffin*, [1956] S.C.R. 186 at 187, 7 D.L.R. (2d) 568 at 570.

dered. Moreover, it can hardly be considered to preclude further contestation by anyone, whether parties or non-parties to the reference, because it does not render the issue *res judicata*.[79] It may be argued further that the Supreme Court, as successor to the Privy Council and as the final appellate court, should no longer consider itself bound by any previous decisions, its own or the Privy Council's, in any type of proceeding. The Privy Council asserted such freedom, but rarely exercised it. The Supreme Court has recently reversed some of its own decisions and has declined to allow a Privy Council decision.[80]

Should the provincial courts follow reference opinions? To opinions rendered in the Supreme Court and Privy Council, in federal references, it is submitted that the lower courts should certainly show great respect. It should be kept in mind that these opinions are not judgments, though they are certainly of great weight and where directly relevant will normally be so persuasive as to be determinative. Mr. Justice Locke in *C.P.R. v. Estevan*,[81] by holding that the Supreme Court was not bound by its own or the Privy Council's opinions, clearly implied, however, that such opinions were not binding on any court.

The position might be distinguishable where a provincial court is faced with a previous decision of a higher court on a provincial reference. Most of the provincial reference statutes state that the opinion of the court "shall be deemed a judgment". In *Milk Bd. v. Hillside Farm Dairy Ltd.*[82] the British Columbia Court of Appeal considered itself bound by an earlier decision of the Supreme Court of Canada in an appeal on a provincial reference. At issue in both cases was the validity of a particular British Columbia statute. Two of the judges in the Court of Appeal, writing for the majority, took the position that all reference decisions are binding. In this they ignored the *Estevan* case and relied on an earlier but emphatic Supreme Court decision[83] to this effect. While this authority would now be questionable, Mr. Justice Sheppard also stated a second ground for his decision: "the opinion, although a reference, is by statute stated to be a judgment. . . . This court is therefore bound by that judgment and is restricted to matters not determined thereby".[84] With respect, this conclusion appears unnecessary. It is clear from the statute that the opinion is deemed to be a judgment for the purpose of appeal. The Supreme Court itself has held that the statute, by stating that an opinion shall be "deemed" a judgment, indicates that it is not a judgment.[85] And even if

---

[79]See, *supra*, at pp. 194, 195. *Coffin* case, *supra*, note 78.

[80]See, *supra*, at p. 28.

[81]*Supra*, note 78, at p. 368 S.C.R., pp. 659–60 D.L.R.

[82](1963), 43 W.W.R. 131, 40 D.L.R. (2d) 731 (B.C. C.A.).

[83]*A.G. Can. v. Higbie*, [1945] S.C.R. 385, [1945] 3 D.L.R. 1.

[84]*Supra*, note 82, at pp. 144–45 W.W.R., p. 746 D.L.R.

[85]*Union Colliery Co. v. A.G. B.C.* (1897), 27 S.C.R. 637.

it is a judgment, it is obviously of a very special kind, limited in its effect. Consequently, provincial courts should be free in a proper case to ignore their own or the higher courts' decisions in provincial references.

Combined with the abandonment of *stare decisis* with respect to reference opinions, there should be a more discriminating use of such opinions when invoked for persuasive purposes. In analyzing what a reference actually "decided", the opinion should be carefully examined in relation to the precise hypotheses put to the court and the facts, if any, before it. Such analysis may reveal that the opinion decided very little, in which case it ought not to be an embarrassment in subsequent cases.

In sum, it is suggested that if references have created premature or overly broad precedents the fault lies more in judicial practice than in the reference system. An appropriately critical approach by the courts to such decisions can remove the substance of this complaint.

C. CONCLUSION

The controversy over references is really an aspect of the larger controversy with respect to the role of the judiciary in interpreting and applying the constitution. Judicial activists will generally approve of a system which overcomes obstacles to judicial review. Those who take a more restricted view of the role of the judiciary will see it as a hazardous procedure, burdening the courts with hypothetical questions and producing premature decisions with mischievous consequences.

On balance the case for the use of references seems more supportable. If one accepts the courts as the best arbiters of constitutional rules, one should favour a system which facilitates judicial review. There are some situations where a reference will be justified in the interests of speed, clarification for the benefit of many individuals who would not readily be able to seek judicial review, or the elimination of technical barriers to bringing actions or taking appeals.

Several caveats must be entered, however. In the first place, some of the justifications for the use of references have been attenuated by developments of the last decade. The obstacles to standing for individuals to seek declarations on constitutional issues, the nearest substitute for a reference, have largely disappeared.[86] With almost universal legal aid for the needy and numerous special interest groups able to undertake or support litigation, Government initiatives by way of a constitutional reference are now not as necessary to ensure judicial review. At the same time the development of a more functional jurisprudence with greater emphasis on the factual context tends to militate against the use of the

---

[86]*Supra*, at pp. 148–65.

reference which often lacks factual substance. So although there is still a role for the reference it has been somewhat reduced by events.

Where there are reasons for resorting to a reference, Governments should still avoid doing so if the issue to be referred is not justiciable in the sense that it is one better left to another branch of Government or one which lacks objective criteria for its determination. The principal danger to be avoided here is the reference of essentially a political issue to the courts: where there are few, if any, genuinely legal criteria to which courts can resort for a rationale for their decision, they may be perceived as making a political judgment which may impair their long-term credibility.

Once the decision is taken to refer a constitutional question, then care should be taken in its framing so that the issues are precisely defined. The referring Government and counsel on all sides should make every effort to ensure that all relevant facts are placed before the court.

As for the courts, they should be prepared to refuse answers to questions that are non-justiciable, or too vague to be effectively answered. They should have regard to gleaning all relevant evidence, including an active resort to judicial notice. They should also examine critically earlier opinions and be prepared to disregard or distinguish those which were too general, too vague, or too abstract.

Even a carefully controlled reference system must play a secondary role in judicial review, however. A decision based on complete facts and real issues is to be preferred to one based on incomplete facts, or hypothetical problems, and a binding authority is likely to be more reliable than an advisory opinion. Thus, if other circumstances are equal and judicial review through a concrete case is feasible, it should be preferred. The reference should be seen as a useful supplement to our judicial review system, but one to be resorted to with caution and perhaps, in the future, with diminishing frequency. The second century of Confederation has so far seen a sharply reduced rate of references in comparison to the volume of ordinary constitutional litigation,[87] and this trend is likely to continue.

---

[87]From 1867 to 1966, of the 197 constitutional cases reaching the highest available court (the Judicial Committee of the Privy Council until 1949, the Supreme Court of Canada thereafter), 68 or roughly 35% were references; in the period 1967–1986, of 155 constitutional cases in the Supreme Court, 23 or roughly 15% were references.

Chapter 10

The Future of Judicial Review

The last 15 years have seen the strengthening and enlargement of the role of judicial review in enforcement of the constitution, with its rapid future growth firmly assured. To the judicial responsibility of applying the rules of federalism was added, by the adoption of the *Canadian Charter of Rights and Freedoms* in 1982, the task of protecting a wide range of human rights. This task has already become so large as to overshadow in many ways the more traditional role of enforcing federalism. These developments give cause, and an opportunity, to consider briefly the future role of judicial review, and the prospects as to its scope and continuing legitimacy.

A. NEED FOR JUDICIAL REVIEW

It can be assumed that the distribution of powers between federal and provincial authorities will continue to generate regular disputes. In spite of suggestions such as that "continual negotiations and political compromise"[1] are generally a better device than judicial review for solving such disputes, experience has shown that political resolution is not always possible. An obvious example in the last decade has been the increasing conflict over resources, the control of their development and production and the taxation of their revenues. Probably no issue, short of constitutional reform, has been the subject of as much intergovernmental discussion, and yet many issues have not been resolved without resort to the courts. Longer term constitutional solutions through agreed constitutional amendment have also been modest in scope.[2]

While it is unlikely that federalism issues will fail to be discussed in federal-provincial fora before litigation occurs, it is difficult to envisage negotiations as a substitute for all judicial review. Indeed, judicial review provides both an ultimate alternative to, and a framework for, political negotiation. The agenda of negotiations and the relative negotiating strength of the parties are strongly influenced by what the courts have done or

---

[1]Weiler, *In the Last Resort* (Toronto: Carswell, 1974), at 175; *cf.* Strayer, Review (1975), 13 *Osgoode Hall L.J.* 311.

[2]See *Constitution Act, 1867*, s. 92A and the Sixth Schedule, as added by the *Constitution Act, 1982*, ss. 50, 51.

may be expected to do. It can scarcely be doubted that federal-provincial discussions of resource jurisdiction in the early 1980s were occasioned and shaped by important Supreme Court decisions of the 1970s,[3] or that the negotiations at the First Ministers' Conference on the Constitution of November, 1981, where agreement was reached among ten Governments on constitutional change, were influenced strongly on both sides by the Supreme Court decision in the Patriation Reference.[4]

So without minimizing the importance of political compromise, judicial review can be seen as an important adjunct to the negotiation process in the solution of federal-provincial conflicts. It cannot preclude political solutions, nor need it detract from their use.

The use of judicial review in the protection of individual and group rights is practically a new venture for Canadian courts, however. Prior to 1982 there were only limited constitutional guarantees of rights, such as those pertaining to language or denominational schools in ss. 133 and 93 of the B.N.A. Act, 1867, which could be invoked as a basis for judicial review. Now the *Canadian Charter of Rights and Freedoms* guarantees a wide range of rights, and it makes them judicially enforceable in relation both to laws and to administrative practices that abridge those rights. If there were any doubt that these rights and freedoms were to be judicially enforced, it is dispelled by s. 24 which says that anyone whose rights or freedoms are infringed "may apply to a court . . . to obtain such remedy as the court considers appropriate". This is in addition to s. 52 of the *Constitution Act, 1982*, which reaffirms the supremacy of the constitution and thus, implicitly, the legitimacy of judicial review in Charter and other matters.

So the role of judicial review in this field is not only assured but greatly enlarged. This again is not to say that other techniques for the protection of human rights are not worthwhile, or indeed not better. The adoption of the Charter has caused, and will continue to cause, careful reconsideration, at the legislative and administrative level, of laws and practices to see if they conform to its standards. This should and no doubt will make unnecessary much judicial review, and for the individual will bring about relief which will be more effective, timely, and inexpensive than resort to the courts. Administrative machinery such as human rights commissions and ombudsmen can do more on a systematic basis to protect individual rights, with less delay and expense, than can the courts which

---

[3]*Canadian Industrial Gas & Oil Ltd. v. Govt. of Sask.*, [1978] 2 S.C.R. 545, 80 D.L.R. (3d) 449; *Central Canada Potash Co. Ltd. v. Saskatchewan*, [1979] 1 S.C.R. 42, [1978] 6 W.W.R. 400, 88 D.L.R. (3d) 609, 23 N.R. 481, 6 C.C.L.T. 265.

[4]*Re Resolution to Amend the Constitution*, [1981] 1 S.C.R. 753, 11 Man. R. (2d) 1, 34 Nfld. & P.E.I.R. 1, [1981] 6 W.W.R. 1 (*sub nom. A.G. Man. v. A.G. Can.*), 125 D.L.R. (3d) 1, 39 N.R. 1, 1 C.R.R. 59.

are only reactive to isolated instances of rights violations somewhat for-
tuitously brought before them. But again judicial review will provide the
"back-stop", the "fail-safe" mechanism, where other devices prove to
be inadequate, and judicial interpretation of Charter rights will permeate
the governmental system and the way it responds to the requirements of
the Charter.

The adoption at last of a Canadian amending procedure will not
obviate the need for judicial development of the constitution on a case
by case basis. Many aspects of the new amending procedure, as provided
in Part V of the *Constitution Act, 1982*, are inflexible because they require
unanimity of the provinces for amendments to be made. In the critical
area of distribution of powers, any amendment derogating from provincial
rights or powers will be subject to opting out by individual provinces,
and this may make the federal Houses of Parliament reluctant to agree
to any such amendment which will not become law uniformly across the
country. The net result may be that such amendments will not occur
without unanimous provincial agreement, a rare event as experience has
shown. Consequently, it is difficult to envisage frequent amendments of
the constitution as a major substitute for its continuing judicial development.

B. SCOPE OF JUDICIAL REVIEW

In the context of the enforcement of federalism, we have seen in
the last 15 years the expansion and consolidation of the judicial role.

First we have seen further decisions striking down barriers to judicial
control of jurisdictional questions, whether such barriers involved an
attempted denial of remedies for acts done under invalid laws,[5] the attempted denial of supervisory power of superior courts over the jurisdiction of inferior tribunals,[6] or the attempted denial of judicial review power
of provincial superior courts in favour of federal superior courts.[7]

Second, the courts have steadily reduced, almost to the point of
vanishing, the barriers to standing to raise constitutional issues before
the court.[8] The Supreme Court has essentially taken the position that if
there is a justiciable issue and no other way to raise it in court, virtually
anyone should be allowed to do so. In other words, no justiciable constitutional issue should fail of review for want of a party with a recog-

---

[5] *Amax Potash Ltd. v. Govt. of Sask.*, [1977] 2 S.C.R. 576, [1976] 2 W.W.R. 61, 71
D.L.R. (3d) 1, 11 N.R. 222; *Air Canada v. A.G. B.C.*, [1986] 2 S.C.R. 539.
[6] *Crevier v. A.G. Que.*, [1981] 2 S.C.R. 220, 127 D.L.R. (3d) 1, 38 N.R. 541.
[7] *A.G. Can. v. Law Society of B.C.*, 37 B.C.L.R. 145, [1982] 5 W.W.R. 289, 137 D.L.R.
(3d) 1, 43 N.R. 451, 19 B.L.R. 234, 66 C.P.R. (2d) 1.
[8] *Supra*, at pp. 148–65.

nizable legal interest to raise it. And in other contexts the court has not worried unduly about justiciability either, treating as justiciable matters which in some other jurisdictions would be regarded as political.[9]

No longer, then, need we fear for the future that our courts will be reticent in undertaking to adjudicate issues of federalism. Indeed, it is arguable that the pendulum of judicial activism has swung about as far as it should in the other direction. This question will be addressed more fully in the next section.

Apart from the growing activism of the courts in taking on constitutional issues for decision, we have also seen in recent years a greatly enhanced attention to constitutional facts and the means for their consideration by the courts. This has been a combined effort of a bar more conscious of the importance of facts, and courts which have become much more receptive to their introduction. Unlike the past, we have more recently seen a judicially articulated rationale for the use of such facts, and the long-needed distinction between the processes of constitutional characterization and those of statutory interpretation. While the fact processes in constitutional litigation can no doubt profit from further sophistication, the necessary groundwork has been laid.

This growing attention to facts can be seen as a shift away from the conceptual jurisprudence which was the hallmark of the Judicial Committee of the Privy Council and was long hallowed by the Supreme Court of Canada. It represents a move to a more functional jurisprudence which focusses on what impugned laws actually do, rather than seeking intuitively their theoretical essence. Of course this shift is not complete nor can it ever be, as facts may not be available or may not provide the answers. But their importance is increasingly recognized and their use increasingly sought. This is a healthy development which is likely to produce more realistic results and also reinforce the legitimacy of the judicial review process.

What has been said above in the context of federalism concerning the guarantees for judicial review which the courts have discovered, and the relaxation of standing requirements, would appear to have ready-made equivalents in the judicial enforcement of the Charter of Rights.[10] The judicial role appears here not only to have been assured from the outset, but also to be in a state of rapid expansion.

First, the obvious may be noted that potential Charter issues abound. A brief look at current law reports confirms the frequency of Charter challenges in today's jurisprudence.

Second, the Supreme Court has seemingly broadened the concept of justiciability under the Charter. In the *Operation Dismantle* case it

---

[9]*Patriation Reference, supra*, note 4.
[10]*Supra*, at pp. 185–87.

rejected the doctrine of "political questions" as a test of justiciability, holding that it could decide such questions.[11]

Third, the Court appears to have rejected the presumption of constitutionality in Charter cases on the grounds that, the Charter being in constant evolution, Legislatures cannot be presumed to have intended to comply with it as its requirements are ever changing.[12] This frees the courts from important constraints in finding laws to be invalid for inconsistency with the Charter.

Fourth, in its interpretation of the Charter the Court has made several decisions which enlarge the role of the judiciary *vis-à-vis* the legislative and executive branches of government. A few salient examples will be mentioned. The use of s. 1 of the Charter to defend legislation has been limited by the decision in the *Big M* case that a limit of a right or freedom prescribed by law can never be "justified" under s. 1 if the very purpose of that law is to limit such rights.[13] Resort must be had to the blunt instrument of s. 33 to achieve such a purpose. Limits can only be "justified" under s. 1, no matter what the evidence, if it is just their *effect* which tends to restrict a right or guarantee, and then only if that effect is not substantial.[14] Further, it was suggested by 3 of the 6 judges in the *Singh* case that administrative concerns for savings in time and money could never constitute a justification under s. 1 for qualifying rights under s. 7.[15] That is, although legislators may have to settle for less-than-perfect public health care or public safety measures or national defence due to time and money constraints, such utilitarian considerations can never be applied in relation to individual rights under s. 7 nor presumably in attenuating the perfect fulfillment of any other right under the Charter. The potential for extensive development of s. 7 guarantees was further opened by the Court in the *Motor Vehicle Act Reference* where it was held that such guarantees are not confined to procedural matters but "are to be found in the basic tenets of our legal system";[16] tenets which, it may be assumed, will be intuitively discernible by the courts as and when required.

These few examples of Charter interpretation by the Supreme Court

---

[11][1985] 1 S.C.R. 441 at 459, 472, discussed, *supra*, pp. 216–19. This was consistent with what the court did previously in a non-Charter case, the *Patriation Reference*, *supra*, note 4.

[12]*A.G. Man. v. Metro. Stores (MTS) Ltd., et al.*, [1987] 1 S.C.R. 110, discussed, *supra*, 252–54, 293, 306.

[13][1985] 1 S.C.R. 295 at 353.

[14]*Edwards Books & Art Ltd. v. The Queen*, [1986] 2 S.C.R. 713.

[15]*Singh et al. v. Min. of Employment and Immigration*, [1985] 1 S.C.R. 177 at 218–19. But see *Jones v. H.M.*, [1986] 2 S.C.R. 284 at 304.

[16][1985] 2 S.C.R. 486 at 498, 503.

demonstrate that the scope of judicial review under the Charter is enlarging rapidly.

C. LEGITIMACY OF JUDICIAL REVIEW

We have seen that judicial review was accepted almost at the outset of our constitution as a legally legitimate part of the governmental system. We have also seen how it can be reconciled both with parliamentary supremacy and majoritarian democracy.[17] Yet its political legitimacy continues to require regular care and nurturing and this need cannot be fulfilled by reiterating its legal legitimacy.[18]

That is, the courts must command the respect, or at least maintain the acquiescence, of other branches and levels of Government, and of the public, to be effective. They have no armies or police forces to enforce their will in constitutional matters.

If they do not preserve that respect, their decisions on issues of federalism will not be accepted in the resolution of federal-provincial conflicts. In judicial review under the Charter a lack of general acceptability of the role of the courts will not only plunge them into the middle of political disputes, but will also strengthen those who may wish to resort to s. 33 to override dispositions of the Charter as judicially interpreted. This is not to say that judicial review ought not to produce results contrary to conventional wisdom or current public opinion: indeed, that is the very purpose of having a Charter. What is required is a proper balancing n continuity and change; between interpretivism and non-tivism.

important condition for preserving the legitimacy of judicial is the perceived exercise of self-restraint. If courts do not appear to confining their decision-making to truly justiciable issues, they will attract the criticism that their decisions represent political interference by non-elected bodies. While our courts have generally avoided this pitfall, they have on occasion undertaken to deal with issues which in some countries would be viewed as political, or not ready for adjudication. This is a constraint which will require careful judicial attention in the future.

But it is also a constraint which Governments should be astute to observe, particularly because of the seemingly unlimited power which they have to refer questions to the courts. Governments must appreciate that when they refer questions which cannot be answered by discernible

---

[17]*Supra*, c. 2, *passim*.
[18]See, *e.g.*, *Motor Vehicle Reference* case, *supra*, note 16 at p. 497.

legal (as opposed to political) standards, they force the courts into a political role which must in the long run undermine respect for them.

The courts must also protect this legitimacy by decisional processes which are logical, reasoned, factually sound, and well articulated. As experience with the U.S. Supreme Court, particularly the Warren Court, has sometimes shown, decisions which constantly discover principles or distinctions heretofore unknown to the constitution undermine their acceptability. Frequent fluctuations in decisions harm it even more.

So legitimacy of judicial review must be nourished carefully by both courts and Governments.

D. CONCLUSION

The last 15 years have made us more aware both of the potential and the perils of judicial review in the enforcement of the constitution.

On the one hand, it has been a time of growth in judicial activism, particularly with reduced requirements of standing for individuals to raise constitutional issues and a more casual approach to justiciability. These trends have been reinforced with the adoption in 1982 of the *Canadian Charter of Rights and Freedoms* which multiplies the grounds for constitutional attacks on laws and administrative actions and assures the availability of judicial remedies. Jurisprudence to date suggests it will involve the courts in many issues of a social, economic, and to some extent, political, nature.

In the same period we have also seen the development of a more functional constitutional jurisprudence, particularly exemplified by its greater attention to current events and the facts which surround a challenged law or governmental practice.

On the other hand these developments bring with them added hazards for the political legitimacy of judicial review. Greater activism involves the courts in more governmental processes; decisions pronouncing on what are reasonable or justifiable laws or official conduct appear at least to involve the making of public policy; and functional jurisprudence ventures forth, from the realm of logic and deductive reason, to the realm of empirical fact-finding combined with value judgments that, however necessary, may seem to many to be more legislative or executive in nature. These tendencies open the courts to accusations that they are behaving more as political, than as judicial, bodies, and to that extent their political legitimacy will be questioned. Experience in the United States has shown that such questioning can become very widespread indeed and can provoke counter-measures.[19] We are far from this state of affairs in Canada but closer than we were on our first centennial. What is now a greatly improved judicial review process should be carefully guarded by all those responsible.

---

[19]See, *e.g.*, the many proposals introduced in Congress to limit the jurisdiction of U.S. federal courts, as described in Tribe, *Constitutional Choices* (Cambridge, Mass.: Harvard University Press, 1985) at 47–64.

INDEX

Abbott J., 131

Act respecting the Constitution Act, 1982, An, 62, 63, 223

Act to prevent frauds, etc. 1696 (Imp.), 6

Actions: *see also* Remedies
certiorari, for, 166-68
class, 169, 180-81, 184
declaration, for, 119-21, 148-65, 183
denial of right of, as bar to judicial review, 97-110, 129-30
see also Exclusion of judicial review
governments, against:
see Governments, actions against
injunctions, 165-66
mandamus, 169-70
private and public, distinguished, 145-46
prohibition, 168-69
references: *see* References
standing to bring, generally 145-46
see also Standing to sue
statutory rights of action, 121-24, 174-75

Adderly C.B., 18

Admissions: *see* Facts

Advisory opinions, judicial
Australia, in, 141-42
Canada, in, *see* References
United States, in, 140-41

Aeronautics Act (Can.), 287

Amicus curiae; 196n
see also Non-governmental interveners

Aspect doctrine: *see* Double-aspect doctrine

Atkinson, Lord, 213

Attorney General
action by, on behalf of public, 161-63, 166, 180, 192, 193
declaratory action against:
at common law, as Crown representative, 107-09, 119-20, 124, 127-28, 195
declaratory action by, statutory right, 121-22, 162-63, 174-75, 194, 322
failure to notify, of constitutional issue, effect, 76, 78-79, 84-86
injunction, right of action for, 166
intervenant in constitutional cases, as
appeal, right to, 81-83, 171, 174, 214, 319
costs against, 81-82
notice to, concerning constitutional issue, 73-86, 170-71, 174, 191, 313
party, as, 81-83, 174, 191-95, 214
relator action in name of, 161, 163-64
statutory 121-22, 194-95

Australian constitution
generally, 177-78
judicial power in, generally, 141-42
separation of powers in, 141-42

Barwick C.J., 178

Beetz J., 253, 254, 280, 306

Benjamin, J.P., Q.C., 74

Bill 101 (Que.), 287

Bill of Rights, Canadian, 33, 43-44, 157, 159, 186, 202, 259, 290

Bill of Rights, 1688 (Imp.), 36, 224

Blake, Edward, 312-13, 316

Boothby J., 7

Brewin, F.A., 128